D0918951

Linking

Community and Corrections

in Japan

Linking

Community and Corrections

in Japan

Elmer H. Johnson with Carol H. Johnson

Southern Illinois University Press
Carbondale and Edwardsville

Library of Congress Cataloging-in-Publication Data
Johnson, Elmer Hubert.
    Linking community and corrections in Japan / Elmer H.
Johnson with Carol H. Johnson.
        p. cm.
    Includes bibliographical references and index.
1. Corrections—Japan. 2. Juvenile corrections—Japan.
3. Community-based corrections—Japan. 4. Probation—Japan.
5. Juvenile probation—Japan. I. Johnson, Carol H., 1922–   .
II. Title.
HV9813.J66 2000   99-17489
364.6'0952—dc21   CIP
ISBN 0-8093-2279-X (cloth : alk. paper)

The paper used in this publication meets the minimum requirements
of American National Standard for Information Sciences—Perma-
nence of Paper for Printed Library Materials, ANSI Z39.48-1992. ⊚

*This book honors the Japanese dedicated
to meeting the frustrations and challenges
intrinsic to careers in corrections*

Contents

Figures

Tables

ix

Preface

THIS IS THE THIRD OF THE books reporting my research on
the operations of Japanese correctional agencies. The first
book, *Japanese Corrections: Managing Convicted Offenders in an
Orderly Society* (1996), outlines features of the Correction Bureau and the Rehabilitation Bureau. I intended this to be my
complete and final report, but, during the research and the
preparation of the first book, I discovered unexpected aberrations from the general decline in Japan's imprisonment rate.
The second book, *Criminalization and Prisoners in Japan: Six
Contrary Cohorts* (1997), deals with six kinds of offenders who
have entered Japanese prisons in increasing numbers: *yakuza*
(members of crime syndicates), women drug offenders, adult
traffic offenders, juvenile drug and traffic offenders arriving
at training schools, foreigners, and elderly Japanese.

This third book turns the focus to the Rehabilitation Bureau and its responsibilities in probation, parole, and aftercare, but the Correction Bureau also has functions in Japan's
particular version of community-oriented corrections. When
I arrived in Tokyo in 1988 to begin my field research, Keiji
Kurita, then director general of the Rehabilitation Bureau,
invited me to expand the scope of my investigation to include
the merits and shortcomings of the Rehabilitation Bureau. For
this book, I have endeavored to search out the fundamental
facts and have sent chapter drafts to Japan so that the facts as
presented could be checked for accuracy. However, the interpretations of the facts and their theoretical contexts are exclusively mine. The conclusions and interpretations do not necessarily mirror the points of view of the Ministry of Justice, the
Rehabilitation Bureau, and the Correction Bureau.

In my career as a professional observer and researcher, I have conceived myself as a kind of *amicus curiae*, "friend of the court," who is not a party of a particular litigation but offers expert advice on some matters affecting the case. My role is that of a person who is not "of the criminal justice system" but strives to know the practicalities of correctional work. Professional obligations as scholar and researcher press me to be "critical" and "comparative." Several interpretations of "critical" come to mind: hypocritical (judging something by unreasonable standards), faultfinding (habitual complaining), or impartiality (objective pursuit of fundamental meaning). Impartiality comes closest to my approach.

Durkheim (1938, 136) distinguishes three versions of the comparative method: "They can include facts borrowed from either a single and unique society, from several societies of the same species, or from several distinct species." Clinard and Abbott (1973, 1) have noted a theme characteristic of all three versions: "A truly comparative criminologist must approach existing data and conduct new research by using theoretical frameworks, propositions, or models that can be tested across various societies."

My research qualifies as Durkheim's first version—facts borrowed from a single and unique society—and, in keeping with the dictum of Clinard and Abbott, draws on the theoretical frameworks of sociology and criminology. My three books do not pursue directly any comparison of Japanese and American practices, but my exposure to the workings of correctional agencies in the United States and elsewhere have influenced indirectly my choice of topics for research in Japan and my interpretation of the findings.

Early in my professional career, I recognized that textbooks then had little relevance to the working of law enforcement, probation, prisons, and parole. Dr. Clarence Patrick, chair of the North Carolina Board of Paroles, employed me as a parole supervisor in three rural counties for the summer of 1956. For the years 1958–60, William F. Bailey, then director of the North Carolina Prison Department, appointed me as assistant director, while I was on academic leave from North Carolina State University. In subsequent years, I observed correctional practices in many sections of the United States, Canada, Europe, Australia, People's Republic of China, South Korea, and Japan.

As a member of the faculty of Southern Illinois University at Carbondale, I interacted with some forty staff members of the Correction Bureau of Japan who studied over decades at the Center for the Study of Crime, Delinquency, and Corrections. Myrl Alexander, first director of the Center and later a director of the Bureau of Prisons of the federal government of the United States, had arranged their study program.

My earlier visits to Japan in 1970 and 1985 and my direct exposure to the correctional programs there and elsewhere had whetted my interest in learning more in the approach Foucault (1980, 38) advocates: "With the prisons there would be no sense of limiting oneself to discourses *about* prisons; just as important are the discourses which arise within the prison, the decisions, and regulations which are among its constituent elements, its means of functioning, along with its strategies."

Anticipating my retirement as a member of the faculty in 1987, I suggested to Minoru Shikita, then director general of the Correction Bureau, that I prepare a book on the operations of the Correction Bureau. With his acceptance of my proposal, he arranged for a grant from the Takeuchi Foundation of Hitachi, Ltd., to support preliminary research in 1988. A Fulbright award supported nine months of field research in 1990–91. I returned to Japan in 1992 to complete the field research.

Scientific research usually first frames hypotheses that point the investigation toward particular unresolved issues and thereby promises to push back the frontier of the unknown. Second, collection of basic information bears precisely on the hypotheses. The approach has much merit, but, for examination of the full scope of Japanese corrections, the research project would require great financial investment, a large staff of researchers, and years of investigation.

To bring the project within the grasp of a single criminologist (me), the project was tailored to already existing resources through field visits, interviews, documents, and annual statistics. The hypotheses emerged out of the preexisting information. Although the statistics were gathered for administrative purposes, they lend themselves to insight-stimulating analysis.

A series of the directors general of both bureaus gave indispensable support: Keiji Kurita, Kunpei Satoh, Tsuneo Furuhata, Hiroyasu Sugihara, Tatuzo Honma, and Shigeo Kifuji of the Rehabilitation Bureau and Hazuyoshi Imaoka, Kazuo Kawakami, Kiyohiro Tobita, Noboru Matsuda, Shinichiro Tojo, and Ichiro Sakai of the Correction Bureau. Many staff members contributed their time and knowledge; this book is dedicated to them in special appreciation. Others of exceptional service are Tatsuhiko Araki, Masatoshi Ebihara, Takashi Kubo, Seji Kurata, Masaru Matsumoto, Mitugi Nishinakama, Yoshiaki Okumra, Ken-sichi Sawada, and Koichi Watanabe. The staff of Southern Illinois University Press—represented directly in this instance by John Wilson and Karl Kageff—deserve my sincere appreciation. Marie Maes, as a competent copy editor, raised questions that rescued me from unintended but grave mistakes. Walter Stubbs of Morris Library, Southern Illinois University at Carbondale, provided access to references.

This research has given me a number of piquant pleasures. Chief among them has been Carol Holmes Johnson's increasing contribution as an advisor on Japanese customs and constructive critic when jargon eludes practical understanding. Even after a half-century, our marriage is an adventure of new experiences. In addition to that vital part of my life, her participation in this project has become that of a research colleague. The cover of this book announces this special partnership.

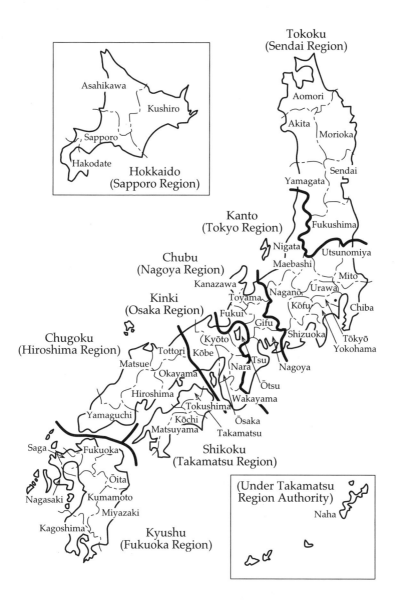

Map of Regional Parole Board and Probation Office Jurisdictions in Japan. Heavy lines indicate the jurisdictional boundaries of the eight regional parole boards. Broken lines indicate the jurisdictional boundaries of the probation offices within each region.

Linking

Community and Corrections

in Japan

1
Introduction: The Setting and Tasks of the Rehabilitation Bureau

"IN JAPAN THE PUBLIC PROSECUTOR IS vested with wide discretion to suspend the institution of prosecution even when there is sufficient evidence for conviction," Watanabe (1979, 1, 5), a public prosecutor, declares. "We must make efficient use of [this discretion] as a kind of community-based treatment of offenders, only when we get the feeling that [this] is the best way for the correction of offenders. . . . Justice or the seriousness of crime is first consideration to us, secondly comes the feelings of the public and victims, and at last offenders." To illustrate the use of prosecutorial discretion, Watanabe presents this case history:

> A farmer, aged 50 years, living on the coast of Iwate Prefecture, had a mentally deranged wife and a mentally-handicapped son, aged 20 years. His sickly sister also lived in his house. One fall morning when he was working in his field, he heard his wife crying: "I want to die". He saw her trying to hang herself from a beam in the house. He calmed her and returned to the field. She became excited again and tried to choke herself with a rope. In a struggle to control her, he struck her against the wall. She fell senseless; an ambulance took her to a hospital where she died from brain damage. He was arrested on a charge of homicide.
>
> Prosecutor Watanabe questioned him in keeping with the investigative function of Japanese public prosecutors. The farmer admitted that, while struggling with his wife, he had thought that he would be free of her if she was

killed. He offered no defense or plea of innocence; instead, he was prepared to go to prison.

He could be convicted of homicide, Watanabe summarized, and the judge might have granted a suspension of the prison sentence so he could be returned to care for his son and sister, but, even then, there would be a delay in his return to his home while being prosecuted and tried. In interviews, other poverty-stricken relatives and neighbors were found to be unprepared to provide assistance. Most of the interviewees said: "We were very sorry that she was killed, but his family cannot get along without him."

Watanabe selected the charge of bodily injury resulting in death. Relatives promised to serve as informal supervisors of his future conduct. Watanabe decided to suspend prosecution and return the man to his farm. The chief prosecutor agreed with the decision.

Announcing This Book's Agenda

Prosecutor Watanabe lends a personal quality to the discretion given Japan's public prosecutors. Although the farmer accepted the prospect of imprisonment for murder as the appropriate penalty, Watanabe suspended prosecution because of the negative consequences for the family and because the local community favored leniency "because the family cannot get along without him."

Prosecutorial discretion and judges' suspensions of prison sentences are vital elements in the processing of defendants that results in a very low imprisonment rate. The processing returns to the community many of those persons who would be prisoners in most other countries. The Japanese reluctance to employ imprisonment rests in part on a faith that most offenders have the capacity for self-correction without intervention of the criminal justice system. The officials have that faith, but, even more important for community-oriented corrections, the general public believes that if the criminals are repentant and capable of self-correction, they should be returned to the fellowship of the family and community.

When considered part of governmental services, community-oriented corrections is conceived as probation, parole, and prisoner aftercare. However, as Watanabe implies, and as a later portion of this chapter will explain, public policy radiates beyond the usual conception of formally designed and implemented programs and enlists the motivational forces of community life. Chapter 2 will elaborate on the several relationships between community and corrections.

The rise and perdurability of prosecutorial discretion and suspension of sentences—as well as probation and parole in the Japanese version—stem from the particular history, social structure, and cultural perspectives of Japan. This introductory chapter will review the particular history and sociocultural system of Japan and, more specifically, the Rehabilitation Bureau's history and its place in the organization of corrections. This book as a whole is dedicated to offering practical and theoretical answers to three general questions about the Rehabilitation Bureau and its linkages with the community: What are the characteristics of major programmatic elements (probation, parole, and aftercare)? How do various personnel carry out programmatic responsibilities? Why are the various duties and activities carried out in a particular way? These abstract questions and answers will be fleshed out in two chapters on adult probation and parole, two chapters on juvenile probation and parole, one chapter on supervision of probationers and parolees in the community, and a final chapter on programmatic outcomes and aftercare.

The knowledge and experience of the officials and staff members of Japanese agencies have been probed to learn their perceptions of the realities of correctional work. What they presented as verified facts were not necessarily certain, without question, and self-evident, but what they present as "truths" pattern what they do and, thus, offer insights into the Japanese version of correctional work. The body of theoretical criminology offers conceptual schemes by which the informational bits could have been assembled, classified, and interrelated in a systematic way. The "actualities" of Japanese correctional practice could be selected and given order to produce reliable understanding through application of the general principles of theoretical criminology.

A Particular History and Philosophy

The feudal principles of hierarchical social order of the Tokugawa era in Japan persist today in the great importance placed on duty, on maintaining social harmony, and on the place of individual within status-oriented relationships in groups. DeVos (1973, 3) declares: "What makes a Japanese 'Japanese,' that is to say, what comprises Japanese cultural psychology, has persisted in spite of changes in legal institutions, in technology, and in spite of an absorption of a great deal of scientific and aesthetic tradition from the industrial West."

Japanese commentators often claim that social homogeneity and consensus is basic to the social psychology of the Japanese (Kasai 1973, 134; Suzuki 1979, 144). The people are attracted to one another by their similarities; they share general cultural agreements. "Japan has been an exceptionally homogeneous nation for a long time," Ishida (1971, 9) says, "because of the cultural unification of different influences in a relatively isolated chain of small islands." Historically, under rural circumstances, unity had been extended from the Japanese family to the nation-state. "The family spirit can be found in most segments of society," Shikita (1985, 144) declares. "Very few Japanese feel alienated from society."

Social ties are along the horizontal dimension through attachments of *oyabun* (persons of superior rank: parent, patron, boss, and so on) with the *kobun* (persons of subordinate rank: child, client, employee, and so on). That dimension favors group cohesion in spite of rank differences among members, Nakane (1984, 44–46) notes. Different roles and degrees of authority are to be respected, and each should be loyal to his or her rank. Like fathers, leaders are responsible for the welfare of followers. Group consensus inhibits conflict among members. Self-gratification at the expense of the collective welfare is unspeakably reprehensible, explains Christopher (1987, 53). He notes a Japanese proverb: "The nail that sticks up gets pounded down."

"Sociologists have often observed that Japanese believe in no absolute standards of morality or deity," says Becker (1988, 432–33), "but rather that all standards of behavior are relative and contextual. . . . Contextualism has come to mean a distrust of dogma and the written word, a recognition that the spirit of a person's morality was more important than the letter of the law." This relativism helps explain the willingness of the Japanese people and officials to twist the meticulousness of the written law to extend leniency to the lawbreaker who appears to be genuinely penitent and capable of moral redemption.

Reischauer (1988, 144–45) attributes the relativism to child-rearing practices: "Japanese children are nursed for a relatively long period, are fed more at will, are constantly fondled by their mothers, are still often carried around on the back when mothers go out—once an almost universal practice—and often sleep with their parents until quite large." The growth of dependence on the mother becomes "psychic dependence for gratification from the warmth and approval of the group." From the general relativeness of Japanese attitudes, Reischauer says, "Japanese are more likely to emphasize extenuating circumstances and the pitifulness of the miscreant." The attitude contributes to the official leniency in prosecutorial discretion and the judges' suspension of prison sentences (to be discussed below).

Within that normative system, criminal behavior is prevented, and the lawbreakers are pressed to be repentant. To qualify for official leniency, the criminals must be repentant and adapt the moral stance of the rehabilitated person. An innate capacity for self-correction is taken for granted. If the lawbreaker fails to exhibit the capacity, the spirit of forgiveness is withdrawn: Ostracism appears and punishment under law become probable. Wagatsuma and Rosett (1986, 47) note, "Japanese not only believe that human character is mutable but view an excessively bad person as 'non-human'." The undeserving felon is shunted off to prison and its meticulous and exacting regimen.

Corrections and the Community: A Prelude

As social creatures, the Japanese relate to one another in many community activities: work, education of children, recreation, buying and selling of goods and services, dealing with illness and death, and coping with disasters and crime. As in other societies, these activities reflect an interdependence among residents that is the substance of community.

The ideal "well-organized" society probably does not exist, but the possibility is greatest as a people approach the universal sharing of beliefs that certain things and behaviors are desirable, proper, moral, or legitimate. (A moral principle or behavioral standard is "legitimate" when the persons who are expected to conform to it regard it as binding on their own conduct.) As individuals, each of us enter into relationships with other persons in efforts to solicit, direct, command, restrict, or otherwise influence their behavior toward outcomes that are congenial to our personal interests. A society exists because the collection of such personal strivings (each individual trying to get his or her own way) are successful only when the other persons cooperate. These strivings become disciplined (self-control consistent with group interests) because they are regulated by agreed-on rules of behavior (normative system) and patterned relationships among participants (social structure).

The term *community* has a variety of meanings—meanings not necessarily consistent with one another—that have different kinds of significance for the analysis of the relationships between community and the operations of the Rehabilitation Bureau in Japan. For the moment, however, I call attention to "social psychological community" based on the sentimental bonds evoked by shared experience to discipline the strivings for self-interest and to weld residents into an organized society. Relative intimacy and common interests create communal bonds when residents have lived and worked with one another over a long period of time and when they hold similar cultural beliefs. Self-control by individuals becomes an instrument for sustaining community order. This version of community is especially pertinent to the high degree of social homogeneity and normative consensus many commentators have attributed to the Japanese people.

The criminal justice system stands in sharp contrast to those elements of the social psychological community. First, many people view criminals as abnormal beings incapable of the self-control conducive to the maintenance of community order, and the social disrepute accorded criminals is likely to extend to police, parole supervisors, and prison officers, who are often denied the social acceptance derived from sharing the sentimental bonds of neighbors. Second, criminal justice personnel work in bureaucratic organizations, performing their duties within the framework of written laws and administrative guidelines under the coercive authority of the criminal law. Even their contacts with private citizens—presumably the persons they protect from criminals—tend to be characterized by formality and by the priority of organizational interests over those of private citizens. In short, the bureaucratic character of the criminal justice system opposes the intimacy of contacts and development of common interests that fuel the social psychological community.

Urban conditions have contributed to the rise of the monolithic criminal justice system, but the system does not capture all elements of society relevant to the appearance of criminality and the efforts to deal with it. The concept of community alerts us to the fact that change is endemic to the relationships among residents and among urban social institutions. The ideas inherent to community-based corrections call for recognition of the importance of maintaining the relevance of criminal justice practice to community affairs. To avoid the counterproductive effects of obsolete law enforcement measures, criminal sanctions are withdrawn or modified to keep public policy consistent with cultivation of the potential of social psychological community for preventing lawbreaking and returning offenders to the group of conformists.

When the field of corrections is linked with the community, workers in probation and parole are seen as participants in a network of family members, teachers, employers, fellow workers, and others who supplement the "natural" influences of social psychological community. Rather than depending only on the formidable coercive force of the criminal law, Japan's policy of official leniency operates on the broad social tapestry of community relationships. The sentimental bonds are especially likely to produce habitual and rather voluntary compliance with sociocultural expectations, resulting in a level of effectiveness and economical savings that no deliberate management of behavior can duplicate.

In keeping with the effects of social psychological community, the Japanese philosophy underlies the policies of public prosecutors and sentencing judges that divert a large share of accused persons back into the community. The officials assume that the Japanese-style conscience will press most offenders to abandon criminal conduct. Public prosecutors are authorized by the Code of Criminal Procedure to decide whether or not accused persons go on to formal trial. Some 95 percent of the defendants are convicted in a formal trial, but the judges return many of them to the community with or without probation. Suspensions of the sentences to prison that had just been pronounced are among the reasons for a remarkably low rate of imprisonment. The number of offenders entering Japanese prisons has declined from 96.9 per 100,000 Japanese in 1950 to 29.9 in 1994. The American imprisonment rate has shot up from 109 per 100,000 in 1950 to 401 in 1994 (Research and Statistics Section 1996a, 18; Maguire and Pastore 1995, 540).

By sharply restricting the use of imprisonment, the Japanese unintentionally have created a testing ground for the latent implications and long-term consequences of a national commitment to community-based corrections. Some Western prison systems have suffered the impact of multiplicative imprisonment rates. Some critics of this public policy have called for a turn to community-oriented corrections. The historical, cultural, and political factors stimulating the Japanese forbearance are not matched by Western societies, but study of the Japanese model offers warnings of potential deficiencies and reveals possible benefits of community-oriented corrections.

The Rehabilitation Bureau: Its Place in Japanese Corrections

The Rehabilitation Bureau assumed its current form in 1952 after six years of organizational experimentation. Within the Ministry of Justice, the "Prison Administration Bureau" and the "Rehabilitation Section" had been named in 1946. Three units—Correction General Bureau, Adult Correction Bureau, and Juvenile Correction Bureau—were created in 1947. The three units were merged in 1949 into the "Correction and Rehabilitation Bureau." In 1952 the Correction Bureau and Rehabilitation Bureau assumed their separate statuses among the seven bureaus of the Ministry of Justice (Correction Bureau 1967).

The Civil Affairs Bureau drafts laws and ordinances pertaining to civil matters and deals with nationality as a status, registration of family matters, and registration of immovables and commercial enterprises. The Criminal Affairs Bureau

supervises the work of prosecutors and drafts relevant legislation. The Litigation Bureau is involved in civil and administrative suits of interest to the government. The Civil Liber-
ties Bureau is concerned with the protection of basic rights of
the people. The Immigration Bureau specializes in the movement of persons in and out of Japan and the registration of
alien residents. The United Nations Asia and Far East Institute
for Prevention of Crime and Treatment of Offenders (UNAFEI),
another independent organization within the structure of the
Ministry of Justice, was established in 1962 in Fuchu, a sub-
urb of Tokyo, under the joint auspices of the United Nations
and the Ministry of Justice. In 1970 the Ministry assumed sole
responsibility for financial support of the institute.

All correctional functions in Japan are concentrated in the
Correction Bureau and Rehabilitation Bureau, twin components of the national Ministry of Justice. The Correction Bureau manages all prisons, juvenile training schools, and pretrial detention facilities. Fifty probation offices, thirty branch
probation offices, and eight regional parole boards (RPBs)
disperse the Rehabilitation Bureau's operations throughout
the nation. The probation offices supervise all adult probationers granted supervision in the community, juvenile probationers from the family courts, and inmates paroled from prisons
and training schools. Almost all supervision is carried out by
fifty thousand unsalaried volunteer probation officers. Aftercare hostels are operated by voluntary organizations and partially subsidized by the Ministry of Justice.

The field of Japanese corrections, the Rehabilitation Bureau (1990) acknowledges, cannot be solely immune from "a
rapid social change" in the form of "industrialization, cultural
sophistication, and accelerated mobility of population." The
Bureau predicts future trends: "ever growing use of behavioral sciences, diversification of treatment, and deeper concern with human rights of offenders." Article 1 of the Juvenile
Law expresses the aspirations of Japan's system of community-
oriented corrections: "The object of the Law is, with a view

to the wholesome rearing of juveniles, to carry out protective measures relating to the character correction and environmental adjustment of delinquent juveniles and also to take special measures with respect to the criminal cases of juveniles and adults who are harmful to the welfare of juveniles."

The term *protective measures* is frequently expressed in the administrative documents, instructions, and reports of the Rehabilitation Bureau. The term conveys the general philosophy that the restrictions going with supervision in the community are expected to serve the ultimate interests of the probationers and parolees. The safeguarding of the community in general is obtained by terminating delinquent tendencies through measures intended to protect them from environmental circumstances opposing their "wholesome rearing." The law implies recognition of both positive and negative influences in the community on the possibility of delinquencies.

The Correction Bureau is a full-fledged partner directly in the community-oriented corrections of Japan in at least two ways. First, juvenile classification homes (discussed in chapter 5) were established in 1949 as a component of a modernized juvenile justice system. They were placed within the juvenile justice programs of the Correction Bureau but serve as the diagnostic instrument of the family court. Second, pre-parole service units were introduced in 1979 in ten correctional institutions. Investigative officers of the regional parole boards and staff members of the correctional institutions collaborate in preparing documents for early consideration of parole cases (see chapter 3).

Concentration of services at the national level has advantages: minimizing inappropriate and differential influence of local political bodies, cultivating uniform policies and procedures, lending more efficiency in the use of limited resources, raising the quality of services to clients beyond the possibilities of local criminal justice agencies, and promoting quality of staff through centralized recruitment and training programs. However, centralized agencies are less likely to take local conditions into account. Staff members tend to be less familiar with the traditions of the locality and attitudes of its residents; in Japan that tendency is strengthened by the frequent transfers of personnel among localities. National agencies are less likely to experiment with new approaches because their greater size elevates the costs of any administrative error. Local communities may resent the policies framed in central headquarters without due consideration of local needs and situations.

Personnel Recruitment and Training

The position of director general of the Rehabilitation Bureau occupies a place in the career system of the Ministry of Justice for public prosecutors and judges. Otherwise, executive positions are part of the Bureau's career system. Recruitment benefits from the nationwide system administered by the National Personnel Authority (NPA) for all the national government. The NPA I examination is prepared for graduates of senior colleges and universities who had majored in psychology, sociology, education, law, economics, architecture, public administration, physics, chemistry, and so on. The NPA II examination is for graduates of junior colleges or those graduates of senior colleges who have not obtained a college degree in a particular academic specialty. The NPA III examination is for high school graduates.

If university graduates pass the NPA I examination and wish to become a professional probation officer (PPO), they will be interviewed at the Rehabilitation Bureau and, if hired, assigned to a probation office or regional parole board. After six months of practical experience, they become full-fledged PPOs. After another year, they come to the Research and Training Institute at the Tokyo headquarters of the Ministry of Justice for a primary course of 180 days. Fifty days are in Tokyo, followed by on-the-job-training at a probation office.

After six months, the PPO returns to Tokyo for the thirty-day terminal phase. The junior college graduates passing the NPA II examinations become PPOs after four to six years in administrative tasks. The high school graduates completing the NPA III have had eight years of administrative tasks before becoming PPOs. In that status they are eligible for the primary course.

The Research and Training Institute conducts the training for all subdivisions of the Ministry of Justice, except the Correction Bureau, which has its own program of in-service training. The full-time instructors are assigned to particular subdivisions in the multiagency model of in-service training. Two instructors specialize in the training of probation officers. Adjunct instructors are recruited from experienced staff of probation offices and regional parole boards.

The secondary courses are intended to stimulate personnel and instruct a few participants in practical matters. A parole board will plan the course and invite personnel in the area—Japan is divided into east and west areas for this purpose—to attend the course. The Research and Training Institute will bear the costs.

The central office of the Rehabilitation Bureau plans special courses that deal with treatment methods or rehabilitation aid hostels, for example. One year the theme was counseling and casework. Participants interested in the topic of a particular course are invited to Tokyo. Senior courses are devoted to personnel with fifteen or twenty years as probation officers and who are to be appointed as supervisors of sections in probation offices or for regional parole boards.

Pardons: General and Individual

The Offenders Rehabilitation Law, Articles 3–10, authorizes the National Offenders Rehabilitation Commission. The commission makes recommendations directly to the Minister of

Justice "with respect to enforcing special amnesty, reduction of sentence, excuse from the execution of sentence, or restoration of rights of specific persons." Pardon is the only means available to probation offices to discharge an adult parolee or probationer from supervision before completion of the full length of supervision.

Pardons can be traced back to the Nara era (710–784), when they were granted for major events such as deaths in the imperial or shogunate households. These general pardons continue to be issued on rare occasions such as on the occasion of Emperor Hirohito's death in 1989, when granted to persons convicted for violating the Election Law by failing to report political contributions. The general pardons (amnesties) arbitrarily benefit certain categories of offenders according to particular offenses, length of sentence, or other broad variables. The benefits may include commutation of sentence (reduction of its severity) or restoration of rights (Shikita and Tsuchiya 1990, 229).

Individual pardons are awarded according to the qualities of the individual or his or her case. Public prosecutors, prison wardens, or directors of probation offices may originate applications or may certify applications of probationers, former prisoners, or parolees. From the legal point of view, the pardon is a means of removing the statutory bar to specific professions, such as medical practitioner, school teacher, practicing lawyer, real estate dealer, and the like (Rehabilitation Bureau 1990, 51).[1]

From Severe Sanctions to Supervision in Community

From the year 1336, feudal Japan was "torn by factions and plagued by incessant civil wars until late in the sixteenth century, when a process of national unification by force of arms was begun" (Sansom 1963b, v). Ieyasu Tokugawa established the Tokugawa state (the *bakufu*) based upon hierarchical control of all phases of life: occupation, behavior, and the possession of weapons. (The contemporary heavy emphasis on gun control began then.) The era was transitional between feudalism and the modernization undertaken during the Meiji Restoration.

The Taiho Code of 701 named five modes of punishment: strangulation or beheading, transportation to varying distances, imprisonment with labor for one to three years, flogging with a stick, and flogging with a whip. For crimes against an individual or individuals, the offender was not imprisoned but placed in the charge of a relative until coming before a court to confront accusers (Ogawa and Tomeoka 1910, 290).

"Throughout the whole Tokugawa period," Ooms (1985, 147) summarizes, "criminal punishment was cruel, public, and exemplary." The public was supposed to respect bakufu authority by witnessing vicariously the pain inflicted on criminals: decapitation, crucifixion, bodily mutilation, and parading the criminals through the streets. However, exile from the family and village was a formidable sanction in an age of limited mobility and conveyed a message that community forces would manage criminality with minimum cost to governments. Ostracism set the deviant adrift, and acceptance was crucial to reintegration within local life. Violators of village behavioral standards were punished with monetary fines, surrender of rice or sake, and service as night watchmen (Sato 1990).

In Japan juvenile delinquents have received greater tolerance than adult offenders. As early as 668, persons less than seven years of age were assumed to be free of culpability. The premise of limited culpability freed those aged eight to sixteen years from the use of torture to force confession. Offenders less than age sixteen years, convicted of a theft or injury, could benefit along with adults from the *shoku* provision of the *ritsurei* judicial system introduced between 668 and 718. Punishment could be waived on payments according to a schedule of fines. Persons ten years or younger, when convicted of a felony, were confined without pillories or manacles. Imperial approval was necessary for death sentences of persons less than eleven years of age.[2]

Penological history in Europe also begins with organized cruelty. In the Middle Ages, the serf, servant, vagabond, lunatic, and petty offender were whipped. Imprisonment was for pretrial detention, exerting pressure to pay fines, and temporary confinement before servitude on galleys. Outlawry, mutilation, and the death penalty (after 1688) were early punishments (Ives 1944). King (1958) notes that the Statute of Athelstane in the tenth century was exceptional in freeing the offender of grim punishment if the family would assume responsibility.

Probation grew out of a number of early methods in the West of alleviating severe punishments. Christian churches provided sanctuary from secular law for clericals; gradually, the right of the clergy was broadened to cover all who could read (Ives 1944). "Criminal-policemen" were granted a pardon if they betrayed their accomplices (Radzinowicz 1956, 40). In 1841 John Augustus, a boot maker with a shop near the police court in Boston, came forward to ask the judge to permit him to sponsor as a voluntary supervisor for an offender about to be sentenced to prison. In 1878 the Massachusetts legislature provided that the mayor of Boston should annually appoint a salaried probation officer as part of the police force (Moreland 1941).

In 1820 the English magistrates of Warwickshire Quarter Sessions, King (1958) reports, began releasing suitable young offenders on condition that they return to their parents or guild masters who would supervise them. The Temperance Society of the Church of England had gone beyond coping with drunkenness to accept wider responsibility for social work. In 1976 the society installed a "police court missionary" to work with drunkards facing prison sentences and to obtain their release on bail. "Thus," King (1958, 3) summarizes, "the legal and religious approaches converged toward the conception of probation as we know it today."

Parole developed in the West from a number of independent measures: indenture, penal transportation to America and Australia, the English and Irish experiences with the "ticket-of-leave" system, and the work of nineteenth-century American reformatories. Indenture began in eighteenth-century England, when prisoners as laborers were consigned to contractors or ship masters who transported them to the colonies, where the felon's services were given to a successful bidder. Released conditionally, the prisoners agreed to certain conditions (Moran 1945). For criminals transported to Australia, the governors there after 1790 would issue a ticket-of-leave to released prisoners permitting them to seek employment elsewhere. The English Penal Servitude Act of 1853 specified the length of imprisonment before a ticket-of-leave would be granted and specified misconduct justifying forfeit of the ticket-of-leave. Walter Crofton in Ireland provided for a system of police supervision of released prisoners. In Dublin a civilian employee helped former prisoners to find jobs, required them to report to him periodically, and visited their homes biweekly. After 1864 prisoner aid societies employed agents for supervision in England and Ireland, with the government contributing half the costs (Moran 1945).

The Emergence of Probation and Parole in Japan

"As in those other countries where community-oriented treatment of offenders has a far longer history, Japanese corrections have also arrived at the stage where probation and parole play a crucial part in the administration of criminal justice" (Rehabilitation Bureau 1990, i). "It can probably be correctly assumed that probation and parole were able to be initiated in Japan two decades ago," Shiono (1969, 25) insists, "only because there has been a long history of public participation in the rehabilitation of offenders in the community."

In 697 Emperor Shohmu released a robber and gave him

clothing; a moratorium on the death penalty lasted for 347 years from the early ninth century (Satoh 1989). For centuries, each small community was expected to be responsible for crime prevention and aid to former offenders.

The House Laws of the Imagawa clan during the period 1467–1590 emphasized protection of the ruling family and its domain. The doctrine of joint responsibility (*enza*) required the family or servants to share responsibility for the guilt of an offender (Sansom 1963b, 254–55). The principle was extended to require both parents and the children to be punished if the parents were involved in their children's quarrels. That principle was included in the October 13, 1655, municipal ordinance of Edo (now Tokyo). An article of a criminal law of Edo (the *kujikata gojyosho* compiled in 1742) specified that a juvenile killing a person or committing arson would be left in the care of a relative until age fifteen and then exiled. Exile of the juvenile murderer was regarded then to be more lenient than the death penalty imposed on the adult murderer. To avoid exile, some guardians then would report the fifteen-year-old had left for unknown places. That juvenile was called an *otazunemono* and, if apprehended, would be executed. The authorities would require the responsible relative to search for the absconder. After a year and three reports of "futile" search, the relative would be fined.

As an official in the Tokugawa government, Matsudara Sadanobu, an advisor to the shogun, established in 1790 a workhouse oriented to easing the reentry crisis. In the *ninosuka-yoseba* (Ishikawajima Workhouse for Criminals and Homeless Paupers), inmates made lime, charcoal balls, and paper. They were paid to give them economic resources when released and were to find work from skills learned in the facility. Rehabilitated ex-prisoners were given land for farming or a small shop for a business (Hiramatsu 1972; Takigawa 1972; Satoh 1989).

On January 3, 1868, a group of feudal lords initiated the Meiji Restoration when they terminated the Tokugawa state, restored the emperor's direct responsibility for government, and began a series of reforms for a "new" Japan (Beasley 1972). By appearing in 1854 to force open Japanese ports to American ships, Commodore Matthew C. Perry and his squadron of American warships added to the collapse of the feudal system already in decline (Craig 1961).

For centuries, Japanese villagers had assumed responsibility for crime prevention and assistance to ex-offenders (Shiono 1969), but formally implemented community strategies appeared later in Japan than in most Western countries. Lack of sufficient resources had motivated the Meiji government to ask voluntary organizations to assist ex-offenders. I doubt that the public issue of crime per se was the first priority and that establishment of community-oriented corrections was really considered in the policy deliberations during the Meiji Restoration and in the decades that followed. Nevertheless, indirectly—probably inadvertently—a community orientation has entered an official debate in Japanese corrections. The nature of the policy debate, in Japan as well as elsewhere, falls semantically between "rhetoric" and "discourse." Rhetoric conveys a theme of effective speaking or writing (that I prefer) or a theme of insincere and grandiloquent language (that I reject as inappropriate). Discourse implies either a formal expression of opposing views on a public issue (that I accept) or rational thought (a term that overestimates the deliberate and logical nature of the Japanese movement toward community-oriented corrections).

In the Meiji Restoration,[3] the reformers gave priority to establishing a criminal justice system: the first Penal Code (1880), the Code of Criminal Procedure (1880), Law for Suspension of Execution of Sentence (1905), and another Penal Code (1907) that exists today with revisions. The latter code adopted a parole system but was not carried out by the government (Nishikawa 1994). The code would have put parolees under police surveillance, requiring them to report any travel and changes of address and to come to police stations

each month. The Offenders Rehabilitation Law (1949) terminated the police surveillance and expanded parole as a means
of shortening imprisonment. The postwar chaos had produced
a prison crisis: the fiscal burden of excessively populated prisons, aggravated sanitary conditions, and the limited supply
of food for all Japanese (Shikita and Tsuchiya 1990, 209–10).

Ogawa and Tomeoka (1910, 319) wrote: "A law of reprieve
was promulgated in 1905, and two other excellent laws about
leaving offenses of a trifling nature unpunished, and postpon-
ing a criminal action at the discretion of the judge, were published at the same time and are now in force." They reported
that the government has not undertaken "the work of protecting ex-convicts, who may otherwise return to their old evil
ways." Rather they said the obligation was turned over to a
volunteers group; they note "a remarkable fact" that thirty-
seven private associations were engaged in this work.

A firmer base for juvenile community-oriented corrections emerged with the "old" Juvenile Law of 1923 and the
Reformatory School Law. The age limit for juveniles was set
at eighteen years; nine kinds of "protective treatment" were
defined: warning; entrusting the juvenile to a school principal; assigning him or her to a guardian; assigning them to a
temple, church, or welfare institution; putting them on probation; sending them to a juvenile reformatory; sending them
to a training school at Tama (Tokyo) or Naniwa (Osaka); or
referring them to a hospital. The Juvenile Law was a milestone
in calling for the juvenile tribunal (a predecessor for contemporary family courts), for the nine kinds of protective treatment, and for authorizing parole under the supervision of
juvenile probation officers. Initially the tribunals were established only in Tokyo and Osaka, and the rehabilitation services were offered only in five metropolitan prefectures. The
services became nationwide only in 1942 (Shikita and Tsuchiya
1990, 253–54).

From 1948 to 1950, the fundamental legislation for modern community corrections was enacted in Japan. Ono (1970, 8)

calls this development of noninstitutional treatment "the most significant development in criminal policy after the war." The juvenile tribunal was abolished in 1949 when the new Juvenile Law and the Offenders Rehabilitation Law established the family court, the juvenile parole board, and the juvenile probation office. The juvenile probation office was responsible for supervision of juveniles granted probation by the court or parole from training schools. In 1950 the Law for Aftercare of Discharged Offenders and the Volunteer Probation Officer Law drew on traditions to give a special twist to the supervision of probationers and parolees. The new Juvenile Law (1948) established age twenty as the maximum for treatment of delinquents as juveniles, made family courts the gateway to the juvenile justice system, and created the juvenile classification homes. The Law for Probationary Supervision of Persons under Suspension of Execution of Sentence (1954) initiated probation for convicted adults (Nishikawa 1990; Hyotani 1985; Shiono 1969).

Suspension of Prosecution: A Form of Diversion

Public prosecutors occupy a special place in the Japanese criminal justice system, Ito (1986, 67) argues, because they alone can participate in proceedings from investigation, through prosecution and conviction, to sentencing and execution of the sentence. Prosecutors' offices in Tokyo and Osaka, he reports, have Special Investigation Departments for prosecution of illegal political and economic activity. More generally, public prosecutors have authority (Article 248 of the Code of Criminal Procedure) to decide which offenders go to the district courts where convictions are well over 90 percent. "It is a unique characteristic of Japanese criminal procedure that the prosecutor is granted wide discretionary power to decline any prosecution," Ito (70) observes, "even after he has obtained sufficient evidence to establish the guilt of a suspect. This system is called *kiso-yuyo* (suspension of prosecution)."

In addition to suspension of prosecution, the public prosecutors are able to divert suspects to summary courts and to drop doubtful cases from further action. Summary courts may impose sentences of imprisonment at forced labor not exceeding three years for crimes such as the following: habitual gambling and opening a gambling place, larceny, embezzlement, dealing in stolen property, and intrusion upon a habitation.

Suspensions of prosecution have lost percentage representation among all decisions of the public prosecutors (see table 1.1). In spite of the decline of percentage share from 52.1 in 1931 to 28.7 in 1988, suspensions of prosecution have continued to hold a significant proportion of the dispositions. Two safeguards exist against the public prosecutors' inappropriate exercise of discretion in deciding not to prosecute (Tanaka 1986, 25–26). First, established in 1948, the Inquest of Prosecution is carried out by an independent committee of eleven laypersons chosen by lot from citizens eligible to vote in general elections. The victims or other persons may file a criminal complaint applying for examination of the public prosecutor's decision. Second, Articles 262–68 of the Code of Criminal Procedure provide for a complaint asking that a nonprosecution decision be reversed and the case committed to trial. If the complaint is granted by a court, a practicing lawyer is appointed to serve as public prosecutor.

The public prosecutors and judges hold in common a faith in the principle that "worthy" defendants should be diverted from imprisonment. By exhibiting a willingness to be "rehabilitated" and taking action to ease the crime's impact on the victim, the offenders are deemed eligible to return to the community, where "natural" social and psychological forces have greater deterrent effect on them than that initiated by the criminal justice system. "Imposing on an offender the stigma of an ex-convict," Shibusa (1985, 3–4) explains, "often makes

Table 1.1

Public Prosecutors' Dispositions of Suspects for Penal Code and Special Law Violations, 1931–1988

Year	Decisions	Percentage Change[a]		Percentage Distribution of Prosecutors' Decisions			
		Total Decisions	Prosecution Suspensions	Prosecution Suspensions	Other Non-Prosecutions[b]	Formal Trials	Summary Proceedings
1931	334,277	—	—	52.1	22.9	9.2	15.8
1936	388,446	16.2	28.3	57.6	15.6	10.5	16.3
1941	310,901	-20.0	-26.9	52.5	10.5	9.8	27.2
1946	512,982	65.0	34.7	42.9	7.1	23.5	26.5
1951	1,057,303	106.1	172.9	56.8	10.8	13.6	18.8
1956	651,786	-38.3	-53.1	43.2	15.4	20.8	20.6
1961	544,085	-16.5	-24.7	39.0	9.2	22.3	29.5
1966	478,806	-12.0	-19.9	35.5	8.3	21.9	34.3
1971	434,139	-9.3	-4.6	37.3	8.2	20.3	34.2
1976	395,372	-8.9	-25.7	30.5	7.5	29.6	32.4
1981	343,880	-13.0	-23.0	27.0	7.0	34.3	31.7
1986	281,923	-18.0	-19.6	26.5	6.5	38.2	28.8
1988	241,819	-14.2	-6.9	28.7	8.3	38.5	24.5

Source: Shikita and Tsuchiya (1990, tables 22 and 24).

Note: Traffic violations are excluded.

[a]Difference between previous and current year is divided by figure for previous year.

[b]Includes insufficient evidence, nonexistence of valid complaint, and lack of mental capacity.

his reintegration more difficult and recidivism more likely. . . . In general, Japanese public prosecutors consider that their discretionary powers have been granted for the purpose of obtaining effective crime prevention rather than their energy-saving in disposing of a number of cases." Hirano (1963, 299) also sees suspension of prosecution as an instrument for rehabilitation: "Because the investigation and disposition of the matter were carried out by the procurator in closed chambers, the identity of the offender . . . was rarely disclosed to the public. Consequently the offender could continue in the community as a good citizen rather than with the stigma of a criminal."

As for other elements of the contemporary society, discretionary prosecution combines the traditional with the modern. When taking control from the feudal Tokugawa regime in 1868, the Meiji government faced the grave and practical problem of stretching limited resources to create the infrastructure of a modern society. The Satsuma Rebellion of some of the feudal lords and their *samurai* added to the difficulties. Rice warehouses and stables had to be converted as temporary prisons for captives (Hiramatsu 1973; Beasley 1990).

In 1885, Akiyoshi Yamada, minister of justice, declared at a meeting of all chief judges of courts that prisons were crowded because even offenders were being punished for insignificant offenses.[4] "Those persons should be admonished," he said, "instructed for the future, and released instead of being punished" (Asano 1991, 2). The minister had discovered that the largest group of inmates had been imprisoned for thefts (half of them for stealing vegetables or firewood), the second largest group had been imprisoned for fraud (most cases could have been settled by civil litigation), and the third largest group had violated administrative regulations (many did not know the regulations existed) (Maeda 1982, 15–16).

Suspended prosecution emerged informally as an immediate and practical solution, without being incorporated into the legal code. Public prosecutors seized opportunities to avoid prosecution of minor offenses, if reasonable grounds existed, even when evidence was sufficient for conviction. Well after its empirical introduction, suspended prosecution was formally recognized in the 1922 Code of Criminal Procedure (Nishikawa 1990; George 1988).

The practice of suspended prosecution initially was severely criticized by legal scholars and the public, fearing the unusual unrest existing at the time. The scholars, Satsumae (1977, 6–7) says, argued that the practice would violate the principle of equality under law and the deterrent effects of prosecution. He doubts that the public prosecutors' preference for the practice would have survived if they had argued only that the time and costs of trials would be saved and the negative effects of crowded prisons be avoided. The public prosecutors won the argument, Satsumae contends, because they emphasized rehabilitating minor offenders in keeping with the "spirit of generosity" in Japanese traditions and the faith in family influences in aftercare.

The present Code of Criminal Procedure offers general criteria but leaves to the public prosecutor the rationale for excusing the suspects from trial in district courts. Sakai (1985, 9) sees a problem in the variations in criteria among public prosecutors due to the code's abstractions. The code implies that the public prosecutors must have particular reasons for choosing trial over return of the individual to the community as a person likely to correct his faults without formal intervention. In addition to the authorization of leniency by the code, the occupational subculture of Japanese public prosecutors endorses the philosophy of studied leniency. New prosecutors are advised to avoid being too strict for fear of being deceived by the criminal or his family, Ito (1986, 70) says. Without adequate consideration of the case, they should not "impress the label of criminal upon a person who shows a reasonable possibility of rehabilitation."

Article 248 of the Code of Criminal Procedure states: "If after considering the character, age and situation of the offender, the gravity of the offense, the circumstances under which the offense was committed, and the conditions subsequent to the offense, prosecution is deemed unnecessary, prosecution need not be instituted." In 1993 public prosecutors suspended 38.5 percent of the Penal Code cases they received. Of the 79,755 non-traffic cases that were not prosecuted, 79.1 percent were suspended, 14.6 lacked sufficient evidence, 23 percent did not entail a valid complaint, 0.6 percent lacked mental capacity, and 3.4 percent were based on other justifications. The suspension rate (number of suspects granted suspensions divided by the cases prosecuted plus suspended) varied among crimes: robbery, 6.0; homicide, 6.7; indecent assault, 13.2; bodily injury, 26.0; fraud, 32.0; larceny, 41.9; gambling, 46.6; and embezzlement, 80.1 (Research and Training Institute 1994, 57–58).

Sasaki (1995, 1–2), a public prosecutor, supplements the criteria given in the Code of Criminal Procedure. The situation of the offenders goes beyond the conditions of his personality development to include the "prospect that someone will be able to supervise or prevent the offender from committing a new offense." The gravity of the offense means "whether the result of the offense is serious or not," as well as whether it is minor or not. The circumstances under which the offense is committed include the offender's mental state, the motive, whether premeditated, the persistence of criminal intent, the method and means of the offense, and the social impact of the crime. The conditions subsequent to the offense means the offender's repentance, the completion of a restitution arrangement, the victim's attitude, and possibility of change in the social situation affected by the offense. To illustrate the actualities of decision by the public prosecutor, Sasaki (1995, 2–3) presented a case, summarized as follows:

> A male, aged 22 years without a fixed residence or income, was accused of fraud for not paying a 2,000-yen restaurant bill. He had been previously arrested. He said his family

had abandoned him and would not compensate the restaurant and no private party was available for supervision. Sasaki believed that extenuating factors existed: the offender was young, a first offender, and willing to work; the restaurant's loss was small. Eager to help offenders toward rehabilitation, a voluntary probation officer offered to compensate the restaurant and to find a job for the young man. When a job was found, Sasaki suspended prosecution. A few months later the offender was arrested for larceny. The reports on the case and an interview convinced Sasaki that the offender suffered an abnormal mental state. A psychiatric examination found slight schizophrenia. In keeping with the Mental Health Law, Sasaki informed the prefectural governor that the prosecution of the case would be suspended. The offender was hospitalized for psychiatric treatment.

Corrections in the Community: Probation and Parole

Suspended prosecution contributes to diversion from imprisonment, of course, and in this respect is part of community-oriented corrections. Among the justifications for suspended prosecution, the diversion offers the opportunity for communal forces to end criminal tendencies when the offender is capable of self-correction. However, this form of leniency does not include the element of supervision that goes with probation and parole in their modern form.

The Japanese model of probation does include supervision through the sentencing judges' authority to suspend the sentence they have just pronounced. However, the suspension of a sentence need not entail probationary supervision. In fact, suspensions of sentence *without* supervision are much more common than suspensions *with* supervision. Both suspended sentences and suspended prosecution depend on the redemptive pressures of communal influences but, without requiring supervision, do not qualify as community-oriented *corrections*. Otherwise, probation in Japan—entailing supervision as one of the conditions for suspension of sentence—qualifies for community-oriented corrections.

Parole in Japan always includes supervision and comes under the authority of one of eight regional parole boards located in Tokyo, Osaka, Nagoya, Hiroshima, Sendai, Sapporo, Takamatsu, and Fukuoka. These cities are sites of high courts and high prosecutors, but that choice of location does not imply any administrative dependence on the judiciary or procuracy. The regions are part of the organizational scheme of the Ministry of Justice and distribute the functions of the Correction Bureau and regional parole boards.

In the Japanese version, the regional parole boards have these major functions for community-oriented corrections. They grant paroles, grant provisional release from the detention houses (all pretrial detention in Japan is under the Correction Bureau), and revoke paroles from prisons. Penal detention in a detention home is for one to thirty days for persons unable to pay a fine in full. RPBs may revoke paroles when parole conditions have been violated or a new crime committed. They decide when inmates serving indeterminate sentences will be released. They grant paroles and irrevocable releases from training schools. Finally, the Ministry of Justice may delegate to the RPB chairs the authority to appoint the volunteer probation officers.

Administrative Niches of the Agencies

The chapters to follow will be concerned with two major aspects of the community-oriented operations of probation and parole. The programs of the Rehabilitation Bureau are responsible, first, for exaction of the penalty authorized by law. A dichotomy between the purposes of control and treatment exists on the operations. The prisoner has lost the status of a free person in the community; the parolee gains some of the privileges of the free person but continues to be subject to the authority of the state; the probationer draws the least penalization but still is not in a full-fledged free status.

Second, the probation offices, the RPBs, the district courts, family courts, the prisons, and voluntary organizations are an aggregate of elements in the organizations making up the system of community-oriented corrections. In the totality of their relationships with one another, the elements are supposed to contribute to concurrent achievement of three major purposes: protection of the community from future crimes; reintegration of adjudicated offenders into the community; and furthering justice by monitoring the obligation of probationers and parolees and, at the same time, respecting their civil and human rights.

Article 18, Offenders Rehabilitation Law, makes crime prevention one of the responsibilities of the probation offices. They are expected "to indoctrinate, and guide the public to arouse their opinion, to make efforts to improve the social environment, and to promote the activities of the local residents which aim at the prevention of offenses." To that end, the Rehabilitation Bureau has sponsored an annual nationwide campaign, "Movement Toward a Brighter Society," since 1950. Demonstrations and parades are held in the municipalities, with literature distributed that encourages citizens to become involved and community organizations to join in moving toward a crime-free society. Roundtable seminars and programs on radio and television carry the theme. Voluntary probation officers and professional probation officers strive to diffuse resentment against offenders and urge citizens to prevent recidivism by accepting and helping convicted offenders.

Coordinating the functions is crucial for community-oriented corrections. "It is indispensable to keep good relations between the correctional institution and the aftercare agency," Namiki (1980a, 1–2) comments, "for the transfer of offenders from the institution to the community, but officers working in both fields in reality do not always recognize its importance." He notes that both fields publish journals in Japan but that "activities of one field are seldom introduced in the other field's journal." As he implies that immiscibility of staff as individuals may be cultivated unintentionally by the special functions of the agencies themselves. In Japan the functions essential to probation and parole are distributed among agencies in a particular fashion differing from organizational patterns in other nations. That particular fashion reaps advantages and disadvantages.

A fundamental difficulty for agencies of community corrections is their marginal position between the judicial and executive branches of government; the Rehabilitation Bureau is not an exception. If probation were completely the responsibility of the courts, the judges would be able to manage probation services and enlist their influence in acquiring needed resources. The judges' direct contact with probation supervision would alert them to the realities of case supervision and the practical effects of granting of probation to unqualified defendants. The courts' selection of probationer may become more effective in the long run.

In Japan probation already is in the executive branch of the national government but, being a component of the Ministry of Justice, presumably enjoys some of the advantages of being associated with the public prosecutors. Judges are oriented to and trained for adjudication rather than the delivery of human services. The purposes of probationary supervision are monitoring both for protection of the community and for prevention of further crimes by serving the ultimate interests of probationers. Judges are unlikely to be prepared to direct intelligently the service function of probation. As members of the executive branch, probation offices have reasonable access to the social services of other departments and agencies.

Combining probation and parole supervision. Probation offices supervise both parolees and probationers. The RPBs do not carry out supervision but have the right to ask the probation office how parole supervision is being carried out. Although the staffs of probation offices are full-time professional probation officers, most case supervision is carried out by unsalaried volunteer probation officers (VPOs). Chapter 7 will concentrate on case supervision, including the heavy reliance on VPOs.

The combining-clienteles model of supervision raises difficulties that should be assessed in light of other characteristics of the Japanese system of criminal justice. The combining-clienteles model arouses doubts because diversion strengthens the differences between Japanese probationers and parolees, on average, in public attitudes toward their restoration to life in community and the offenders' attitudes toward other persons, their belief in self-redemption, and their expectation of the perceptions of significant others toward them. However, the differences between Japanese probationers and parolees are narrowed by the adult court judges' perception of probation as a punitive sanction short of imprisonment; they avoid probation if the defendants have any capacity for self-correction when restored unconditionally to the community.

Usually, the combining of two clienteles receives objections because of the necessity to accommodate two masters during the supervision process: the judges for probation versus an element of the executive branch of government for parole. As just noted, the peculiar arrangement in Japan allocates authorization of case terminations to the regional parole board but, as an example of an arguable approach, places supervision under the authority of the probation office's chief.

The third issue is that the functions of presentence investigation and supervision impose duties in excess of the capacity of personnel. In Japan the issue applies only to juvenile probation and parole; there joint supervision has an advantage because probation offices are relieved of presentence investigations for juvenile cases.

Issue of presentence investigations. The presentence investigation provides the court with sufficient and reliable information essential for intelligent decisions. Ideally, the report includes a history of family; personal, social, and economic factors in the offender's life; a description of the offense; any previous criminal record; an evaluation of the offender's personality and potentialities; and a plan for treatment. By conducting the presentence investigation of an individual who later is added to his or her supervision caseload, the probation officer is already informed about the background and needs of the probationer.

In the organizational scheme of Japan, the probation officers suffer disadvantages because they have no hand in the selection of the persons who become their responsibility; they have no function in case intake. The regional parole boards decide which prisoners will be granted parole. Probation officers do not conduct presentence investigations. The family courts decide whether or not a juvenile will be granted probation. The hearing officers on the staff of the family court carry out the presentence investigations. Their reports include any diagnostic information acquired by the juvenile classification homes.

The procedures of adult courts in Japan combine fact-finding and fixing the type and amount of punishment. As Ogawa (1976, 620) points out, "[T]he system of presentence investigation has not yet been introduced in criminal courts except for juvenile delinquents who come before the family courts." Lacking the system of presentence investigation, judges depend on the public prosecutor and defense counsel for presenting evidence and for information relevant to the suspension of a sentence and whether or not probationary supervision would be appropriate.

Issue of the difficult probation cases. As noted above, judges prefer to avoid probationary supervision when prison sentences are suspended. Moreover, the Penal Code insists that probation be employed when the defendant commits a crime during a suspension for a previous crime. Kouhashi (1985, 6) comments: "It seems to be inevitable that difficult cases . . . are committed to probation. It is not desirable, however, for the Probation Office to be burdened with too many difficult cases. . . ."

RPB's unusual functions in supervision. As an organizational feature of community corrections in Japan, the regional parole boards are required to turn supervision of parolees over to the probation offices, but the RPBs control termination of both probation and parole cases. Under Article 8 of the Law for Probationary Supervision of Persons under Suspension of Execution of Sentence, the RPBs may terminate probationary supervision when so requested by the chief of a probation office. The board also may reverse that termination in the event of the probationer's misconduct.

Divergence of juvenile case-investigation functions. The family courts disperse the responsibilities of case investigation between the juvenile classification homes (operated by the Correction Bureau) and the courts' own "investigative officers."[5] The juvenile classification homes prepare psychological reports on juveniles, while the courts' own staff are responsible for investigation of community factors. The division of labor hinders the easy transfer of information on cases to probation officers but has advantages: The judges control the development of case histories vital for informed decisions, and the probation officers are freed of the responsibilities of preparing presentence investigation in addition to case supervision.

Length of supervision in juvenile probation. A family court judge cannot fix the length of supervision when placing a juvenile on probation. Kouhashi (1985, 8–9) notes that the "legally prescribed maximum period is two years or until twenty years of age, which ever is longer." That provision reduces the willingness of family courts to use probationary supervision. The judges are reluctant to order probation for a very young juvenile, he explains, because the especially long period of supervision "might place new hurdles on the road to finding employment and so forth." For adult probation,

Article 25 of the Penal Code specifies the length of the suspension of the execution of the sentence (whether with or without probationary supervision): "[T]he execution of the sentence may, according to the circumstances, be suspended for a period of not less than one year nor more than five years as from the day when the sentences became finally binding."

2
Community and Corrections:
Historic and Contemporary Japan

THE ADMINISTRATION OF CRIMINAL JUSTICE and the affairs of the community appear at first glance to be polar opposites. Criminal justice agencies are frequently conceived to be only instruments of written laws and bureaucratic entities that implacably search out criminals; impersonally set out to punish, deter, or otherwise motivate them to abandon forbidden conduct; and discharge them back into the community cleansed of aberrant tendencies. The community is usually extolled as a more humane and compassionate enterprise. "Relatedness is the essence of community, the foundation of community, and involves the reciprocity of caring and being cared for," the Asia Crime Prevention Foundation (1993, 108) declares.

The concept of community-oriented corrections advances the proposition that the connection of the two fields would be worthy in outcomes. The Rehabilitation Bureau is dedicated to implementing that proposition. This book is intended to explore the nature of the implementation, its premises, and the significance within the history and current setting of Japan. As background for the exploration, this chapter considers why that linkage is a promising approach for the field of community, how the concept of "community" has several meanings, the grounding of the concept in Japan's history, and the effect of more recent developments in Japanese society. Two aspects of public policy stand out in the Japanese setting for community-oriented corrections: the special attention given to the family as a social institution and the public policy depending heavily on the private sector for delivering services usually considered functions of the government (the state). This chapter will explain that special attention.

Why Explore the Linkages Between Criminal Justice and the Community?

In reviewing a literature on the appearance and early operations of the penitentiary in the West, Ignatieff (1981) presents three fundamental misconceptions that weaken the efficacy of the analysis. His choice of faulty ideas about the meaning of penal confinement incidentally embody a well-designed justification for community-oriented corrections.

The first misconception: The state has a monopoly over the punitive regulation of behavior. Ignatieff (1981, 162) says: "[T]he emergence of the modern prison cannot be understood apart from the parallel history of the other total institutions created in this period—the lunatic asylum, the union workhouse, the juvenile reformatory and industrial school, and the monitorial school."

His comment is consistent with a principle of comparative criminology: The nature and the purposes of criminal justice activities are derived from the broad setting within which they are located. To understand community-oriented corrections in Japan, we must examine the history and the macrosystem (the totality of social institutions) of Japan.

In essence, the arguments for community-oriented corrections pivot on two fundamental ideas. First, the administration of justice, rather being autonomous, is part of the much broader area of the planned and unplanned processes by which persons are taught, persuaded, or forced to conform to the behavioral standards that sustain the social order. The police, public prosecutor, courts, prisons, parole boards, and probation agencies are elements in the criminal justice system, but their ultimate effectiveness is dependent on the other sectors of the social organization. Second, to understand the possibilities of community-oriented corrections in Japan, we must examine the history from which Japanese corrections emerged and the contemporary sociocultural environment within which the programs of the Rehabilitation Bureau operate.

The second misconception: The state's moral authority and practical power are the primary instruments for maintaining the social order. Ignatieff (1981, 186–87) points out that the crimes referred to the state's apparatus are only a "small part of those disputes, conflicts, thefts, assaults too damaging, too threatening, and too morally outrageous, to be handled within the family, the work unit, the neighborhood, the street." He calls attention to a social network that "handled the 'dark figure' of crime" (offenses not referred to the police) and "recovered stolen goods, visited retribution on known villains, demarcated the respectable, hid the innocent, and delivered up the guilty."

In general, correctional policy is to be revised to make possible closer collaboration of practice and the potentialities of the community in motivating its residents for habitual and rather voluntary compliance. In that respect, any deliberate management of behavior cannot match the community for effectiveness and economy.

The offenders can be turned from a life of criminality by recognizing that otherwise they would be deprived of the social bonds that give purpose to their relationships with other important persons. They may see themselves being shut out of the network of services that are coordinated to meet the basic economic and social needs of residents of contemporary communities. Similarly, the growth of future caseloads would be slowed by prevention of delinquency and crime.

The third misconception: All social relations can be described in terms of power and subordination because, it is assumed, "individuals are naturally unsocial or asocial, requiring discipline and domination before they will submit to social rules" (Ignatieff 1981, 182–83). The misconception lies in "neglect of large aspects of human sociability, in the family and in civil society generally, which are conducted by the norms of cooperation, reciprocity, and the 'gift relationship.'"[1]

Conventional criminal justice practice is dedicated to immediate response to the threat of crime. Coercive authority is expected to achieve compliance. In community-oriented corrections, the community is expected to become an ally.

The alliance promises to be fruitful for the government. Some of the expense and effort of continuous surveillance will be avoided. Unprecedented public support will enhance agency budgets. Volunteers will supplement the professional staff. The public will be encouraged to give moral support to the government's various efforts to deal with crime and criminality.

Diversion reduces the caseload of correctional agencies. Rolls of probation offices would be relieved of those suspects and defendants who could be returned to the community without excessive risk. Even among the convicted offenders there are individuals ready to respond positively to the community's inducements for restoration to ranks of the law-abiding persons. Diversion would dilute the flow of convicted persons to juvenile training schools and prisons.

Arguments in favor of community-oriented corrections lend singular importance to the benefits of curtailing prison admissions. Whereas probation (especially) and parole have the obligation of reintegrating the offender into the community in the senses of its fellowship and service system, the counterproductive consequences of imprisonment are emphasized: the high rate of recidivism among the prison's "graduates," the shutting out the reformatory possibilities of fellowship with law-abiding citizens, possible conversion of experimental into confirmed criminality by thrusting unsophisticated first offenders into the environment dominated by experienced criminals, and the increased difficulty of resuming a normal life the greater the offenders' penetration of the criminal justice system. Probation and parole is supposed to impose less burden on the government's budget because the prison buildings need not be constructed and maintained, a staff of guards around the clock is not necessary, and a full range of inmates' basic needs need not be supplied.

Prelude: Trends in Japanese Corrections

Japan is prominent among the countries committed to exploiting the benefits of community-oriented corrections. That commitment is expressed within a conceptual scenario of traditions that, from a Japanese perspective, are supposed to persist despite the contingencies of a highly industrialized society. The traditions, as will be made clear later in this chapter, were screened by the Meiji Restoration when a group of reformers were thrust into the awe-inspiring complications of bridging the past, present, and future. Their policy decisions have had fundamental effects on the nature of "new Japan." Their influences, as modified by subsequent developments, have given special facets to "community" in Japan that justifies our exploration of Japanese corrections.

As table 2.1 illustrates, the Japanese commitment to community-oriented corrections has been a product of the urge to minimize the use of prisons and juvenile training schools. Second, probation—the most direct evidence of this preference—has increased its advantage over juvenile training schools (JTSs) and has narrowed its disadvantage with adult prisons. In the course of some thirty-five years, the juvenile justice system has halved the rate of admissions to juvenile probation and reduced threefold the admissions to JTSs. Both community-oriented corrections and institutional corrections have lost clientele. The age-specific rates support this conclusion on the potential pool from which juvenile offenders can be drawn: the population of Japanese aged fourteen to twenty years. The number of persons in this age group has increased over the last thirty-five years.

The age-specific rates demonstrate that the number of young probationers and inmates have failed to keep pace. The

Table 2.1

Comparing Courts' Referrals to Correctional Institutions and Probation, Juveniles and Adults, 1951–1987

Years	Family Court Dispositions			District Court Dispositions		
	Probation (A) Age-Specific Rates[a]	JTS (B) Age-Specific Rates[a]	Ratio A/B[b]	Probation (A) Age-Specific Rates[c]	Prison (B) Age-Specific Rates[c]	Ratio A/B[b]
1951	242.8	115.9	209.5	127.8	256.1	49.9
1955	144.1	71.6	201.4	100.5	211.7	47.5
1960	176.8	75.2	235.1	80.6	158.0	51.0
1965	149.2	54.8	272.1	68.8	127.5	54.0
1970	114.1	33.7	338.1	55.2	45.6	57.7
1975	90.9	23.4	388.2	53.9	90.3	59.7
1980	141.9	40.0	354.0	56.9	94.2	60.4
1985	137.1	47.2	290.5	51.6	90.1	57.3
1987	120.3	38.2	314.3	47.9	82.2	58.2

Source: Adapted from Shikita and Tsuchiya (1990, 369, 382).

[a]Rates are probationers or juvenile training school inmates per 100,000 Japanese aged 14–19 years of age.
[b]Ratios: Number of probationers per 100 inmates.
[c]Rates are probationers or adult prisoners per 100,000 Japanese aged 20 or more years of age.

juvenile justice system has given exceptional priority to probation over the JTS. The age-specific rate for probation exceeded that of the JTS for each year, but, as the ratios show, probation's advantage has been great and has tended to expand with the passage of time.

The conclusions also hold for adults, but in a particular way. Probation has surrendered numerical priority to imprisonment, indicating that adult offenders benefit less than juveniles from the preference for community-based alternatives. Of course, there are more adult offenders because of the greater span of adult ages. Later in this book, the noteworthy leniency of family courts will be discussed. Nevertheless, the age-specific rates of adults have dropped for both probation and prisons, and the ratios show that probation has slightly narrowed the primacy of imprisonment.

Divergent Connotations of "Community"

The concept and explication of "community" defy simple definition because of the sentiments evoked. It is a "glow word" in that its widespread appeal and agreeableness attracts universal acclaim, whereas its advocates disguise profound differences in interpretation and ultimate purpose. It is a "cue word" that draws forth sentimental images of the relationships among residents of past society that are unlikely to square with the realities of those relationships and that are even less likely to be consistent with contemporary conditions. "Expending much ink and paper in writing about the contemporary community," Schore (1967, 79) comments in a detailed survey of that writing, modern intellectuals usually contrast it "with some 'ideal state of nature'—past or future—in which the raucous problems of the day are not heard, or are somewhat muted."[2]

One of the definitions of *community* suggests many of the elements it covers: "a complex system of friendship and kinship networks and formal and informal associational ties rooted in family life and ongoing socialization process" (Kasarda and Janowitz 1974, 329). The definition mentions "formal associational ties" and thereby reflects recognition of the impact of urbanization upon the "ideal state of nature" but properly identifies the concept with ties of social intimacy— exemplified by the family—and with the key importance of socialization—the coupling in personality development of learning the behavioral standards of one's society and the development of a sense of self. The "formal associational ties" will take us into the organizational structure of community.

The consensual community. In this version, the emphasis is on a shared sense of belonging to intimacy groups that gives them great influence over its residents. Kawamura (1994, 97) finds that the term *community* is generally linked in Japan with this type of organization.[3] "Traditionally, a community was a village made up of fifty to one hundred households," he explains, "based on living under a system of communal land ownership and irrigation." As a second feature, the Tokugawa government treated the village as the lowest administrative unit.

The consensual community, when existing in reality, has a great capacity to influence the behavior of its residents. A sense of mutuality emerges from intimate social contacts within a relatively small population. The other fellow's fate is bound up with one's own over a long period of time. Uniformity of behavior is favored by common customs and similarity of occupational experiences. Successive generations are exposed to about the same circumstances of living; slow and gradual changes lend stability to the relationships among residents.

Territorial community. Several notions underlie the conception of the community as occupying a particular place on the earth's surface. The geographical boundaries are mountains, bodies of water, or the location of natural resources. Other boundaries, more indirectly associated with territory, are common sentiments, beliefs, ethnicity, and other bases for social solidarity. In those several ways, the locality may generate a sense of belonging and identification that encloses an in-group and excludes strangers. The nostalgia of the hometown is a sentimental attachment to a special place where the family and other associates had influence during childhood and adolescence. The hometown's capacity to discipline its members is indicated by the greater temptations to steal, lie, or commit adultery in foreign lands than at home.

The local resource base may be primary (extraction of raw materials, agriculture, forestry, fishing, or mining); secondary (fabrication or processing of raw materials); or tertiary (distribution of products, finances, communications, military, education, recreation, or government). The resource base affects the community's size, the typical occupations of its residents, the distribution of income, the range of lifestyles, the rate of in-migration or out-migration, and the relative presence of strangers. Through those linkages with the resource base, territorial communities differ in the level of crime, the nature of offenses, and the strength of local normative consensus in preventing and responding to crime.

Community and social organization. Persons turn to one another for companionship, for collaborative efforts in meeting basic needs, and for giving purpose to their lives. A great variety of groups exist as platforms upon which their members contribute to the achievement of social and personal purposes and receive those benefits. These groups also are instruments for the general social order—they are part of the social organization—through their regularized, recurrent, and predictable behaviors that are consistent with society's behavioral scheme.

The social organization entails the coordination of the regularized behaviors to meet the physiological, psychological, and social needs of all members of a society. The two-person groups are the elementary building blocks of social organizations. Social institutions specialize in serving particular needs: providing income, education, medical care, distributing goods and services, communication, transportation of goods and people, and so on. The family as a social institution meets a great number of fundamental needs but, especially in modernized societies, depends on other social institutions for services. Cities, prefectures, and the nation-state are social organizations that deliver services but also comprise an organizational context for the special functions of the various social institutions. The community fits into the system by being the first organization beyond two-person groups, the family, and other social institutions that serve the full range of physiological, psychological, and social needs of its residents.

From the perspective of economics, Wuthnow (1991, 7–10) lists three sectors of society ("various zones or regions of activity") that help clarify the relationship between community and social organization. The three sectors are the state, the market, and the voluntary component. The state "reserves for itself the right to enforce compliance" in activities ranging "from military conscription to taxation to the issuance of subpoenas." (I add probation and parole as parts of the state's compulsory authority).

He defines the market as "the range of activities involving the exchange of goods and services for profit." The "principle of noncoercion" of this part of the private realm is derived from the buyers in the free market to choose among sellers because of competition among profit seekers.

Free of the state's coercion and of the economic constraints of the market, the voluntary sector involves the "freedom of association for purposes of mutuality, camaraderie, or services rendered free of obligation or remuneration." For the analysis of community-oriented corrections, the voluntary sector becomes the target of the Rehabilitation Bureau in recruiting allies from the community in general in meeting the public issues of crime and corrections. The voluntary probation officers and rehabilitation aid organizations are obvious examples; beyond them would be public participation in maintaining a social consensus opposing crime and criminality, in giving moral support to crime prevention and the Bureau's programs, in urging financial support for its operations, and in bolstering efforts to revise public policy for gaining the benefits of community-oriented corrections.

Community of interests. Unlike the premises of consensual community, contemporary urbanites are involved in substantial anonymity in their contacts with other persons, high territorial and social mobility, and a diversified occupational structure, but unprecedented dependence on a network of social organizations for meeting their fundamental needs. In light of these conditions, Janowit

z (1967, 211–12) advanced the concept of "community of limited liability" as descriptive of life in metropolises. Although exposed to behavioral standards intended to maintain the solidarity of the general community, urbanites are likely and usually to prefer their privacy within the family and the groups that capture their special interests. The individual will withdraw conformity to communal expectations when their needs as individuals are not served. The point of withdrawal varies among groups, "but, for each individual, there is a point at which he cuts his losses."

In that light, unlike the pervasive authority postulated by consensual community, the organization of the urban community is grounded in "communities of interest," each gaining the allegiance of members because their conformity with behavioral standards has been rewarded. The concrete aspects of life mirror the urban conditions outlined above; lacking the foundation of a general sense of mutuality, the metropolitan community must find a balance among the claims of special interest groups. Taking the individualistic emphasis of this approach, Hirst (1994, 49–51) argues that all associations should be "communities of choice" in which members "freely choose associations and enjoy the benefits of cooperating with others." He believes that membership of an association goes beyond mere utilitarian convenience. As a chosen means to pursue some common purpose and "through fellowship with others, the individual enhances his or her personal qualities." The urban community also benefits, he says: "[T]he need to build a community out of choice, to win members and to keep their trust is not merely a fundamental discipline or a protection of individual rights, but also helps to make real the cooperation that is built-up and the trust that is created."

Villages in the Tokugawa Period

For almost three centuries, Japan suffered incessant civil war between the feudal lords (the *daimyo*), until the late sixteenth century, when a process of national unification by force of arms was begun (Sansom 1963b, v.). The Tokugawa Shogunate (1603 to 1867) extended its direct rule to all major cities and, through selected daimyo, elsewhere in Japan. Rural fiefs were divided into districts and *mura* (villages) within the districts. Cities were divided into *cho* (wards). The villages and wards were subdivided into neighborhood groups (*gonin-gumi*).

During the struggle for unification, the daimyo had required their samurai to be ready for warfare by living close to the castle. Over time, the removal of them from the land contributed to an arbitrary division between cultivators of the land and warriors. The Tokugawa regime's authority was extended to reregistering agricultural land for taxation. The farm fields were recorded in the names of free cultivators who headed the smaller individual families. The families were grouped in mura that became the standard unit for rural administration (Hall, 1966).

In the Tokugawa era, as will be explained, the village combined the elements of consensual community and territorial community. The consensual community was partly the consequences of territorial isolation but also of decades of a common life. A special feature of the feudal village, however, is the use of the villages by the rulers to serve the rulers own interests. Incidentally to that feature, the rulers pressed the villagers to join together in a common defense. The nostalgia of the consensual community was an insufficient explanation in itself.

"All members of the entire samurai class were forced to choose," Najita (1974, 21) says, "either to live in a single class town where the daimyo resided and serve as stipended bureaucrats or on land and surrender their aristocratic status." Disconnected from the land and no longer expected to use the swords that had given them high status, former warriors were transformed into salaried bureaucrats dealing with the abstract elements of fiscal, educational, and agricultural matters.

The peasants had practical farming skills not familiar to the samurai bureaucrats, but cultural differences also separated them. "Whether of not their estates produced rice," Tonomura (1992, 189–90) asserts, "the aristocrats of the capital in their silken robes had little inclination to interfere directly in the peasants' social system." In the feudal setting, the government did not deliver services. "Feudal government was primarily government of the people by the lord's officials for the benefit of the lord," Steiner (1965, 13) declares. "What the lord required above all was revenue and peace and order." The result was not self-government but a vacuum of government because of the daimyo's lack of concern about the lives of the peasants, except for taxes and maintenance of social order. This arrangement, Steiner (1965, 15) explains, "lacked the political significance that characterizes the notion of autonomy."

With minimal involvement of the castle bureaucrats, the bakufu (the Tokugawa state) appointed a headman from the mura's population to represent them and to be accountable for the village's meeting the demands of the district's representative of the daimyo. The headman disseminated the lord's orders, oversaw tax collection and household registration, signed deeds of land transfers, and represented the village in appeals to the daimyo. The headman had to strike a delicate balance between the demand of the daimyo's representatives and holding the respect and support of the villagers.

The history of Japan has given unusual importance to consent and consensus in governance. Haley (1991, 195) cites the Tokugawa mura being able to be "relatively free of direct, obtrusive governmental supervision or control by paying their rice tax due . . . and otherwise maintaining outward, visible conformity with official policies and community peace and harmony." The mura controlled the details of carrying out the instructions of the Tokugawa rulers. When the mura was able to satisfy the rulers, freedom from obtrusive external supervision continued, but that autonomy persisted because the mura residents agreed to meet the demands of the ruler's representative. Agreement was struck consensually within a local community of near equals in legal status because the residents maintained order and paid taxes in rice but also because of the sociocultural cohesion of the villages.

The sociocultural cohesion of the mura has been attributed to the ostracism and censure of fellows in the consensual community produced by generation of common life. Its social unity was supposed to be due to the central concern as the mutual benefit of its members, a community closed to outsiders, intimate personal relationships, and an atmosphere of relaxed and unguarded contracts among members (Hayashi, 1988). Thereby, the consensual community was able to employ censure and ostracism as social control measures.

The territorial community also strengthened group solidarity; the mountain terrain tended to isolate the villagers.[4] Fukutake (1989, 34) goes so far as declaring that "membership in the village is a territorial rather than a social-relational definition, and this has served historically to reinforce 'village consciousness'." He pronounces this to be "a particularly Japanese characteristic not to be found in other Asian countries." The economics of rice cultivation had its particular effects.

Intensive labor demanded close and habitual cooperation with little need for leadership. Everyone performed all chores, and their total effort was especially essential in planting and harvesting. Residents of a village had to cohere in disputes with other villages over water sources and access to common pastures and forests (Hayashi 1988; Tonomura 1992).

In Kyushu the peasants and Christians rebelled against their daimyo in 1637–1638. As an aftermath, the bakufu began household registration at a temple in 1645. The temple certified the household's lack of a tie to Christianity. By the 1660s, household registration became more systematic as a control device by recording fundamental information about all members of a household: name, sex, age, occupation, birth, marriage, divorce, death, and transfer (Tonomura 1992).

The five-household group (*gonin-gumi*) emerged during the Tokugawa era as a system of mutual responsibility imposed by the rulers. The households in each group were collectively responsible for one another's conduct and the payment of taxes. The village register listed the duties of residents that in practice were more to impress the authorities than to describe the actual behavior of residents. Sansom (1963c, 102–3) lists the provisions of one register: how to receive visiting officials; how to clear roads; how to clean wells and ditches; cultivation of all arable land; trees and bamboo to be cut only when authorized; rules for sale of horses and oxen; and forbidding gambling, bribery, and hospitality for unknown outsiders and members of forbidden sects.[5]

The gonin-gumi was an agency of self-government, not arising from popular initiative, to preserve order. It promoted mutual dependence and consensus as an instrument of control that entrusted the detailed governance to the residents of the mura. "Outside the family (*ie*), Tonomura (1992, 176) says, "it was the minimal and, socially, the most powerful collective unit that—ideally—fostered the state ideology of a docile and productive peasantry." Intended to preserve order and to keep the authorities informed of conditions in the village, Sansom (1963c, 102) pronounces it to be "in fact a police organ for spying and delation." Each group's head had to make certain that the peasants lived frugal lives, worked hard, and paid taxes (Braibanti 1948). The arrangement first imposed joint responsibilities on the offender's relatives (*enza*) or unrelated persons in the household (*renza*). Later the responsibility was extended to neighbors (Ishii 1980).

The Community in Contemporary Japan

The Meiji Restoration had been preceded by a variety of discontents, Beasley (1990, 54–55) summarizes, "but proposals for overcoming them tended to focus on the familiar issue of substituting rule by emperor for rule by shogun." Not inheriting a blueprint for reform, the new leadership began "a period of largely administrative experiments, which only gradually took coherent shape." I am reminded of the "critical time" of the Great Depression of 1929–1940 in the United States, when the administration of Franklin Delano Roosevelt, facing a grave crisis without an advance and consistent program of reform, experimented with a variety of possible solutions. The New Deal has left strong marks on the American infrastructure. Similarly, the changes introduced by the Meiji reformers provided a supporting structure as Japan moved through the stages of Japanese militarism and occupation by a foreign power, the stages of modernization and industrialization, and emergence as a major economic power.

The mura became a building block for creation of a nation-state. "A wedge had been driven between the village as a cooperative living arrangement functioning in a governmental vacuum," Steiner (1965, 24–25) concludes, "and the village as a unit that served the needs of the state." Compulsory conscription was introduced, replacing the samurai, to create a modern army. Because the procedures for conscription required some record of the population, the House Registration Decree of 1871 merged villages into districts that were the elements of prefectures as administrative units for the central government.

To strengthen mobilization of civilians in the war effort,

the Home Ministry in 1940 ordered revival of the neighborhood association. The *chonaikai* (a district or block association) was composed of four hundred to six hundred households. The *burakukai* (hamlet association) was the village unit. A wide variety of functions were carried out: certification of changes of address and vital statistics; administration of rationing and sanitation regulations; distribution of commodities; sale of bonds; collection of certain taxes and scrap metal; supplying labor; air raid defense and certification of war damage; cooperation with the police; and dissemination of government propaganda (Masland 1946).

The Allied Occupation Forces after World War II called for the dissolution of the chonaikai because of its feudal identification with totalitarianism and its wartime functions, but it was revived by 1956 in most cities. Aoyagi (1983) summarizes several explanations for the revival: The chonaikai represented a basic cultural pattern; or, although such a pattern, it would not have survived without government control and guidance; or, although a culture pattern, it was a local phenomenon strengthening democratization.

"If one emphasizes neighborhoods' political and administrative functions," Bestor (1985, 122) points out, "it is easy to see the chonaikai and other neighborhood institutions are little more than extensions of municipal government—created largely at the government's instigation, subservient to it, and manipulated by it to serve the government's ends." But he goes on to note the underlying assumption the chonaikai and local administrative agencies share common interests; and that neighborhoods are social arenas for their residents; and that the social functions cultivate the community solidarity making the neighborhoods effective in playing administrative and political roles.

Aside from the dispute about the double-barreled orientation of the urban chonaikai, the loss of universal acclaim of the Japanese merits recognition. In his study of suburban Tokyo, Allinson (1979, 114) discovered that "well-educated, white-collar workers and their wives, who often came from urban backgrounds, found such associations troublesome intrusions on their private lives." The chonaikai drew more favorable opinions from long-term farmers and older retirees from commercial and professional occupations.

The attitudinal environment for the concept also has changed over the decades. In recent years, Imamura (1987, 7–8) states, the press and officials have preferred to speak of "community" rather than the Japanese word *kyodotai* because the latter carries the meaning of a binding social relationship *without* individual freedom and privacy. "This type of solidarity involves a greater consideration of the individuality of the members," she (1987, 7–8) says, more emphasis on horizontal rather than vertical (hierarchical) relationships, and the responsibility of local residents to deal with local problems rather than expecting the government to take care of everything."

Assessment of the contemporary meaning and functions of community must allow for the special features of its setting within Japan's sociocultural setting, but those features do not exempt the Japanese from the effects of modernization. "Village society has lost the community-like character of a closed local society that it once was," Fukutake (1989, 132–36) announces. "In town neighborhoods, where those constraints had in any case been weaker, their loosening has gone further. . . . Rapid economic growth and urbanization have also changed the structure of cities." He ticks off the underlying developments. Non-farmers commute from villages because they cannot afford urban housing; their presence dilutes village solidarity. The villagers have more contacts outside the locality, and the villages have been regrouped into larger governmental districts. New factories have invaded some villages. The small neighborhood group has become the end-of-the-line of governmental activities; it has lost its many functions of mutual aid. New towns lack any community traditions.

Participation in local affairs has become more specialized; "communities of limited liability" have emerged in Japan, according to Ben-Ari (1991, 9–11), raising doubts that Japan, as a singular exception to other industrialized societies, has undergone modernization without losing the qualities of consensual community. Drawing on a literature of community life in contemporary Japan, he makes a number of conclusions: Participation in local affairs has become more specialized according to sex, age, and occupational status; it serves the interests of specific community groups. At least some of the sentiments and loyalties of traditional consensual communities have transferred to the workplace, weakening the commitment by community residents per se.[6]

Local communities have become more and more dependent on external government agencies because the delivery of services has assumed an unprecedented scale and complexity. Local services have become integrated with wider urban and state systems: schools, public utilities, welfare bureaucracies, commercial firms, transportation services, and communication enterprises. This development was stimulated initially, Ishida (1983) pointed out, by the Meiji regime's policy of minimizing conflicts among villages by turning the previous linkages between peasants and the local daimyo toward loyalty to the central government. The contemporary local communities exceed the mura in the capacity to adapt consciously and intentionally to changes in external circumstances. The concept of limited liability, Ben-Ari says, is relevant in two senses: Only some individuals or households are active, and, when communal effort is not personally rewarded, they may withdraw participation either physically or emotionally. In spite of greater dependence on systems external to the locality, residents of local communities today are less passive and submissive to the demands of those systems than were the members of traditional villages.[7]

In traditional communities, collective cooperation was based on kinship, joint residence, and common sentiments (the consensual community), but in contemporary Japan, collective cooperation in localities is oriented to limited, usual instrumental goals and involves only part of the local population.

The culture and history of Japan continues to shape in peculiar fashion the emergence and operation of voluntary organizations. "Village consciousness" in the territorial sense is more relevant here than in other societies. Many local voluntary organizations are directly linked, and encouraged, by various branches of government. Local organizations tend to have longer organizational life spans than in the United States. Some critics have noted the linkages and questioned whether or not the organizations are examples of local initiative by socially aware citizens, or are they locality groups subject to manipulation by centralized government.

Community as an Alternative to Government

The correctional agencies of Japan were modeled and currently operate as part of a government that seizes opportunities to draw upon the community in lieu of investing in the delivery of services. The consensual community is expected to prevent delinquency and crime; as part of the social organization of society, the communities are pressed into service for supervision of probationers and parolees. This governmental policy can be traced back to the Meiji Restoration.

The Meiji reformers "were not the kind of bureaucrats one can call 'faceless.'" Beasley (1990, 58–59) declares. "They were men of initiative, even idiosyncrasy, who had risked their lives and in some cases an established position in society to break free from the trammels of upbringing and tradition." There were heavy demands for expenditure, but an efficient tax system had to be created. Many sources of discontent had to be managed. A modern army and its supporting infrastructure had to be created to cope with the threat of foreign intervention and the violent reactions of discontented daimyo and samurai. In the development of industry, how far should the state be involved—another heavy burden on the public purse—and how much should private enterprise be summoned?

While introducing modern social institutions and their infrastructure, the Meiji regime could amass only a fraction of the material and social-psychological resources that this movement required. The slender material resources of the state were to be stretched by limiting the functions of government. In the early years of the Meiji Restoration, private enterprise was reluctant to risk investments in unfamiliar sectors of the economy because of the shortage of capital and the technical and organizational complexities of machine production (Smith 1955). Following a brief flirtation during the immediate post-Restoration period with state establishment and control of vital industries such as munitions, shipbuilding, coal mining, and communications," Pempel (1982, 14) declares, "the government withdrew from direct ownership and management, leaving these aspects to the private sector."

During the Meiji era, prison labor was directly involved in the economic development. Prisoners were employed in land reclamation and mining projects in Hokkaido, Japan's frontier at that time. The Asahikawa-Abashiri highway, traversing Hokkaido, was constructed between 1886 and 1891. Sorachi Prison provided labor for coal mines (Yokoyama 1982, 3–4; Hiramatsu 1973, 35–36). Later the government reversed the relationship by turning to private business and industry to ease the burden of prisoners on the government's budget. The industrial prison continues to thrive because of linkages with the private industrial sector. Through subcontracting with private companies, the products of prison workshops have access to the free market.

Public prosecutors and sentencing judges return a substantial proportion of apprehended suspects to the community without supervision. The consensual community is expected to deter further lawbreaking by suspects and defendants; again the costs of correctional agendas are reduced. Suspended prosecution emerged informally when public prosecutors seized upon this way to avoid prosecution of minor offenses if reasonable grounds existed (Nishikawa 1994). In the Meiji era, the public prosecutors faced a horde of accused persons among the samurai defeated in battle. They seized upon this immediate and practical solution; later the procedure was incorporated in the Code of Procedure. Article 25 of the Penal Code authorizes the judge, who has just sentenced a defendant to prison, to suspend the sentence and either place the offenders on probation or release them unconditionally.

Japan is unusual among contemporary industrial societies in the relatively small size and curtailment of the growth of its governmental personnel. "Attention has been focused primarily on reducing the size and cost of the national bureaucracy" (Pempel 1982, 9). The National Personnel Authorization Law of 1969 set a maximum fixed number of officials and required each ministry to eliminate one of its bureaus and reduce personnel by 5 percent over a three-year period. In 1980, the size of government was restricted when the rate of economic growth slowed and the governmental deficit grew (Verba et al. 1987).

Until the 1970s, Japan demonstrated the policy of limiting governmental functions by lagging behind countries of Western and Northern Europe in health insurance and pension schemes. "In 1955 Japan was spending only 5.3 percent of its national income on social security payments," Watanuki (1986, 259) reports, "while at that time West and North European countries were already allocating nearly 20 percent of their national income for that purpose."

The word *welfare* has been reinterpreted in Japan, Kinoshita and Kiefer (1992, 9) assert, in mirroring changing and ambivalent attitudes. In the years before Japan gained the reputation of being prosperous, the word was pejorative and associated with needy, low-income persons who could not take care of themselves. Now, the word is more likely to be regarded in the sense of government being successful in delivering services in the spirit of "public well-being." The limited scope of governmental services is being questioned because of changing conditions in the Japanese society.

Although political discussions are too confusing for clear

definitions, Watanuki (1986) sees the "Japanese-type welfare society" centered on lower governmental expenditures for social security functions than in the "welfare state" and greater reliance on the family, community, and private companies. He reports that in light of the unprecedented aging of the Japanese population, social security benefits began to rise during the 1970s.

Familialism as a Foundation for Community

Familialism is a social pattern that gives the interests of the family priority over the interests of its members as individuals. In feudal Japan, the ie household was an extreme example of familialism and its capacity to dominate the lives of its members. As a kind of social organization, the ie was a basic element in the Tokugawa community in its function for social control, economic production, socialization, and monitoring of morals. The Meiji reformers continued these functions of the ie household in their program to modernize Japan after the collapse of the Tokugawa bakufu.

The values of familialism have lingered in contemporary Japan—which helps to explain its relatively low crime rate for an industrialized society. Familialism colors every stage of criminal justice processing, Moriyama (1995, 57) insists, in relationships "between the policeman and the offender, the judge and the defendant, and the prison officer and the prisoner." The linkages between consensual community and the remnants of familialism are a basis for community-oriented corrections. Fundamental changes in Japanese society, however, challenge the continued efficacy of the linkages.

The ie was an agricultural or small-business enterprise that possessed the property and was controlled by the "family" head in the paternalistic mode. It was a "corporate residential group," rather than qualifying as the usual conception of a family, because its members were not necessarily blood relatives." Not only may outsiders without the remotest kinship ties be invited to be heirs and successors," Nakane (1984, 5) explains, "but servants and clerks are usually incorporated as members of the households." The wife and daughter-in-law (especially if she gave birth to a male heir) from the outside became members, whereas sisters and daughters went to other ie households. The oldest son continued to live after marriage in the same house as the father (the ie head) and his mother in a household of two or three generations.

Members, Fukutake (1981, 34) declares, "were trained to suppress individual desires and make the goal of their lives to maintenance of the ie and the enhancement of its name." The Tokugawa era (1603–1867) transmitted feudal characteristics that still linger in contemporary Japan; Confucian morals were among the characteristics. The teachings were dedicated to strengthening the family and assuring its continuity through filial piety (Sansom 1963c, 88).[8]

The Meiji Restoration switched the political emphasis gradually from the Tokugawa fief as the focus of loyalties to focus on loyalty to the nation as a whole. Smith (1983, 17, 31) emphasizes that the Meiji political rhetoric was revolutionary but was essentially conservative. "Since they believed a stable family meant a stable society," he comments, "the oligarchs took a bold step and as if by a slight of hand converted filial piety from a private duty into a civic virtue." The Meiji civil code made the ie the basic unit of Japanese society until 1947, when this aspect of the legal system was abolished (Iwao 1993).[9] The emperor was portrayed as the patriarch of the common main family, Ishida (1983) explains, and the tradition of ancestor worship and the subordination of branch families to the main family were enrolled in the development of the spirit of nationalism. To that end, Professor Hozumi Yatsuka of Tokyo's imperial university declared that to be obedient to the family head is to be obedient to the spirit of the ancestors, and, since the present emperor sits on the throne in the place of the imperial ancestors, obedience to him is obedience to them (comment cited by Beasley 1990, 80).[10]

The ie system had much to do with the rapid industrial-ism of Japan. The eldest son inherited the family household property. As long as there were new labor markets to receive them, Fukutake (1989, 27–28) says, "the younger sons . . . took positive steps to leave the family and seek a livelihood else-where." While promoting the process of industrialization, the ie system also delayed social policy, Fukutake notes, by "keeping wages low and working conditions harsh, and pre-venting any demand for social services from becoming pow-erfully articulated."

"As industrialization progressed," Ishida (1983, 11) notes, "the workers came to feel more and more estranged from their village, which ironically heightened their nostalgia for tradi-tional village life." Government and management had the opportunity to portray relationships between employees and management as an "enterprise family." The ie imagery lingers in the conception of the employer as the head of the company existing as a pseudo-family. Nakane (1984, 8) explains: "[T]he employer readily takes responsibility for his employee's fam-ily for which, in turn, the primary concern is the company, rather than relatives who reside elsewhere."

Lincoln and Kalleberg (1990, 140–41) measure the com-mitment to this approach by the agreement or disagreement with this statement: "A company should take care of its em-ployees, since a company and its employees are like a family and it's employees are like a family and its members." They report: "Past surveys have shown that most Japanese work-ers respond positively to questions of this sort."

Familialism in Japan has suffered in recent decades from the impact of a set of far-reaching developments that favor the nuclear family over the extended family. The birthrate dropped by half between 1947 and 1957; the replacement rate (suffi-cient babies to equal the number of parents) has hovered around one. The Eugenic Protection Law (1948) legalized abortion, and the use of contraceptive methods became widespread (Hodge and Ogawa 1991). Women aged 25 to 35 years delayed marriage and motherhood, divorced more freely, and had fewer children. The number of divorcees receiving child allowance rose considerably in the seventies and eighties (Rosenberger 1996).

Since 1973, the percentage of women employees (as opposed to those in family businesses or self-employed) topped 70 percent (Ueno 1994). Prosperity has made higher education and other opportunities available to daughters as well as sons. Improvements in home facilities have lightened the burden of housework and freed women for other pursuits (Pharr 1981).

Using "privatization" to review the changes in the Japanese family since World War II, Morioka (1986) emphasizes the functions of the ie as a basic unit of the social structure and its deterioration because of the private nature of the emergent nuclear-family household. With the decline of the ie as the primary workplace, the traditional household lost its public nature as a unit of the overall social organization. It became a private entity based on the "consummatory values": sexual intercourse within a private conjugal relationship, mutuality in affection, sharing the pleasures and crises of marital life, and other elements of the nuclear family. This "privatization" of the nuclear family has eroded the *public* functions of the traditional ie.

The privatization has been promoted, Morioka points out, by the Residents Basic Register Act (1967), which called for registration of individuals and the shift from arranged marriages to love matches. The average size of households has declined, signaling the loss of close kin (other than children) as coresidents. Rest and relaxation has gained popularity, and rearing of children has lost emphasis among family functions. The divorce rate had declined but has begun a recent increase with the gain of employed wives and of public aid for fatherless households.[11]

With the privatization of family life, Morioka believes, the social functions of the ie have been lost. With the disappearance of occupational cooperation and mutual aid, visiting is more rare, houses are secluded from the outside world, and

families are virtually isolated functionally from other families. Traditions of kinship have lost much of their influence.
The child-training function of the family has waned.

Balancing the Past and the Future

In restricting the use of imprisonment, Japan offers an exceptional opportunity for examining the sources of a community-
oriented corrections. The history of the mura and the ie household carries implications that the source has been the consensual
community, but closer examination suggests that neither justify the nostalgia evoked by images of the past consensual
community. The cohesiveness of the mura is a product of the
combination of sense of unity of its residents, a common reaction against the threat of bakufu and competing villages, the
demands of a rice economy, and the isolation of the feudal village from the rest of Japan and the world.

The field of corrections in Japan has avoided the rush to
imprisonment as the primary answer for the criminality that
goes with benefits of industrialism and urbanization. This
noteworthy development may be attributed to survival of
elements of consensual community, but that belief overlooks
the exploitation by the Meiji reformers of that imagery in
maintaining social stability in developing the foundations of
"new Japan" during a short slice of history. Now the Japanese
society is undergoing the effects of massive socioeconomic
changes that have fueled the movement away from the ie
toward the nuclear family. Meanwhile, the rise to the status
of one of the world's economic powers complicates the future
of Japan's uniqueness as an exception to the deterioration of
the traditional community. The community of interests is becoming more of a model for relationships among the Japanese
and Japan's place among nations.

Community-oriented corrections has been and will be an
instrument in Japan for a composite of social institutions and

their history. As the society changes, familiar practices of probation, parole, and aftercare will be pressed to adapt. The community of interests will gain importance as a model. The traditions of Japan will be too influential to justify any assumption that the experiences of Western corrections will be followed. In its own way, Japan will continue to link corrections and the community as units of social organization and sociality.

3
Adult Probation and Parole:
Administrative Features

THE POSSIBLE RELATIONSHIPS BETWEEN the community and correctional practice are promising means of accomplishing the ultimate goals of the regional parole boards and probation offices, but, as chapter 2 demonstrates, the potentialities are elusive. These two social units are components of the administrative and functional structure given a mandate to realize their potentialities. In targeting adult probation and parole, this chapter turns to the main point of this book: the management of probation and parole as the programmatic elements for accomplishing the potentialities of community-based corrections in Japan.

Comparing Adult Probation and Parole

Probation and parole are similar in being substitutes for imprisonment. Probation offers full-fledged diversion, especially for offenders not previously exposed to incarceration; parole shortens the exposure to imprisonment. Both approaches are less costly to administer than the prisons because full surveillance and provision of basic needs for life are not necessary and because human services in the community—those accessible to all residents—can become available. To differing degrees, the two approaches contribute to preserving family ties—when such ties exist—and enable willing offenders to provide economic support for dependents.

63

Table 3.1
Adult Admissions to Probation and Parole, 1950–1995

Years	Probation Admissions		Admissions to Parole			Probationer-Parolee Ratios[c]	Parolee Percent of Releases[d]
	Number	Age-Specific Rates[a]	Number	Age-Specific Rates[a]	Approval Rates[b]		
1950	221	0.49	43,106	95.36	78.5	0.51	73.2
1955	4,361	8.58	32,435	63.78	94.4	13.44	63.7
1960	8,525	15.21	30,824	55.00	91.2	27.66	68.4
1965	8,350	13.41	19,430	31.21	84.1	42.97	57.2
1970	6,908	9.89	17,861	25.58	86.2	38.68	61.8
1975	7,048	9.19	14,933	19.46	84.3	47.20	56.0
1980	8,058	9.92	15,206	18.72	84.4	56.72	51.8
1985	7,180	8.35	17,795	20.69	91.2	40.35	55.7
1990	4,793	5.28	14,896	16.41	92.5	32.18	56.3
1995	4,856	5.02	12,138	12.55	94.1	40.01	56.8

Sources: Shikita and Tsuchiya (1990, 194, 372–74); Research and Statistics Section (1986a, 7; 1990a, 2–3; 1991a, 76; 1991b, 76, 162; 1996a, 2–3, 55; 1996b, 76, 162).

[a] Age-specific rates are the number of admissions per 100,000 Japanese over 19 years of age.
[b] Parole approval rates per 100 prisoners considered by regional parole boards.
[c] Number of probationers per 100 parolees.
[d] Percentage share of parolees among all prisoners released from prisons.

Probation avoids at least some of the stigmatization that breeds the offenders' alienation from prosocial values and norms and excludes the psychic pains of forced confinement. In Japan, those advantages over parole are narrowed by the very factors that minimize the use of imprisonment. Judicial policy relegates probation to the arsenal of punitive sanctions and prefers that "worthy" persons be restored to the community without probationary supervision.

Unlike probation, parole is expected to confront the reentry crisis that is aggravated when the individuals are rejected by their families or have lost contact with families. Rejection of former prisoners encourages repetition of crimes. Serial inmates face especially difficult reentry. However, parolees leave before their full sentences have been served; gaining a parole suggests more favorable attributes and past behavior that could ease reentry difficulties.[1]

Paroles in Japan had a minor place among releases from prison before World War II ended; Shikita and Tsuchiya (1990, 373) offer these percentage shares of paroles among all releases from prison: 5.7 in 1926, 3.7 in 1930, 13.3 in 1935, and 12.7 in 1940. The representation of paroles surged to 73.2 percent in 1950, when the socioeconomic chaos after World War II crowded the Japanese prisons (see table 3.1). After 1960, parole's percentage share declined to hover in the 50 percentages.

The parole rates per 100,000 Japanese link the use of parole to the probable number of candidates, assuming no major change in the likelihood of being imprisoned. The pool of persons from which parolees are selected may broaden in time, but this rate would not change if the chances for being paroled remain the same. The percentage share of all releases from prison is another possible barometer of trends in the use of parole, but a sharp decline in all releases from prisons could indicate a relative gain in parole even though the absolute number of paroles actually declined. Again we find the highest rate in 1950. The rate of 95.4 is low, and means that only 95 of every 100,000 adult Japanese are parolees.

In absolute number of cases, adult parole admissions have greatly exceeded probation admissions—43,106 versus 221 in 1950, or only 1 probationer per 200 parolees. Adult parole held that great advantage immediately after World War II, when there was an urgent need to relieve the crowding in prisons. Second, adult probation was just being established as a well-developed approach. The ratios in table 3.1 record a long-term gain in the number of adult probationers when compared with admissions to adult parole.

The table also makes visible the general decline—although always a substantial proportion, 73 percent in 1950—in the representation of parolees among all adults released from prison. In the following years, the parolees lost share to reach 56.8 percent in 1995. Most of the inmates discharged in 1995 (56.8 percent) had been paroled. Of the remainder, 40.3 percent had not been the subject of a parole application. I word the statement in that fashion because approval of the prison warden, not simply the inmate's request, begins the regional parole board's procedure. Only 2.9 percent of the applicants had been denied.

Probation: Its Tie to the Suspended Sentence

When promulgated in 1905, the Law for Suspension of Execution of Sentence gave legal recognition to the suspension of the sentences the courts had ordered. The law authorized suspension of a sentence without labor for one year or less, under specified circumstances, and set the period of suspension as two to five years. To be qualified, the defendant could not have been previously sentenced to imprisonment with labor or, if so previously sentenced, it had to have occurred more than ten years earlier. In 1907, the Penal Code reduced the latter disqualification to seven years and permitted suspension of prison sentences, with or without labor, for lengths of two years or less. An amendment to the Penal Code in 1947 allowed suspensions for three years or less. Still another amendment in 1953 shortened the disqualification due to a previous criminal record from seven to five years and allowed judges the opportunity to grant a second suspension when the defendant had violated the first suspension. More important to our study, probation was made mandatory if the second suspension were granted. In 1954 an amendment to the Penal Code authorized probation also for the first suspension (Shikita and Tsuchiya 1990, 110–11).

The national judicial system covers all courts in Japan: the Supreme Court, fifty district courts, fifty family courts, and 452 summary courts handling minor cases. Nakajima (1991) reports that well over 90 percent of adjudicated cases are concluded within six months after prosecution is initiated. Three judges preside in district court trials of "specified serious or sophisticated cases," and a single judge otherwise. If a defendant cannot afford a defense counsel, the court appoints one from among "practicing lawyers." The indictment outlines the basic facts of the crime, but the judge relies for detailed information on the prosecutors, the defense counsel, and the witnesses they bring.

The Japanese use of suspended sentences was modeled on the French-Belgium system (Ancel 1971). Conditional suspension of prison sentences emerged in Belgian law in 1888 and French law in 1891, when Meiji reformers were examining European legal systems. In Belgium and France, the prison sentences were pronounced in courts to intimidate the convicted offenders, but the sentence was lifted without probationary supervision for casual offenders believed to be capable of voluntary rehabilitation after being intimidated.

Courts about the world may suspend their sentences either before or after they have pronounced sentence; in Japan, suspension comes afterward. The suspension continues the action of the court rather than being an entirely distinctive measure. Moreover, the suspension provides an opportunity to alleviate the excesses of the high conviction rate (approaching 99.9 percent in 1995) of cases the public prosecutors send to district courts for trial. Ishikawa (1986, 8–10) explains the high conviction rate as the consequence of the "precise and minute fact-finding" by the "professionally-minded" officials in law enforcement, the procuracy, and judiciary who are "diligent toward their task of discovering the so-called objective truth in each case."

Sentences to prison are among those that may be suspended by the courts and return the defendant to freedom in the community without probationary supervision. The Japanese criminal justice system defines these as *simple* suspensions. Suspension *with* probation becomes a stern measure when compared with simple suspension and, thereby, is supposed to lull any public fear that dedicated criminals have been turned loose in the community.

Judges sometimes are reluctant to require probationary supervision as a condition of the suspension, Kouhashi (1985, 4–5) says, when there are extenuating circumstances, since the offender will be denied by law another suspension if a new crime is committed while on probation. If granted a suspension for the earlier crime without being placed on probation, the person committing a new crime still has the possibility of receiving a suspension again.

Article 25 of the Penal Code authorizes the judge to suspend a sentence to prison "under extenuating circumstances" when certain conditions exist. The length of sentences would be not more than three years. If previously imprisoned, the offender must have completed that sentence at least five years ago; the requirement could be canceled if there are "extenuating circumstances" and the new sentence is no more than one year. If the person "had committed a crime again within the period of such supervision for a previous crime, . . . the subject person shall be placed under protective supervision during the period of suspension." The length of probationary supervision is specified by the sentencing judge and ranges from one to five years, corresponding to the length of the sentence being suspended. In practice, "extenuating circumstances" are specified by Kouhashi (1985, 3) as the defendant has no or a minimal criminal record or is young enough to change attitudes and lifestyle. The victim excuses the offender, the victim and the defendant have agreed to terms for restitution, and the offender exhibits readiness for rehabilitation. The offense was accidental, not deliberate.

Prison sentences were rather few from 1931 until World War II, and suspensions of prison sentences were even more rare (see table 3.2). In the years immediately after the war, social chaos brought unprecedented numbers of prisoners and an upsurge in the suspensions. Prison admissions had slackened off in the following decades, but the suspension rates climbed to hover around the high 50 percents and lower 60 percents. Official statistics do not report until 1956 on the use of suspensions to put adjudicated offenders on probation. Afterward, suspensions with probation have held shares of all suspensions ranging from 14 to 19 percent. Failures (revocations of all suspensions) were 18.3 percent in 1956 and have declined since then, reaching 8.2 percent momentarily in 1971 but usually in the lower teens.

The probation caseload is affected by two opposing factors. The caseload is reduced by the judges' preference for outright release without probation. The caseload is expanded by the Penal Code's insistence on probationary supervision when the defendant is charged with a new crime while on suspension of a previous sentence. Suspensions of sentences at first court appearance are much more frequent than second suspensions of offenders who, while already freed on suspension for a previous crime, were granted suspension again for a new crime. In 1979, first court appearances held 95.6 percent of the suspensions and second suspensions only 4.4 percent. Second suspensions lost even that small share over time, reaching 2.1 percent in 1994. However, mandatory second choices of suspensions *with* probation have occupied an important, although declining over time, share of all suspensions

Table 3.2.

Suspended Prison Sentences, Probation, and Revocation for Adults, 1931–1993

Year	Prison Sentences(A)	Suspensions Number(B)	Suspensions Rates B/A	Suspensions with Probation Number(C)	Suspensions with Probation Rates C/B	Suspensions Revoked (%)
1931	35,219	4,817	13.7	NA	NA	10.5
1951	118,229	54,272	45.9	NA	NA	NA
1956	102,275	48,969	47.9	6,922	14.1	18.3
1961	83,249	43,142	51.8	8,067	18.7	13.6
1966	78,814	42,142	53.5	8,012	19.0	11.2
1971	69,467	40,361	58.1	6,451	16.0	8.2
1976	75,498	45,892	60.8	8,238	17.9	10.1
1981	76,219	44,269	58.1	8,217	18.6	14.2
1986	74,856	42,589	56.9	6,242	14.7	13.8
1991	54,522	32,668	59.9	4,647	14.2	11.4
1993	56,480	34,458	61.0	4,944	14.3	11.1

Sources: Shikita and Tsuchiya (1990, 165); Research and Training Institute (1993, 71, 73; 1995, 62, 64).

with probation. From 25.1 percent in 1979, the share has dropped irregularly to 15.1 percent in 1994 (Research and Training Institute 1984, 106; 1989, 109; 1994, 62; 1995, 63).

The net effect is the weighting of probation caseloads with many unpromising candidates for rehabilitation. Nishikawa (1994, 221–22) reports that a considerable number of adult probationers have committed serious crimes or have a propensity for repeating crimes. Some persons convicted of homicide, robbery, and rape, for example, would present "extenuating circumstances" and draw a prison sentence for no more than three years. Bodily injury and theft, crimes with high levels of recidivism, drew the highest suspension rates (Shikita and Tsuchiya 1990, 156–64).

Outcomes of Suspensions with Probation

How had probation compared with outright releases by suspension of sentences in regard to revocations of suspensions? Table 3.2 shows the revocation rates (the number of canceled suspensions per 100 cases) for all suspensions, whether for outright release or for probationary supervision. These rates are approximations because the failures did not necessarily occur in the year the suspension was granted. The greatest number of prison sentences were in 1951, when the number of suspensions was highest. The number of prison sentences has dropped over the subsequent years; the rates have done likewise but not in tandem with the drop in number of sentences. Table 3.2 does not compare probation outcomes with outcomes of suspensions without probation. Other data are unfavorable to probation in rate of revocations per 100 cases: 26.2 versus 10.4 in 1981, 29.6 versus 10.5 in 1984, 28.3 versus 9.5 in 1987, 25.5 versus 8.3 in 1991, and 24.9 versus 8.0 in 1994 (Research and Training Institute 1984, 106; 1987, 98; 1990, 121; 1993, 73; 1995, 64.

The inferior record for suspensions with probation is al-

most the inevitable consequence of the court's policy in selecting the least promising probationers among the convicted offenders granted suspension of prison sentences. As Kouhashi
(1985, 5) explains: "A lot of difficult cases are recommended
for community-based treatment." When there are circumstances favorable to the offender, the judges are inclined to
choose suspension of a prison sentence *without* probation.
Other offenders also are believed to be worthy of a suspension (not going to prison) but not to outright release into the
community. These are the "difficult cases" among candidates
who would be on probation for the first time but who, the
judges believe, do not deserve outright release because they
lack a strong innate capacity for self-correction. Probationary
supervision is deemed more stern than unconditioned return
to the community—although short of imprisonment—and
is necessary for deterrence and for protection of members of
the community.

Second, among the convicted offenders just sentenced to
prison, there are individuals who had been in prison for a previous crime and that earlier incarceration had been completed
five years or less ago. If other qualification are satisfied, these
individuals may be granted suspension of the new prison
sentence, but, if they committed a new crime while benefiting from an earlier suspension, they must be placed "under
protective supervision during the period of suspension" (Penal Code, Article 25.2–1). In effect, the probation offices *must*
accept "difficult cases," contrary to the common assumption
that probation specializes in "deserving" offenders.

In 1988 the Research and Training Institute published
results of a survey of the criminal records of 45,755 multiple-
offense recidivists spanning ten years (Research and Training
Institute 1988, 31). One table focuses on whether or not a
prison sentence was suspended by the court as the recidivists
underwent each of an increasing number of sentencing experiences. The rate of suspensions dropped from 56.4 per 100
sentenced individuals at first sentence to 5 percent at six or

more sentencing experiences. For suspensions with probation, the rate dropped from 11.8 for first sentenced to 1.5 for six or more sentencing experiences.

The declining rates seem to be due to greater care in selecting those recidivists who were granted suspensions. Failures were reduced with greater degree of recidivism. The percentage share of suspensions resulting in revocations decreased from 62.9 for first sentencing incidents to 39.7 for six or more incidents. Suspensions with probation also exhibited fewer failures with greater recidivism but trailed revocations in general, decreasing from 78.6 percent failure for first sentencing incident to 51.2 percent failure for six or more incidents.

Parole and an Integrated System

The RPBs begin their deliberations with the advantages of an integrated correctional system and the classification procedures of a nationwide prison system. As components of the national Ministry of Justice, the Rehabilitation Bureau and the Correction Bureau manage all correctional affairs of Japan in their respective responsibilities. The Rehabilitation Bureau is responsible for parole decision making through the RPBs but depends on probation offices (also managed by the bureau) for supervision of parolees. In their decision making, the RPBs rely on the classification procedures of the Correction Bureau that, beginning in the detention houses, distribute prisoners among specialized prisons to which regional parole boards come to assess inmates for eligibility for early release.

At the detention houses, classification workers assemble information from documents developed by the police, public prosecutors, and courts and add their own information acquired by interviews and psychological testing. On the basis of the collected information, the classification section—subject to the approval of the detention house's warden—

decides which of the prisons in the correction region is appropriate for the particular convicted inmate. The Correction Bureau's scheme of prison types takes into account basic characteristics of prisoners: sex, age, length of sentence, recidivism, nationality, possession of "criminal tendencies," and physical or mental disabilities. Females (class W) go to five women's prisons distributed about Japan and a branch prison in Sapporo. The women's prisons receive all classification classes, whereas male prisoners are distributed among prisons according to the general scheme. Housing assignments within women's prisons take the scheme into account.

Foreigners (class F) who cannot tolerate the Japanese menu or housing arrangement and cannot understand the Japanese language are assigned to special units. Civilian males go to either of two prisons: Fuchu in Tokyo or Osaka Prison. American military males convicted for violations of Japanese laws go to Yokosuka Prison on the shore of Tokyo Bay under a formal agreement with the government of the United States.

Juveniles sentenced to adult prisons (class J), aged less than twenty years, have been sentenced in district courts for especially serious crimes. The family courts had referred them to public prosecutors because of the circumstances of the crime or personal characteristics of the young defendant. The public prosecutors referred them to the district courts for trial as adults. The number of class J inmates has dropped from 2,259 in 1945 to 47 in 1995 (Shikita and Tsuchiya 1990, 311; Research and Statistics Section 1996c, 124).

Persons serving sentences of more than eight years (class L) are referred to one of seven prisons, including four reserved for them alone. Adults less than twenty-six years of age (class Y) go to one of seven juvenile prisons. Prisoners sentenced to imprisonment without labor (class I) were only 112 in 1995 (Research and Statistics Section 1996b, 26). These *kinko* inmates (imprisonment without labor) have committed "non-infamous" crimes and are worthy of greater tolerance than *cho-eki* offenders (imprisonment with labor), whose crimes are "infamous" (Research and Training Section 1969, 18). However, kinko inmates usually accept the opportunity to volunteer for work in prison industries.

The major classification distinction is between class A (persons without "advanced criminal tendencies") and class B (those with "advanced criminal tendencies"). Among prisoners in 1995, A class per se composed 17.8 percent and B class pee se 53.6 percent, but, since the distinction also applies to other classification types, A class holds 33 percent of all inmates and B class 67 percent. Four criteria are used in selection of B class: previous imprisonment within the previous five years, association with crime syndicates (yakuza), nature of the offense, and persistent departures from rectitude.

Duties of the Regional Parole Boards

The offices of the eight regional parole boards are located in Tokyo, Osaka, Nagoya, Hiroshima, Fukuoka, Sendai, Sapporo, and Takamatsu, where the high courts and high public prosecutor offices are located. The Offenders Rehabilitation Law, Articles 12–17, outline the organization of the RPBs. They will have more than two but less than thirteen members who are appointed for three-year terms. The chair of the board is appointed by the Minister of Justice from its membership. When the chair is prevented from presiding, a substitute is selected from the RPB membership in a prearranged order. Each board has its secretariat according to the organizational scheme set by the Ministry of Justice Ordinance.

Located in Tokyo, the Kanto RPB is the largest in the dimensions of its business in eleven prefectures including fifteen juvenile training schools, eighteen prisons, three detention houses, and a women's guidance home. The secretariat has six sections: general affairs, research and liaison, first investigative section (chief and seven staff), second investigative section (chief and staff), third investigative section (chief and four staff), and case management section. The first investigative section gathers information on parole applications from juvenile training schools. The second investigative section deals with adult parole applications. The third investigative section administers parole revocations, other terminations of juvenile parole supervision, and provisional discharge from adult probationary supervision.

Articles 28 and 30 of the Penal Code set two general requirements for being considered for parole: the inmate "evinces general reformation" and has served one third of a determinant sentence or ten years of a life sentence. The regional parole boards are authorized to grant paroles from prisons and juvenile training schools and provisional release from detention houses. Of the 13,156 parole applications in 1995 for inmates serving determinant sentences, 94.2 percent were approved, 2.4 percent were denied, and 3.3 percent were withdrawn by either the prisons or probation offices. The RPBs considered paroles for thirty-two inmates serving life sentences; twenty-five were approved and seven denied. The life inmates granted parole had served an average of seventeen years, two only eight years, and two only twelve years (Research and Statistics Section 1996a, 30–31, 44).

A person on penal detention or detained for nonpayment of a fine, Article 30 states, may be granted "provisional release" whenever "circumstances warrant." Article 16 specifies that penal detention shall be for one to thirty days and shall be served in a detention house. Article 18 authorizes detention from one day to two years for persons unable to pay a fine in full. The length of detention is reduced by partial payment according to the ratio of the amount paid to the total fine originally imposed. RPBs received a few applications from detention houses in 1965 to 1980, but none since then except for one application in 1990 that was withdrawn (Research and Statistics Section 1996a, 4–5).

The RPBs decide when inmates serving indeterminate sentences will be released. In indeterminate sentences, the court sets a minimum (say, one year) term and a maximum term (say, three years), leaving the precise time of release from prison to the correctional authorities. In Japan the RPBs make the decision. Of the 13,222 cases before the boards in 1995, only thirty-four were for indeterminate sentences. One warden withdrew two cases from board consideration because of violations of prison rules, and the RPBs denied three of the remaining twenty-nine cases (Research and Statistics Section 1996a, 31).

The RPBs grant paroles from prisons and juvenile training schools and absolute (irrevocable) releases from juvenile training schools as authorized by the Offenders Rehabilitation Law, Articles 12, 19, and 43. These RPB functions will be considered in chapter 5.

According to the Offenders Rehabilitation Law, the RPB may revoke parole when the persons do not reside at a place they had reported, had been arrested under a warrant of arrest (*inchi-jo*), or otherwise violated the conditions of parole. The length of supervision usually is for the unserved part of the prison sentence, but the board may extend the parole period for an absconding adult parolee (escape from supervision) by eliminating from the time of supervision the months from disappearance to the date when the parolee was located (Article 42-2-4).

The Minister of Justice may delegate to the RPB chair the power to appoint the VPOs according to the qualifications listed in Article 3, Volunteer Probation Officer Law. The authorization exists in spite of the RPBs' exclusion from supervision of parolees and probationers. The boards do have the right to contact the probation offices on how supervision is being carried out.

Procedures in Parole Decision Making

As parole decision makers elsewhere, the RPB members ask practical questions when they consider the parole application. Are new crimes likely if parole is granted? Will members of the community tolerate the early release from prison of this criminal? Is this prisoner repentant and has already demonstrated progress toward being a law-abiding member of the community? In that spirit, Article 34, Offenders Rehabilitation Law, announces the purpose "to promote the improvement and rehabilitation of the person under probationary supervision, by leading and supervising him to observe the conditions [of parole], and giving him guidance and aid, in recognition of the fact that he naturally has the responsibility to help himself."

In Articles 34, 35, and 36, the law hovers between the treatment and control goals that complicate the administration of community-based corrections. "Someone may understand that parole constitutes some sort of permissive indulgence and represents 'mollycoddling' of convicted criminals by shortening their sentences," Hagiwara (1982, 1–2) comments. "However, society which has a right to safety and immunity from criminal harm must pay attention to smooth reintegration of offenders into society." He sees parole's purpose to be the balancing of "maximum protection for society and maximum opportunity for reintegration for conditionally released prisoners."

From the control perspective, Article 34 speaks of "leading and supervising him to make him observe conditions . . . to live at a fixed residence and engage in an honest calling; to be on good behavior, to keep away from persons who are of criminal or have delinquent tendencies; to ask his supervisor for permission in advance for changing his residence or going on a long journey." Article 35 continues to specify control measures common among probation and parole agencies. The meaning of *guidance* is elaborated as methods "to watch the behavior of the person under probationary supervision by keeping proper contact with him." The suggestion of the control purpose is strengthened by instruction "to give the person under probationary supervision such instructions as are deemed necessary and pertinent to make him observe the conditions."

A broad conception of *treatment* is implied in Article 35, when calling for "measures necessary to aid him to become a law-abiding member of society." The article plunges into the topic of "rehabilitation aid" for methods "necessary to accomplish rehabilitation": to help probationers and parolees obtain means for education and training, medical treatment and recreation, lodging accommodations, vocational guidance, and a job. Parolees are to be helped to "adjust their environments," including help toward returning "to a destination deemed most suitable for rehabilitation."

Japanese researchers gathered data on 1,200 parole candidates to determine factors that induced RPB members to deny parole at first application (Ifukube and Sugihara 1979). For rape and indecent assault, denials were linked to sentences over five years, more than four victims, and the offender's failure to compensate victims. Sentences over ten years and more than two victims worked against prisoners convicted of homicide. Robbery was penalized when imprisonment exceeded ten years, death or rape was involved, offenses were more than two, and the victim's injuries took more than three months to heal. First denials of all offenses were linked to an inmate older than forty years, with a history of misconduct while drunk, who had no fixed residence or job before imprisonment and expected to live with a relative, acquaintance, or at a hostel.

Usually five to seven times a month, each of the ninety-four investigative section probation officers assigned to the RPBs visit the several correctional institutions that are their responsibility. From information derived from interviewing inmates, the officers prepare reports for the RPB summarizing their life history; criminal record; motives and reasons for the crime; source of income; hobbies; addiction to tobacco, alcohol, or drugs; mental and physical health; conduct in prison or juvenile training school; family relationships; the employment-residence plan for life after release; and the assessment of the officer preparing the report (Namiki 1980b, 4).

At the request of the director of the probation office, a

VPO is assigned to visit the prospective residence to which the released inmate will return, as specified in the inmates employment-residence plan. The VPO assesses the family situation, the attitudes of the members toward the inmate's return, and any problems in the setting. When appropriate, the VPO advises the family on how any problems can be overcome. The VPO's report, including comments of the probation officer's chief, goes to the prison and RPB. If the home situation is unsatisfactory, the VPO continues contacts for obtaining improvement. Another relative, employer, or friend may be a substitute for the prisoner's immediate family. Otherwise, assignment to a hostel may be recommended.

The Offenders Rehabilitation Law, Articles 29 and 30, requires that the RPBs "conduct an examination in order to decide whether to permit such release or not." An RPB can dismiss an application without a hearing "when such application has been made contrary to the established formality or has not met legal requirements." The hearing "shall be conducted by investigating into the subject person's character, behavior while in the prison or juvenile training school, vocational knowledge, way of living before commitment to the prison or juvenile training school, family relations and other relevant matters." The RPB member must personally interview the candidate unless the "subject person is seriously ill or seriously injured." The member may request the opinion of the correctional institution's head or his or her presence at the examination session.

The RPB membership is divided into several panels, say three members in each of four panels. The number of members depends on the RPB's caseload. The member is assigned to certain prisons or training schools for face-to-face interviews with eligible persons. On average, 63.6 days were required in 1995 for cases ultimately to be approved, 75.4 days for those puzzled over and then denied, and 58.2 days when withdrawn from consideration either because of the inmate's violation of a prison rule or an unsatisfactory parole plan (Research and Statistics Section 1996a, 10).

After interviewing the inmates at correctional institutions, the board members prepare a handwritten report. If the parole is approved, a copy of the report goes to the probation office. The standard form of the report calls for the following information: names of the inmate and institution; outline of the inmate's personal problems and criminal tendencies (alcohol, drugs, gambling, yakuza affiliation, etc.); conduct during any previous probation or parole; any experience with hostels; behavior in prison (excellent, good, or poor); grade in progressive stages; number of rule violations; self-examination: the inmate's thoughts about the offense, former life, and the future; whether or not the victim feels vindictive toward the inmate; recommended parole conditions; and specific matters to be emphasized in supervision.

A panel meets once a week, when the members report on their interviews. Most decisions are made by full consensus. Otherwise, the responsible member reinterviews the inmate to clarify any remaining issues or to obtain another impression of the inmate. When parole is denied, the inmate is informed, but not about whether the case will be reconsidered. If the warden again approves a recommendation, the possibility of a parole will be considered six months later. The rejection rate for adult parole applications is very low because, I was told, the candidates are first selected by the prison officers who know the individual quite well. Usually gangster-inmates are unlikely to be released on parole when they are reluctant to comply with the instructions of VPOs or PPOs. Yakuza who are paroled are very obedient.

Putting the Approval Rate in Context

"When a person sentenced to imprisonment at or without forced labor evinces genuine reformation," Article 28 of the Penal Code states that "he may be paroled by an act of the administrative authorities after he has served one-third of the sentence for limited term or ten years of a life sentence." From

1985 through 1995, those lifers receiving paroles had served an average of twelve to eighteen years, with the average escalating as the years passed (Research and Statistics Section 1990, 44; 1993a, 44; 1996a, 44).

"The sentence for a limited term" is the determinate or definite sentence that specifies a certain number of years. The indeterminate sentence sets fixed maximum and minimum years and leaves to the paroling authorities the time of release from prison. Of releases in 1995, the RPBs acted on twenty-nine indeterminate cases, releasing twenty-five inmates after the minimum had been served and four before the minimum (Research and Statistics Section 1996a, 40).

Releases from prison are either on parole or at expiration (discharged when the prison sentence has been completed), if we ignore escapes (very rare in Japan) or deaths. In 1995 there were no escapes, 118 deaths, 9,233 releases at expiration, and 12,138 paroles.

Addressing expiration and parole as the sole departures from prison, table 3.3 tells us that paroles comprised 56.8 percent of all 1995 discharges. A few of the inmates discharged at expiration had failed to obtain RPB approval when the prison warden recommended their parole. Most of the "expiration" inmates completed their sentence without being a candidate for parole. As will be discussed below, a variety of sound reasons explain the release of many prisoners without parole. When we turn from all releases from prison to take up the Rehabilitation Bureau's report on RPB decisions, table 3.3 reports the high approval rate (94.2 percent) for the 13,190 RPB cases. Of the remaining cases, 324 (2.5 percent) had been denied approval and 440 (3.3 percent) had been withdrawn by the prison wardens or probation offices.

The prison warden, not the inmate, initiates the application for parole. Article 29, Offenders Rehabilitation Law, puts parole among the measures available to the prison for control of inmates. It instructs the RPB to conduct an examination "when the RPB has received an application for parole or provisional release from the warden of the prison."

Table 3.3
Parole Decisions by Length of Prison Sentences, 1995

	Total RPB Cases	Length of Prison Sentences in Months					
		Under 6	6–12	12–24	24–36	36–60	60–240
Prison Releases							
Total cases	21, 371	2,111	4,876	8,542	3,749	1,487	606
Expiration	9,233	1,663	2,000	3,120	1,493	716	241
(Parole denials)	(614)	(16)	(72)	(257)	(167)	(80)	(22)
(No parole request)	(8,619)	(1,647)	(1,428)	(2,863)	(1,326)	(636)	(219)
Parole	12,138	448	2,876	5,422	2,256	771	365
Percent Distribution							
Prison releases	100	100	100	100	100	100	100
Expiration	43.2	78.8	41.0	36.5	39.8	48.2	39.8
(Parole denials)	(2.9)	(0.8)	(1.5)	(3.0)	(4.4)	(5.4)	(3.6)
(No parole request)	(40.3)	(78.0)	(39.5)	(33.5)	(35.4)	(42.8)	(36.2)
Parole	56.8	21.2	59.0	0.2	60.2	51.8	60.2
RPB Decisions							
Total cases	13,190	207	1,952	5,698	3,363	1,411	559
Approvals	12,426	204	1,869	5,431	3,154	1,299	469
Denials	324	2	18	73	98	77	56
Withdrawals	440	1	65	194	111	35	34
Percent Distribution							
Total cases	100	100	100	100	100	100	100
Approvals	94.2	98.5	95.8	95.3	93.8	92.1	83.9
Denials	2.5	1.0	0.9	1.3	2.9	5.4	10.0
Withdrawals	3.3	0.5	3.3	3.4	3.3	2.5	6.1
Share of First Termers among RPB Approvals							
Total cases	12,397	204	1,868	5,424	3,144	1,295	462
Percentages	59.1	89.2	63.2	52.9	59.9	65.2	78.3

Source: Research and Statistics Section (1996a, 18–19, 36).

Note: "Parole denials" plus "no parole requests" equal expirations.

RPB members explain their reliance on prison officials in the selection of candidates for parole. I was told that decision making is based on "philosophy," not on accumulated statistics on previous parolees. "We do not like automatic decision-making," a board member explained. "We do not have statistics that go back on violence and other misconduct of previous parolees." The RPB members tend to share the previous experiences of prison staff with attitudes of inmates. "The recidivists think they know the outer demeanor we expect of them and adjust their visible conduct toward us accordingly." Prison officers have had direct contact with prisoners over a span of time and are expected to be especially familiar with the ways of the people—including prisoners—in the particular prefecture. Unlike the members of the RPBs and their staffs, who are usually transferred every two or three years, the prison officers are "locals" who may be natives of the area or, at least, have resided there for a considerable period.

The diversionary policies of public prosecutors and the judges' use of suspended sentences magnify among prisoners the presence of questionable prospects for rehabilitation on parole. Paroling authorities in Japan have special reason to grant parole to such questionable candidates as a measure for "control and assistance" of such inmates. "It is expected that release on parole to be followed by supervision," says Hagiwara (1982, 2), "will serve his rehabilitation. Otherwise, he would be discharged without supervision. Such practice has some additional significance in Japan since a good-time system is not in existence."[2]

The high approval rates convey the impression of limited chances for denial of applications, but, of the 13,222 candidates in 1995, only half (51 percent) were being considered for the first time (see table 3.4). The rest had appeared before RPBs multiple times. Each time they had high but slightly declining chances for being approved. Denials assumed increasing—but also low—shares of the decisions as the number of appearances accumulated. Withdrawal of applications were more stable but also held small percentage shares.

Table 3.4

Parole Decisions by Number of Appearances Before RPB, 1995

Number of RPB Appearances	Total RPB Appearances		Percent Distribution of Decisions			Approvals per 100 Appearances
	Number	Percent	Approvals	Denials	Withdrawals	
1	6,737	51.0	96.0	1.5	2.5	96.0
2	2,020	15.3	93.6	2.4	4.0	46.8
3	1,306	9.9	91.7	3.5	4.8	30.5
4	1,011	7.6	91.9	3.7	4.4	23.0
5	650	4.9	92.2	4.6	3.2	18.4
7.5	1,498	11.3	91.2	4.8	4.0	12.2
Total	13,222	100	94.2	2.5	3.3	37.5

Source: Research and Statistics Section (1996a, 26).

Approval per 100 previous appearances takes into account the inmates' history of contacts with the RPB in the course of their current sentence. As the number of appearances accumulate, long-term imprisonment comes to the fore because shorter sentences do not provide sufficient time for multiple applications. Table 3.4 demonstrates the approval rate per 100 appearances dropped sharply as the number of appearances grew.

Withdrawals of applications were few in table 3.3; the withdrawals were due to new rule violations or unsatisfactory arrangements for residence and employment of the prospective parolee. The withdrawals did not cancel all hope of parole. In 1995, 56 percent of the withdrawals resulted in subsequent approval of a new application, 31.3 percent were denied parole, and 12.7 percent received no further consideration (Research and Statistics Section 1996a, 45).

Complex Influences in RPB Decisions

Selective diversion of some Japanese defendants and convicted offenders has transfigured the pool of prisoners from which parolees are chosen, but, as in other correctional systems, the biographical differences and other characteristics of prisoners influence the RPB decisions. The differences among parolees, as portrayed by Rehabilitation Bureau statistics, will be the subject matter of chapter 4. Here the focus is on what that data tell us about RPB decisions.

Table 3.5 relates RPB approvals to general categories of crime. Judges include crimes as defined in codes of law among the criteria for setting the length of sentence. Crimes differ in lengths of imprisonment legally possible and thereby differ when completion of a third of the sentence opens the possibility of parole. But explanations and motives for behavior seep beyond the distinctions. The inmate's crime is a criterion for simplistically determining parole eligibility, but it is not sufficient for reliably predicting future conduct. Crime categories tell us more about the administrative patterns of parole boards than the qualities of the persons who are subject to their decision making.

As we should expect, property crimes are most common in the cases presented for RPB deliberations. Larceny is especially numerous because of the wide variety of incidents the term encompasses: housebreaking theft, bicycle and motorbike theft, theft from vehicles, shoplifting, theft from vending machines, and so on. Inmates convicted of larceny have a high average number of previous incarcerations, but their relatively minor threat of violence raises their chances for RPB approval. Fraud—seeking an illegal economic advantage—is recidivistic, but previous exposure to imprisonment is short of larceny. Arson and embezzlement draw a high percentage of first exposures to prison. I could say these inmates tend to be "first offenders," but, in light of the heavy use of diversion in Japan, we cannot be certain that these persons engaged in arson or embezzlement for the first time. Arson incidents differ in length of sentence, depending on whether or not an inhabited structure was burned. Embezzlement, typically a white-collar offense, is high among approval rates and first exposure to prison.

The Stimulant Control Law of 1951 as subsequently amended has been the major vehicle for the imprisonment of drug abusers and traffickers. Recidivism is high because of the habitual abuse and the gangsters' persistent pursuit of the profits of drug trafficking. Sniffing of toluene and acetone in a plastic bag also has placed some adults in prison. The Narcotic Control Law was amended in 1953, but the number of cases has declined. The greater number of first termers— when compared with the other two types of drug offenders— helps explain the high approval rate for narcotic offenders.

Traffic offenders drew almost a perfect approval rate and a very high proportion of first termers. Japan suffered a crisis of traffic fatalities and accidents because of urban congestion, narrow streets, a postwar expansion of car ownership, and an increased number of irresponsible drivers. Criminalization of more traffic offenses followed the escalating number

Table 3.5
RPB Approvals by Crimes, 1995

Selected Crimes	RPB Cases		RPB Approvals		First Termers' Pct. Share of Decisions	
	Number	Percent	Number	Percent	Total Cases	Approvals
Violence against persons	1,784	13.5	1,632	91.5	82.0	83.2
Bodily injury	422	3.2	400	94.8	70.1	70.5
Bodily injury with death	94	0.7	85	90.4	90.4	90.6
Homicide	434	3.3	376	86.6	85.5	87.5
Robbery	204	1.5	193	94.6	88.2	88.6
Robbery with death or rape	214	1.6	194	90.6	82.7	86.1
Rape	285	2.2	268	94.0	89.5	90.3
Indecent assault	112	0.8	97	86.6	76.8	79.4
Societal violence	553	4.2	505	91.3	60.0	60.8
Extortion	337	2.6	308	91.4	61.1	62.7
Firearms	136	1.0	123	90.4	69.8	69.1
Violence law	74	0.6	68	91.9	39.2	39.7
Property	5,568	42.1	5,245	94.2	52.6	53.9
Larceny	4,274	32.3	4,035	94.4	47.4	48.6
Fraud	832	6.3	776	93.3	62.5	64.2
Embezzlement	164	1.2	162	98.8	90.8	91.4
Arson	138	1.0	125	90.6	89.8	91.2

Table 3.5 cont. on next page

Table 3.5 continued

Selected Crimes	RPB Cases		RPB Approvals		First Termers' Pct. Share of Decisions	
	Number	Percent	Number	Percent	Total Cases	Approvals
Forgery	116	0.9	107	92.2	81.0	84.1
Drugs	3,953	29.9	3,730	94.4	44.7	45.7
Stimulants	3,762	28.4	3,549	94.3	43.6	44.5
Organic solvents	128	1.0	120	93.7	55.5	56.7
Narcotics	63	0.5	61	96.8	87.3	88.5
Illicit trades	81	0.6	75	92.6	63.0	64.0
Traffic	1,093	8.3	1,082	99.0	90.8	91.3
Total crimes	13,222	100	12,451	94.2	58.2	59.2

Source: Research and Statistics Section (1996a, 12).

Note: Excludes crimes not specifically defined and those with few numbers in source report. Included crimes do not equal total of of accidents and traffic fatalities. More drivers were sent to prison; some became candidates for parole.[3]

Illicit trades cover entrepreneurs in prostitution, gambling and lotteries, and traffic in pornography. The yakuza (Japanese crime syndicates) are active in these illicit enterprises.[4] Societal violence also involves gangsters, although the Law for Punishment of Acts of Violence also was directed against the rallies of the *bosozoku,* motorized gangs of adolescents and young adults. The offenses of societal violence share the image of violence but differ from violence against persons by being directed against the corporate order. Societal violence and illicit trades are characterized by high probation rates because the laws being violated call for comparatively short sentences. Some of the cases involve defendants who are otherwise reputable. Some of these offenders have been before the courts frequently.

Among crimes of anti-person violence, homicide and indecent sexual assault have comparatively low approval rates and proportions of first termers. We are surprised by the recidivism of homicide cases; usually, murderers are first offenders, but, in the context of Japanese diversionary practices, most of these recidivists have probably been involved in other kinds of offenses.

Death and serious injury in bodily injury cases are first termers to a greater extent than simple bodily injury. Bodily injury includes an array of violence-prone individuals, but extreme violence is less frequent. Rape cases also draw a high proportion of first termers when compared with indecent assault. Robberies involving homicide or rape do not differ from simple robbery in level of recidivism, but simple robbery gains a better approval rate.

Regardless of the length of the prison sentence, first termers hold the advantage in gaining RPB approvals (see table 3.3), but that advantage is greatest for sentences of less than six months. When debating whether or not to suspend a prison sentence, judges are likely to decide against a convicted defendant with a history of repetitive imprisonments. The history grows as the serial prisoner ages. Half of the new parolees had been in prison previous to the sentence just completed. That rate per 100 parolees rose from 10.3 for ages less than 25 years to 70.2 for ages greater than 59 years. Another bit of evidence is the growing average number of appearances before the RPBs with advancing age of inmates: 1.08 for ages less than 25 years, 1.43 for ages 25–29 years, 2.20 for ages 30–39 years, 3.02 for ages 40–49 years, 3.56 for ages 50–59 years, and 4.34 for ages 60 years and more (Research and Statistics Section 1996a, 26–27, 90).

Length of sentence, in and of itself, is important in parole decision making, although its influence is not fully consistent. Table 3.3 reports a general (although irregular) relationship between parole's share of prison releases and length of sentences. The percentage of RPB approvals drops consistently from 98.5 for sentences less than six months to 83.9 percent for sentences of five years and more. The length of sentence, of course, determines when serving a third of the sentence opens eligibility for parole, but the length is related to the perceived degree of seriousness of the crime and the court's evaluation of the defendant's past behavior and character.

Rule violations are among the reasons for the reluctance of wardens to recommend parole. Infractions become more likely as the sentence lengthens. The frustrations of being locked up may multiply with time. Skill in evading punishments may evaporate with repeated attempts to manipulate prison situations. Among prisoners leaving prison in 1995, the infraction rates per 100 inmates rose consistently from 4.01 for inmates completing a sentence less than three months in length to 322.8 for sentences of ten years or more. The percentage of inmates without rule violations dropped from 95.6 for sentences less than three months to 26.8 for sentences of ten years or more with the same consistency (Research and Statistics Section 1996b, 190).

Simple rates do not take into consideration the possibility that the number of rule violations do not rise consistently with prolongation of the stay in prison. The 674 inmates serving less than 3 months had 27 rule violations for a rate of 2.67 per 100 estimated months served. For inmates serving 3 to 6 months, the rate per 100 estimated months was 6.42. From that point, with increasing number of months served, the rate declined to reach 1.93 for 15 or more years served. The rate grew from 64.3 per 100 discharged prisoners for first admissions to 117.6 for inmates in prison five or more times. For first termers, 69.7 percent had no infractions, and the percentage dropped with the greater number of exposures to incarceration (Research and Correction Statistics 1996b, 192).

Time Served Before Parole

As for other parole systems, the collection of information and the deliberations of decision makers take time. Any unnecessary delays are especially unfortunate because in Japan the length of parole supervision is only the unserved portion of the prison sentence. In collecting information for RPB consideration, the RPB staffs encounter particular difficulties because of the accumulation of many cases in the final portion of the inmates' sentences, the relatively average short lengths of prison sentences when compared with American prisons, and the Japanese policy of giving prison wardens the authority to determine whether or not an application for parole is filed. The low imprisonment rate of Japan eliminates the use of parole as a means of reducing the overpopulation of prisons.

Parole's share of discharges from prison remained at more than 60 percent until 1971, Satoh (1989, 35) recalls, but the percentage dropped to about 50 and stabilized at that level (see table 3.1). Hyotani (1985, 1) attributes that decline to the many inmates being granted parole when only 10 percent of the prison sentence remained to be served. "The parole system," he asserts, "was not functioning as satisfactorily as it should for rehabilitation of offenders. . . . The Rehabilitation Bureau . . . decided, in March 1983, on a policy of promoting increased utilization of parole, which included earlier granting of parole release to first offenders in order to give them longer parole periods and, at the time, to achieve a little higher rate of parole release."

The Penal Code specifies that before parole can be authorized, the prisoner must serve a third of a determinant sentence or ten years of a life sentence. However, of all paroles granted in 1995, only 8.3 percent were authorized before 70 percent of the prison sentence had been served before the parole. Of the parolees, 30 percent had served 90 percent or more of the sentence; less than 10 percent of paroles came before 70 percent of the sentence had been served.

Those conclusions are derived from data reported in the Annual Reports of Statistics reported for the Rehabilitation Bureau and are the basis for our table 3.6. The table relates the crimes to the respective array of lengths of sentence imposed by district courts: less than 12 months, 12 to 18 months, 18 to 24 months, 24 to 36 months, 36 to 60 months, and 60 and more months. For each of those categories, the proportion of the sentence served before parole is specified: 70 percent or less, 70–79 percent, 80–89 percent, and 90 percent and over.

By the time 80 percent of the sentences had been served, 36 percent of the paroles had been granted. Inmates serving their first prison sentence had a great advantage over serial inmates: 58.4 versus 2.5 percent. The positions were reversed for paroles obtained after at least 90 percent of the sentence: 11.9 versus 56.1 percent.

For all RPB cases, the importance of length of sentence for parole approvals is demonstrated by statistics on whether approvals came when 80 percent or 90 percent of the sentence had been served. For sentences less than a year, 30.5 percent of approvals came before 80 percent of the sentence had been completed. That percentage increased irregularly with prolonged incarceration, topping at 40.2 percent for sentences of

Table 3.6
Proportion of Sentence Served Before Approval of Parole by First or Multiple Imprisonment of Inmates, 1995

Length of Sentence by First Term or Serial Terms	Number of RBP Cases	Proportion of Sentence Served Before Parole					
		Less than 70%	70–79%	80–84%	85–89%	90–94%	95+%
		Percent Distribution of Parole Approvals					
Less than 12 months	2,072	7.1	23.5	25.9	18.4	20.8	4.3
First	1,362	10.8	33.5	27.1	14.8	9.4	4.4
Serial	710	—	4.2	23.7	25.5	42.7	3.9
12–18 months	2,853	9.3	26.0	13.6	28.7	22.1	0.3
First	1,560	16.8	44.8	14.8	15.2	8.1	0.3
Serial	1,293	0.2	3.4	12.1	44.9	39.1	0.3
18–24 months	2,571	6.7	27.8	14.0	19.4	17.9	14.2
First	1,312	13.1	52.2	14.8	9.9	6.1	3.9
Serial	1,259	—	2.4	13.2	29.3	30.3	24.0
24–36 months	3,144	8.6	29.4	11.8	15.9	24.6	9.7
First	1,882	14.2	48.5	15.7	10.3	9.1	2.2
Serial	1,262	0.1	0.9	5.9	24.4	47.8	20.9
36–60 months	1,295	9.9	30.3	9.9	12.5	17.0	20.4
First	844	15.1	46.1	13.0	11.7	7.7	6.4
Serial	451	0.2	0.9	4.0	14.0	34.4	46.5

Table 3.6 cont. on next page

Table 3.6 continued

Length of Sentence by First Term or Serial Terms	Number of RBP Cases	Proportion of Sentence Served Before Parole					
		Less than 70%	70–79%	80–84%	85–89%	90–94%	95+%
		Percent Distribution of Parole Approvals					
60+ months	462	9.5	25.8	16.2	12.3	14.1	22.1
First	362	12.2	32.3	19.6	12.4	11.6	11.9
Serial	100	—	2.0	4.0	12.0	23.0	59.0
Total months	12,397	8.3	27.3	15.0	19.5	20.8	9.1
First	7,322	13.9	44.5	17.3	12.4	8.4	3.5
Serial	5,075	0.1	2.4	11.6	29.8	38.8	17.3

Source: Research and Statistics Section (1996a, 36–37).

three to five years. At the other extreme (at least 90 percent of the sentence being served), the percent share increased from 25.1 to 36.2 for sentences of five years and more.

When we consider the differences among crimes (see table 3.7), the differences in lengths of sentence influence whether or not a substantial portion of the paroles come early in the imprisonment stay. Violence against persons is associated with 10.8 percent of the paroles being granted before 70 percent of the sentence being served; the sentences averaged 48.1 months. Homicide and aggravated robbery respectively (with death, serious injury, or rape of the victim) had 19 percent paroled for those who had less than 70 percent of the sentence being served when parole was authorized. What appears to be unintelligible is explained by the long average sentences plus the natures of the offender and the crime situation that justified earlier release. Bodily injury (especially) and indecent assault received shorter sentences but also had few paroles early in the period of imprisonment.

Traffic cases had short sentences and also relatively more earlier paroles. Here, the most culpable violators of traffic laws had the greatest chance of being imprisoned, but they were regarded usually as "decent" persons unlike the "typical criminals."

Property offenses have sentences averaging in the low twenty months, except for arson. Larceny is the most numerous of RPB property cases; the diversity of its criminal incidents results in considerable average delay in approvals. Fraud draws a slightly earlier parole on average. Embezzlement and forgery, as white-collar offenses, benefit from the earliest paroles.

As drug crimes, stimulant drugs (especially numerous) and organic solvents ("paint thinner" sniffing that drew very short sentences) suffer greater delays for paroles than the few narcotics cases. Other factors than the long sentences (40.3 months on average) appear to be operating to effect the very early paroling of many of the narcotics offenders. Perhaps because there are fewer narcotics drug offenders, traffickers are less prevalent among narcotic offenders than for stimulant drugs and organic solvents.

Societal violence differs from violence against persons in that the community order is the target in extortion, firearms and swords, and violations of the Law for Punishment of Acts of Violence. Firearms has the longest average sentences, but all three crimes have few early paroles and a high average number of months before parole. The yakuza are predominant among these offenses, although the young adult members of the bosozoku also have been prosecuted for violations of the Law for Punishment of Acts of Violence. Illicit trade (prostitution, gambling, and pornography) is identified with the yakuza and their illicit enterprises. The sentences are rather short, and timing of paroles is in the intermediate range.

The Pre-Parole Service Program in Prisons

On October 1, 1966, the Rehabilitation Bureau introduced the pre-parole service program as a means of initiating administrative processing of applications as early as possible in the inmate's stay in the institution. The Rehabilitation Bureau (1990, 29) outlines the idea: "In this scheme, a certain parole officer[5] of the board visits the correctional institution regularly to interview inmates and discuss cases with correctional officers. In contrast to conventional practice where a parole officer interviews inmates only after application for parole has been filed, the unit officer visits inmates at the optimal time for the parole preparation."

The program was expanded, the statement of the Rehabilitation Bureau (31) continues, in 1979 for the benefit of long-term prisoners. A parole officer would interview inmates serving sentences of eight years or more when they had served two-thirds of a determinate sentence. This action is a change from the usual procedure of awaiting the warden's recommendation.

Table 3.7
Proportion of Sentence Served Before Parole by Crimes, 1995

Selected Crimes[a]	Number of RPB Cases	Mean Length of Sentence	Pct. Share of Sentence Before Parole	Proportion of Sentence Served Before Parole			
				Less than 70%	70–79%	80–89%	90+%
				Percentage Distribution			
Violence against persons	1,608	48.1	80.6	10.8	34.8	31.0	23.4
Bodily injury	400	19.1	83.9	3.0	24.2	43.0	29.8
Bodily injury, death	85	42.6	78.3	17.6	36.5	25.9	20.0
Homicide	364	87.9	80.4	12.6	33.0	28.3	26.1
Robbery	193	42.4	77.2	19.2	42.0	21.2	17.6
Robbery, death or rape	182	69.9	77.7	19.8	39.6	18.1	22.5
Rape	268	36.8	79.6	9.0	43.7	29.8	17.5
Indecent assault	97	26.8	82.2	3.1	35.1	40.2	21.6
Societal violence	505	23.1	84.3	5.2	19.4	39.8	35.6
Extortion	308	21.2	84.0	5.2	22.4	36.4	36.0
Firearms	123	33.1	84.0	4.9	20.3	42.3	32.5
Violence law	68	18.7	86.2	4.4	5.9	48.5	41.2
Property	5,244	23.5	82.8	6.7	28.2	32.7	32.4
Larceny	4,035	22.9	83.7	5.2	25.4	33.2	36.2
Fraud	776	23.2	81.0	9.4	33.4	33.2	24.0
Embezzlement	162	21.7	74.9	17.9	59.9	16.7	5.5

Table 3.7 cont. on next page

Table 3.7 *continued*

Selected Crimes[a]	Number of RPB Cases	Mean Length of Sentence	Pct. Share of Sentence Before Parole	Proportion of Sentence Served Before Parole			
				Less than 70%	70–79%	80–89%	90+%
				Percentage Distribution			
Arson	124	50.4	80.5	8.1	36.3	39.5	16.1
Forgery	107	23.9	74.0	20.6	40.2	28.0	11.2
Drugs	3,730	23.6	83.7	6.3	21.1	38.7	33.9
Stimulants	3,549	23.7	83.9	5.6	21.2	38.8	34.4
Organic solvents	120	10.8	84.6	3.3	16.7	50.0	30.0
Narcotics	61	40.3	69.9	52.5	26.2	11.5	9.8
Illicit trade	75	19.2	82.4	6.7	29.3	34.7	29.3
Traffic	1,082	10.4	78.0	16.9	36.7	32.9	13.5
Total crimes	12,426	25.5	82.7	8.3	27.3	34.5	29.9

Source: Research and Statistics Section (1996a, 32–35).

[a]Excludes crimes not specifically defined and those with few numbers in source report.

Life termers would be interviewed automatically after serving twelve years. As a second policy change, the life termers would receive the opportunity of a special halfway house program immediately after release on parole.

In addition to preparation for parole beginning as early as possible in the stay in prison, the pre-parole service units are intended to consolidate all relevant information, regardless of the originating agency, and to relate the inmate's situation in the institution to what he or she will encounter upon return to the outside community. Presumably, the eligible prisoners will be released from the correctional institutions at an optimal time for their integration into the legitimate activities of the community. The RPB's investigation section benefits from reliable information on the inmate's current status and experiences in the prison and any changes in the residence-job plan; up-to-date information provides opportunity to readjust the plan.

The programmatic objective was to expand the program to all correctional institutions, but the number of professional probation officers had been insufficient for full coverage (Namiki 1980b). In 1979, full-time investigative officers of the RPBs were introduced in ten correctional institutions.

The correctional institution is directly involved in the selection of parolees and also alerts newcomers to the qualifications and procedures for obtaining a parole. When the inmates are admitted, they are oriented to parole requirements and procedures as well as told what they should expect in the prison. During the inmate's prison career, the classification committee of the prison or juvenile training school receives reports from supervising officers of the institutions; the reports are used otherwise for evaluating eligibility for promotions along the stages according to the progressive-stage system. New inmates are in the lowest stage (stage four) and promoted on the way to stage one according to the criteria intended to improve institutional adjustment and self-responsibility. That evaluation process and the reports are enlisted when the classification committee rates the inmate for parole. The recommendations of the classification committee go to the warden or superintendent, who decides whether or not an application will be filed with the RPB.

For those inmates expected to be granted parole ultimately, the prison sponsors pre-parole orientation for one or two weeks before the date of parole. The format differs among the institutions, but usually prison officials, PPOs, and employment security officials deliver lectures. Sometimes inmates—escorted by prison officers—visit probation offices and public employment security offices.

Variations among the Rehabilitation Regions

The administration of correctional affairs is centered in Tokyo, but the nation is divided into regions for the intermediate level of national administration. The regional parole boards and probation offices operate within each of the eight regions that manage rehabilitation services within a set of prefectures. Their jurisdictional boundaries correspond with those of the high courts of Japan, reflecting the functional linkage of the Rehabilitation Bureau with the judiciary of Japan. In a more general sense, the establishment of the boundaries may be traced historically to feudal Japan and the changes introduced during the Meiji Restoration. The boundaries also mirror roughly and less directly the cultural and social structural differences among the Japanese.

In early Japan, the Code of Taiho (646), meaning "great treasure," adapted some features of the Chinese model of government in an attempt to establish the authority of a central regime. The land was divided into prefectures and subprefectures, and officials were appointed to assure that the tax revenue from agriculture would be collected. But the appointments usually went to local feudal lords, and the centralization of authority was blunted (Sansom 1963a, 67–69; Reischauer 1988, 44–46).

In replacing the Tokugawa government (the bakufu), the Meiji reformers set out to strengthen centralized government "by transferring sovereignty over the land and people from the feudal lords, or daimyo, to the emperor (1869) and then abolishing the feudal domains and establishing a centralized prefectural system [1871]" (Kishimoto 1988, 2). The reformers accepted the boundaries of the ancient provinces in establishing strongly centralized government under the Home Ministry in 1873. By the end of 1889, Kishimoto (1988, 143) reports, the Home Ministry and prefectures had eliminated four-fifths of the villages existing before the Meiji Restoration in the course of centralizing governmental authority.

Castle towns of the Tokugawa era remain among the contemporary cities that are elements in the system of centralized government, but Sonoda (1985, 201) cautions against any assumption that cultural and social pluralism has disappeared: "From region to region, there are astonishing differences in the various forms that social structure and cultural life take in the Japanese provinces." Geography has cultivated regional independence, and a national educational system has had to cope with dialects "that were unintelligible to peoples from other regions."

The forty-seven prefectures differ considerably in a number of socioeconomic variables: population density, age distribution of the population and its flow, kinds of households, income, employment, social welfare expenditures, incidence of crime, and so on. Analysis of the reports of the Statistics Bureau, Management and Coordination Agency, unveiled intrinsic diversity among the prefectures in such characteristics. For example, the Tokyo Prefecture has the greatest population density per square kilometer (8,782) and Hokkaido the least (259). Their ratios of one-person households per all ordinary households are 19.3 versus 16.3. However, when a set of prefecture is merged into one of the eight rehabilitation regions, the general averages wipe out at least a portion of the differences among the constituent prefectures in terms of demography and socioeconomic activities.

The Annual Reports of Statistics on Rehabilitation provide some insights into the differences among regional parole boards. As table 3.8 documents, the volume of their cases vary; the differences stem from the varying size of the population from which prisoners have been drawn. Eight regions differ in the number of prefectures represented and the quantity and demographic qualities of the prefecture's people.

More directly, the RPBs depend on the prisons of the region for the pool of candidates for parole. The Tokyo region has the greatest number of candidates; 6,470 inmates were released from its prisons in 1995, of whom 55.8 percent were paroled. At the other extreme, the prisons in the Takamatsu Rehabilitation Region—on the island south of Hiroshima—released only 1,011 inmates, but 59.1 percent were paroled. The Osaka Rehabilitation Region also had a large number of releases (4,048) and paroled 55 percent of them. The other regions had fewer releases but paroled larger portions. Sapporo—on the large island of Hokkaido to the north—had comparatively few releases but paroled 75.2 percent of them.

At least by implication, laws obligate the Rehabilitation Bureau to recognize differences among the regions of Japan. Article 18-2, Offenders Rehabilitation Law, instructs probation offices to engage in crime prevention by arousing public opinion, making "efforts to improve social environments," and promoting "the activities of local residents." Similarly, Article 1, Volunteer Probation Officer Law, requires VPOs "to contribute to the welfare of the individual and the public by helping persons who have committed criminal offenses to improve and be rehabilitated and at the same time by leading public opinion for the prevention of offenses and by cleaning up the community, in the spirit of social service."[6] Article 2 tells the minister of justice to assign VPOs to each of the "rehabilitation areas" and adds: "The number of Volunteer Probation Officers in each rehabilitation area shall be fixed by the

Table 3.8
Adult Parole Decisions by Rehabilitation Region, 1995

RPB Decisions	Tokyo	Osaka	Nagoya	Hiroshima	Fukuoka	Sendai	Sapporo	Takamatsu
Total cases	3,777	2,315	1,454	873	2,045	925	1,235	598
Approvals	3,609	2,227	1,374	815	1,857	865	1,147	557
Denials	68	15	29	28	109	16	46	20
Withheld	100	73	51	30	79	44	42	21
Released inmates	6,470	4,048	2,260	1,375	3,135	1,429	1,643	1,011
Pct. paroled	55.8	55.0	64.3	63.5	63.5	64.7	75.2	59.1
Pct. decisions	100	100	100	100	100	100	100	100
Approvals	95.6	96.2	94.5	93.5	90.8	93.5	92.9	93.1
Denials	1.8	0.6	2.0	3.2	5.3	1.7	3.7	3.4
Withheld	2.6	3.2	3.5	3.4	3.9	4.8	3.4	3.5
Proportion of Average Sentence Served Before Parole Approval								
Sentence	26.09	24.25	25.03	27.13	24.79	26.09	25.04	27.78
Months served	21.26	20.46	20.73	22.71	21.16	22.39	21.51	22.35
Pct. served	81.49	84.37	82.82	83.71	85.36	85.82	85.90	80.45

Table 3.8 cont. on next page

Table 3.8 continued

RPB Decisions	Tokyo	Osaka	Nagoya	Hiroshima	Fukuoka	Sendai	Sapporo	Takamatsu
			Distribution of Proportions of Sentences Served Before Parole					
Less than 70	8.7	9.1	6.7	11.6	6.6	7.6	2.4	19.5
70–79	34.5	22.1	31.0	22.3	22.5	23.8	26.0	23.3
80–89	31.5	34.3	35.8	29.7	39.8	34.3	39.8	29.7
90+	25.3	34.5	26.5	36.4	31.1	34.3	31.8	27.5
Total	100	100	100	100	100	100	100	100

Sources: Research and Statistics Section (1996a, 18–20, 36–39; 1996b, 172–75).

Minister of Justice in consideration of the population, economy, criminality, and other circumstances in the community."

The Rehabilitation Bureau sponsors each year a particular purpose of the crime prevention program known as "Movement Toward a Brighter Society," but, Tanigawa (1982, 338) comments, "the initiative must come from local residents themselves and not from some higher governmental source. . . . Crime and delinquency trends vary widely from community to community. In some, a serious substance abuse problem exists which can and should serve as the focus of movement activities, while in relatively crime-free locales, a sub-theme of child rearing and adolescence might be selected."

Differing but universally high rates of approvals in case decisions characterize all RPBs. Although clinging to the policy of usually respecting the wardens' recommendations, the boards were unlike in denial and withdrawal rates. The absolute numbers and rates are small, but the Fukuoka RPB had the most denials in spite of a high percentage of paroles among all prison releases. Cases withdrawn after submission were roughly the same among the RPBs; the 100 instances for Tokyo were relatively few when the number of cases is taken into account.

The regions also differed in the time taken in parole decisions after the inmates became eligible for consideration (see table 3.8). In Japan a third of the prison sentence must be served before the prisoner technically becomes eligible to be considered for release or parole. However, on average, paroles were grated after 82.7 percent of the prison sentences had been served.

The discrepancy between time of eligibility (after a third of the sentence has been served) and average approval of paroles (82.7 percent of sentence served) occurs because of several factors. Not all applications are approved upon first appearance before the parole board. For some prisoners, multiple appearances before the RPB precede final approval. Each denial requires a delay of months before recommendation, if reconsideration occurs. Candidates are not necessarily qualified according to announced criteria or in terms of an acceptable residence-employment plan for an effective return to the free community. The prison wardens are gatekeepers in the sense that they—not the prisoners—file applications for parole. The prison staff takes time in preparing dossiers for the warden's examination, and the warden then decides whether the application goes forward. The RPB's staff and its functions necessarily add to the administrative process.

For the regions, the portion of the average sentence completed before parole ranged from 80.45 to 85.90 percent. The distribution of the percentage of sentence served before parole provides a more understandable description. The earliest parole decisions were before 70 percent of the sentences had been served. The most tardy decisions are reported as 90 percent or more of the sentence had been completed.

The Takamatsu Rehabilitation Region scored the best record (table 3.8): Of the cases, 19.5 percent were concluded before 70 percent of the sentences had been served, and 27.5 percent of the cases were left for the 90 percent completions. The 19.5 percent explains the relatively early average time (80.45 percent of the sentence) of the paroles in the Takamatsu Region. The Tokyo and Nagoya Regions had fewer most-delayed cases but had to rely on the 70–79 percent or 80–89 percent decisions to reduce their overall delay. Hiroshima has a mixed record: a high 11.6 percent of decisions early in the sentence but also the highest percentage (36.4) of very tardy decisions. Sapporo confirms its least adequate decision making performance (85.9 percent of the sentences) served before parole.

Classes of Prisons and RPB Decisions

The RPBs are dependent on prisons for their candidates, of course, and the quality of most of those candidates is related to the administrative process determining which offenders go to prison. Upon admission to prison, the adults denied suspension of their prison sentence are classified at the detention houses. Broadly speaking, they go to either A- or B-class prisons, where they usually spend their penal confinement in that classification and the particular prison. A few new prisoners are added to the "permanent party" of a detention house to work in the kitchens, perform institutional maintenance, or join the few inmate workers in small industrial shops. Some of these inmates are paroled from detention houses. Women are sent to one of the five women's prisons. Some prisoners are incarcerated as patients in medical facilities operated by the Correction Bureau. Two regions (Fukuoka and Sapporo) have prisons that serve also as remand (detention) centers and medical facilities; two of those prisons are listed on table 3.9 as "multifunctional prisons."

Table 3.9 distinguishes the eight correction regions of the Correction Bureau and, second, two methods of legally returning prisoners to the general community: early release on parole or upon expiration (completion) of the number of months of the prison sentence that the court had imposed. (Correction regions of the Correction Bureau have the same jurisdictional boundaries as those of the Rehabilitation Bureau.)

The table also uses five of the classes of Japanese prisons: B-class, A-class, medical (hospitals), women's, and "multifunctional" prisons. The Correction Bureau also operates all the detention centers (also called "remand" facilities) in Japan. The detention centers hold pretrial inmates and carry out initial classification of convicted offenders received from the trial courts. The detention facilities have been removed from table 3.9 to avoid further complications of an already differentiated system of correctional facilities. The focus here is on the major trends in paroling of inmates of the Japanese prisons. The vast majority of inmates in detention houses are not yet candidates for parole.

Those prisoners evaluated as A-class (not possessing "advanced criminal tendencies") upon entering the prison system dominate the chances for gaining parole. B-class inmates, who have been evaluated as "possessing advanced criminal

Table 3.9

Releases from Prisons in 1995: Parole or Expiration of Sentence by Class of Prison and Correction Region

Correction Regions	Total Cases	B-Class Prisons	A-Class Prisons	Medical Units	Women's Prisons	Multiple-Functions
Sapporo	1,643	864	295	—	66	418
Percent	100	52.6	18.0	—	4.0	25.4
% Parole	65.2	63.3	90.5	—	81.8	48.6
% Expiration	34.8	36.7	9.5	—	18.2	51.4
Sendai	1,429	1,153	276	—	—	—
Percent	100	80.7	19.3	—	—	—
% Parole	59.7	51.9	92.4	—	—	—
% Expiration	40.3	48.1	7.6	—	—	—
Nagoya	2,183	1,592	584	97	—	—
Percent	100	68.8	26.8	4.4	—	—
% Parole	58.1	48.5	84.6	48.4	—	—
% Expiration	41.9	51.5	15.4	51.6	—	—
Fukuoka	3,100	2,104	599	42	96	259
Percent	100	67.9	19.3	1.3	3.1	8.4
% Parole	57.4	48.2	89.3	69.0	72.9	50.6
% Expiration	42.6	51.8	10.7	31.0	27.1	49.4
Hiroshima	1,319	1,004	189	—	126	—
Percent	100	76.1	14.3	—	93.6	—
% Parole	56.6	47.7	79.9	—	6.4	—
% Expiration	43.4	52.3	20.1	—	3.6	—
Tokyo	6,163	3,686	2,121	136	220	—
Percent	100	59.8	34.4	2.2	3.6	—
% Parole	55.7	39.7	80.1	52.2	89.6	—
% Expiration	44.3	60.3	19.9	47.8	10.4	—
Takamatsu	1,011	730	281	—	—	—
Percent	100	72.2	27.8	—	—	—
% Parole	52.7	39.2	87.9	—	—	—
% Expiration	47.3	60.8	12.1	—	—	—
Osaka	3,787	2,673	857	—	257	—
Percent	100	70.6	22.6	—	6.8	—
% Parole	52.5	33.1	83.9	—	87.6	—
% Expiration	47.5	60.9	16.1	—	12.4	—

Source: Research and Statistics Section (1996b, 38–43).

tendencies," are in the majority among released prisoners but, because of the negative prognosis, attain a lower parole rate. Parolees from medical facilities also have a low parole rate, but the rate reflects in part the reluctance of outside communities and their hospitals to accept inmate-patients on parole. Women's prisons receive both A- and B-class adult women; their parole rate is high in spite of the inclusion of B-class inmates among the women. The inmate population of "multifunctional prisons" also is too mixed for reliable comparison with other prisons.

Public prosecutors and district court judges divert from imprisonment those offenders who are believed to be capable of self-correction, who regret the misconduct of which they are accused, and who have made reparations to their victims. The public prosecutors divert an important proportion of accused persons from trial in district courts. Those referred for trial have very great chances for conviction, but district courts suspend a goodly share of the prison sentences. Of offenders considered socially worthy, the majority are skimmed off, and the least promising individuals go to prison. Compared to B-class prisoners, a smaller proportion of the new prisoners go to A-class prisons and, evaluated officially as more amenable persons, ultimately would especially merit RPB approvals. The least promising prisoners would have less chance for parole, although the situation is muddled by the policy of granting them a tardy parole with the hope that supervision will improve the possibility of their rehabilitation.

In short, the particular functions assigned each type of prison mirrors the qualities of those inmates assigned to it, and, therefore, the type of prison reflects the probability that its inmates typically will be granted parole. The eight correction regions differ in the classes of prisons each possesses. It seems to be reasonable that, since regions differ, they will vary accordingly in their percentage of releases from prison allocated to parole. For example, as table 3.9 documents, A-class and women's prisons have the higher parole rates, but their shares of all prisoners are less than those of B-class prisons.

However, table 3.9 tells us that the actual situation is more complicated. The table shows the highest (Sapporo) to lowest (Osaka) percentage shares of all discharges on parole from prisons. The array deviates from an expectation that the total number of releases determines the share of paroles. Otherwise, the Tokyo Correction Region would head the table. Another explanation is unsatisfactory: that among the regions, Sapporo should have the highest parole rate for A-class prisons, but Sendai has the highest rate.

To my surprise, B-class prisons—which usually have the lowest rates for correction regions—impel the general trend for correction regions. Sapporo has the highest rate among the correction regions (63.3) for B-class prisons, and the equivalent rates drop to the lowest rate (33.1) for Osaka. The concurrence of two factors explain the general trend. First, the relatively higher parole rate for A-class prisons is often countered by their loss of percentage share of total number of prisons for some correction regions; the high parole rate of those A-class prisons has less effect on the parole rate for all prisons in the regions. Second, the particularly low parole rate for B-class prisons in some regions is more significant because the qualitative primacy of B-class prisons enhances the impact of those low rates on the correction regions that have low parole rates for all their types of prisons.

Adult Probation and Parole by Regions

For adults, parolees are more numerous than probationers; for every person admitted to probation in 1995, there were 2.52 parolees in 1995 (see table 3.10). Parole's advantage differed among the general categories of crime according to the doubts of courts about the feasibility of placing on probation those who had violated certain kinds of crime. Of course, earlier parolees had been denied probation by sentencing court and sent to prison.

The particular crime is an inferior criterion for evaluating the total personality of a given offender or for predicting future conduct, but there are differences among crimes in the relative importance of probationers or parolees in the caseload of probation offices in Japan. The number of parolees per probationer (the ratio) measures the level of difficulties faced by released prisoners, compared to probationers, in finding a legitimate place in the community. Since the chances for an earlier probation vary with the category of crime, a crime with a higher ratio suggests greater difficulties for both the former offenders and the case supervisors.

The ratios also are useful summary indicators for comparing the rehabilitation regions in regard to the relative importance of probation versus parole admissions. How did the regions stack up in narrowing the numerical superiority of parole admissions over probation admissions? How do the clusters of crimes differ in that respect? The differences are pivotal to the examination of table 3.10. The absolute number of admissions becomes less important than the movement of probation admissions toward being on par with parole admissions. For a few offenses, the number of probationers exceed the number of parolees, but the absolute numbers were so small that reliable conclusions are denied. Except for some twenty specific offenses, there are insufficient admissions for reliable comparisons. The general categories were constructed to meet that difficulty.

Violence against persons is associated with the highest ratio (3.51), mostly because of homicide (ratio of 18.60) and robbery (9.86). The three subclasses of robbery had high ratios, but robbery resulting in serious injuries or death (16.50) and the few incidents combining robbery with rape (18.00) tended more toward parole (ratio of 5.20). Rape (4.39) was less likely to draw probation than forcible indecent assault (1.58).

Bodily injury has numerous incidents because of its wide variety of situations. That variety increases chances of probation (ratio of 1.77). Sendai and Tokyo Rehabilitation Regions (4.68 and 4.65) had the greatest tilt toward parole because of their unusual proportion of homicide and robbery cases. Sapporo had the lowest ratio (1.90) among the regions because of a relatively high number of probation admissions for bodily injury, one of the offenses likely to receive the courts' leniency.

Adult drug offenders differed greatly in their relative numbers and presence on either probation or parole rolls. For adults, stimulant abuse was definitely most common and narcotic offenses most rare. With their greatest absolute numbers, the stimulant abusers (ratio of 3.12) had most influence on the general ratio (3.07) for drug offenders. Narcotic abusers (ratio of 9.14) definitely were likely to be on parole, but their absolute numbers (only 64 parolees compared to 3,424 parolees for stimulant drug offenses) lessened their influence. Drug offenses were prominent in all regions, but stimulant drugs were especially operative in raising the proportion of paroles and ratios of three regions: Osaka (ratio of 4.09), Takamatsu (3.91), and Fukuoka (3.67).

Crimes against property (ratio of 2.43) are most numerous, challenged moderately by drug offenses, because of the many cases of larceny and fraud occupying the second position. Fraud (ratio of 3.43) is less likely to draw probation than larceny (2.25). Three regions record an unusual number of probation admissions for larceny. For Osaka (ratio of 2.91), Fukuoka (2.68), and Tokyo (2.61), probation admissions also benefit from fraud and embezzlement, crimes that sometimes draw otherwise reputable persons.

Societal violence is oriented against the community's public order as an abstract target rather than against persons per se. The component incidents were more likely to gain probation (ratio of 1.78) because extortion (1.57), a highly diverse form of aggression that carries elements of crimes against property, was the most numerous offense of societal violence. Violation

Rehabilitation Regions	Number of Admissions[a]	General Categories of Adult Crimes				
		Violence Against Persons	Societal Violence	Property	Drugs	Traffic
All Regions						
Probationers	4,689	448	268	2,067	1,182	724
Percent	100	9.6	5.7	44.1	25.2	15.4
Parolees	11,830	1,571	478	5,022	3,626	1,133
Percent	100	13.3	4.0	42.5	30.6	9.6
Ratios[b]	2.52	3.51	1.78	2.43	3.07	1.56
Tokyo Region						
Probationeers	1,613	8.3	6.3	45.2	27.0	13.2
Parolees	4,489	13.9	3.3	42.4	30.5	9.9
Ratios[b]	2.78	4.65	1.47	2.61	3.14	2.10
Osaka Region						
Probationers	680	9.0	3.7	46.8	25.7	14.8
Parolees	2,076	11.5	4.3	44.6	34.5	5.1
Ratios[b]	3.05	3.90	3.56	2.91	4.09	1.05
Nagoya Region						
Probationers	577	8.3	4.7	44.9	26.3	15.8
Parolees	1,045	12.5	4.6	45.6	25.2	12.1
Ratios[b]	1.81	2.73	1.78	1.84	1.73	1.38
Hiroshima Region						
Probationers	339	8.9	4.4	44.5	19.2	23.0
Parolees	688	15.3	3.8	41.4	28.0	11.5
Ratios[b]	2.03	3.50	1.73	1.89	2.97	1.01
Fukuoka Region						
Probationers	628	13.2	6.4	41.4	20.5	18.5
Parolees	1,636	13.4	4.2	42.7	29.0	10.7
Ratios[b]	2.60	2.65	1.70	2.68	3.67	1.52
Sendai Region						
Probationers	297	8.4	5.7	48.5	19.9	17.5
Parolees	724	16.2	5.0	42.7	22.0	14.2
Ratios[b]	2.44	4.68	2.12	2.15	2.69	1.98
Sapporo Region						
Probationers	337	11.6	8.9	33.8	36.2	9.5
Parolees	742	10.0	5.5	39.5	37.7	7.3
Ratios[b]	2.20	1.90	1.37	2.57	2.29	1.69

Table 3.10 cont. on next page

Table 3.10 continued

Rehabilitation Regions	Number of Admissions[a]	General Categories of Adult Crimes				
		Violence Against Persons	Societal Violence	Property	Drugs	Traffic
Takamatsu Region						
Probationers	218	12.8	5.5	42.2	20.2	19.3
Parolees	430	14.7	4.6	30.5	40.0	10.2
Ratios[b]	1.97	2.25	1.67	1.42	3.91	1.05

Source: Research and Statistics Section (1996a, 78–85).

[a]Excludes other penal law, other special law offenses, and crimes with very few cases; pornography, gambling, lotteries, prostitution, and various public order offenses.
[b]Number of parolees per probationer.

of the law against firearms and swords (4.17) was an exception, but the Law for Punishment of Acts of Violence (1.57 also) drew a sufficient number of otherwise reputable persons to permit a number of probationers. Extortion has been especially instrumental in differentiating the regional ratios from 1.37 for Sapporo to 3.56 for Osaka.

Traffic offenses (ratio of 1.56) is especially oriented toward probation because, compared to the so-called "traditional" offenses, the public is inclined to regard them as only "minor" rule breaking. Traffic offenders often agree with the public tendency to believe they are not "real criminals." The "daring heroics" of exhibitionistic driving attracts the admiration of some members of the general public. Imprisonment and subsequent parole is more likely for traffic law violators whose offenses are regarded to be flagrant. In all the regions, a higher percentage of traffic offenders are granted probation than those being paroled. Probationers gain almost numerical equality with parolees in three regions: Hiroshima, Osaka, and Takamatsu. At the other extreme, parole (ratio of 2.10) gains the upper hand.

As fundamental elements of community-based corrections, probation and parole have potentialities to be realized by effective selection of those accepted for the program and their supervision out on the streets. Rehabilitation Bureau statistics have made possible our introduction to the patterns of the selection of probationers and parolees. The next chapter turns to the account of the Bureau's statistics about the qualities and backgrounds of adult probationers and parolees.

4
Adult Probationers and Parolees

AS ALREADY CONSIDERED, ADULT PROBATION and parole are managed by the courts and regional parole boards as elements of community-oriented corrections. They make the decisions of whether or not convicted offenders return to the community under supervision. The return is authorized with some degree of official optimism that the selected *individuals* will undertake positive behavioral change either because of their self-correction or the influence of benign community forces.

Now we turn to the individuals who have survived the decision making to become probationers or parolees. The decision making and its implications will be considered on what the statistics published by the Ministry of Justice tell about the human side of community-oriented corrections. Crime is an aspect of human behavior and thus representative of the frailties, inconsistencies, sometimes even susceptibilities, and sometimes in particular ways the affinities among human beings. As abstractions, statistical reports do not capture the quintessence of the individuals collectively described as probationers and parolees, but they sustain a beginning toward understanding their biographical background, their characteristic as occupants of the statuses of probationers and parolees, and their prior exposure to the criminal justice processing.

Trends in Admissions since 1950

The diversionary practices rely on the Japanese values that favor leniency if the defendants accept obligations to the community and abandon criminality. Table 4.1 traces the absolute number of prison admissions and the age-specific rates to document the remarkable decline in imprisonment rates. The table compares probation admissions with parole admissions in absolute numbers, age-specific rates, and ratios. The number of probationers per prison admission has remained rather constant since 1960. Suspensions without probation have given many convicted defendants the benefits of outright release into the community; therefore, probation offices have not experienced the full effect of the retreat from imprisonment. The judges assess probation as less punitive than imprisonment but unnecessarily inconvenient to "worthy" defendants deserving restoration to the streets without probationary supervision.

In absolute numbers, only 221 releases on probations were granted in 1950, when the 60,040 admissions were at the peak for prisoners. During the socioeconomic crisis immediately following World War II, the prisons were greatly overcrowded, and the government's formal resources were gravely strained. The very low probation ratio (only .004) attests to the modest beginning of the program. Probation admissions reached the 8,000s in the 1960s, a figure subsequently matched only in 1980. The admissions have been rather stable after 1955, if compared by ratios with prison admissions. The rates per 100,000 adult Japanese for probationers have rather corresponded over the years with the rate for prison admissions.

Parole has had a clear numerical superiority over probation for adults. From its heavy use in 1950, parole admissions have dropped rather consistently to reach 12,138 in 1995, but the other form of release from prison (release on "expiration," completion of the prison sentence) also tended to decline. Both versions of release have mirrored the general movement downward of prison admissions. The ratios show that the number of releases on parole in 1950 were two and three-quarters greater than releases at expiration. The admissions had dropped in 1955, when socioeconomic conditions moved toward normalcy. Parole regained some of its earlier numeri-

Table 4.1

Admissions to Adult Probation, Adult Parole, and Prisons, 1950–1995

Years	Admissions of Adults			Releases from Prisons		
	To Prisons	To Probation	Ratios[a]	At Expiration	On Parole	Ratios[b]
			Number of Persons			
1950	60,040	221	0.004	15,445	42,141	2.73
1955	54,035	4,361	0.81	18,322	32,198	1.76
1960	41,008	8,525	0.21	14,179	30,751	2.17
1965	33,935	8,350	0.25	14,596	19,432	1.33
1970	25,890	6,908	0.27	11,015	17,855	1.62
1975	26,175	7,048	0.27	11,736	14,933	1.27
1980	28,374	8,058	0.28	14,140	15,202	1.07
1985	31,656	7,180	0.23	14,143	17,795	1.26
1990	22,745	4,753	0.21	11,557	14,896	1.29
1995	21,838	4,856	0.22	9,233	12,138	1.31
		Rates per 100,000 Japanese, Ages 20+ years				
1950	132.8	0.49	—	34.2	93.2	—
1955	106.3	8.58	—	36.0	63.3	—
1960	73.2	15.21	—	25.3	54.9	—
1965	54.5	13.41	—	23.4	31.2	—
1970	37.1	9.89	—	15.8	25.6	—
1975	34.1	9.19	—	15.3	19.5	—
1980	34.9	9.92	—	17.4	18.7	—
1985	36.8	8.35	—	16.4	20.7	—
1990	25.0	5.23	—	12.7	16.4	—
1995	22.6	5.02	—	9.5	12.5	—

Sources: Shikita and Tsuchiya (1990, 172-73, 194, 374); Research and Statistics Section (1991b, 44, 162; 1996a, 55; 1996b, 44, 170).

[a]Number of probationers per inmates admitted to prison.
[b]Number of parolees per inmate released at expiration of sentence.

cal superiority in 1960, when prison admissions continued to have high numbers and parole clung to the earlier enthusiasm for supervision after discharge from prison.

In chapter 3 we noted that RPB decisions are subject to a complex characteristics of prisoners in the pool of parole candidates: biographic characteristics, length of sentence, distributions of crimes, and previous exposure to the several segments of the criminal justice system. Although parole has always been favored over discharge at expiration of the prison sentence, the ratios reflect a general trend toward less favor along with a drop in the size of prison admissions. The rates per 100,000 adult Japanese link both kinds of release from prison to the demographic trends in the society at large. Additional support is given the conclusion that parole has lost some of its official favor with the decline in prison admissions. Possibly, the prison wardens have found a smaller proportion of the fewer prisoners eligible for a recommendation for parole. The complex factors involved suggest caution is appropriate, but the decline in prison admissions, in addition to its own affect, supplements the influence of other elements in the complex of factors. Parole always has the higher rate, and both kinds of release score general, although irregular, declines over the decades. The differences have narrowed between the two kinds of prison release with the passage of decades.

Status Differences Between Probationers and Parolees

In relationships with other persons, each of us occupy particular social positions (statuses) within groups. In the family, there are the statuses of mother, father, sons and daughters—perhaps grandmothers, grandfathers, cousins, and so on. Each status is tied to a social role consisting of a set of expectations for the status occupants. The expectations are the criteria for evaluation of role performance by significant other persons and also for self-appraisal by the status occupants.

Status in the Japanese context is basic to the relationships between supervisors and probationers and parolees (see chapter 7). Here the concept is applied to the differences between probationers and parolees in personal and social characteristics. Attributes of the probationer and parolee influence the probability of criminal conduct and how they have been processed during the decision making that had placed them in the status of probationer or parolee.

Adult probationers are younger (mean 33.9 years) than parolees (40.3 years). In 1995 admissions, 32.6 percent of 4.856 probationers and 8 percent of 12,138 parolees were less than 25 years of age. The relative youth of probationers mirrors the greater likelihood that they have been on the caseload of the public prosecutors and judges for the first time. That initial involvement in the criminal justice system is favorable for assignment to probation. Moreover, the higher mean age of parolees implies that previous exposure to prison requires more time and attainment of more advanced chronological age. The relative concentration of younger adults among probationers is shown by the ratio of the number of probationers per parolee: 1.64 for ages less than 25 years but no more than a ratio of .42 for the other age categories (Research and Statistics Section 1996a, 89).

Both probationers and parolees averaged 10 years of schooling in 1995, but slightly more had attended college (6 versus 4 percent). Three parolees and ten probationers had no schooling (Research and Statistics Section 1996a, 87). Compulsory education through the ninth grade narrows the differences. Probationers had higher proportions with less than attendance in high school and also at the college level. The opposing proportions held down the mean schooling of probationers. Adults admitted to prison in 1995 had only a mean schooling of 7.16 years (Research and Statistics Section 1996b, 118–19). Selection by sentencing courts and by the RPBs gave the advantage to probation and parole, but the selection probably was the indirect consequence of favoring certain crimes that are related to younger ages and also favoring first offenders who tend to be younger. The average schooling of Japanese has risen over the decades; the older mean age of parolees suggests that more of them, compared to probationers, were in the earlier generations leaving schools in the lower grades.

The Ministry of Justice publishes two very general statistics on the economic status of probationers, prisoners, and parolees. Both are too general to be of weighty importance. The comparative statistics suggest that as in Western societies, the criminal justice agencies take in a disproportionate number of persons in the lower socioeconomic statuses. The quality of employment is not specified, and the definition of *jobless* may be too broad. The data are too general for incisive analysis, but the impression is consistent with the American experience.

At admission to prison, inmates trail probationers in employment (44.0 versus 55.5 percent) and suffer more unemployment (51.3 versus 44.1 percent). Students (0.09 percent) and household workers (0.34 percent) are greatly underrepresented (Research and Statistics Section 1996b, 106–17). The higher employment rate of probationers suggests closer linkages with the community, and the sentencing judges taking that into consideration when deciding whether probation or imprisonment is the better choice for those convicted offenders deemed ineligible for return to the community without supervision. Parolees have a disadvantage in employment when compared with the employment new inmates had left. The newly arrived prisoners have left the jobs they had before apprehension and sentencing, but the parolees may or may not be successful in developing a satisfactory employment-residence plan.

Employment status at admission to probation or parole is described only in four variables: employee, student, household work, and jobless. The statistics ignore the possibility of student status and appear to underestimate "household work." Household work includes the possibility of assigned tasks in an economic enterprise of the family. The percentage shares of all probationers in 1995 admissions are employed 53.3, jobless 44.1, household work 2.3, and student 0.3. The shares for parolees are employed 28.6, jobless 70.1, household work 1.2, and student 0.1 (Research and Statistics Section 1996a, 88).

In a very broad way, income levels suggest, along with the data on employment, that either the economically well-to-do have less reason to violate criminal laws or their rule breaking is not necessarily forbidden by the laws. However, from the perspective of community-oriented corrections, probationers have the better prospect for the economic status favorable to a satisfying return to community life. The preliminary statistics signal the relatively higher economic status of the probationers; the share devoted to below average income was 23.7 percent for probationers, 33.6 percent for parolees, and 45.7 percent for prisoners. The rest of the percentage distribution of inmates was above average 0.5 and average 53.8 (Research and Statistics Section 1993b, 117). Tabulations deal with the broadly defined income statuses: above average, average, and below average. Few are "above average," and "below average" generates the most interesting differences. The distribution of adult probationers in 1993 was 1.5 percent above average, 74.8 percent average, and 23.7 percent below average. Parolees tilted toward below average; the distribution was 1.0 percent above average, 65.5 percent average, and 33.5 percent below average (Research and Statistics Section 1993a, 88).[1]

Psychometric test scores give preliminary and general information about the psychological characteristics of probationers and parolees. Probationers have the highest mean scores (89.1) compared with parolees (80.1) and prisoners at admission (78.4). Of the respective categories, this was the percentage share of scores of 100 or more: probationers 23.5, parolees 7.6, and prisoners 6.5 (Research and Statistics Section 1996a, 87; 1996b, 128).

Mental health diagnoses indicate the majority are without discernible defects: 95.6 percent of probationers, 97.7 percent of the parolees, and 96.3 percent of the prisoners. Mental retardation is the most numerous defect. In contrast to a frequent classification of prisoners as psychopaths, the diagnosis was applied to only 82 (.004 percent) Japanese inmates, 20 (.006 percent) probationers, and 18 (.001 percent) parolees (Research and Statistics Section 1996a, 87; 1996b, 130). Perhaps the rebellion frequently associated with psychopathy of prisoners is less prevalent in Japan.

Age and Trends in Community Corrections

Age and sex are examples of ascribed status that affect individuals' self-perceptions and other persons' perceptions of their conduct that led to their conviction in court. Achieved status, produced by the efforts of the individuals, has similar effects. Clear-cut separations of the two kinds of status is difficult because both stem from complex relationships that immerse research in the physiology of organic maturation and senescence, the psychology of learning and personality development, and the sociology of family and other relationships within the community.

Age status has more than ordinary importance as an analytic instrument for understanding the workings of probation and parole. The importance follows age status as an element in the definition of a person's place in the social structure, the changes with age in the degree and kinds of responsibilities expected of a person, and the impact of major social changes on age status. Age status systems exist in all societies, but Japanese society traditionally has accorded greater esteem to the elderly than in Western societies. The escalating number of elderly in the society has raised the number of older parolees without any necessary change in the criminalistic tendencies of the elderly.

Table 4.2 documents the proportional growth of prisoners considered for parole by RPBs from 1970 through 1995. The average age of males interviewed for parole consistently increased from 32.4 years in 1970 to 40.2 years in 1995. In 1970, men aged 40 years and over constituted 18.4 percent of all applicants; that share rose to 43.5 percent in 1995. Men aged 50 years and over gained at an even more impressive rate, from 5 percent of all parole candidates in 1970 to 21 percent in 1995. Women applicants were older on average than the men; their

Table 4.2
Ages of Prisoners Interviewed by
Regional Parole Boards by Sex, 1970–1995

Ages in Years	1970	1975	1980	1985	1990	1995
Mean Ages						
Males	32.4	34.0	36.4	37.5	38.8	40.2
Females	37.7	38.6	39.9	40.5	41.3	41.4
Percentage Distribution by Sex						
Under 25						
Males	23.3	15.9	10.2	12.4	11.1	9.2
Females	9.7	9.8	4.3	8.4	7.3	7.9
25–29						
Males	25.9	25.6	17.8	14.3	16.6	16.1
Females	15.2	18.0	12.1	10.1	12.7	17.6
30–39						
Males	32.4	35.3	40.5	35.5	27.2	26.7
Females	38.3	28.3	35.2	31.2	24.9	23.9
40–49						
Males	13.4	17.2	23.5	25.8	29.1	27.0
Females	25.3	29.9	33.5	31.4	34.0	25.4
50–59						
Males	4.0	4.7	6.6	10.2	13.1	16.0
Females	9.4	10.6	12.2	15.8	16.8	17.0
60+						
Males	1.0	1.3	1.4	1.8	2.9	5.0
Females	2.1	3.4	2.7	3.1	4.3	8.2
Total Number						
Males	20,507	17,423	17,495	18,872	15,270	12,386
Females	434	378	696	1,056	946	836

Sources: Research and Statistics Section (1971a, 26–27; 1976a, 26–27; 1981a, 26–27; 1986a, 26–27; 1991a, 26–29; 1996a, 26–29).

average was 37.7 years in 1970 and rose consistently to reach 41.4 years in 1995. The percentage distributions reveal the greater concentration of women in the ages over 39 years and even more so for ages over 49 years.

The trend toward more advanced age of parolees mirrors

the aging of the Japanese population as well as the effects of public prosecutors and judges in diverting defendants and convicted offenders away from prison (and subsequent eligibility for parole) for earlier offenses of persons while younger. "Japan faces a rapid demographic transition in the years ahead," Jones (1988, 958) warns, "in part because of an increase in average life expectancy which climbed from only 50 years for men and 54 for women in 1947 to the longest in the world in 1986 at 75.2 years for men and 80.9 for women." Minami (1991, 9) lists several problems thrust upon local governments in Japan. Health care must be provided the bedridden and the increasing number of victims of Alzheimer's disease. Recreation centers are needed by elderly without economic resources. Residential facilities are needed for those reluctant to leave hometowns to be with their adult children or for the elderly without the assistance of families. The adult children who care for elderly parents often require assistance in the forms of advice, home helpers, and nurses.

The size of the population is determined by birthrates and death rates, with in-migration and out-migration having little influence in Japan. Death rates have diminished over the decades. Increased longevity adds to the accumulation of older persons. Concurrently, a number of factors have reduced the birthrate: a high abortion rate, delay of marriage for the sake of the pleasures of single life, the trend toward nuclear families, more women gaining economic independence through employment, and so on. The young adults have lost their proportional share of the Japanese population.

Analysis of the trends in admissions to probation and parole benefits from a point made by Riley (1987, 4): "People in the several age strata differ not only in age but also in historical experiences to which their cohorts have been exposed." Her second point is relevant to the relationships between age and community corrections in Japan. Relationships between persons are shaped by Japanese cultural perspectives, but differences in historical experiences also have influence. The several age strata "are further differentiated by age criteria (customs, laws, or bureaucratic rules) for occupying and performing social roles," she continues.

"Each cohort is born at a particular date," Riley explains, "lives through a unique segment of historical time, and confronts its own particular sequence of social environmental events and changes." Defining *cohort* as a set of people born at the same time (2), she treats the concept as a device for tracing the aging of persons in each cohort who are exposed to (and contribute to) social changes as they "grow up, die, and are replaced by other people." Aging and social change are interdependent, she says, because "each transforms the other."

Over time, the demographic trends of Japan have altered the age distribution of persons entering prison and, later, of the cadre of prisoners considered for parole. The number of parole candidates is modified, but, in addition, differences in life experiences of successive cohorts of prisoners affect the psychology of parolees (and probationers), their attitude toward being thrust into the status of parolee (or probationer), and their participation in the relationships with case supervisors.

For those prisoners appearing before RPBs from 1970 to 1995, table 4.2 illustrates the relevance to community corrections of movement of each cohort through the decades in the course of their socioeconomic changes experienced by the Japanese. The first major point is that the particular age cohort in 1970 occupies a different share of all parole candidates than the similar age cohort of 1975, 1980, and so on. Males in ages less than 25 years held a 23.3 percent share of the male parole applicants in 1970, but the share dropped over the years to only 9.2 percent in 1995. For the similar comparison for ages 60 years and over, the percentage grew from 1.0 in 1970 to 5.0 in 1995.

The percentage shares shifted over the years to produce the gain in the average age of parolees. Changes in the tendencies toward criminality probably have accompanied the socioeconomic and political changes over the years, but, even when such possibilities are held constant, the dynamics of birthrates and death rates have produced the proportional decline of young adults and proportional gain of parole candidates 40 years and older. The volume of male cases have dropped because of the loss of young adults who usually are the major contributors to the crime rate.

Table 4.2 lends itself to demonstrating the differential exposure to socioeconomic changes of the cohorts. We take the age cohort 60 years and older as an example. The cohort aged 60 years and over in 1970 had been born in the years 1890–1910. The members would have experienced the war years (1935–1945) when 25 to 55 years of age, the postwar years (1945–1950) when 35 to 60 years of age, and the era of economic expansion (1960–1970) when 50 to 80 years of age. The cohort aged 60 years in 1995 (born in 1935) would have experienced three "slices of history" at different ages: less than 10 years of age in the war period, ages 10 to 15 in the postwar chaos, and ages 25 to 35 years during the economic expansion.

The qualities of the parole caseload are influenced by changes in the age status of approved applicants. The volume of males has dropped also, primarily because of the proportional loss of young adults in the demographic development. Note that women differ from men as parole applicants. Population trends in the Japanese population have produced an increasing representation of females over the decades, although they remain a small minority when compared with male parole applicants.

As suggested by Riley's second point, the conditions and guidelines for case supervision are apt to be modified in response to the qualitative changes in the clientele. Age affects case supervision in another way: the number of appearances before the RPB before the parole application is approved. The increased average number of appearances suggests a decline in the perceived quality of parole candidates as an affect of differences in the life experiences and distribution of ages in cohorts. Male applicants averaged 2.44 appearances, and only 51.5 percent were approved in 1995 at first appearance. Women averaged fewer appearances (mean of 2.07 appearances), and

59.1 percent gained approval when first considered by the RPBs. There were only 807 women compared with 11,644 men. The mean number of appearances increased with greater age: for males from 1.08 for ages less than 25 years, to 4.18 for ages 60 years and older, and the equivalent ages of women drew 1.05 to 3.63 mean number of appearances (Research and Statistics Section 1996a, 26–29).

Exploring the Human Qualities of Cases

The age status turns attention away from the administrative processing by courts and regional parole boards exclusively to the qualities of the persons who become objects of this processing. Because this chapter has been assigned the responsibility of concentrating on individuals, a number of case histories of particular adult probationers and parolees were gathered from probation offices. Professional probation officers selected cases illustrating the background and conduct of adult offenders who became probationers or parolees and mirror the events typical of their experiences while being supervised. Their case summaries take us beyond the abstractions of statistics into the human dimensions of probation and parole.

Male probationer, aged forty-seven years, embezzlement. At age thirty years, he changed his job from a securities company to a real estate firm. Four years later he turned to employment in a travel agency that captured his keen interest. His salary exceeded $70,000 a year, and he hoped to open his own agency. *Pachinko* became his other passion. He spent an average of $850 a month in the gambling halls based on the Japanese version of pinball machines (pachinko). Encountering financial difficulties, he borrowed some $84,000 and embezzled another $350,000 from the travel agency.

Suspending a prison sentence of eighteen months, the judge substituted a probation term of three years for several reasons: The embezzler expressed repentance, agreed to pay the travel company $825 a month in restitution for ten years, probation appeared to be the means of his restitution, and this was his first offense.

While on probation, he worked initially in a factory, but, wanting a higher income, he switched to truck driving after three months. The hours and physical exertion had adverse effects on his health, so he became a salesman for a construction firm.

After a year on probation, he returned to the pachinko parlors and failed to meet the payments to the travel agency. He had married his paramour (the mother of his fourteen-year-old son), and she pressed him to contact the VPO. He resisted the VPO's advice for three months but finally agreed to give up pachinko and support his family. The travel agency agreed to his request to reduce the monthly payments for restitution by half and extend the payments to twenty years.

After two years on probation, he injured a boy in a traffic incident. He apologized and agreed to pay some $84,000 as compensation. For the following six months, he avoided further problems, supported his family, and had regular contacts with the VPO. Probationary supervision was ended. The PPO finds the case successful because the probationer exhibited a capacity for self-correction in spite of problems raised, because the family lent him support and encouragement, and because the PPO and VPO provided appropriate advice and encouragement.

Male probationer, aged fifty-four, bodily injury. He was sentenced to prison for eighteen months for inflicting bodily injury during a scuffle among homeless people. He had been a vagrant for years and, the PPO reported, was ready to continue vagrancy without a "will to work." The court suspended the prison sentence and substituted probation.

Supervision depended on finding a place of residence, the PPO recalled, but the probationer had no money, and the social agency refused to help a client without a will to work and to rebuild his life. The rehabilitation aid hostel had similar reluctance. Hoping to instill a more congenial attitude in the vagrant, the PPO scheduled interview after interview to help the probationer get a job. The hope proved futile, and contact with the probationer was lost.

Male probationer, aged eighty-seven years, attempted murder. The defendant had been sentenced to five years of imprisonment for attempted murder at a home for the aged. He was placed on three years probation after suspension of the prison sentence. The defendant had lived for years at a home for the aged, had no relatives or income, and was unable to work because of physical infirmity. Only with the intervention of municipal authorities was the probation office able to place him in a home for the elderly.

The PPO describes the case as an example of the difficulties of coordinating probationary supervision with services of other public agencies. The case involves the need to gain access to hospitals or domiciliary institutions for persons in urgent need of care. Offenders are not easily accepted by such agencies because their status is tainted by social deviance and the assumption that they are incapable of responsible conduct. Homes for the aged lack the capacity to satisfy the volume of applications for entry. A waiting period of two or three years for all applicants is inconsistent with meeting the needs of the elderly defendant abruptly returned to the community.

Male parolee, aged about forty years, yakuza member. After graduating from high school, "Mr. D" attended a school specializing in commercial art for two years. He worked for a wholesaler in textiles owned by the brother of the woman he married at age twenty-three years. When customers failed to pay their bills, the wholesale enterprise became bankrupt. Mr. D became a truck driver.

The brother-in-law had some connections with the yakuza. To deal with the customers who had not paid their bills, the former wholesaler made an agreement with the gangsters and ultimately became a loan shark and then a trafficker in stimulant drugs. The brother-in-law invited Mr. D to join the illicit trade. In February 1978, Mr. D. was arrested in Kyoto, and his wife sued for divorce.

After ten years in prison, Mr. D was pressed to sever connections with the yakuza as a step toward qualifying for parole. In spite of his anxiety about the gang's retaliation, Mr. D was able to withdraw for two reasons. First, the yakuza organization was eager to divorce itself from the brother-in-law who was engaged in drug trafficking. The organization made a public statement, although insincere, of its abstinence from any drug trafficking. Second, the boss of this yakuza gang had been killed in an intergang conflict, and this gang had collapsed.

During the first nine months of his parole, Mr. D worked at his ex-wife's restaurant, and then moved to Tokyo for a job, through a friend's recommendation, at a computer part's shop. The shop went bankrupt, but he became a salesman for medical instruments, completing parole in May 1991.

The PPO considers Mr. D's successful completion of supervision to be typical of selected yakuza granted parole and offers an explanation. The regional parole boards give especially careful attention to yakuza cases before granting parole because of their handicaps. They usually have grown up in disorganized families and have fragile attachments to parents. They tend to be undermotivated students. Adolescents and youth recruited by yakuza frequently are runaways contacted on the streets. Mr. D sprung from a middle-class family, and graduated from high school, and benefited from firm family support. The PPO and VPO were able to join these "significant others" in encouraging Mr. D to reorient his life in spite of problems in finding job stability.

Male parolee, aged thirty-nine years, counterfeiting. Mr. A was one of four persons arrested for passing 72,166 counterfeit notes for 5,000 yen from September 1981 to February 1982. Twenty-one false bills were used to purchase betting tickets at a horse-racing track and nine notes to buy cigarettes in Osaka. In 1983 he was sentenced to ten years imprisonment. He was also convicted of violation of the Law of Firearms and Swords because gangsters had given him two shotguns as security for counterfeit money. Mr. A's former wife was given three years imprisonment as one of the four defendants.

Starting a printing company in 1974, Mr. A moved to a new four-story building in 1977, but his management ability did not equal the demands of business expansion. Facing bankruptcy, a codefendant suggested that, since he had printing equipment, production of counterfeit money would solve the problem.

He was the second and favorite son of an office worker for the railroad. The level of family income was average. His school performance was uneventful, except for an incident of sexual promiscuity. He dropped out in the second year of high school. His employment was in a succession of occupations: automobile mechanic for a year, at a shop for western pastries for a year, an apprentice cook for thirty months, and a taxi driver in Kyoto for two years. Then he returned to Ohita. Except for three violations of the Road Traffic Law, he had no previous criminal record.

For parole, his father was the sponsor. During the trial, his wife had divorced him; he had no further word from her. Before the counterfeiting, he had used his father's real estate as collateral for a loan. Because the real estate had been auctioned to satisfy the loan, his parents had moved to public housing in Ohita and were living on the father's pension ($2,083 a month). The family also included Mr. A's mother, who had heart trouble, and Mr. A's physically handicapped daughter.

In the pre-parole interview, the father was indignant that Mr. A had received the maximum sentence for his offense. The problems were adverse public opinion, unpaid restitution, and arrangements for a job when paroled. A neighbor sympathized with the father but condemned Mr. A. Mr. A's four-story building was auctioned. His parents hoped he could be a construction carpenter. That plan did not work out.

He was released on parole at the rehabilitation aid hostel in Hiroshima under a plan that he be a taxi driver, but his driving license had lapsed. A job for a water purifying company was substituted. Although he was a good employee, he withdrew from the hostel after a month and returned to Ohita and supervision by a VPO there. He worked as an apprentice cook at a coffee shop but resigned after five days because people gambled at pachinko in the shop. He worked part-time as a baggage sorter for a transportation company and, mainly, at installing vending machines. Obtaining his driver's license, he became a chauffeur.

The PPO's report ends with thirteen months remaining on the parole period. Mr. A was a dedicated worker. His family had given him firm and loyal support. Consultations with the VPO were regular (two or three times a month), and advice was sought. He avoided alcohol and gambling. He was giving priority "to establishing his basic life" and was not trying to reduce the debt remaining from bankruptcy of his printing company.

Male parolee, aged thirty-three years, fraud. Mr. A. T. defrauded nine elderly women for a total of $250,000 by telling them, "If you put your money in our company, it will yield 60 percent interest annually." His first offense resulted in a prison sentence of four years.

He had worked for T Company; the company claimed to be selling to elderly people gold and membership cards to golf courses. When the fraud was detected and received wide publicity, T Company became bankrupt. His job salary had been $12,500 a month, enabling him "to spend money like water." Along with other employees of T Company, he established F Company and continued to obtain a high income. Management of the new enterprise was faulty, and the members turned to defrauding elderly women as a means of raising capital.

Born in Hyogo Prefecture, he completed junior high school and, at age fifteen years, attended high school part-time while working at a department store. He had an above-average intelligence (105 intelligence quotient). When twenty-one, he became a clerk in a wine shop. After two years, he joined T Company.

The PPO reports the transactions preceding authorization

of parole. The VPO investigating the pre-parole plan issued six reports. The first report: Mr A. T.'s father, dealing in real estate, agreed to be sponsor. The mother owns a beauty parlor and agreed their home had space enough for the inmate with his grandmother and son already residing there. He was divorced from his wife. Employment had to be arranged. The second, third, and fourth reports offered no further information, except that Mr. A. T. wanted to be a shop assistant at a fish store. The fifth report: His parents wanted him to do handicrafts; he wanted to be a shop assistant. Sixth report: The VPO had told the inmate that "if you want, I can recommend you as a shop assistant to one of my close friends who owns a fish store." Mr. A. T. and his parents agreed.

He was paroled after his second appearance before the parole board and after serving 82 percent of the prison sentence. He reported to the Kobe probation office. Initially he told the PPO that he wanted to work at his mother's beauty parlor, not the fish store, but he failed to work at the beauty parlor. After two months, he found a job selling telephones. After a month, he became a salesman for a real estate company.

The VPO and his parents kept telling him "don't change jobs." The PPO believed that "the offender lacked a moral sense of responsibility. He thought that he had committed a fraud under direction of his company. That way he didn't think he was to blame for the crime." However, he continued his residence in his parents' home and observed the conditions for parole.

Living Arrangements Before Adjudication

The statistics on "living arrangements" prior to adjudication offer clues on the viability of the probationers' and parolees' contacts with their families. Those contacts are given weighty emphasis in Japan. The criminal justice system relies substantially on the family for controlling the conduct of its members indirectly if not directly. The distributions in table 4.3 suggest a heavy policy reliance on the family, especially if broken families are included. The reliance is less justified for parolees, especially for persons accepted for parole more than once.

Among the specified arrangements is living alone and apart from the residence of one's own family. The term *alone* carries alternative meanings: self-reliant maturity versus disaffected withdrawal from the family. Probationers exceeded parolees in the percentage of their number who lived alone, but other probationers were more likely to have linkages with intact families. Parolees were very dependent on hostels, primarily because they had experienced through imprisonment greater physical withdrawal from family relationships. Even parolees who had been in prison for the first time had a considerable number (21.5 percent) requiring hostels upon release.

Linkages with a spouse or both parents would be identified as "normal" family contacts; the two versions take up more than half of the arrangements. The broken family is also well represented; because of divorce or death, a single parent was expected to assume family obligations. The mother-stepfather version is more common than the father-stepmother version because of the mother's greater involvement in family relationships, the continued preference of the mother into adulthood, and the greater longevity of females. Other relatives sometimes have been substituted for parents.

Some Japanese employers provide dormitories for their unmarried employees as a side effect of welfare corporatism. Paternalistic management emerged in the early decades of the twentieth century to correct "appallingly primitive working conditions" in the early industrialization of Japan and also to prevent unionization of labor. "The paternalistic management ideology based on family tradition," Yoshino (1968, 84) explains, "was a deliberate and rational response on the part of Japanese business leaders to the specific and social strains they faced." Employers' housing is an extraordinary resource for probationers and, especially, parolees who lack helpful family linkages.

Table 4.3

Adults' Living Arrangements Prior to Adjudication
of Probationers and Parolees Admitted to Programs
in 1995 by First Versus Multiple Admissions

Living Arrangements	First Admission			Multiple Admissions		
	Probation	Parole[a]	Ratio[b]	Probation	Parole[a]	Ratio[b]
Alone	658	144	4.57	99	123	0.80
With spouse	922	1,183	0.78	176	1,055	0.17
Both parents	1,060	1,540	0.69	141	644	0.22
Father	172	243	0.71	26	117	0.22
Mother	534	849	0.63	99	584	0.17
Other relatives	269	521	0.52	36	456	0.08
Employer	112	119	0.94	19	207	0.09
Hostel	162	1,269	0.13	19	2,629	0.007
Totals	3,889	5,861	0.66	615	5,765	0.11
Percentage Distributions						
Alone	16.9	2.5	—	16.1	2.1	—
With spouse	23.7	20.2	—	28.6	18.3	—
Both parents	27.3	26.3	—	22.9	11.2	—
Father	4.4	4.1	—	4.2	2.0	—
Mother	13.7	14.5	—	16.1	9.3	—
Other relatives	6.9	8.9	—	5.9	7.9	—
Employer	2.9	2.0	—	3.1	3.6	—
Hostel	4.2	21.5	—	3.1	45.6	—
Totals	100	100	—	100	100	—

Source: Research and Statistics Section (1996a, 86).
[a]Admissions are number of times individual was imprisoned.
[b]Ratios: The number of probationers per parolee.

The rehabilitation aid hostels, operated by private associations and partially subsidized by the Rehabilitation Bureau, receive even greater numbers of probationers and parolees who require interim housing. They will be described in chapter 8. The hostels are part of a system of assistance to those probationers and, mostly, parolees and released prisoners who are in special need of help in the early stage of return to the community.

The primary purpose of table 4.3 is to compare the living

arrangements of probationers and parolees. The ratios (the number of probationers per parole) measure the differences in degree of advantage held by probationers. The general advantage is measured against a ratio of one when neither probation nor parole hold an advantage. Most of the ratios are less than one because parolees are more numerous than probationers. In other words, for those living arrangements, parolees turn to them because of their vulnerability when they lack support of their families. Alone, and for first admissions, probationers have a positive ratio.

Probationers had a positive ratio—a greater presence of probationers in the particular living arrangement—for living alone and had a high, although negative, ratio for the employer's dormitory. Those instances were for first admissions to probation only, implying higher probability of favorable case outcomes. Living apart from the parental family suggests a capacity to be self-supporting. Residing in an employer's dormitory indicates a history of employment.

Recidivism: Fostered by Leniency

Some convicted offenders continue a life of crime; others abandon criminality after the first, second, or additional crimes. Some continue law violations until the end of their lives. Why the differences? The riddle of recidivism resists easy and final explanation because of opposing factors: the offender's trouble-ridden biography or preference for a life of predation; the errors of the criminal justice agencies in deciding who goes free and who is imprisoned; the inadequacies of correctional programs; and the community's failure to reward the genuinely rehabilitated probationer, parolee, or discharged prisoner.

The leniency of public prosecutors and sentencing judges may interrupt the drift toward dedicated criminality but, contrary to an unexamined opinion, may be among the explanations for the accumulation of serial offenders on probation, in prisons, and on parole. Yesteryear's leniency does not guarantee the end of law violations by resolving the riddle of recidivism. But the puzzle of recidivism also includes the possibility of delayed abandonment of criminal ways. Responsible and careful assessment of multiple offenders justifies placing trust in some of them again because of changes in their living situations and their attitudes.

Among admission in 1995, the 4,783 probationers averaged 1.78 admissions to the program and 56 percent were admitted for the first time. Repeated admissions were more characteristic of parolees, 2.76 mean number of admissions and only 43 percent on parole for the first time. The RPBs approved the applications at a rate of 91.1 percent in 1970 to 95.9 percent in 1995, but, for serial parolees, the approval rate increased from 78.7 percent in 1970 to 91.8 percent in 1995. The percentage of recidivists among parole candidates resembled the similar figure for prison admission: 39.2 versus 52.7 in 1970; 36.5 versus 57.3 in 1975; 36.7 versus 58.4 in 1980; 39.3 versus 60.3 in 1985; 43.6 versus 62.3 in 1990; and 41.8 versus 60.1 in 1995 (Research and Statistics Section 1971a, 12; 1971b, 74; 1976a, 12; 1976b, 78; 1981a, 12; 1981b, 78; 1986a, 12; 1986b, 74; 1991a, 12; 1991b, 76; 1996a, 89; 1996b, 76).

The probability of RPB approvals in 1995 was affected by the particular crime that sent the parole candidate to prison, but the person imprisoned for the first time had a better chance of being considered than the serial inmate. Table 4.4 arrays, by the percentage of cases approved, the crimes of the parole candidates who numbered 70 or more. For each crime, the percentage of recidivists (two or more exposures to imprisonment) is given for the approved cases, the denied cases, and the cases withdrawn because of a rule violation in prison or inadequacies of the employment-residence plan for parole.

Traffic and embezzlement gained the highest approval rates and the lowest recidivism rates (8.7 and 8.6 percent) of the approved cases. There were few denials and withdrawals; for the traffic offenders all denied cases were recidivists

Table 4.4
Regional Parole Board Approvals of Adult Parole Applications by Selected Crimes, 1995

Selected Crimes	Number of Parole Candidates	Number Not Approved	Approval Rate	Percent of Recidivists		
				Approved Cases	Denied Cases	Withdrawn Cases
Traffic	1,093	11	99.0	8.7	100	50.0
Embezzlement	164	2	98.8	8.6	—	50.0
Larceny	4,274	239	94.8	51.4	90.8	63.2
Stimulants	3,762	213	94.3	55.4	79.5	66.9
Bodily injury	516	31	94.0	25.9	44.4	22.7
Rape	285	17	94.0	9.7	30.8	—
Organic solvents	128	8	93.7	43.3	66.7	60.0
Fraud	832	56	93.3	35.8	63.6	56.5
Robbery	418	31	92.6	14.2	15.8	25.0
Illicit trades	81	6	92.6	36.0	50.0	—
Forgery	116	9	92.2	15.9	60.0	50.0
Violence law	74	6	91.9	60.3	100	60.0
Extortion	337	29	91.4	37.3	50.0	57.9
Arson	138	13	90.6	8.8	14.3	33.3
Firearms	136	13	90.4	30.9	12.5	40.0
Homicide	434	58	86.6	12.5	30.3	24.0
Indecent assault	112	15	86.6	20.6	50.0	28.6
Total	13,222	771	94.2	40.8	63.4	55.4

Source: Research and Statistics Section (1996a, 12–13).

and half of the withdrawals. None of the embezzlers were denied, but half of the few withdrawals were recidivists. In short, first termers were highly represented among approvals but less so among the rare non-approvals.

Larceny and stimulant drugs were very numerous among the parole candidates and gained a high approval rate, but the RPB approvals were granted in spite of a high proportion (over 50 percent) of candidates with records of serial imprisonment. Recidivism was even more common for the non-approvals. Larceny is especially common among prison admissions, and its perpetrators tend to be repetitive and to be regarded as minor transgressors. Stimulant drug abusers include persons otherwise with good reputations, but drug abuse tends to be habitual.

Bodily injury and rape share the 94 percent rate of approvals, but rape is especially identified with first admissions to prison, although bodily injury draws a goodly share of recidivists. Courts regard rape as a serious crime; in 1992 the courts suspended a third of the cases, compared to 58.6 percent of all Penal Code cases (Research and Training Institute 1994, 57). However, the low level of recidivism among RPB approvals suggests corrigibility. Organic solvents and fraud drop slightly in approval rates and also share intermediate degrees of recidivism. Abuse of organic solvents is attributed mostly to adolescents and young adults, and fraud carries elements of misconduct tinged with white-collar respectability. Fraud is identified in the Penal Code with "a person who has illegally obtained or causes another to obtain illegally an economic advantage" or "a person who, by taking advantage of the lack of knowledge or experience of a minor or the weak-mindedness of another, obtains the surrender of such a person's property."

Robbery, illicit trades, and forgery receive 92 percent approvals, although illicit trades have higher recidivism than the other two. The illicit trades are prostitution, gambling and lottery, and dealing in pornographic materials; in addition to the few such cases, they usually represent minor figures in the trades. Forgery and robbery involve many first termers, a factor especially important in easing the negative image of this combination of force and property crime.

Extortion and the fewer violations of the Law for Punishment of Acts of Violence[2] share the 91 percent approval rate, but prosecution of the violence law draws heavily on recidivists. Extortion, an element in societal violence, has an intermediate level of recidivism. The recidivism associated with the violence law mirrors the targeting of the aggressive misconduct of the yakuza, but the approval rate is raised by the inclusion of generally conventional persons among those convicted of violating the law. Among those persons are the young adults who, as members of motor vehicle groups (the bosozoku), engage in aggressive public demonstrations.

Arson and firearms move in tandem down the continuum of approval rates but differ considerably in level of recidivism. Arson and its lower recidivism is related to a variety of fire setting either deliberately or through negligence. The Penal Code speaks of burning "a building, railroad train, electric car, vessel or mine actually serving a human habitation or in which persons are actually present." However, the articles also refer to structures not serving as habitations.

The intermediate level of recidivism suggests a mixture of offenders, including members of criminal gangs. Stringent control of firearms has been traced back to the end of the sixteenth century, when a sword hunt removed weapons from the farming class and, by distinguishing soldiers from civilians, gave the samurai a monopoly on them (Sansom 1963b, 331). Japanese robbers seldom use firearms, Moriyama (1995, 52) says, preferring a knife or sword. However, Shikita and Tsuchiya (1990, 95–97) describe fluctuations from 1958 to 1987 in the number and kinds of weapons seized from the yakuza. The general trend has been from swords and daggers toward guns. The greatest number of confiscated firearms was in the latter 1980s.

Homicide and indecent assault (a sex crime) drew the lowest (87 percent) approval rates but still at a remarkably high level when the notoriety of the crime is considered. First termers were favored in RPB deliberations for persons sentenced for homicide. "Indecency through compulsion" is an "indecent act upon a male or female person." Rape is "sexual intercourse with a female person" through "violence or intimidation." Recidivism was at the moderate level.

The Rehabilitation Bureau reports the record of previous contacts with the workings of the criminal justice system (see table 4.5). The most severe experience was selected for each individual. The contacts were imprisonment, suspended sentences with or without probation, fines, and suspended prosecution. The number of parolees exceeded that of probationers; their prior experiences with imprisonment and parole also were greater. Overall, the probationers had less experience with the sanctions of the criminal law. That experience was less severe; probationer's representation increased as the rigor of the official reaction declined. That trend held for suspended sentences without probation, fines, and suspension of prosecution. Probation also drew the larger proportion of persons without previous experience with the criminal justice system.

Ratios are the number of probationers per 100 parolees; the ratios measure the relative importance of probation with changes in age relative to parole. As the ratios move toward 100, the number of probationers approaches the number of parolees. For total persons, the ratios decline with advancing age. Probation comes chiefly to the young adults. The comparisons by age reflect the underrepresentation of probationers among those experiencing imprisonment, but the representation rose gradually with advancing age.

Suspensions with probation were few in the records of both probationers and parolees, but compared with imprisonment, current probation moved even closer to the number of parolees. That trend grew with advancing age. Suspensions without probation were most numerous; the ratios declined

Table 4.5
Previous Experiences with Criminal Justice System of Adults Admitted to Probation and Parole, 1995

Ages	Number of Persons[a]	Sentences to Prison			Fines[b]	Suspended Prosecution	No CJS Experience
		Prison	Suspension, Probation	Suspension, w/o Probation			
Adult probationers							
Number	4,888	536	295	1,299	830	149	1,719
Percent	100	11.1	6.1	26.9	17.2	3.1	35.6
Adult parolees							
Number	11,950	6,096	1,088	2,254	801	24	1,687
Percent	100	51.0	9.1	18.9	6.7	0.2	14.1
Ratios[c]							
Under 25	165.3	2.0	12.2	81.0	344.7	1,125.0	291.4
25-29	42.6	1.1	13.1	47.2	123.8	566.7	100.0
30-34	30.9	6.2	20.3	52.7	108.6	800.0	57.8
35-39	30.7	8.7	39.8	57.8	66.3	400.0	51.5
40-49	25.1	9.5	46.9	56.8	56.6	566.7	30.7
50-59	24.6	12.1	49.0	64.6	42.6	280.0	27.4
60+	22.0	13.3	88.2	67.9	43.6	—	15.4
Total	40.4	8.8	27.1	57.6	103.6	620.8	101.9

Source: Research and Statistics Section (1996a, 90).

[a]Excludes persons whose previous experiences were not reported.
[b]Includes general fine, traffic fine, and fine with penal detention.
[c]Number of probationers per 100 parolees.

along with increasing age to show that the leniency had been extended especially to the younger adults. Fines were fewer but duplicated the trend. Suspended prosecution was too rare for a reliable comparison.

Probationers and parolees had about the same absolute number without previous contact with the criminal justice system. The advantage was greatest for the twenty-year-olds in age. Their fewer total numbers gave the percentage advantage to the probationers. Along the age continuum of ratios, the absolute number of probationers exceeded that of parolees less than age thirty years. From that point, the ratios dropped consistently with heightened age.

The official ideology of the juvenile justice system of Japan is expressed in Article 1 of the Juvenile Law: "The object of this Law is, with a view to the wholesome rearing of juveniles, to carry out protective measures relating to the character correction and environmental adjustment of delinquent juveniles." When younger, some of the adult probationers and parolees had experiences with the range of "protective measures": juvenile training schools, juvenile probation, referral to social agencies,[3] case dismissals after a formal hearing by the family court, and case dismissals without a hearing. The protective measures in table 4.6 are arrayed from most to least restrictive. The majority of the adults had no experience with these protective measures—slightly more of the parolees. The ratios show that probationers less than twenty-five years of age were more numerous than the equivalent parolees for adults without exposure to protective measures. From that age, the advantage for probationers slipped back.

The two versions of community corrections are portrayed in table 4.6 according to protective measures experienced by a minority of adult probationers and parolees. Of those experiencing juvenile corrections previously, parolees were more apt to have been in training schools and probationers on juvenile probation, but the youngest adults gave the probationers the numerical advantage for both programs. For all ages,

Table 4.6
Previous Exposure to Protective Measures of Adults Admitted to Probation and Parole, 1995

Ages	Number of Persons[a]	Training Schools	Probation	Social Agencies	Case Dismissals		No Record of Measures
					Hearing	No Hearing	
Adult probationers							
Number	4,586	730	919	12	215	90	2,620
Percent	100	15.9	20.0	0.3	4.7	2.0	57.1
Adult parolees							
Number	11,599	2,212	1,693	90	348	42	7,254
Percent	100	19.1	14.2	0.8	3.0	0.4	62.5
Ratios[b]							
Under 25	165.2	130.8	191.9	900.0	201.6	323.1	172.1
25–29	41.7	22.5	45.5	—	49.4	112.5	52.6
30–34	30.7	13.5	31.2	5.9	37.3	116.7	37.1
35–39	29.6	13.3	35.1	—	15.2	120.0	32.4
40–49	24.2	10.0	22.7	8.7	21.4	550.0	26.7
50–59	22.6	11.0	20.3	—	10.5	—	25.0
60+	17.9	12.8	40.0	—	—	—	17.6
Total	39.5	33.0	55.6	13.3	61.8	214.3	36.1

Source: Research and Statistics Section (1996a, 91).
[a]Excludes persons whose exposure to protective measures was not reported.
[b]Ratio: Number of probationers per 100 parolees.

probationers had the higher ages for previous juvenile parole when compared with training schools. Only a small proportion of the adults had been exposed to the other protective measures. All three earned very high ratios for adults less than twenty-five years of age. The trend suggests that the youngest of the probationers had greater access to protective measures. If older individuals had had such earlier access, more of them might not have become adult probationers in 1995.

Referrals to social agencies were too few for a reliable assessment. Adult probationers had the greater exposure to case dismissals, especially those without a formal hearing. As characteristic for all these comparisons, the youngest probationers gained the largest ratios. The ratios trickled down with advancing age.

Some of the adult probationers and parolees were on the programs again. For admissions to probation in 1995, 44 percent had been on probation previously. The mean number of admissions was 1.78. The mean number was greater at the extremes of ages rather than rising with increasing age. The mean number of admissions to adult probation by age were 2.03 for ages less than 25 years, 1.69 for ages 25–29 years, 1.58 for ages 30–34 years, 1.52 for ages 35–39 years, 1.63 for ages 40–49 years, 1.73 for ages 50–59 years, and 2.12 for ages 60 years and over (Research and Statistics Section 1996a, 89). From age 35 years, the adult probationers exhibited increasing recidivism with advancing age, but the majority of them were on probation for the first time regardless of age at the time of entering the current probation status.

Adult parolees averaged more previous times on parole (2.76) than probationers on previous probation. Only 35 percent were serving their first parole assignment. The number of times on parole grew with greater age, from 2.40 for ages less than 25 years, to 3.77 for persons 60 years and over. The development is a side effect of the diversionary policies that minimize resort to imprisonment. As noted earlier, admissions to parole resemble the trend of prison admissions toward greater proportions of serial prisoners. The selective criteria of public prosecutors and sentencing courts color the quality of prison admissions, and the RPBs adjust to the effect upon the parole candidates they consider.

Multiple exposure to parole had modest effect on the RPBs' approval rate; in 1995 the rate was 95.9 percent of candidates considered for the first time and 91.8 percent of those who had been on parole previously. The single admissions had the higher mean length of prison sentences (27.14 months versus 23.99 months) because of the difference in the distribution of sentences according to length. The percentage share of sentences of three years and more was 16.6 for single exposure to parole and 10.9 for multiple exposure (Research and Statistics Section 1996a, 18–21).

Crimes and Community Corrections

Criminal behavior is related to the sociocultural organization of the given society rather than being merely the individuated conduct of pathological beings. Because crimes are related to collective life, Durkheim (1938) sees them as a normal symptom of social morbidity (the "ill health" or faulty functioning of society.) Only when crime rates exceed those usual in a given society does the patterning of criminality qualify as abnormality. He believes a crimeless society to be a sociological impossibility because of the diversity shaping human personality. If the hypothetical society of saints were to emerge, the abhorrence previously directed against murder (becoming nonexistent in the perfect society) would be shifted to offenses previously considered less serious. He argues (Durkheim 1947, 81) that the public conscience makes certain behavior a criminal act because it reproves it.

Erikson (1966, 6–7) defines *deviance*[4] as conduct "which the people of a group consider so dangerous, or embarrassing, or irritating that they bring special sanctions to bear against the persons who exhibit it." To him, deviance is a property (trait or attribute) *conferred upon* that behavior by the people who come in direct or indirect contact with it. Rather than emphasizing the behavior of the person called a criminal, Erikson concentrates on the relationship between that behavior and the standards applied to persons occupying their status in the community. A social audience passes judgment on the nonconformist. The legal definition of theft is one of a variety of judgments of the taking of property the taker does not own, including "borrowing," "confiscating," "commandeering," and "snatching."

This approach emphasizes the "criminalization" of marginal nonconformists who previously stood somewhere between complete conformists and criminals. In a complex society, a multitude of ethnic, regional, and occupational groups differ from one another in language, clothing, etiquette, beliefs, and lifestyles. The term *criminalization* refers to the assignment of criminal status to individuals through the political use of the criminal law to deal with what is perceived to be a public issue. Traditional crimes, such as homicide and larceny, were criminalized decades or centuries ago. New (nontraditional) crimes have been incorporated more recently in the criminal law because marginal deviance, previously tolerated, has been reassessed in the attitudinal environment of a public crisis.[5]

In Japan, traffic and drug offenses are the prominent examples of the workings of criminalization for new crimes. Traffic fatalities and injuries soared from 1948 to 1970 because of the great expansion of automobile registration, urban congestion, and narrow streets and roads. A series of governmental reactions included greater use of fines in an administrative rather than a penal way, but also new legislation to further criminalize traffic offenses, to increase the level of penalization, and to strengthen the rigor of law enforcement. Abuse of stimulant drugs (amphetamines) grew during the chaos after World War II, when the public gained access to the stimulant

drugs produced for the military during the war. Penalties of
the law were strengthened and hospitalization made mandatory. In prison admissions, traffic offenders and drug abusers (drug convictions are proportionally high among women)
have become prominent.[6]

In 1995, adult traffic offenders held higher shares of probation admissions (14.7 percent) than of prison admissions
(8.8 percent) and of parole admissions (9.3 percent). Drug offenders assumed greater shares of admissions than of traffic
admissions: 24.3 percent for probation, 28.7 percent for prison,
and 29.8 percent for parole. Stimulant drugs were dominant;
organic solvents (paint thinner, for example), absent from 1995
prison admissions, were in small proportions in probation
and parole. Involvement with other drugs were most numerous in prison admissions but in very small numbers in all three
admissions (Research and Statistics Section 1996a, 78–85).

Regional parole boards took less time on average to decide traffic cases than drug cases because traffic offenders are
eligible for parole earlier in the prison sentence. Of the total
length of the prison sentences for traffic offenders, 79.1 percent was consumed when they were released on parole. For
drug offenders, the equivalent percentage was 85.0, compared
to 83.5 percent for all RPB decisions. Stimulant drugs had
brought the vast majority (3,549 of 3,730) of the drug offenders among the approved RPB cases; the decisions took 85.8
percent of the time of the full sentence, compared to 85.3 percent for the organic solvent cases and 70.4 percent of the other
drug cases (Research and Statistics Section 1996a, 78–85).

In the RPB cases considered in 1995, 58.2 percent were for
inmates in prison for the first time. Traffic offenders were
considerably more likely to be "first timers" (90.8 percent).
Drug abuse generated greater recidivism, 44.7 percent for all
inmates interviewed by the RPBs were in prison for the first
time. The percentages of first termers was 43.6 for stimulant
drugs, 55.5 for organic solvents, and 87.3 for other drugs (Research and Statistics Section 1996a, 12).

Over the decades, drug and traffic offenders have assumed

Table 4.7
Adult Admissions to Probation and Parole by Crimes, 1970–1995

Selected Offenses[a]	Percentage Distribution					
	1970	1975	1980	1985	1990	1995
Adult Probation						
Violence against persons	21.1	15	9.7	8.6	11.1	9.4
Bodily injury	(10.0)	(8.3)	(5.2)	(4.9)	(7.2)	(5.6)
Rape	(6.6)	(3.2)	(2.1)	(1.0)	(1.1)	(1.2)
Robbery	(1.4)	(0.9)	(0.5)	(0.7)	(0.7)	(0.8)
Homicide	(0.8)	(0.7)	(0.5)	(0.6)	(0.5)	(0.4)
Societal violence	13.1	9.2	5.3	4.6	4.7	5.7
Extortion	(8.7)	(5.3)	(3.1)	(3.4)	(3.7)	(4.1)
Violence law	(2.9)	(2.1)	(1.5)	(0.7)	(0.6)	(0.8)
Property	46.2	46.4	37.9	41.1	41.8	43.7
Larceny	(36.5)	(37.7)	(30.4)	(32.3)	(34.5)	(35.7)
Fraud	(5.6)	(4.6)	(3.8)	(5.0)	(3.5)	(4.7)
Embezzlement	(1.4)	(0.9)	(0.8)	(0.6)	(0.7)	(0.6)
Forgery	(0.9)	(1.2)	(1.4)	(1.9)	(1.1)	(0.8)
Drugs	0.7	7.8	22.2	23.7	19.2	25.0
Traffic	12.3	18.5	23.3	20.5	21.3	15.3
Illicit trades	6.5	3.1	1.6	1.5	1.9	0.9
Total percent	100	100	100	100	100	100
Total number	6,738	6,830	7,841	7,004	4,665	4,731
Adult Parole						
Violence against persons	22	22.8	16.4	12.6	12.1	13.2
Bodily injury	(5.3)	(5.9)	(5.2)	(4.2)	(4.0)	(3.9)
Rape	(6.7)	(6.6)	(3.2)	(1.8)	(1.9)	(2.1)
Robbery	(4.7)	(4.2)	(3.3)	(2.9)	(2.6)	(3.1)
Homicide	(4.1)	(5.0)	(3.7)	(3.0)	(3.0)	(3.1)
Societal violence	6.9	6.1	5.7	3.5	4.5	4.0
Extortion	(4.2)	(3.8)	(3.4)	(2.4)	(2.9)	(2.6)
Violence law	(1.7)	(1.4)	(1.1)	(0.7)	(0.6)	(0.5)
Property	53.3	46.4	45.4	42.8	41.0	42.2
Larceny	(41.1)	(35.2)	(33.9)	(31.6)	(30.8)	(31.9)
Fraud	(7.6)	(6.6)	(7.2)	(7.3)	(6.5)	(6.4)
Embezzlement	(1.8)	(1.6)	(1.6)	(1.4)	(1.0)	(1.3)
Forgery	(0.9)	(1.4)	(1.3)	(1.2)	(1.0)	(1.0)
Drugs	0.5	3.7	17.8	29.1	30.9	30.4
Traffic	15.7	19.5	14.0	11.4	10.6	9.5
Illicit trades	1.6	1.5	0.7	0.6	0.9	0.7
Total percent	100	100	100	100	100	100
Total number	17,652	14,728	14,978	17,473	14,669	11,915

Sources: Research and Statistcs Section (1971a, 88–95; 1976a, 86–93; 1981a, 76–83; 1986a, 76–83; 1991a, 78–85; 1996a, 78–85).

[a]Excludes "other" and public order crimes.

increasing proportions of admissions to probation and parole (see table 4.7). The upsurge for drug offenders has been most noteworthy, but both adult probation and parole have scored gains since 1970. Leniency has characterized the resort to criminalization, but drugs have sustained an upward trend most consistently. Other offenses are in the so-called traditional mode and have lost percentage share to drugs and traffic. Along with the decline in total admissions, violent offenses have lost proportional representation over the decades. Bodily injury (an offense encompassing a variety of aggressive incidents) were most numerous in violence against persons by probationers, but other violent crimes joined in the erosion of violence against persons over the decades. Rape, robbery, and homicide held greater shares of violence against persons by paroled inmates and worked against the declining percentage share of those parolees. Nevertheless, parole admissions also retreated from the relatively greater presence of violence in earlier decades.

Societal violence entails threats to the community as a corporate entity rather than victimizing individuals directly. Mostly because of extortion (a property crime suggesting violence), probationers had the greater involvement in those threats, but parole joined the downward trend over time. Property crimes cling to the majority of all admissions, especially for parole, but lost shares over the decades. Larceny (another multifaceted offense) is dominant, and fraud lends minor support. Embezzlement and fraud are also involved in a fragmentary way. The illicit trades are prostitution, gambling and lottery, and dealing in pornography—offenses linked with crime syndicates. Those offenses are of minor and declining importance; probation holds a larger share of cases than parole.

Probation and imprisonment are alternatives for sentencing courts; how do probation admissions compare with prison admissions among the categories of crime (see table 4.8)? The ratios for all crimes have a slight decline over the decades; the general trend has been a modest loss of the representation

Table 4.8

Comparing Admissions to Adult Probation and Prisons by Crimes, 1970–1995

Crimes	Number of Probation Admissions per 100 Prison Admissions					
	1970	1975	1980	1985	1990	1995
Violence against persons	27.3	20.6	18.3	14.1	16.6	15.1
Bodily injury	29.7	24.2	19.4	15.7	20.4	22.8
Rape	38.0	23.4	31.0	16.5	13.6	14.8
Robbery	12.3	8.8	6.7	7.7	8.9	5.5
Homicide	7.0	7.3	6.3	5.8	5.2	3.9
Societal violence	36.2	25.4	18.4	14.0	12.7	19.8
Extortion	48.7	31.1	22.5	20.0	19.1	27.5
Violence law	21.3	16.5	14.1	7.6	6.8	16.0
Property	24.5	26.2	27.1	24.3	23.6	24.6
Larceny	24.9	28.0	29.4	26.6	26.0	27.4
Fraud	20.7	16.5	15.9	15.3	11.7	15.9
Embezzlement	31.8	23.5	24.1	13.8	20.4	14.8
Forgery	23.0	31.9	51.4	62.8	46.1	30.4
Drugs	34.6	31.0	27.8	19.3	15.2	18.8
Traffic	20.9	32.1	47.9	40.8	38.0	37.7
Illicit trades	49.7	43.2	39.2	29.6	31.8	32.6
All crimes	27.3	26.9	28.4	22.7	21.9	21.3
No. of probationers	6,908	7,048	8,058	7,180	4,793	4,856
No. of prisoners	25,322	26,175	28,374	31,656	21,838	22,745

Sources: Research and Statistics Section (1971a, 92–95; 1971b, 66–69; 1976a, 90–93; 1976b, 70–73; 1981a, 80–83; 1981b, 66–69; 1986a, 82–85; 1986b, 66–69; 1991a, 82–85; 1991b, 66–69; 1996a, 82–85; 1996b, 66–69).

of probationers, but the representation has hovered around 25 percent.

Probation of traffic offenders was most impressive, peaking at a ratio of 47.9, then tail off. Drugs also held a high ratio initially but consistently lost out to imprisonment in subsequent decades. Illicit trades were few in absolute numbers, undermining the importance of their very high ratios, but the unusually high reliance on probation suggests the apprehension of minor participants in illicit trades.

The declining use of probation for violent crimes is noteworthy. Societal violence (especially extortion) had a very high ratio in 1970, but the value of the ratios dropped subse-

Table 4.9
Comparing Admissions to Adult Probation and Parole by Crimes, 1970–1995

Crimes	1970	1975	1980	1985	1990	1995
	Number of Probation Admissions per 100 Parole Admissions					
Violence against persons	36.9	30.5	30.8	27.4	29.0	28.5
Bodily injury	72.5	64.6	51.9	46.5	56.4	56.6
Rape	37.6	22.8	34.6	22.4	19.2	22.8
Robbery	11.6	10.1	7.6	9.6	9.3	10.1
Homicide	7.0	6.7	7.5	8.6	5.6	5.4
Societal violence	72.0	70.4	49.0	52.3	32.9	56.1
Extortion	79.2	64.9	48.4	56.8	40.1	63.5
Violence law	65.0	71.8	68.6	40.9	32.6	63.5
Property	33.1	46.3	43.6	38.5	32.4	41.2
Larceny	33.9	49.7	47.0	41.0	35.7	44.4
Fraud	28.3	32.4	27.6	27.8	17.2	29.1
Embezzlement	29.9	26.0	28.6	16.5	22.8	18.9
Forgery	36.9	40.3	55.4	61.9	36.5	33.3
Drugs	56.6	99.1	65.3	32.7	19.8	32.6
Traffic	29.8	43.9	87.3	72.3	64.2	63.9
Illicit trades	150.9	95.5	124.5	100.0	65.9	50.0
Total ratios	38.7	47.2	53.0	40.3	32.2	40.0
No. of probationers	6,908	7,048	8,058	7,180	4,793	4,856
No. of parolees	17,861	14,933	15,206	17,795	14,896	12,138

Sources: Research and Statistics Section (1971a, 88–95; 1976a, 86–93; 1981a, 76–83; 1986a 76–83; 1991a, 78–85; 1996a, 78–85).

quently. For violence against persons, probation for homicide and robbery was unusual, but the ratios dropped here as well as for this general brand of violence. The representation of probation for rape and bodily injury was high in 1970, but the ratios (especially for rape) dropped in the following decades. Rape cases are less common than for bodily injury (an offense involving many kinds of incidents), and a few cases of probation can inflate the ratio unduly.

When compared with parole admissions, probation had the advantage of fewer parole admissions than prison admissions; the ratios in table 4.9 were inflated, but the total number of parolees differ from those of prisoners in the denominator. The changes in ratios among crimes are worthy of examination. Parole always had the numerical advantage over probation, but probation gained representation from 1970 to 1980 but dropped away afterward for all crimes. Probation of drug offenders followed the trend, holding a respectable position. The position at 1970 for traffic offenders was less impressive, but the ratios rose sharply and clung to a high representation from 1985 through 1995. Again, the performance for illicit trades is not reliable.

Extortion and the violations of the Law for Punishment of Acts of Violence held higher percentages of probationers than parolees. Extortion is grouped with fraud in the Penal Code, but its definition conveys the theme of violence: "a person who, by intimidation, causes another to surrender property." The violence law has been directed against public demonstrations, including that of motor-vehicle groups, as well as the violence of gangsters. Both versions involve a variety of incidents; the courts find reasons to dismiss the suitability of imprisonment for cases not qualified for outright release into the community. In violence against persons, bodily injury has high ratios; again, the miscellany of incidents raises chances for relative leniency. Robbery and homicide illustrate a preference for imprisonment for extreme violence. Rape occupies an intermediate position.

As would be expected, property crimes usually attract probation, but, in the Japanese context, the most favorable cases are drained off by the judges' preference for suspension of sentences without probation. Documentary forgery is the only numerous property crime that approaches the volume of larceny cases and that exceeds larceny's ratio. As for larceny, forgery includes a wide variety of law violations but, for forgery, tends toward white-collar offenses: forgery of "imperial state documents," "a public official who prepares or alters a document," "a doctor makes a false entry in a medical certificate," and so on. Fraud and embezzlement gain less opportunity for probation because their definitions move closer to public conceptions of ordinary thievery.

Final Comment

In summary, the judges' preference for suspensions without probation is one of the elements of Japan's particular approach to community-oriented corrections. The preference expresses the general Japanese faith in leniency toward offenders when they express repentance and show willingness and capacity for self-correction, but Abe (1963, 332–38) argues that public prosecutors go beyond the general public in general understanding of the sources of crime, are less emotionally shocked by offenses, are more humanitarian, and usually believe they are broad minded in their decision making.

The diversionary policies are key elements in Japan's very low imprisonment rate, and the screening of offenders shapes the characteristics of the residue who go to prison. The ultimate consequence is the higher average ages, and criminal record, and previous contacts with the criminal justice system of that residue. The characteristics of adult parolees take on unusual qualities. For adults, the number of parolees exceed that of probationers. Prison populations are the demographic reservoir from which parolees are drawn. Expiration of the prison sentence is the other sort of prison release. Both expiration and parole have declined over the decades in concert with the reduction in prison admissions. Parole has settled down since 1970 with a rather stable and major share of releases.

Adult probation has clung to a considerably small share of the court's extension of leniency to convicted defendants. Due to the preference of sentencing judges, probation loses out to the alternative of suspended sentences without probationary supervision. Whether consciously or not, the judges bet that the controls of the community will be sufficient for offenders who are believed to be capable of self-correction. Probation is reserved for a smaller number who need prodding but do not require imprisonment.

*The Rehabilitation Bureau, Ministry of Justice of Japan, spon-
sors the annual nationwide campaign called "Movement Toward
a Brighter Society." Volunteers and the probation offices orga-
nize public events to urge public participation in prevention of
crime and delinquency. (Courtesy of Rehabilitation Bureau)*

*Since 1950, volunteers have distributed pamphlets and other
materials in main terminals of mass transportation during the
annual campaign in support of crime prevention activities.
(Courtesy of Rehabilitation Bureau)*

A psychologist interviews a juvenile referred to the classification home for diagnosis and evaluation. (Courtesy of Tokyo Juvenile Classification Home)

The psychologist responsible for interviewing and preparing the study of a juvenile client reports findings at a case conference when the final report to the family court is decided. (Courtesy of Tokyo Juvenile Classification Home)

Psychological tests are often used to analyze the juvenile's personality trend, self–image, relationship with others, and so on. (Courtesy of Tokyo Juvenile Classification Home)

The "observation staff" of the juvenile classification home is responsible for daily care of residents. The staff observes the conduct of residents for clues to reasons for their behavior. Here the choice among books may be a clue to be reported to psychologists. (Courtesy of Tokyo Juvenile Classification Home)

A staff member poses as a juvenile taking a vocational aptitude test at a juvenile classification home. (Courtesy of Tokyo Juvenile Classification Home)

In sandbox diagnosis, the juvenile is asked to assemble plastic objects in a sandbox into a scene such as a farm, home, or park. Here a psychologist is asking the juvenile to explain a scene he has assembled. (Courtesy of Tokyo Juvenile Classification Home)

At a juvenile classification home, staff members play the roles of resident and psychologists in the use of technology to measure aptitude for driving motor vehicles. (Courtesy of Tokyo Juvenile Classification Home)

Classification Division staff members are shown here at work— which includes a pre-parole unit. (Courtesy of Kawagoe Juvenile Prison)

A probation officer, who is assigned to the regional parole board, interviews an inmate of a prison. Staff members represent the two participants. (Courtesy of Kawagoe Juvenile Prison)

At the Classification Division, the staff discusses the case of an inmate-candidate for parole. (Courtesy of Kawagoe Juvenile Prison)

Japanese prisons provide a dormitory or special building for inmates scheduled for parole. This facility is the pre-release building at Kawagoe Prison. (Courtesy of Kawagoe Juvenile Prison)

Interior of the pre-release building at Kawagoe Juvenile Prison for inmates scheduled for parole. (Courtesy of Kawagoe Juvenile Prison)

Korakukai Rehabilitation Aid Hostel was established initially on this site when a former warden of Fuchu Prison provided a house. This modern building was constructed later. (Courtesy of Rehabilitation Bureau)

Senshuryo Rehabilitation Aid Hostel is located in Osaka. (Courtesy of Rehabilitation Bureau)

Hakkosya Rehabilitation Aid Hostel is located in Tokyo. (Courtesy of Rehabilitation Bureau)

Wachukai is the largest rehabilitation aid hostel in Japan. It was established in 1912 by the Federation of Buddhist Temples. This multistory building was opened in 1987. (Courtesy of Wachukai Rehabilitation Aid Hostel)

Keiwa-en Rehabilitation Aid Hostel, located in the Nakano district of Tokyo, specializes in male juveniles who need assistance during the reentry crisis. (Courtesy of Rehabilitation Bureau)

5
Juvenile Corrections in
the Community: Family Court and
Juvenile Classification Homes

UNLIKE COMMUNITY-ORIENTED CORRECTIONS for adults, admissions to juvenile probation have held the advantage over juvenile admissions to parole. Table 5.1 offers evidence that the absolute number of probation admissions increased through 1965; the trend is similar for adult probation but for much fewer cases. The dip of 1970 and 1975 in absolute number of probation admissions is due to the fewer cases reaching family courts, a tendency toward more dismissals without a hearing, and fluctuation in the number of traffic cases. Probation admissions have soared since 1977, when short-term probation for juvenile traffic offenders was introduced (Shikita and Tsuchiya 1990, 270–72, 347).

The juvenile probation admissions also held the advantage in age-specific rates when compared with probation of adults. The magnitude of increase over the years was as impressive as the relative consistency of the increase for juvenile probation. The probation-parole ratios underscore the relative magnitude. Parole admissions of juveniles are comparatively few in absolute numbers. The pattern is due to the few admissions to juvenile training schools, shrinking the human reservoir from which parolees are recruited. Nevertheless, paroles take up a high proportion of releases from training schools, reaching well over 90 percent in 1980 and thereafter. Releases at expiration of sentence (completion of time at training school as set by the family court) lose shares as the years pass.

Table 5.1

Juvenile Admissions to Probation, Training Schools, and Parole, 1950–1995

Years	Probation Admissions		Parole Admissions		Probationer-Parolee Ratios[b]	Parolees as Percent of Releases[c]	Juvenile Admissions per 100 Adult Admissions	
	Number	Rate[a]	Number	Rate[a]			Probation	Parole
1950	13,291	128.0	3,121	30.0	426.9	97.6	6,014.0	7.2
1955	17,094	161.4	7,375	69.6	231.8	84.1	392.0	22.7
1960	24,408	225.6	7,797	72.1	313.0	83.2	286.3	25.3
1965	28,173	218.3	6,301	48.8	447.1	85.0	337.4	32.4
1970	27,383	256.7	3,167	29.9	864.6	71.4	396.4	17.7
1975	21,384	224.7	1,593	16.7	1,342.4	81.1	303.4	10.7
1980	56,322	579.6	4,063	41.8	1,386.2	91.5	699.0	26.7
1985	71,411	651.4	5,585	50.9	1,278.6	93.1	994.6	31.4
1990	73,779	616.8	4,333	36.6	1,702.7	94.4	1,539.3	29.4
1995	51,075	513.8	3,782	38.0	1,350.5	95.6	1,051.8	31.2

Sources: Shikita and Tsuchiya (1990, 374); Research and Statistics Section (1996a, 54–55).

[a]Age-specific rates are numbers of admissions per 100,000 Japanese 14–19 years of age.

[b]Number of probationers per 100 parolees.

[c]Percentage share of parolees among all inmates released from juvenile training schools.

Compared with adults, juveniles are much more apt to receive probationary supervision but are less numerous on parole rolls (see table 5.1). During the chaos immediately after the end of World War II, juvenile admissions to probation were comparatively heavy, then the rate per 100 adult parolees dropped but reflected a continuing major advantage over adult probationers. After 1960, the rate increased significantly but not with full consistency.

Of all releases from juvenile training schools, the parole share grew remarkably over the years and always exceeded the equivalent figure for adults. Nevertheless, the rates of juvenile paroles per 100 adult admissions to parole always have been low. The explanation lies in the much greater absolute number of adult paroles. The greater number of inmates of correctional institutions, of course, affects the supply of possible candidates for parole.

Family Courts: Functions and Philosophy

Established on January 1, 1949, the family courts specialize in family affairs and juvenile delinquency cases. The Law for Determination of Family Affairs states its purposes to be "to establish the peace of family and to maintain a wholesome cooperation among relatives upon the basis of the individual and the essential equality of both sexes." The law expects that family problems normally will be conciliated rather than adjudicated. Later the law and the Juvenile Law were amended to place both family affairs and juvenile delinquency cases in the family court. The court's jurisdiction covers three kinds of problems: (1) *ko*-type matters—declarations of absence or of incompetence and correction of household registers; (2) litigation matters—a divorce or adoptive relationship, for example; and (3) *otsu*-matters—such as distribution of matrimonial property or partition of co-owned property (Supreme Court of Japan 1989, 18).

For household registration, the policemen visit every residence in the neighborhood twice a year for any changes in the number and characteristics of all residents. The register establishes legal residence for voting, schooling, pension benefits, and so on. Divorce by mutual agreement exists in Japan; when difficulty cannot be conciliated by the family court, it is necessary for formal referral to a district court.

The Juvenile Law (therefore, the family court) is concerned with three classes of juveniles: "delinquents," "child offenders," and "predelinquents." "Delinquents" are those aged fourteen through nineteen who are accused of breaking the Penal Code or special laws. "Child offenders" are those less than age fourteen, who are subject to prosecutions under criminal laws because of referral to the family court by two agencies responsible under the Child Welfare Law for treating persons less than fourteen years of age. The agencies are, first, child guidance centers and, second, child education and training centers managed by the prefectural government. The "child offenders" sent to the family court have been found to have high risks of repeated offenses and likely to injure themselves and others. The "predelinquents" are deemed to need "protective measures," such as the Juvenile Law proposes, in keeping with "the wholesome rearing of children."

The law defines a predelinquent as "any juvenile who is prone to commit an offense or violate a criminal law or ordinance in view of his character or environments, because of the existence of the following reasons: (a) that he habitually does not subject himself to the reasonable control of his guardian; (b) that he stays away from his home without good reason; (c) that he associates with a person of criminal propensity or of immoral character or frequents places of evil reputation; (d) that he has the propensity to commit acts harmful to the moral character of his own or of others."

The personnel of family courts are judges, court clerks, investigative officers, medical officers, and auxiliary employees. The judges are appointed for ten-year terms from a list of candidates supplied by the Supreme Court. (For clarity in distinguishing the respective positions, we have reserved the term *probation officer* for staff of the probation offices responsible for supervision of probationers and parolees. We call the supervising personnel of the family court "investigative officers.") Each prefecture has one family court, except Hokkaido, which has four, for a total of fifty courts. In addition there are 242 branch offices and 59 sub-branch offices throughout Japan. The fifty family courts and ten large branch offices have a clinic for medical examination, diagnosis, and short-term treatment of adult and juvenile clients. Most medical officers specialize in either internal medicine or psychiatry (Supreme Court of Japan 1989, 12–13; n.d., 30).

Candidates for the position of judges must pass two national examinations to be eligible for a two-year course of the Supreme Court's Legal Training and Research Institute. Upon successful completion of the training, the apprentice is qualified to be an assistant judge, prosecutor, or lawyer. Full judges have at least ten years experience in such roles (Abe 1963).

The investigative officers have completed a four-month course offered by the Research and Training Institute that is an organizational component of the Supreme Court. The trainees are appointed from among university graduates in social or behavioral sciences who have passed a national examination held by the Supreme Court. After that course, the trainees are apprentices to family courts for a year. After the apprenticeship, a practical course is attended for eight months (Supreme Court of Japan 1989, 14).

Intake and Processing of Delinquents

As the first of five routes by which juveniles arrive at family courts, the police are most likely to have initial contact with juveniles either as delinquents or as individuals vulnerable to exploitation. Police are likely to withdraw charges that an offense has occurred, without formal action, against juveniles involved in minor offenses punishable by fines or lesser penalties. Yoshitake (1989, 93) notes that the police are obligated to send juvenile delinquents to the public prosecutors "when the offenses are very grave or the juveniles seem to be habitual offenders in spite of their offenses." The police also are in a position to observe directly "juvenile conduct that suggests symptoms of personal maladjustment or undesirable social circumstances injurious to the youngster's own interests."

As the second route, juvenile offenders who would be subject to imprisonment if they were adults go to the public prosecutors, who have the authority to confirm that a crime is involved and to refer them to the juvenile court. Article 42, Juvenile Law, instructs public prosecutors to send juveniles to the family court when, "upon investigation of a suspected juvenile case . . . there is suspicion of an offense."

Third, parents, teachers, and other members of the community may bring predelinquents to the family court (Juvenile Law, Article 6). Fourth, as already implied, the prefectural governor or the chief of a child guidance center is responsible for treating troubled and troublesome children under the Child Welfare Law. If these children are found unmanageable in those centers, they may be referred to the family court, which has authority (lacked by the centers) to assign predelinquents to an institution without agreement of the juveniles or their guardians (Juvenile Law, Article 6-3).

Fifth, family court investigators may discover a juvenile who is eligible for appearing before the family court. The investigator is authorized by the Juvenile Law, Article 7, to conduct the necessary investigation through contacts with the juveniles, their guardians, and other persons and, second, to refer to the family court the cases found appropriate for that action.

From that point, the family courts move toward deciding what should be done. Among the dispositions available to the courts, the judge may dismiss the case without a hearing after reading the investigator's report or after conducting a hearing in a rather informal manner but not open to the pub-

Table 5.2
Family Court Dispositions, 1951–1991

Dispositions	1951	1961	1971	1981	1991
		Percentage Distribution			
Dismissals					
Without hearing	39.8	53.2	60.1	70.4	72.0
With hearing	25.9	23.2	25.6	19.1	17.0
Probation	18.8	13.7	9.8	7.5	7.8
Training school	9.0	5.8	2.6	2.2	2.3
Public prosecutor					
Deserves prosecution	5.6	2.8	1.3	0.4	0.4
Over age limit	—	0.6	0.3	0.2	0.2
Welfare agencies[a]	0.9	0.7	0.3	0.2	0.3
Number of cases	134,946	138,143	112,340	188,541	157,610

Sources: Shikita and Tsuchiya (1990, 382); Research and Training Institute (1993, 97).

[a]Includes child guidance centers responsible to prefectural governors, child education and training homes, and homes for dependent children.

lic. A single judge presides, with these persons present: the investigative officer, the juvenile, the parents or guardians, perhaps a concerned teacher or employer, and the court clerk. The juvenile and parents or guardian may appoint an "attendant" who serves as a kind of defense counsel and is present at the hearing with permission of the family court. If a lawyer serves as attendant, the court's permission is not necessary (Supreme Court of Japan 1989, 26).

After considering the information incorporated in the investigator's report, the judge may decide to dismiss the juveniles unconditionally without a formal hearing. This disposition maximizes the policy of avoiding punitive sanctions, when feasible, in favor of the "wholesome rearing of juveniles" prioritized by the Juvenile Law. These boys and girls go home, perhaps because the offense is minor, perhaps because the individual is deemed to be capable of self-correction, or perhaps because the informal controls of family and other reference groups are expected to produce compliance. Table 5.2 documents the frequency of this disposition and its increased dominance over the decades. Dismissals have increased their percentage share of the dispositions: 65.7 percent in 1951 and 89 percent in 1991. Meanwhile, other dispositions have lost share to reach the following shares in 1991: 7.8 percent for probation, 2.3 percent for referrals to training schools, 0.6 percent for referrals to public prosecutors; and 0.3 percent to welfare agencies.

Dismissals after a formal hearing occupy second place among total dispositions over the decades, but their share declines, mostly because of the greater proportion of dismissals without hearings. The judges prefer to meet directly with the juveniles and the parents or guardians. Their responses will strengthen evidence that a dismissal of the case is justified, that further investigation is necessary, or that other dispositions are preferred.

Probation returns the youngsters to the community but under supervision, mostly by unsalaried probation officers. In keeping with the philosophy expressed by the Juvenile Law, the family courts prefer, when feasible, either of the two versions of case dismissals. Probation usually is considered to carry some taint of criminalization. As will be discussed later in this chapter, the director general of the Rehabilitation Bureau introduced a special short-term program for juvenile traffic offenders in 1977. In this manner, the treatment possibilities of probation were given greater emphasis.

That theme was extended in 1992, when a "community participation program" for juveniles was introduced. The new program has similarities to the community service orders of Britain and other Western countries, Imafuku (1997, 26–27) explains, but places greater emphasis on development of "a sense of responsibility" and "a sense of self-worth" than on punishment and reparation. The juveniles are expected to "know different types of people" and "learn their way of life." Sound relationships and use of leisure time are to emerge through contacts with "an identifiable role model." Four kinds of community participation are defined: (1) community service in social welfare institutions such as the elderly or physically handicapped; (2) labor in farms or public areas; (3) "observation tours of historical spots, public facilities or construction areas"; and (4) recreational activities "such as skiing, soccer, cooking, fishing and camping."

In 1993 a similar program was introduced, Imafuku (1997, 26) says, but directing short-term probation (six to seven months) toward the "individual's specific and limited problem which prevents his adaptation to the society." For that focus, the family court selects the appropriate scheme for the particular juvenile, perhaps community service, recreational activity, or a drug abuse program. The juvenile is required to implement the scheme and submit a monthly report on performance. The special short-term program is oriented to non-traffic offenders who are not committed to delinquency, lack serious deviant tendencies, and enjoy a reasonably constructive social environment.

Few juveniles are sent to juvenile training schools, and that number has declined over the decades. From the family court's point of view, the juvenile training schools are the next step beyond probation along the punitive continuum. The referrals constitute an abandonment of community-oriented corrections, but the Juvenile Training School Law buttresses the Correction Bureau's policy of offering "correctional education" as another example of "protective measures." Article 4 specifies that correctional education shall consist of "school courses, vocational training and guidance, appropriate training, and medical treatment, while it aims at making them live an orderly life based on the stimulated spirit of self-help, in order to help them adjust themselves to social life."

The family court is authorized to send individuals, ages sixteen years and over, to the public prosecutor for handling as an adult criminal when the offense is punishable by death or imprisonment, and when the juvenile classification home (JCH) regards these older juveniles to be as responsible as an adult. Nevertheless, Japan has avoided any tendency to arbitrarily withdraw protective measures from violent crimes of juveniles, such as homicide or killing in the course of robbery.[1] Table 5.2 attests that few juveniles, aged sixteen to twenty years, are returned to public prosecutors. The modest share has declined at a great rate.

The public prosecutors may detain such juveniles in adult detention centers, where they are quartered separately from adults, and order that they stand trial in district courts. If convicted and receiving a prison sentence, the juveniles will be assigned to juvenile prisons. The eight juvenile prisons receive first offenders less than twenty-six years of age and emphasize vocational training to a greater degree than other adult prisons. The number of persons less than twenty years of age admitted to prison has dropped from 63 in 1983 (none less than eighteen years of age) to 22 in 1995 (1 person less than eighteen years) (Research and Statistics Section 1988a 25; 1993b 25; 1996b 25).[2]

Two other dispositions are based on age of the offender rather than the policy preference for "protective measures." Persons over twenty years of age do not qualify as juvenile delinquents. They were few in number and are removed from the comparison of dispositions in table 5.2. Child offenders (those less than fourteen years of age) and youngest predelinquents are usually treated under the Child Welfare Law and not subject to Juvenile Law. Except for referrals from these social service agencies, the family court is responsible to send the youngest offenders to child guidance homes, child education and training schools managed by the prefectural governors, or homes for dependent children.

Family Courts' Dispositions and Offenses

The criminal laws endeavor to relate each crime of adults along a scale of impact on victims directly and to the community in general. In addition, sentencing judges are expected to take into consideration the qualities of the defendant: previous history of misconduct, personality traits, qualities of the defendant's immediate environment, and any extenuating circumstances.

The Juvenile Law instructs the family courts to place special emphasis on the latter matters. Article 1 speaks of "the wholesome rearing of juveniles" and of "protective measures relating to the character correction and environmental adjustment of delinquent juveniles." For the young, there is hope that criminal tendencies have not been set firmly in the character. The "protective measures" just outlined are conceived as means of "character correction" and "environmental adjustment." Table 5.3 relates the range of protective measures to the offenses bringing the majority of juveniles before the family courts.

In the various annual editions of the *Summary of the White Paper on Crime,* the Research and Training Institute uses a typology of offenses that takes a Japanese point of view in assessing the offenses of juveniles against the decisions of family courts. The typology converts the diversity of the offenses in full specificity into an understandable representation of the relationship between the courts' dispositions and the offenses of juveniles. Table 5.3 applies the typology to all those relationships reported for 1990. The table arranges the courts' dispositions from most severe (referrals to public prosecutors for possible trial in adult courts) to least severe (dismissals without a hearing). Our interest here is in probation that occupies an interim position in that continuum. Referrals to juvenile training schools usually culminate in juvenile parole; the referrals also are significant for community-oriented corrections. Case dismissals can be an example of community-oriented corrections, at least in spirit, because of the courts' covert assumption that the controls of the family and community will be brought to bear on these juveniles.

Table 5.3 illustrates the differences among offenses in the distributions. Table 5.2 already presents the distributions for total offenses over four decades.

The Research and Training Institute refers to homicide

Table 5.3

Family Court Dispositions of Juvenile Delinquent Cases by Offenses, 1990

Offense Categories	Total Number	Public Prosecutor	Training Schools	Probation	Welfare Agencies	Case Dismissals Hearing	Case Dismissals No Hearing
Heinous	493	25	168	185	1	95	19
Percent	—	5.07	34.08	37.53	0.20	19.27	3.85
Robbery	443	14	137	179	1	95	17
Homicide	50	11	31	6	—	—	2
Violent	15,235	200	649	2,376	91	5,754	6,165
Percent	—	1.31	4.26	15.59	0.60	37.77	40.47
Bodily injury	8,201	143	339	1,406	56	3,469	2,788
Extortion	4,260	35	259	715	27	1,471	1,753
Violence law	1,288	7	24	168	3	451	635
Assault	1,187	9	12	75	5	316	770
Firearms	299	6	15	12	—	47	219
Property	130,352	248	1,891	6,248	272	16,485	105,208
Percent	—	0.19	1.45	4.79	0.21	12.65	80.71
Larceny	104,170	200	1,795	5,822	254	14,880	81,219
Embezzlement	23,480	18	27	246	17	1,171	22,001
Intrusion	1,070	16	25	108	—	230	691
Stolen property	1,064	1	3	16	—	103	941
Fraud	496	10	16	36	—	82	352
Arson	72	3	25	20	1	19	4

Table 5.3 cont. on next page

Table 5.3 continued

Offense Categories	Total Number	Public Prosecutor	Training Schools	Probation	Welfare Agencies	Case Dismissals	
						Hearing	No Hearing
Sex	360	21	171	123	—	30	15
Percent	—	5.83	47.5	34.17	—	8.33	4.17
Rape	332	21	170	112	—	23	6
Prostitution	28	—	1	11	—	7	9
Drugs	17,642	230	529	2,294	27	5,974	8,588
Percent	—	1.31	3.00	13.00	0.15	33.86	48.68
Stimulants	583	30	198	259	—	81	15
Organic solvents	17,059	200	331	2,035	27	5,893	8,573
Traffic[a]	252,753	26,561	463	61,317	—	122,094	42,318
Percent	—	10.51	0.18	24.26	—	48.31	16.74
Predelinquency[b]	1,948	—	303	610	217	562	256
Percent	—	—	15.56	31.31	11.14	28.85	13.14
Total	418,783	27,285	4,174	73,153	608	150,994	162,569
Percent	—	6.51	1.00	17.47	0.14	36.06	38.82

Source: Research and Training Institute (1992, 148–50).

[a]Excludes referrals to public prosecutors of persons above age 20 years or referrals to social agencies.
[b]Excludes referrals to public prosecutors.

and robbery as "heinous" offenses. The term brands them as shockingly evil, but, along with sex offenses, they were quantitatively least among the offenses. Robbery was more common than homicide, raised the number of probation referrals, and contributed almost all of the dismissals for heinous offenses. Otherwise, the serious concern about these offenses is signaled by the high rate of referrals to training schools and public prosecutors.

Bodily injury and extortion were heavily represented among violent incidents. They were particularly influential in the high proportion of violent offenders granted case dismissals and the moderate number of referrals to probation offices. This category in general entails a variety of incidents, some of which mute the naked aggression identified with "violence" as a term; the diversity justifies moderation of some referral dispositions.

Crimes against property received a high degree of leniency—80.7 percent of dispositions were dismissals without a hearing and another 12.6 percent dismissals with a hearing. Crimes against property are dominated by larceny, a collection of diverse crimes: entering a house for theft (although housebreaking is a distinctive offense), bicycle and motorbike theft, theft from vehicles, shoplifting, and theft from vending machines (those machines are prominent along urban streets).[3] These offenses are characteristic of the very young (note the many referrals to welfare agencies) and those lacking economic means of satisfying a craving for material goods. If referrals to welfare agencies were removed, the high number of dismissed cases nevertheless would reflect the family courts' perception of these juveniles as lacking tendencies toward confirmed criminality. Probation takes up more of the remaining cases than the training schools.

In definitions of the Penal Code, intrusion upon habitation (housebreaking) and embezzlement resemble larceny in some respects. Housebreaking is regarded as a bit more serious than larceny in general. Article 130 addresses housebreaking as "intrusion upon habitation: A person who, without good reason, intrudes upon a human habitation or upon the premises, structure or vessel guarded by another or who refuses to leave such a place upon demand. . . ."

The family courts dismissed 86.2 percent of these cases. Embezzlement was treated more leniently than larceny: 98.7 percent (1,171 plus 22,001 divided by 23,480) of the cases of embezzlement were dismissed, and 92.2 percent (14,880 plus 81,219 divided by 104,170) of the larceny cases. The Penal Code (Articles 252–54) distinguishes between wrongful appropriation by a businessman "of a thing in his custody which belongs to another" and conversion of "a lost property of another or drifting or any other property which belongs to another person and is in no one's custody." The latter version is most consistent with the family courts' policy of leniency.

Of crimes against property, arson draws the fewest cases but the greatest penalization in use of training schools and probation. That level of family courts' reactions mirrors the serious nature of the offense, but 32 percent (19 plus 4 divided by 72) of the cases are dismissed. The Penal Code, Articles 108–10, penalize "arson of inhabited structures" by death or imprisonment from five years to life. Inhabited structures include buildings, railroad trains, electric cars, vessels, or mines. "Arson of uninhabited structures" draws imprisonment for at least two years. "Setting fires to objects other than structures" can result in imprisonment of one to ten years.

Represented here by rape, sex offenses resemble the heinous offenses in the distribution of dispositions. There were few case dismissals, especially those without a hearing; referrals to the public prosecutors were noteworthy; and the training schools and probation offices drew the majority of referrals.

Organic solvents have been the predominant drug offenses among juveniles; case dismissals were unusually frequent. Stimulant drugs, proportionally more common for adults, drew less leniency than organic solvents in family court dispositions. The Stimulant Drug Control Law is directed against abuse of amphetamines and methamphetamines. The Poisonous and Injurious Substances Control Law is intended to deal with misuse of organic solvents ("paint thinner," toluene, ethyl acetate, and methanol). Organic solvent abuse cases are in the greater majority. The number of narcotic offenses were only sixteen and were excluded from table 5.3; their numbers could not sustain a meaningful percentage distribution.

In JCH admissions, juveniles involved with organic solvents were younger on average (17.2 years) than those abusing stimulant drugs (18.1 years). The percentages less than 17 years of age (29.8 versus 18.7 percent) confirm that pattern. Organic solvent abusers were more likely than stimulant drug abusers to be members of intact parental families. Organic solvent abusers were more likely to be involved as individuals; if there were codefendants, they would be friends at school or during juvenile recreational activities rather than in delinquent gangs or chance contacts (Research and Statistics Section 1996c, 40–41, 56, 62–63).

Those differences help explain the high percentage share of dismissals (84.8 percent) (5,893 plus 8,573 divided by 17,059) for organic solvents; stimulant drugs drew only 16.5 percent (81 plus 15 divided by 583). Public prosecutors received a small proportion of total cases; more for stimulant drugs. Of the 200 organic abusers sent to public prosecutors, 58 percent were too old to be treated as juveniles, 16.7 percent of the 30 stimulant abusers were over-age. Training schools and probation took up the remainder, with both referrals very strong for stimulant drugs. Probation exceeded the training schools, indicating the family courts' favoring of community corrections in that aspect.

The term *predelinquent* conveys the idea that before any violation of the law has occurred, certain symptoms will move inexorably the juvenile toward being apprehended for a delinquent act, and, possibly, the juvenile may become a criminal after reaching adulthood.[4] Predelinquents composed only .46 percent of the total dispositions, but even more interesting is the dispersal of dispositions. None were referred to public prosecutors, but 15.6 percent were sent to juvenile training schools—not for punishment but as a "protective measure" to rescue juveniles from an unfavorable familial or community setting. From one point of view, probation serves unmet needs of troubled and troublesome youngsters who could be placed in the community. Another indication of unmet needs, case dismissals with a hearing were more frequent than dismissals without a hearing. Certain conduct has been specified as grounds for referring predelinquents to family courts. Of the specified reasons, the percentage distribution is as follows: running from home 59.6, companionship with delinquent friends 16.4, immoral intercourse with the other sex 13.8, truancy 6.4, unsound pleasure seeking 1.4, and pleasure seeking at night 2.4 (Research and Training Institute 1988, 135).

Predelinquents at JCH admission are particularly young (15.5 years on average and 58.2 percent less than 16 years of age) compared with non-predelinquents (17.2 years of age and 10.8 percent less than 16 years of age) (Research and Statistics Section 1996c, 40–41). The family courts found that since many of the predelinquents lacked a satisfactory family environment to which they could be returned through case dismissals, the training schools offered the best alternative for such cases. In even more instances, probationary supervision was seized upon as a means of improving "environmental adjustment." Referrals to welfare agencies were intended to meet at least some of the needs of the youngest predelinquents. However, the family courts have adjudicated fewer predelinquents over the decades: 5,096 in 1951, 7,153 in 1965, 2,662 in 1975, 2,920 in 1985, and 1,948 in 1990 (Shikita and Tsuchiya 1990, 276; Research and Training Institute 1992, 150).

Traffic Offenders and Family Court

The less flagrant traffic violators are siphoned off before referral to family courts. They are diverted to summary justice in lower courts or to pay administrative fines upon notification of a violation by the prefectural police. The family court is left with juveniles charged with more serious traffic charges. The number that remain is considerable, and the dispositions range from the most severe to the most lenient, with a large proportion devoted to probation.

Traffic incidents represented 60 percent of the family court dispositions and these percentage shares of each of the specific referrals: public prosecutors 97.3, juvenile training schools 11.1, probation 83.8, dismissals after a hearing 89.5, and dismissals without a hearing 43.9. Referrals of traffic offenders to public prosecutors were remarkably frequent; many of these referrals were of defendants older than 20 years of age; they were too old to be under the family court's' jurisdiction. (One caution is appropriate: Remember that of all family court dispositions, only 6.5 percent were to the public prosecutors.) The special probation program for juvenile traffic offenders spawned a particularly great number of referrals to probation offices. The traffic cases attracted a large number of case dismissals, but an unusual proportion of the dismissals followed formal hearings. The hearings show that the family courts considered the merits of these cases with special care.

Traffic violators appear before juvenile courts accused of violating either of two laws: professional negligence in death or injury and the Road Traffic Law. Article 129 of the Penal Code attaches the term *endangering traffic through negligence* to crimes of obstructing traffic on roads, railroads, waterways, and bridges. The article refers to a person who "on his professional or occupational duties concerning the traffic, commits the crime." Article 211 deals with "Death or Bodily Injury through Negligence in the Conduct of Occupation." It specifies that "a person who fails to use such care as is required in the conduct of his profession or occupation and thereby kills or injures another shall be punished with imprisonment . . . or a fine." The article was revised in 1968, according to Shikita and Tsuchiya (1990, 9), "for the purpose of imposing more adequate punishment on automobile drivers such as those involved in the most vicious and serious cases, which could elicit a strong public outcry." Yokoyama (1990, 24) describes the background in the earlier history of motor vehicles in Japan. Because most drivers in the earlier years were professional chauffeurs, the public prosecutors and judges adopted that precedent in dealing with the crisis of mounting traffic fatalities and injuries.

The other element of responses to traffic offenses is the Road Traffic Law, one of the "special laws" outside the Penal Code. The Research and Training Institute (1969, 1) interprets the distinction: "The Penal Code comprises such offenses as larceny or homicide, that is acts which have been condemned by all societies as 'natural crimes.' In contrast, the special law offenses, Road Traffic Law for example, are referred to as 'statutory crimes,' in that they are violations of laws specifically promulgated for the purpose of maintaining the administrative control of a given society at a given time."

In spite of the interpretation that negligence of professional obligations is the most serious traffic violation, adjudication of the Road Traffic Law cases leads to the most stern dispositions of family courts: more referrals to public prosecutors and fewer grants of probation, if we cancel the effect of the greater number of Road Traffic Law dispositions. What appears to be a paradox is explained by the diversion to summary justice of the less flagrant Road Traffic Law violations before referral to the family courts. In considering the remaining cases, the family courts find *proportionally* more referrals to the public prosecutors and fewer referrals for probationary supervision than for instances of professional negligence.

Programs for Juvenile Traffic Offenders

In recent decades, Japan has turned to juvenile training schools, probation, and parole in response to growing concern about juvenile involvement in a traffic crisis. The Research and Training Institute (1993, 19) summarizes: "Between 1955 and 1970, the number of persons killed or injured in traffic accidents increased almost parallel with the rise of ownership of automobiles, driving license holders and the distance covered by automobile driving.... Of the casualties noticeable are high rates of teenagers and the youths in their twenties killed while driving automobiles. . . ." The Traffic Safety Policy Office (1994, 9) records fatality rates per 100,000 in 1994 of 15.23 for ages 16 to 24 years and 7.19 for ages 25 to 64 years.

In 1980 representatives of various ministries and agencies framed a strategy that gave priority to preventive measures but included probation and juvenile training schools (Traffic Safety Policy Office 1985, 160–64). By shaping public opinion, "a social environment" was to confront reckless driving. Improper modification of vehicles would be prohibited. Youths were to be "guided" at home and in their communities. In addition, the Road Traffic Law was amended to prohibit side-by-side driving, and putting the public in danger. Revocation of driving licenses was to penalize such misconduct.

A short-term probation program was introduced in 1977 for selected juvenile traffic offenders who had been convicted in family court for violations of the road traffic law for traffic incidents causing death and injury.[5] On recommendation of the family court, probation offices require these juveniles to attend two group sessions and report to the probation office each month for four months. The verbal report is supplemented by a simple written report in which the juvenile is required to answer questions such as these: What did you do this month? Did you drive this month? Do you have a problem that should be discussed with the probation officer? The juveniles answer the questions sincerely, we were assured.

The curriculum for the group sessions relies on manuals and group discussions. The manuals deal with topics such as drivers' responsibilities, methods of safe driving, the functions of traffic rules and regulations, and the need for driving licenses (Research and Training Institute 1993, 30). Full-time probation offices conduct two training sessions. When the training is completed, the probation officer can terminate supervision if the monthly reports have been satisfactory. A few juveniles are kept under supervision for a usual maximum of six months. Probation supervision for more than six months must be authorized by the family court.

At the first session, the nature of the probation program for juvenile traffic offenders is explained, and the conditions to be satisfied are specified. After three or four months, the second session deals with the responsibilities of drivers, the importance of traffic safety, and an audiovisual discussion of ways to avoid traffic accidents. Usually, discussion groups are organized to separate certain kinds of traffic offenders: those who operated vehicles without driver's license versus those possessing the license; the bosozoku versus the non-bosozoku; or offenders convicted of professional negligence causing death or injury versus those convicted of professional negligence not resulting in death or injury.

Juvenile parole also participates in the Rehabilitation Bureau's response to the traffic crisis. Juvenile parole does not match juvenile probation in the volume of cases; as table 5.4 shows, the numerical inferiority is increased by the proportion of juvenile parolees drawn from the short-term program of the training schools. Traffic offenders make up only a small share of the "graduates" of the short-term program. Most parolees come from the long-term program.

Of the juveniles appearing before the RPBs in 1995, none were denied paroles, and only twenty-four had their applications withdrawn. Table 5.4 lists only approved cases but also indicates the distribution of RPB transactions among the rehabilitation regions. Tokyo, Osaka, and Fukuoka contributed the most "graduates" of the short-term traffic programs. They also had the greater number of total parolees, but they had to surrender that advantage to other regions with greater percentage of parole approvals held by short-term traffic programs.

The juvenile training schools were reorganized in 1977 in terms of two short-term programs and one long-term program. The short-term approach was designed for juveniles believed to be most congenial to rehabilitation (not having

Table 5.4
Parole Approvals by Three Programs of
Juvenile Training and Rehabilitation Regions, 1995

Rehabilitation Regions	Number of Approvals	Programs of Juvenile Training Schools		
		Long-Term Program	Short-Term Non-Traffic	Short-Term Traffic
		Percentage Distribution		
Tokyo	1,261	63.2	29.3	7.5
Osaka	617	55.6	35.2	9.2
Nagoya	454	43.4	43.6	13.0
Hiroshima	175	55.4	34.3	10.3
Fukuoka	612	54.3	39.2	6.5
Sendai	280	57.9	32.1	10.0
Sapporo	268	59.0	36.2	4.8
Takamatsu	140	40.7	44.3	15.0
Total	3,807	56.3	35.0	8.7

Source: Research and Statistics Section (1996a, 8–9).

"advanced delinquent tendencies") in a short period of time (from one to four months). One of the two short-term programs targeted juveniles involved in fatalities or injuries through negligent driving or in other serious traffic delinquencies. The other short-term course received similar non-traffic delinquents. The long-term program (up to two years) received juveniles with advanced criminal tendencies and who were believed to require more time for resocialization (Correction Bureau 1990, 57).

In 1991 the short-term approach was transformed.[6] A general program was begun, based on one of three courses: academic education, vocational guidance, or career guidance. Academic education is oriented to individuals not completing compulsory education (to the ninth grade). Two training schools provide senior high school education. Vocational guidance aims at improving motivation, knowledge, and skills for post-release employment. Career guidance also is intended to assist post-release employment but through basic social training for a "disciplined social life." The second short-term program replaced the traffic course by serving "delinquents suited for open treatment." They commute to a community school on weekdays and stay with their families on weekends. Those eligible juveniles with jobs usually commute from the training school to the workplace on weekdays and stay at the training school on weekends.

In 1994 the long-term programs modified the already existing guidance, vocational training, and academic programs. The modifications were implemented to "encourage the smooth re-entrance of society through expanding chances to get timely job training and licenses according to the needs and problems of individual trainees" (Correction Bureau 1995, 158–59). The living guidance courses are intended to cultivate "disciplined social life" among young persons who are socially deviant or immature. Those methods include group activities, lectures, counseling, and therapies. Advanced vocational training courses are offered at Naniwa Juvenile Training School in Osaka Prefecture and Tohoku Juvenile Training School in Miyagi Prefecture. The courses are authorized by various laws such as the Vocational Training Law and Electric Work Specialist Law. At least one training school in each correction region specializes in elementary or junior high school courses. Kitsuregawa School in Tochigi Prefecture and Fukuoka School in Fukuoka Prefecture provide education at the senior high school level.

Summaries of Some Cases
Sent to Training Schools

To promote understanding of the nature of cases reaching the family courts, five case histories were developed by a juvenile classification home staff. These young males were referred to juvenile training schools.

Male, aged fifteen years, eighth grade in school. His parents were divorced when he was three years old. His mother was responsible thereafter, since he had no further contact with his father. She worked as a bar hostess until late at night. Alone at home, he kept company with classmates. At age ten years, he began to shoplift stationery for "fun." In junior high school, he skipped classes and copied older schoolmates by driving stolen motorcycles without a license and sniffing paint thinner. Unable to control him, his mother took him to a child care center, but he rejected the case worker's guidance and continued delinquent associations. He ran from home to continue the delinquent associations. Noting his 20 incidents of motorcycle larceny and 150 of paint thinner abuse, the family court concluded that neither his mother nor the child care center could manage him. The court sent him to a juvenile training school.

Male, aged seventeen years, high school student. He felt free to behave as he wished because of overindulgent parents and grandparents. In high school, he bleached his hair and began a series of shopliftings and bicycle thefts. Rebelling against teachers, he quit school. Several thefts brought him to the family court, where his case was dismissed after a hearing. In less than a month, he stole cigarettes and bicycles, drove a motorcycle into a house while driving without a license, and ran away. The family court sent him to a training school.

Male, aged seventeen years, high school student. A member of an upper-middle-class family, he had been very active and sociable since early childhood. Always wanting to be surrounded by friends, at age thirteen, he stole bicycles and shoplifted for "fun" with friends. The family court put him on probation, but he continued delinquent associations, engaging in paint thinner abuse predominately. The court ordered him to a juvenile training school.

Male, aged nineteen years, graduate of juvenile training school. His father was a member of a yakuza gang, a prison inmate a couple of times, and abandoned his sick wife and four sons to a life of poverty. The boy's crimes began at age fourteen with larceny and extortion. At age fifteen, he was sent to a training school for twenty months because of larceny and more than twenty assaults. At seventeen he was involved in a gang rape and was returned to a training school. After a year on parole, he joined a yakuza gang; a peony tattoo on his back symbolized his affiliation. At age nineteen he knifed a gang rival; the family court returned him to a training school.

Male, aged sixteen years, high school student. His father was an elementary school principal, his mother an elementary school teacher. From his childhood, their frigid relationship affected the familial environment. His older brother quit a university because of neurosis. Also affected by the familial situation, the delinquent felt isolated, became convinced he could not depend on other persons, and suffered insomnia. During his first year in high school, his acting out of hostility reached the point of physical aggression against other members of the family. To obtain rest, he withdrew temporarily from school to go to a spa. Back in school and recovered from insomnia, he was irritated by the necessity, because of his absence, to stay in the same school grade. When a classmate expressed doubts about his sanity, he stabbed him to death in an explosion of hostility. Without a criminal record otherwise, he was diagnosed as having a psychogenic reaction based on neurotic personality and suspected of having a psychopathic personality. The family court recommended treatment at a medical training school.

Juvenile Classification Homes: A Partnership

The Juvenile Law authorizes the family court to send a juvenile to a JCH in two instances. First, the court may issue a warrant "against a person who disobeys the summons for the investigation or hearing of a juvenile case" (Article 11) or "for the welfare of a juvenile who is in urgent need of protection" (Article 12). In either instance, the family court may order detention in a juvenile classification home "not to exceed two weeks. In case particular necessity exists for an extension, the court may, by ruling, renew the term but once." Detention also may be possible "where the Court has received a juvenile under arrest of detention from a Public Prosecutor or judicial police officer" (Article 17).

Second, Articles 8 and 9 call upon the family court to investigate juvenile cases within its jurisdiction through the "pre-sentence investigator" or its staff and the juvenile classification home. Article 9 states that in the investigation, "every effort shall be made to make efficient use of medical, psychological, pedagogical, sociological and other technical knowledge, especially the result of physical and mental examination conducted in the Juvenile Classification Home, in regard to the conduct, career, temperament and environment of the juvenile, his guardians, or other persons concerned."

In an interview, Kazuo Sato, superintendent of the Tokyo Juvenile Classification Home, outlined the background of the JCHs of Japan. A kind of predecessor to the family courts was the Tokyo Shimpan Sho, opened in 1924. Attached to it was a medical section, a branch of the juvenile reformatories existing at that time. A doctor, Katsuro Narita, diagnosed juveniles at the medical section; later he became the first director of the Tokyo JCH. In 1928 the medical section began to confine juveniles while they were being diagnosed.

In 1933 there were fifty-one child education and training schools in Japan. The Juvenile Teaching and Protective Law lent the first formal recognition of the need for diagnoses of neglected and delinquent children in the law's establishment of child education and training homes. Fourteen of those homes performed that function, but the war in the thirties and forties interfered with expansion of the number of homes.

In the reorganization of the juvenile justice system after World War II, Sato recalled, there was a debate about whether or not juvenile classification homes should be started up, but the passage of the Juvenile Law—in which Kasuro Narita and Taro Ogawa, then director general of the Correctional Bureau for Juveniles, were among the influential persons—ended the arguments. Because diagnostic procedures necessitated a residential center, the detention function appeared appropriate for the facility; that function justified, the planners decided, placing the JCHs within the structure of the Correction Bureau. In the course of framing the Juvenile Law, Louis Burdett, a member of the Corrections Division of General MacArthur's SCAP (Supreme Commander for Allied Powers) staff, had discussed the existence of juvenile detention homes in the United States.

The unorthodox organizational arrangement places the JCHs in a marginal position. They are within the structure of the Correction Bureau, a component of the executive branch of the government, but have been intended to serve primarily the family courts, elements of the judicial branch. Coordination is complicated by differences stemming from the marginal position in agency functions, characteristics and perspectives of the family court and JCH personnel, and budgetary practicalities.

The diagnostic services of JCHs are congenial to the ultimate ends and operating philosophy of the family courts. The services are also appropriate for the juvenile training schools of the Correction Bureau and the community-oriented programs of the Rehabilitation Bureau. However, the family courts are uncertain about long-term worth of referrals to institutional corrections—even though the juvenile training schools are committed to a treatment approach—and of probation and parole. Juvenile probation is favored over the JTS referrals when dismissal of cases is not feasible, but otherwise official intervention in the juveniles' affairs is to be regretted. Stationing the JCHs within the Correction Bureau's structure, from the family courts' point of view, strengthens the case for the argument that JCHs are examples of unnecessary intervention into the lives of juveniles.

The JCH model in Japan was framed during the initial phase of the postwar occupation of the country. Introduction of the JCHs was among the major changes of the juvenile justice system during the initial phase, but, later when the Japanese were free to direct their own affairs, the place and functions of the JCH within the juvenile justice system were modified to come closer to Japanese perspectives previous to World War II.

Under foreign military occupation of the first time in Japan's history, the people initially "found their country's administration, like its economy, in chaos," Beasley (1990, 213–14) summarizes, "production at a standstill, few trains, less road transportation, hardly any food, at least in the cities." Defeat opened the way for radical social and political reforms pressed by the victors, he continues, but, "once the shock wore off, the Japanese again began to take the initiative directing their own affairs." As Beasley implies, I see the Japanese leaders adjusting the postwar reforms toward closer conformity with the Japan of the prewar decades. As a corollary, the practicalities of JCH operations were modified.

Juvenile Classification Homes: Functions and Organization

The fifty-three JCHs, including one branch, are located near family courts. They have three major functions. First, upon referrals from the family court, they carry out classification through interviews, psychological testing, behavior observation, and medical-psychiatric examination. Usually the stay is fourteen days, but, if necessary, the family court may authorize a maximum of another fourteen days. From the acquired information, recommendations are reported to the family court for its disposition. Second, the JCHs serve as places of juvenile detention. Third, the JCHs offer diagnostic services to other agencies and the general public.

The largest JCHs (eighteen in number) have a medical section in addition to the two sections found in all of them: the general affairs (administrative) section and the COT coordination section (classification, observation, and treatment). The prehearing investigators on the staff of the family courts probe the juvenile's "social environment" (the family, school, workplace, etc.) to be integrated with the diagnostic information reported by the JCH (Correction Bureau 1995, 67). In other words, the JCHs are limited to psychological diagnoses, whereas the family court's "investigation officers" are responsible for the sociological inquiries.

Before the organizational revision in 1988, there was insufficient coordination between a subsection on classification and a subsection on observation. In classification, psychologists conduct interviews, administer diagnostic tests, and incorporate the information in reports. The observation staff cares for the juveniles in daily life: meals, physical exercise, escort to various scheduled places, and management of visiting. In daily contacts, the observation subsection is able to note the behavior and traits of the juveniles. What is observed is supposed to be written into reports. In practice, however, useful information was not necessarily transferred between the sections. To improve coordination, the new position of "chief specialist in planning and arrangements" was established to receive information from each section and to communicate it to the other section. "Planning" implies assigning tasks to each staff member for the day. "Arrangements" refers to scheduling the daily activities of each juvenile.

Upon arrival, the juveniles are interviewed by a psychologist. What is your name and offense? Do you have a physical problem? Does something worry you? The juveniles are open and honest in their answers, I was told. All valuables, luggage, and personal clothing are deposited, and a uniform is issued. A physician checks for any physical difficulties and questions the juvenile about any injuries. The rules and behavioral expectations are explained before assignment to a one-person room. The juvenile writes a life history, the number and characteristics of members of their family, where the family lives, a description of school life or the juvenile's job, and how the offense occurred. He or she begins the daily diary of what happens during the JCH stay. Both documents serve diagnostic purposes.

The medical examination comes on the second day. The

physician makes a screening examination, determines any health problems, and decides whether or not x-ray and other diagnostic technology should be employed. Juveniles are tested for syphilis; girls are tested for pregnancy. Through information acquired by interview, the psychologist assigned to the case frames a treatment plan and makes written recommendations to the person in charge of the particular housing unit. Perhaps a potential for suicide demands careful observation; this juvenile should be transferred to another room. The afternoon is left open for a visit of family members or the family court investigator.

On the third day, group tests and one-to-one tests are administered (intelligence, sentence completion, and personality inventory.) The tests were developed and financed by the Correction Bureau and the Japanese Correction Association. On the basis of the results, additional tests may be recommended. The psychologist responsible for the juvenile will conduct a more intensive interview and will share the information with the family court's investigator. In turn, the psychologist will receive the investigator's findings on the juvenile's social situation.

The JCH will initiate structured behavior observation. One approach is to have the juvenile write about perceptions of the future, memories of childhood, and occupational hopes. In the second approach, a book is read, and, drawing upon the imagination, a picture relevant to the book is drawn. Third, he or she transforms paper bits into a picture (a montage).

After the tests and interviews, the psychologist will obtain ideas about the case. Further interviews will check on the validity of the initial evaluation. The results will be presented verbally at a case conference; reactions and recommendations of other psychologists will contribute to the consensus incorporated in the treatment plan. After the case conference, the psychologist prepares the written report that goes to the family court for its disposition of the juvenile. Depending on the court's decision, a copy of the report will go, for example, to a child guidance home or juvenile training school. The JCH keeps a copy and maintains a list of clients in case of their referral again.

Family Court Actions Versus JCH Recommendations

In cases reported to the family courts in 1995, the JCHs favored recommendations that most boys or girls be sent to training schools (about 50 percent) or placed on probation (about 40 percent) (see table 5.5). Of the small remainder, referrals to child care agencies were predominant (especially for girls) among recommendations because of low ages. Girls were more likely to draw recommendations that they be sent to child guidance homes or child education and training schools managed by the prefectural governors, or homes for dependent children. These social welfare institutions are outside the juvenile justice system. JCHs suggest that only a few juveniles should go to the public prosecutors or be dismissed ("action not needed").

The decisions of the judges do not necessarily correspond with JCH recommendations because of the court investigator's report on environmental circumstances, the nature of the offense, or the judge's opinions about proper case disposition. Few cases of either sex were recommended by JCHs for dismissal. The courts would send the most doubtful cases to the classification homes; dismissals were frequent for other cases. The few dismissals after JCH study drew heavily on JCH recommendations that no action would be required.

Temporary probation is not among JCH options, but the judges may prefer to delay final action on cases raising particular doubts and ask their special investigators to supervise the juvenile for the time being (temporary probation) as a kind of behavioral diagnosis. Some of the temporary probation actions came after the family court had received JCH recommendations. In those instances, the various JCH recommendations in 1995 were well represented, except that referrals of

Table 5.5
Recommendations of Juvenile Classification Homes Compared with Later Family Court Dispositions, 1995

Family Court Dispositions	Court Disposition	Recommendation of Classification Homes					
		Action Not Needed	Child Care Agencies	Other Community Agencies	Probation	Training Schools	Public Prosecutors
			Percentage Distribution				
Males							
Dismissal, no hearing	2.6	4.0	2.9	—	3.4	1.9	7.9
Dismissal, hearing	2.2	24.0	0.5	—	3.6	1.1	1.0
Social agencies	2.0	2.0	59.8	26.9	0.3	1.3	—
Probation	46.0	52.0	8.4	19.2	78.3	22.5	12.9
Training schools	29.5	4.0	4.4	7.7	1.6	52.7	14.9
Prosecutors	1.2	—	—	—	0.5	0.9	57.4
Temporary probation	16.5	14.0	24.0	46.2	12.3	19.6	5.9
Total number	11,299	50	204	26	4,802	6,116	101
Percent of total	100.0	0.5	1.8	0.2	42.5	54.1	0.9
Females							
Dismissal, no hearing	2.4	—	1.3	5.3	4.3	1.1	—
Dismissal, hearing	2.3	40.0	1.3	—	4.7	0.5	—
Social agencies	4.6	—	60.2	21.0	1.0	2.2	—
Females							

Table 5.5 cont. on next page

Table 5.5 continued

Family Court Dispositions	Court Disposition	Recommendation of Classification Homes					
		Action Not Needed	Child Care Agencies	Other Community Agencies	Probation	Training Schools	Public Prosecutors
		Percentage Distribution					
Probation	37.4	20.0	9.0	10.5	63.7	21.3	50.0
Training schools	26.8	—	6.4	—	1.3	48.0	—
Prosecutors	0.5	—	—	—	—	0.5	50.0
Temporary probation	26.0	40.0	21.8	63.2	25.0	24.5	—
Total number	1,724	5	78	19	680	936	6
Percent of total	100	0.3	4.5	1.1	39.4	54.3	0.4

Source: Research and Statistics Section (1996c, 78–79).

girls to the public prosecutor were absent (see table 5.5). The number of referrals to child care agencies suggests a high representation of very young juveniles. The judges expressed a preference for community-oriented referrals—especially for girls—but reserved judgment by asking their special investigators to test further the JCH recommendations for "other community agencies" and probation. At the other end of the lenient-strict continuum, the judges used temporary probation to question JCH recommendations for referrals to juvenile training schools and (for boys) referrals to public prosecutors.

The judges agreed rather well with the JCH recommendations for those courts' options that square better with the JCH options. For both sexes, family court referrals to social agencies for boys drew heavily on JCH recommendations for child care agencies (59.8 percent) and "other community agencies" (26.9 percent). The same was true for girls (60.2 and 21 percent, respectively). The family courts rank probation at the strict end of the lenient-strict continuum. At the strict end, the dispositions agreed with about half of the JCH recommendations for referrals to juvenile training schools and to public prosecutors. They usually accepted the JCH recommendation that probation be granted, but they also used probation in lieu of training schools.

The Function of Juvenile Detention

Police are obligated to decide within forty-eight hours whether or not apprehended juveniles should be released without detention. If three conditions do not exist, they may be sent home without detention: Is there a valid reason to suspect they may destroy evidence? Are they likely to attempt escape? Is detention necessary for case investigation?

Detention of juveniles is unusual; of the 14,265 JCH admissions in 1995, 11.5 percent were for "protective detention as a substitute for detention" (Research and Statistics Section 1996c, 2). Article 17.2 of the Juvenile Law authorizes the family court, by a special ruling, to place juveniles in the nearest juvenile training school or jail (except for a "house of penal detention") for no more than seventy-two hours from the time of commitment. The length of such temporary placing will be deducted from the two weeks allowed for JCH detention. That two weeks of JCH detention may be extended once for two weeks "in case particular necessity exists."

Shikita and Tsuchiya (1990, 260) explain the relevant functions of the public prosecutors as specified in the Juvenile Law of 1949. When the offenses involve punishment by imprisonment or heavier penalties, the police send the juveniles to public prosecutors. If the investigation determines either of two situations, the public prosecutors must refer the juvenile to the family court. A prima facie case has been made or the juvenile is prone to commit another offense. However, the public prosecutor may institute prosecution only if the family courts send the case back to them. The family courts cannot make such a referral if the given offense is punishable only by fines or lesser penalties or if the juvenile is less than sixteen years of age at the time of the referral.

The Juvenile Law authorizes the family court to issue a warrant of detention in either of two circumstances but requires (Article 17) that action be taken within twenty-four hours after arrival at the court. First, Articles 11 and 26 permit the family court to issue a summons to the juvenile or the juvenile's guardians when necessary for case investigation. If the summons is disobeyed "without good reason," the family court may issue a warrant of detention. Second, Articles 12 and 26 permit a family court warrant against the juvenile when "necessary for the welfare of a juvenile who is in urgent need of protection."

Outpatient Diagnostic Services

Some JCHs have drawn protests of neighbors against the proximity of a delinquent-serving facility. To minimize the possibility of local opposition, the policy of the Correction Bureau is to encourage outpatient services for non-delinquents. Most guidance centers have their own professionals, but the JCHs have experience with juvenile deviants, and the JCH psychiatrists are considered experts in the subject of child abuse. When troubled parents contact the police, they are referred to the JCH, but sometimes the parents will telephone the JCH and perhaps come personally to the clinic. The JCH staff have gone to schools to consult teachers about students in general, will administer psychological tests at annual fairs displaying and selling prison-made goods to the general public, and announce availability of services in articles in neighborhood newsletters.

The Tokyo JCH, and some others, have a separate building for outpatient services to distinguish it from usual JCH affairs. Other JCHs lack a separate building but will display a sign, perhaps designating the Educational Guidance Center for Juveniles, and provide a separate entrance. A brochure of the Tokyo JCH announces: "Juveniles' problems brought to the clinic include not only predelinquent behavior such as truancy or runaway from home but also personality and behavior problems of small children."

The JCHs serve other governmental agencies. Juvenile training schools will call for recommendations of whether or not a young inmate should be transferred to another training school. The family court can order a transfer. The probation office may request diagnosis of some juvenile traffic offenders. The public prosecutor may ask diagnoses of adults at detention centers.

These several sources of referrals have made different contributions to the flow of juveniles. Some decades ago the family courts were the primary contributor—55 percent of all referrals in 1983—but they had lost percentage share by 1995. Other sources had to take up the slack. JCHs have received smaller and smaller shares of the juveniles adjudicated by the family courts. The share was 32.1 percent in 1955, 28.9 percent in 1960, 22.2 percent in 1965, 17.1 percent in 1970, 9.5 percent in 1975, 10.7 percent in 1980, 11.6 percent in 1985, 10.1 percent in 1990, and 11.0 percent in 1994 (Shikita and Tsuchiya 1990, 382–83; Research and Training Institute 1992, 147, 152; 1996, 102–3).

Outpatient diagnostic services to the general public have been the major invigoration, growing at a 122 percent rate between 1983 and 1996 in the ideal of service to the community at large. Nevertheless, the demand for JCH services falls short of the capacity. Table 5.6 makes this point about admissions in 1995. The admissions per JCH for 1995 varied among the categories measuring differences in the family court representation, but the admissions per day were universally very modest. In 1995 the average daily population for the JCHs was only 915 (Research and Statistics Section 1996c, 3). The average of 17.3 juveniles present per unit confirms the underutilization of a promising correctional institution in Japan.

By 1995 the family courts' referrals represented a significant portion of the total JCH admissions for only eight juvenile classification homes (see table 5.6). In most instances, the contribution varied by JCHs but always trailed the contributions of other referral sources. Without other sources taking up a portion of the slack, the general withdrawal of family courts would have been even more devastating.

Because public prosecutors made little use of the investigative and diagnostic services of JCHs, three other sources of referral were crucial: the juvenile training schools of the Correction Bureau, juvenile probation and parole programs of the Rehabilitation Bureau, and requests for services by members of the general public. As table 5.6 records, the juvenile training schools made modest demands for service. As the representation among referrals of family courts declined among JCHs, the referrals of juvenile probationers and parolees assumed increasing importance, although tailing off with "low low representation" by family courts.

The most noteworthy trend has been the upsurge in the

Table 5.6
Sources of Referrals to Juvenile Classification Homes, 1995

Representation of Family Court Referrals[a]	Total	Family Courts	Public Prosecutors	Correction Bureau[b]	Rehabilitation Bureau[c]	General Public
Maximum						
Number (8)	9,511	5,003	14	125	804	3,565
Percent	100	52.6	0.2	1.3	8.4	37.5
Admiss. per JCH	1,189	625	1.7	1.5	100	458
High						
Number (13)	15,824	6,214	2	269	1,332	8,007
Percent	100	39.3	0.0	1.7	8.4	50.6
Admiss. per JCH	1,217	478	0.1	21	102	616
Low high						
Number (12)	10,542	2,563	2	292	3,050	4,635
Percent	100	24.3	0.0	2.8	28.9	44.0
Admiss. per JCH	878	214	0.2	24	254	386
High low						
Number (9)	6,998	1,083	4	241	2,818	2,852
Percent	100	15.5	0.1	3.4	40.3	40.7
Admiss. per JCH	777	120	0.4	27	313	317

Table 5.6 cont. on next page

Table 5.6 continued

Representation of Family Court Referrals[a]	Total	Family Courts	Public Prosecutors	Correction Bureau[b]	Rehabilitation Bureau[c]	General Public
Low low						
Number (11)	13,317	1,155	6	751	2,918	8,487
Percent	100	8.7	0.0	5.6	21.9	63.7
Admiss. per JCH	1,211	105	0.5	68	265	771

Sources: Research and Statistics Section (1988b, 12–15; 1996c, 12–15).

[a]Representation is measured by percentage of total admissions held by referrals from family courts, as categorized: Maximum, 45 to 59 percent; high, 30 to 45 percent; low high, 25 to 30 percent; high low, 11 to 25 percent; and low low, 4 to 11 percent. The numbers in parentheses indicate the number of JCHs.
[b]Referrals from juvenile training schools.
[c]Referrals of juvenile probationers and parolees.

outpatient diagnostic services already discussed as a phase of the JCH efforts to develop cordial relationships with local residents. The calls from the general public were second only to family court referrals where family court referrals were at the maximum, but, as the JCHs lost support from the family courts the outpatient diagnostic services assumed more and more importance, reaching a 63.7 percent share for the "low low" classification facilities.

The referrals from family courts were fundamental to the original design of juvenile classification homes; the JTS referrals are an appropriate benchmark for examining the clientele and the responses to the long-term decline in referrals from the family courts. Table 5.5 distinguishes fifty-three JTSs by the percentage share of all JCH admissions in 1995 held by referrals from the family courts.[7] The JCHs were categorized into five groups, from the highest to the lowest percentage shares. The focus is on how other sources of referral assumed new importance as the family courts' lost share.

Public prosecutors made little contribution to the JCH admissions. The juvenile training schools made modest demands that increased slightly as the family courts withdrew. The chief participants in filling the void were the Rehabilitation Bureau and the general public. The Rehabilitation Bureau sent juvenile probationers and parolees; the share grew from 5.8 percent for the JCHs receiving substantial numbers from family courts to reach 40.3 percent before tailing off. The general public, however, were the most significant users of the diagnostic services—keeping some 40 percent of the referrals and rising to 63.7 percent the units having the greatest loss of family court clients.

Total Admissions: Traffic Offenders a Growing Factor

Through its community-oriented programs, the Rehabilitation Bureau has been summoned to join the governmental effort to deal with juvenile traffic offenders. The resort to probation and parole will be considered later in this chapter. Here the effect on JCH admissions will be considered.

As for table 5.6, the JCH data are arrayed in table 5.7 according to the percentage share of JCH admissions held by referrals of the family courts. As that share declined, the juvenile traffic offenders have assumed greater percentage shares of all JCH admissions. The family courts held a share varying from 4 to 59 percent of admissions to JCHs in 1995. From the peak percentage, the share of traffic offenders rose from 8.9 percent to reach 44.4 percent of admissions when the family court contributed 11 to 20 percent of all referrals (Research and Statistics Section 1996c, 12–19).

Juvenile probationers and parolees were referred to JCH by the Rehabilitation Bureau in greater numbers as the family court referrals became less influential in JCH admissions. Juvenile violators of traffic laws had greater effect as the family court referrals dropped. The number of traffic offenders per 100 non-traffic offender (the ratios for referrals) summarized that important trend.

The general public turned to the JCH for diagnostic services in great numbers as the family courts became less influential in JCH admissions, but that expanded demand primarily for juveniles not involved in traffic law violations. The ratios are very low except for the category of the 4 to 11 percent share of family court referrals. The aberration is due exclusively to the contribution of the Sago JCH in the island of Kyushu of its 1,833 admissions; that facility received 1,616 juvenile traffic offenders referred by the general public (Research and Statistics Section 1996c, 14). Sago consistently presented the anomaly each of the recent years.

Referrals from the juvenile training schools were largely non-traffic offenders. The ratios record the greatest presence of traffic offenders where family court referrals were most common.

Juvenile traffic offenders eased the impact of the family court's decline in the share of JCH admissions. The ratios

Table 5.7
Sources of Referrals to Juvenile Classification Homes by Traffic Versus Non-Traffic Offenders, 1995

Family Courts' Share of JCH Admissions	Total JCH Admissions	Sources of Referral to Juvenile Classification Homes				
		Family Courts	Public Prosecutors	Correction Bureau[a]	Rehabilitation Bureau[b]	General Public
42–59%						
Non-traffic	13,254	6,434	14	175	437	6,194
Percent	100	48.6	0.1	1.3	3.3	46.7
Traffic	1,300	753	—	33	407	107
Percent	100	57.9	—	2.6	31.3	8.2
Ratios[c]	9.8	11.7	—	18.9	93.1	1.7
32–41%						
Non-traffic	8,281	3,128	2	182	11	4,958
Percent	100	37.8	0.0	2.2	0.1	59.9
Traffic	2,500	902	—	4	1,281	313
Percent	100	36.1	—	0.2	51.2	12.5
Ratios[c]	30.2	28.8	—	2.2	116.4	6.3
20–30%						
Non-traffic	6,557	1,837	1	286	37	4,396
Percent	100	28.0	0.0	4.4	0.6	67.0
Traffic	3,351	595	—	1	2,755	—
Percent	100	17.8	—	—	82.2	—
Ratios	51.1	32.4	—	0.3	7,445.9	—

Table 5.7 cont. on next page

Table 5.7 continued

Family Courts' Share of JCH Admissions	Total JCH Admissions	Sources of Referral to Juvenile Classification Homes				
		Family Courts	Public Prosecutors	Correction Bureau[a]	Rehabilitation Bureau[b]	General Public
11–20%						
Non-traffic	4,244	1,015	5	243	—	2,981
Percent	100	23.9	0.1	5.7	—	70.3
Traffic	3,388	199	—	3	3,076	110
Percent	100	5.9	—	0.1	90.8	3.2
Ratios[c]	79.8	19.6	—	1.2	—	3.7
4–11%						
Non-traffic	8,508	952	6	743	2	6,805
Percent	100	11.2	0.1	8.7	—	80.0
Traffic	4,809	203	—	8	2,916	1,682
Percent	100	4.2	—	0.2	60.6	35.0
Ratios[c]	56.5	21.3	—	1.1	1,458.0	24.7

Source: Research and Statistics Section (1996c, 12–15).

[a]Referrals from juvenile training schools.
[b]Referrals of juvenile probationers and parolees.
[c]Number of traffic offenders per 100 non-traffic offenders.

measure the greater representation of traffic offenders among family court referrals when those referrals drop off.

Community Programs among Regions

As for adult probationers and parolees, the rehabilitation regions differ in the volume and characteristics of the juveniles making up the rolls of probationers and parolees. The concentration of Japanese in metro-Japan produces the greatest number of cases, regardless of the characteristics of the juvenile offenders for the Tokyo region. The other regions form an array of differing volumes and qualities of cases. The distributions of offenses offer insights into those patterns.

The family court judges have expressed Japanese values and respected the premises of the laws when they selected relatively few juvenile offenders to go to training schools and a larger number (but a minority among the total juvenile offenders) to be added to the probation roles. Probation held a strong advantage over the juvenile institutions in family court dispositions in 1990, but the general categories varied in number of probationers per parole (see statistics for total regions in table 5.8): 17.54 for traffic offenders, 4.39 for violent offenders, 3.72 for property offenders, 3.03 for drug offenders, 1.60 for predelinquents, 1.70 for heinous offenses, and 1.03 for sex offenders. The less negative the public image of an offense, the greater reliance on probation.

In addition to differences among regions in number of either juvenile probationers or parolees, the relative importance of the several major categories of offenses mirror the workings of the juvenile justice system. Table 5.8 presents the differences between probationers and parolees in the percentage distributions of juvenile offenses.

The short-term program for juvenile traffic offenders augments considerably the caseload of probation offices. For Japan, 7,771 juveniles were admitted as traffic offenders, 41.1

percent of all probation office admissions in 1995. All regions experienced a heavy volume of traffic offenders among their probation admissions. The proportions varied from 38 percent in the Hiroshima Rehabilitation Region to 48 percent in the Sendai Rehabilitation Region. The proportions are universally remarkable, but the regions with few probationers, when compared with other regions, especially reap the benefits. Traffic parolees descended to intermediate importance in share of regional parolees, except for Nagoya, Sapporo, and Takamatsu.

Along with traffic offenses, juvenile drug abusers have received unusual attention from the criminal justice agencies in the atmosphere of a public crisis, but only a minor portion of the probation caseload has been affected. That affect was tilted toward the more urbanized regions. Sendai, Sapporo, and Takamatsu had rather few probationers in general and especially few involved directly with drugs. Organic solvents occupied the greater absolute number of drug offenders on juvenile probation. Tokyo held 54 percent of the stimulant drug probationers and 40.1 percent of the organic solvent; Osaka 23.1 percent of the stimulant drug and 18 percent of the organic solvent probationers. The other regions had minor shares, usually with the share devoted to organic solvents slightly greater than for stimulant drugs (Research and Statistics Section 1996a, 73).

Unlike for juvenile probationers, drug offenders were slightly more numerous than traffic offenders among the juvenile parolees. Traffic offenders had 17.54 probationers per parolee, drug offenders a ratio of only 3.03. Ratios varied among the regions from 7.45 for Hiroshima to only 1.45 for Sapporo (see table 5.8). The ratios were deeply affected by the distinction between stimulant and organic solvent offenses among juveniles. For all juveniles, the ratio was 1.40 for stimulant drugs alone and 5.60 for organic solvents (Research and Statistics Section 1996a, 70–77). That split spread through rehabilitation regions.

Table 5.8
Admissions to Juvenile Probation and Parole by Rehabilitation Region and Offense Categories, 1995

Rehabilitation Regions	Number of Admissions	Major Categories of Juvenile Offenses						
		Heinous	Violent	Property	Sex	Drugs	Traffic	Predelinquent
All Regions								
Probationers	18,928	351	3,372	5,515	196	1,459	7,771	264
Percent	100	1.9	17.8	29.1	1.0	7.7	41.1	1.4
Parolees	3,737	207	768	1,481	191	482	443	165
Percent	100	5.5	20.6	39.6	5.1	12.9	11.9	4.4
Ratios	5.06	1.70	4.39	3.72	1.03	3.03	17.54	1.60
		Percent Distribution of Juvenile Offenses						
Tokyo Region								
Probationers	6,464	2.7	21.0	25.2	1.0	9.9	38.7	1.5
Parolees	1,342	6.6	22.9	34.3	3.0	17.0	11.7	4.5
Ratios	4.82	2.01	4.41	3.53	1.55	2.82	15.93	1.57
Osaka Region								
Probationers	3,431	1.5	14.5	29.9	1.5	9.0	42.5	1.1
Parolees	531	8.3	15.6	43.5	8.8	16.8	5.1	1.9
Ratios	6.46	1.18	6.00	4.43	1.13	3.46	53.96	3.90
Nagoya Region								
Probationers	1,665	1.1	20.1	30.4	0.6	6.6	40.3	0.9
Parolees	434	3.2	22.1	37.1	6.0	8.1	19.6	3.9
Ratios	3.84	1.36	3.48	3.15	0.38	3.11	7.91	0.88

Table 5.8 cont. on next page

Table 5.8 continued

Rehabilitation Regions	Number of Admissions	Major Categories of Juvenile Offenses						
		Heinous	Violent	Property	Sex	Drugs	Traffic	Predelinquent
Hiroshima Region								
Probationers	1,116	2.0	15.6	34.0	1.6	7.3	38.3	1.2
Parolees	175	2.8	28.0	45.7	8.0	6.3	8.6	0.6
Ratios	6.38	4.40	3.55	4.74	1.29	7.45	28.53	13.00
Fukuoka Region								
Probationers	3,166	1.1	14.5	33.7	0.8	5.6	43.0	1.3
Parolees	607	4.8	16.8	48.9	5.3	6.9	10.9	6.4
Ratios	5.22	1.17	4.51	3.59	0.75	4.26	20.62	1.08
Sendai Region								
Probationers	1,317	1.4	17.9	27.2	1.1	3.0	48.3	1.1
Parolees	233	6.4	22.7	42.1	4.3	6.9	11.6	6.0
Ratios	5.68	1.20	4.45	3.65	1.50	2.50	23.55	1.00
Sapporo Region								
Probationers	1,087	2.3	19.4	29.1	0.5	5.3	39.6	3.8
Parolees	272	2.2	18.8	34.9	5.2	14.7	16.5	7.7
Ratios	4	4.17	4.14	3.33	0.36	1.45	9.58	1.95
Takamatsu Region								
Probationers	681	0.6	14.7	35.1	1.3	5.9	41.8	0.6
Parolees	143	4.2	18.2	41.2	5.6	14.7	14.7	1.4
Ratios	4.76	0.67	3.85	4.05	1.12	1.90	13.57	2.00

Source: Research and Statistics Section (1996a, 70–77).

Property offenses usually are preeminent among admissions to correctional agencies; this pattern held for juvenile parole. However, for juvenile probation, the program for traffic offenders thrust property offenses into second place. In all respects, larceny takes up the vast majority of juvenile property offenses. The ratios were at the peak for Hiroshima, Osaka, and Takamatsu. Whether juvenile probation or parole, violent offenses held a sizable portion of admissions and a ratio (4.39) second only to traffic. Bodily injury and extortion were most numerous for both programs, and violations of the Law for Punishment of Acts of Violence were a significant factor for probation. Bodily injury and extortion were prominent factors in determining the ratios ranging from Osaka (6.00) to Nagoya (3.48). Probation admissions were noteworthy even for Nagoya.

Predelinquents and heinous offenses had similar ratios (1.60 and 1.70, respectively) in spite of fundamental differences in policy philosophies they engender. Heinous offenses—robberies and a few homicides—are unlikely prospects for diversion; granting probation implies extenuating circumstances in particular cases of heinous crimes. Probation, however, is possible because, although less drastic than referral to juvenile training schools, the family courts see it as a punitive measure to be employed only when other forms of diversion are not feasible. Predelinquents are regarded as requiring "protective measures" rather than punishment. Measures available to the family courts are expected to protect the predelinquents from the conditions undermining their "wholesome rearing." More of the predelinquents than the heinous defendants have been benefited by case dismissals with or without formal hearings.

For the residue, predelinquents receive probation conceived as a protective measure in these instances. The parolees have been those predelinquents or members of the heinous group who previously have been referred to juvenile training schools. Unlike the members of the heinous groups, these predelinquents have been "rescued" from adverse environments by referrals to the sanctuary the juvenile training schools are expected to constitute in these instances. Juvenile parole takes up almost all discharges from juvenile training schools because it too is intended to be a protective measure for all JTS inmates. The differential images held of the two extreme types of juvenile offenders illustrate the importance of recognizing the distinctive approaches of Japanese corrections. This chapter has applied that principle to the administrative procedures for juvenile probation and parole. The next chapter turns to the characteristics, experiences, and backgrounds of the juveniles exposed to the procedures.

6
Juvenile Probationers and Parolees

ACCORDING TO ARTICLE 2 OF THE Juvenile Law, the division between juveniles and adults stands at age twenty. The family court has jurisdiction over individuals aged fourteen through nineteen years. The age spread for juvenile delinquents is only six years compared to sixty years or more for adult offenders, but that narrow spread has momentous implications. The word *juvenile* in *juvenile justice system* conveys images of immature psychology and underdeveloped social psychology, but the upper and lower age limits are neither fixed nor universal. As elsewhere, legal, historical, and cultural perspectives have influenced the setting of age boundaries for the juvenile status.

Companionate Delinquency
and Marginal Deviance

"Groupism" has been identified as a key characteristic of most Japanese; they are described to be subordinating self-interests to those of the group. Areas of conflict exist, but social harmony is displayed as an ideal to be respected by members of families, communities, and other social groups. Self-discipline is to be rewarded by the personal benefits of prestige, knowing one's place in the societal scheme, and holding the respect of others by observing ethical standards.

The pressure of social control is toward conformity with behavioral standards supposed to be universal in contemporary Japan. Companionate delinquency as a concept focuses attention on the possibility that for juveniles the pressures also come from a combination of a "youth culture" and of changes in the sociocultural environment. In that context, Japanese teenagers try to cope with their difficulties spawned in the course of their passage from childhood to adulthood.

"One of the most consistent findings in criminology," Clinard and Meier (1985, 32–34) attest in discussing the American situation, "is that most illegal acts by juveniles are committed with companions." They see the number of "best friends" varying from two or three engaged in shoplifting or vandalism to a larger number in delinquent juvenile gangs. As will be made clear, the companionate factor has special meaning in Japan. At the moment, the topic serves as an introduction to the chapter.

In the course of coping with the difficulties of their status passage, Japanese adolescents frequently identify themselves with youth culture in its Japanese version and, thereby, weaken their personal commitment to the general culture. The adolescents become marginal deviants who risk being treated as delinquents and subjects for the juvenile justice system.

Whether adults or juveniles, official leniency in Japan is extended to those who qualify as marginal deviants. They stand between full-fledged conformists to the behavioral standards of the community and the flagrant nonconformists whom the Juvenile Law or Penal Code is supposed to capture. Somewhere along that middle of the continuum, between full acceptance and total rejection as members of the community, the questionable conduct is perceived as more annoying or irksome than obstinate and unreasonable and as excusable for only awkward failure to exhibit expected moral commitment. Perhaps the defendant provides evidence of victimization, being denied essential parental instruction or being particularly vulnerability to evil influences. Somehow, the defendants treated as marginal deviants are believed capable of striking a respectable balance between "ought to" and "want to" and between obligation and opportunity.

Does Marginal Deviance Forecast Criminality?

For the juveniles of Japan, we may wonder whether or not one kind of delinquency may lead to other kinds. If so, the official concern about predelinquency is justified. If so, there is reason to withhold punishment when feasible to avoid pressing the juvenile marginal deviant toward more serious offenses. Will the stimulant drug abuser usually become susceptible to narcotic abuse? Is the bosozoku member a likely candidate for dedicated involvement in crimes against property or violence against persons? In other words, can the various juvenile offenses be generalized and, as unified phenomenon, be reasonably explained by a single, generalized theory, or do each of the types of deviance require a specialized explanation? If general principles are reasonably applicable, those supervising probationers and parolees would be free to perceive them as essentially the same, regardless of particular motivations and sociocultural conditions of the various offenses.

Osgood and his colleagues (1988) studied the basic question: Are American high school students involved in one of five kinds of deviance vulnerable to the other kinds of deviance: alcohol use, marijuana use, abuse of other illicit drugs, dangerous driving, and criminal behavior (interpersonal aggression, theft, and vandalism)? For example, does drug use lead to crime, or alcohol abuse to dangerous driving? They note two alternative explanations for any correlation: One type of deviance leads to others, or different deviant behaviors share causal influences. To the extent that the same factors are basic sources of all deviant behaviors, they note, it can be meaningful to speak of the generality of deviance.

Their research is relevant to the juvenile justice system of Japan because the American researchers found that one behavior had only limited influence on another behavior—that people engaged in one form of deviance are not likely to engage in others as well. The Japanese reluctance to apply legal sanctions against young offenders is especially justified when the offenses are comparatively minor or stem from an adverse environment. Conversely, the fundamental argument for formal action against predelinquents is that questionable juvenile conduct will lead to outright criminality. Osgood implies that complex social and psychological factors—rather than a simple and direct effect—shape the criminality outcome of present potentialities. "Involvement in one form of deviant behavior is predictive of later involvement in others, not because of mutual influences," they conclude (91), "but because each partially reflects a general tendency toward deviance." Frequent drunkenness in high school would indicate a willingness to violate conventional norms, and, since that willingness is relatively stable over time, it may be expressed in other kinds of deviance as well as continued heavy drinking.

Marginal Deviance and Official Leniency

Adjudicated offenders in Japan are benefited when they are considered to be exceptions to the outright "criminals" who flagrantly reject the esteemed standards of "proper" conduct safeguarded by the criminal law. Instead of being treated as totally unworthy, public prosecutors and sentencing judges divert from the prisons those defendants who are believed to be capable of self-correction. The family courts are even more forgiving when juvenile defendants are found to deserve "protective measures." Adults in Japan benefited from the official leniency extended to marginal deviants. In 1990, district courts and family courts (for adults violating juvenile welfare laws) made these dispositions: imprisonment (including two capital cases) 41.3 percent; suspended sentences with probation 7 percent; suspended sentence with unconditional return to the community 50.4 percent; fines 1 percent, and other dispositions 0.3 percent (Research and Training Institute 1992, 16).

The juvenile defendants have benefited even more than the adults by being treated as marginal deviants. The family court tends to consider a larger proportion of juveniles as not being genuine delinquents when compared with district courts' handling of adult criminals. Table 5.3 in chapter 5 reports on family court dispositions in 1990: 75 percent were sent home, 36.1 percent dismissed after a formal hearing and 38.8 percent without a formal hearing. JTSs received only 1.0 percent, and 17.5 percent were placed on probation. A few of the very young (0.1 percent) were sent to social welfare agencies. The public prosecutors received 6.5 percent to be considered for trial in adult courts, either because they were older than nineteen years or because their crimes and personal qualities justified that referral. Article 20, Juvenile Law, prohibits the family courts from sending a juvenile to the public prosecutor "if the offense has been committed by a juvenile who is under 16 years of age at the time of sending."

Failure to strike a balance between obligation and opportunity was fundamental to an investigation of 993 JTS inmates who presumably had been found wanting as candidates for leniency of family courts. Questionnaires were designed to measure the "consciousness of norms" of the inmates in their reactions to the JTS setting. Reactions were measured on a descending scale: constructive and democratic, dependent and conforming, evasive and apathetic, and aggressive and selfish. One questionnaire dealt with situations in daily life. In the second questionnaire, the boys were asked to select their level of agreement or disagreement according to practical activities about criminal acts, predelinquent acts, acts incompatible with public norms, traffic violations, and acts "against individual norms" (Tsubochi et al. 1990).

The inmates exhibited less norm consciousness, the researchers concluded, than the respondents in the general public who were subjects in an earlier research project. The boys scored greater norm consciousness with increased time in the training schools. Former members of juvenile gangs had lower scores than non-gang members, but the level of norm consciousness varied according to type of gang. The more "advanced in degree of delinquency," the lower the scores. Fewer violations of training school rules had the same relationship to scores.

Childhood and Adolescence in Earlier Japan

In the Europe of the sixteenth and seventeenth centuries, the modern conception of adolescence emerged as a separate and distinctive rung on the behavioral ladder to be climbed from infancy to adulthood. Through growing and learning, teenagers are expected to find a proper balance between (a) their physical, psychological, and social needs and (b) the behavioral standards of family, peers, and the social institutions of their society (Aries 1962; Gillis 1974; Schlossman 1977). Premodern Japan was predominately agrarian and usually did not regard the ages between childhood and adulthood as a distinctive phase in the life cycle. Japan modernized more rapidly and more recently than Europe, but more recent social changes have focused unprecedented attention on adolescence and its implications for delinquency in Japan.

In the traditional version of the Japanese household (the ie), children were pushed toward adulthood because they were an important labor resource. Yamamura (1986) says that children were treated as "community property"—not as belonging to their parents—within the generalized bond of leader to follower among all household members. In earlier centuries, folk beliefs insisted that if a young child died, the soul would go immediately to the other world and return later in another birth. In the 1970s that belief was expressed in the greater number of small statues at temples to pacify the souls of aborted fetuses. According to another folk belief, women born in the year of the horse would be so strong minded that they would become inadequate housewives and would outlive their husbands. In spite of recent conceptions of child health and welfare, the persistence of traditions is illustrated again by the 25.4 percent decline in 1966 (the year of the horse) compared with 1965 of the number of girls born (Hara and Minagawa 1996).

Studies of small communities in Japan report the persistence of habitual tolerance of the misbehavior of young children. In a fishing community, Norbeck (1954, 169) noted that children, aged two or three years, frequently strike parents with their fists, but the parents usually laugh indulgently. "Discipline is most commonly in the form of reprimand," he says, "and, less frequently, by punishment or threats of punishment." In a small community in Okayama Prefecture, a misbehaving or fretful child would be ignored and isolated from the rest of the family. "Deprived of attention," Beardsley, Hall, and Ward (1959, 297) write, "he may continue to misbehave for a time, but, time and again, instead of seizing upon the moment to follow his own inclinations, the child goes to his mother or grandmother for comfort."

Ages of Youth in a Modernizing Society

Japan modernized more rapidly and more recently than Europe, and, as White (1993, 40) notes, has produced, compared with the United States, "a smaller gap between the goals and rationales of adult society on the one hand and the culture and realities of adolescence." Passim (1968, 248) sees modernization of Japan as an amalgam of the traditions inherited from Japan's own past and ideas and practices imported from the West: "We seem to see a mosaic of the past and present, fragmentation of the total society into old and new sectors, old patterns persisting in their entirety or in parts, new patterns displacing the old or reorganizing total areas of experience." In Japan's recent history, that description also holds for the passage from childhood to adulthood.

The moral unity and structural integrity of Japanese society has persisted sufficiently to extend tolerance to marginal deviants. Those characteristics of Japanese society have preserved the influence of informal social controls through socialization of personality and a common cultural heritage. The characteristics have been preserved in spite of divisive forces usually accompanying urbanization: heterogeneity of cultural norms, functional specialization of occupations and other groupings, population mobility, and impersonality in interpersonal relations.

The tradition of adult humoring and indulging small children persists, Tokuoka and Cohen (1987, 15) declare, in the acceptance of "childish naughtiness," but the "comforting presence of benign adults" also produces the need in adulthood for close intimacy and contact with "people who love and accept them." Since World War II, the pace of social change has quickened appreciatively because of the restructuring of the business infrastructure and revision of the political-legal system. "Individual interests previously submerged within a network of family and community obligations," DeVos and Mizushima (1973, 327–28) point out, "are being asserted more openly as orienting guides for behavior." They note that the changes in social attitudes are most noticeable in the younger generation.

Nevertheless, White (1993, 40, 48) insists, "Japanese adults do not expect young people to be a problem"—even the flamboyant pink-haired rock dancer in the streets does not represent serious individual rebellion or social decline. In abstract language, she attributes this difference from American attitudes toward centripetal rather than centrifugal social forces and a cultural preference for the idea of continuity rather than contradiction between generations. She calls attention to "gaps and loopholes" in the institutional norms that allow for different behaviors—even deviance—"to coexist for the most part within more public 'correct' expectations."

The Japanese teenagers also differ from American peers, White (1993, 103–4) says. Both sets of teenagers are targets for consumer marketing. While also expressing themselves in their clothing and gear, however, the Japanese tend to share a common peer culture on a national scale, although differential access to money has effect. American teen-age styles are split along lines of urban-suburban-rural residence, regional distinctions, and racial and ethnic groupings.

Kawasaki (1994) outlines the complicated dimensions of "youth culture in Japan" and agrees that it is a late arrival and centered on consumerism. Today's adolescents and young adults are the first in Japan to "grow up in truly urban areas and to enjoy an affluent material life." Their use of expressionism as an adaptive style, he believes, is superficial, and still in a conformist mode because it is connected with "soft individualism." A narrow range of social circles has limited the youths' socialization with other segments of Japanese society and has denied the youth the opportunity to learn hierarchical roles, Kawasaki declares, and the older generation is puzzled by the behavior of the young. Yet the Japanese emphasis on total harmony in group sentiment, he says, also produces attitudes of conflict among the youth groups.

Among the social changes have been major declines in birthrate, increased access to the job market for married women, and the trend toward the nuclear family. Iwao (1993) traces the general effects on child rearing. The average number of children per mother is less than two. Consequently, mothers have become more intensely involved with their children. "Parents devote great energy," Iwao (1993, 131) says, "to guiding them down the royal road to success. . . ." For lack of experience with previous parenthood, mothers—and fathers to some extent[1]—are barely trained and uncertain parents. Nuclear families deny novice parents the assistance of older generations. To compensate, they tend to do too much for their children and give them too many material goods. In spite of such changes in the circumstances of child rearing, mothers continue to follow an ie tradition in lavishing care upon sons, but Iwao notes that the small boy fulfills the woman's need for physical contact otherwise denied by the tight cultural restraint on physical expressions of affection. In that respect, Iwao (1993, 127) remarks, the child rearing techniques of contemporary Japanese women "engrave the actual and symbolic warmth and importance of the home managed by the mother in the minds of her children."

Mother-child bonding, Doi (1981) argues, is basic to the dependence of Japanese adults on the group. "When people are children, they depend on their parents, and when they grow up they begin to depend on themselves," a patient told Doi (1981, 57–58). "I've been wishing I had someone to act as a mother to me. Someone I could confide anything to, someone who'd take decisions out of my hands." Doi sees the comment illustrating his concept of *amae* that combines *ninjo* (spontaneously arising feelings) and *giri* (social obligation). He (1981, 34–35) contends that giri obligations are coupled spontaneously with ninjo in the comforting and unlimited acceptance by the intimate group. In Japan, amae represents a merger ("a kind of organic relationship") of group obligations with the personal interests of the individual group member, Doi argues, rather than standing in opposition to one another as conceived in the Western descriptions of personal freedom.

History of Increased Leniency for Juveniles

In the evolution of a society, juveniles are especially eligible for the benefits of any leniency granted violators of the criminal law. The history of Japan conforms to that principle. As early as 668, juveniles were treated differently than adult criminals. Soejima (1974) outlines a literature in Japanese on the history of the policies toward juveniles; his review is the source for the following statements.[2] The Taikwa Reform (645–701) was associated with an early attempt to establish a central government in Japan. Its principles drew heavily on the policies of the Tang Law in China in that period of history. Soejima notes that the Japanese then set sixteen years as the maximum age for juveniles, whereas the maximum was fifteen years under Tang Law. The difference, he says, was taken as evidence of the greater leniency of the Japanese. Why did both the Japanese and Chines at that early time demonstrate that level of concern for juveniles? Soejima cites the explanation offered by Dr. Seiichiro Ono: Even then there was compassion and recognition of the juveniles' immaturity in mental and physical development.

Juveniles were defined as sixteen years or less—those under seven years of age had no culpability, and those eight to sixteen had limited culpability. Juveniles aged eight to ten years could be sentenced to death, but only with imperial approval. Use of fetters was prohibited for inmates less than seventeen years of age. Adults under the death penalty would be in fetters during detention. If the adult defendant, in spite of well-supported evidence, refused to confess, torture would be used because confession was considered necessary to the judicial decision. Beating the suspect's back and hip with a bamboo stick was a method of torture. It could not be repeated more than three times nor exceed two hundred beatings in the three times. A suspect less than sixteen years of age could not be tortured; instead, evidence of several witnesses would be substituted.

The Japanese regulations (ritsurei) established a scale of five grades of punishments. Whipping ranged from 10 to 50 beatings; caning 60 to 100; penal servitude from one to three years; exile from short through intermediate to long distances. Persons aged eleven to sixteen years would be exempt if making particular payments in kim (1 kim equaled 600 grams of copper). The payments were known as shoku. The scale of payments were 1 to 5 kim for whipping, 6 to 10 for caning; 20 to 60 for penal servitude; 100 to 140 for exile.

In the Heian era (794–1185), capital punishment was suspended for three centuries. Census regulations set eighteen years as the minimum age for adulthood, but it is not clear whether or not the maximum age for juvenile delinquency was raised from sixteen to seventeen years.

By 1467, the effects of ritsurei had deteriorated, and the several clan regulations took effect. Two clans recognized the special nature of juveniles. The Imagawa clan set the maximum age for juvenile delinquents at fifteen. Quarrels between children were disregarded, but, if a parent took part, both the father and child should be punished. If a child accidentally killed a friend, punishment would be withheld for an unintentional crime, but persons over fifteen years of age would be punished. The Takoda clan duplicated these provisions. During the Edo era (1603–1867), the municipality of Edo (now Tokyo) issued an ordinance in 1655. First, children's quarrels would be ignored if both sets of parents stopped the quarrel; the parents would be liable if they participated in the quarrel. Second, if a juvenile above the age of thirteen years killed a friend, he should be sentenced to death. In 1723, another regulation authorized exile to an island of an arsonist less than fifteen years of age; arsonists older than fifteen years should be burned at the stake.

In 1742, a composite criminal law in Edo contained one hundred penal articles, including these provisions for juveniles less than fifteen years of age.[3] Juvenile thieves, and later other juvenile offenders, would receive punishment one degree less than that given adults. The juvenile committing deliberate murder or arson would be left in the care of a relative until reaching age fifteen years and then would be exiled. In practice the relative would induce the juvenile to escape just before the fifteenth birthday and would report some excuse for the absconding. The public office would order the relative to find the juvenile within thirty days. After a perfunctory search, the relative would report the failure and be told to search for another thirty days. The third report of failure would result in an order to search for a year. Continuing to report a futile search, the relative would be fined for lack of supervision. If the absconder (called *otazunemono*) were apprehended, the penalty was supposed to be raised from exile to death, but the extreme penalty usually would be avoided by such measures as registration under a false name.

Of particular relevance to community-oriented corrections, a law of amnesty (*sharitsu*) in 1862 provided remission of exile in acknowledgment of either a happy or unlucky happening for the family of the emperor or the shogun. Juvenile exiles to an island for a duration greater than sixteen years would benefit; eligible adults would have been exiled to an island for more than twenty-nine years.

During the Meiji Restoration (1868–1912), imprisonment with forced labor was substituted for whipping, caning, and exile. The Penal Code of 1881 called for a "reform prison," separate from prisons for adults, that suggested the juvenile prisons of contemporary Japan. Inmates less than twenty years of age would be separated by age and previous offenses. However, severe overcrowding frustrated the policy. The Penal Code of 1882 included conditional release of prisoners before completion of their sentences; the police provided surveillance of the prisoners released early, but governmental assistance was not provided for readjustment during return to the community. Private citizens initiated some help. When a discharged prisoner committed suicide, a philanthropist pioneered a private aftercare hostel in 1889 as a precursor to the present rehabilitation aid hostels (Nishikawa 1994, 205).

The earlier version of the juvenile prison was closed in 1907, but another institution for juveniles persisted to become the precedent for contemporary juvenile facilities operated by social service agencies. A second model was authorized by the Reformatory Law of 1900 to be a part of the then Prison Bureau. The Juvenile Training School Law of 1922 (now known as the "Old Juvenile Law") led to the juvenile training schools in the Correction Bureau that today is, along with the Rehabilitation Bureau, a component of the Ministry of Justice.

In 1908 a new Penal Code became effective, adopted parole, and incorporated the suspension of prison sentences of two years or less, but neither supervision (the crucial element in full-fledged probation and parole) nor post-release assistance were provided by government agencies. Voluntary work of private parties was expected to meet the need. Promulgated on two occasions of bereavement of members of the imperial family in 1912 and 1914, general pardons suddenly released 36,731 prisoners. A religious sect mobilized temples to help the released prisoners. The effort was a prototype for VPOs, a key element in Japan's community-oriented corrections. The Rehabilitation Services Law of 1939 provided the basic framework for the early version of VPOs and the privately operated rehabilitation aid hostels (Nishikawa 1994, 206).

The first modern noninstitutional approach to corrections in Japan emerged with the Old Juvenile Law in 1923. It defined juveniles as youths less than eighteen years of age and established the Juvenile Tribunal, a quasi-judicial agency that could send a juvenile to a reform school, conditionally release a reform school inmate, or place the juvenile in the community under supervision. Parole of juveniles came before parole of adults. Lack of financial resources prevented implementation of the law throughout Japan until 1943 (Nishikawa 1994, 206–7).

After World War II, the essence of modern community-oriented corrections was established. The juvenile tribunal was abolished in 1949 when the new Juvenile Law and the Offenders Rehabilitation Law established the family court, the juvenile parole board, and the juvenile probation office. Amendments to the laws integrated the juvenile and adult programs.

Juvenile Contrast: Arrests Versus Training Schools

Juvenile admissions to training schools are only a fraction of adult admissions to prisons, but juveniles hold a greater share of police clearances of Penal Code cases (see table 6.1). Admissions to JTSs in 1950 represented 11.4 percent of the combination of admissions to JTSs and prisons, but juveniles held 34.6 percent of police clearances of Penal Code cases. The

Table 6.1

Juveniles and Adults Compared for Police Clearances and Admissions to Correctional Institutions, 1950–1995

Years	Penal Code Offenders Cleared by Police			Admission to Correctional Institutions		
	Juveniles (A)	Adults (B)	Ratios[a]	Training Schools (A)	Adult Prisons (B)	Ratios[a]
1950	158,426	458,297	34.6	6,868	60,040	11.4
1955	121,753	437,104	21.8	8,604	54,035	15.9
1960	196,682	413,565	32.2	8,992	41,008	18.0
1965	234,959	515,963	31.3	7,874	33,935	23.2
1970	224,943	883,253	20.3	3,965	25,890	13.3
1975	196,946	668,782	22.7	2,549	26,175	8.9
1980	269,718	653,931	29.2	4,720	28,374	14.3
1985	304,070	722,171	29.6	6,029	31,656	16.0
1990	182,328	717,322	20.3	4,234	22,745	15.7
1995	149,137	821,042	15.4	3,828	21,838	14.9

Sources: Research and Training Institute (1996, 43, 97); Shikita and Tsuchiya (1990, 194); Research and Statistics Section, annual reports for given years.

[a]Ratios of A to B are multiplied by 100.

difference has held for all of the following years, although the margin narrowed to a trifle by 1995.

This bifurcation of juvenile justice in Japan—table 6.1 is intended to illustrate the existence of two major and divergent tendencies—confirms the noteworthy tolerance of official policy toward juvenile delinquents. The family courts are a primary instrument of the policy of diverting a very large share of their cases back into the community. The table shows the share sent to training school varies over the decades but always represents a portion of the inmates in all Japanese correctional institutions. However, compared to admissions to correctional institutions, the juveniles have held a larger share of police clearances of Penal Code cases.

The greater degree of tolerance accorded juveniles is confirmed, but, even more significant at the moment, is the appearance of an issue: Why do juveniles hold this larger share of Penal Code offenders as outcomes of police activities? That share has varied over the decades; why? The Penal Code covers the most serious offenses; violations of special laws (such as drug offenses) are not included. Police activities also entail "guidance" of juveniles; those activities are not shown in table 6.1. Penal Code offenses are more likely to represent those juvenile infractions usually regarded as genuine threats to the community. Relative to special laws and police guidance, Penal Code offenses seem to measure juvenile offenses that merit law enforcement measures. Again, the juveniles' share of police clearances differs over the decades.

In discussing the several peaks in juvenile delinquency, Shikita and Tsuchiya (1990, 232–37) explain the 1950 upsurge: "After 1945, the postwar rise in the number of juvenile delinquencies was due largely to social disorder, economic hardships, family breakups and other chaotic conditions in the aftermath of the war." The peak from 1955 through 1965, they say, is explained by the "social changes and frictions" stemming from the rapid industrialization and urbanization. After 1975, their attention turns to the effects of an affluent society: increasing value diversity, the decrease of attention to child care and socialization by families and communities, and unprecedented opportunities for juvenile crimes.

That line of explanation emphasizes the impact of modernization and affluence on the Japanese, especially through deteriorating influence of the families and schools. "Although Japanese society expects young adults to possess traditional values," Vaughn and Huang (1992, 294) summarize, "the institutions of social control are sending young Japanese mixed signals as to what values they should hold in high esteem." In a similar vein, Kashiwagi (1986) describes a new brand of juvenile delinquency as either acting-out behavior toward parents (primarily mothers) or "school-phobic" activity. She attributes them to a combination of socioeconomic affluence and parental overprotection that fails to prepare children for success in academic achievement and interpersonal relationships. In the 1960s, Iwao (1993) says, improper maternal care was frequently blamed for juvenile delinquency, increasing a sense of guilt among working mothers. School bullies have attracted increasing attention; Lanham and Garrick (1996, 117) report that many teachers tolerate bullying for fear of exacerbating it or because of the belief that children should resolve their own interpersonal problems.[4]

Another explanatory approach was discovered by Gillis (1974, 176–78) during his study of the records of the Oxford (England) Police Court for 1870–1914. He discovered a sharp increase in the number of juveniles brought before the court for offenses that previously would not have been treated as juvenile crimes. Many stolen items were of little value and destined for personal use. Offenses often appeared in the course of street games, gambling, and other peer-group activities. The chief complainants, he says, were "school teachers, clergymen, and child-saving groups who liked to think of themselves as protecting youth rather than property."

Similarly, Tokuoka and Cohen (1987, 22) point to increasing public preoccupation with teenagers' problems in Japan and the "willing response" of the police, "who are spending less time on adult crime and on serious juvenile crime." One consequence, they say, is "increasing arrests of children for behavior that was formerly not considered the business of the police." The arrests confirm that "the belief in the rising tide of juvenile delinquency . . . produces an even higher public anxiety about delinquency, and results in . . . more arrests." Since the late 1970s, Yokoyama (1989, 47) reports, the police have been active in "guiding" young people. "Juveniles displaying such bad conduct as smoking or loitering at midnight are more frequently classified as predelinquents."

According to the National Police Agency (1993), the number of juveniles "given guidance for initial-type delinquency"[5] has declined since 1983, but the percentage of all juveniles given guidance who were involved in Penal Code offenses has increased. "This high percentage is attributed to delinquency-inducing social phenomena that are on the rise," the National Police Agency (1993, 83) explains, "such as illegal parking of bicycles and motorcycles, and the increases of large-scale stores where sales clerks cannot keep an eye on shoppers, and also a decline in the morality of juveniles themselves."

Affect of Tolerance on Case Supervision

Family courts follow the policy of tolerance toward marginal deviance among juveniles. Most delinquents are released into the community; referrals to probation and juvenile training schools (and subsequent parole) are limited to the remainder, who appear to require more restrictive management. Tolerance makes sense when most juveniles tend toward conformity because of their socialization to the behavioral standards of an orderly society. The family courts believe that the delinquents will be motivated to join the conformists.

Traffic and drug offenders have assumed increasing shares of juvenile probationers and parolees since 1965 (as shown in table 6.7). These offenses are in the forefront of a movement toward increased involvement of the government's intervention in affairs usually left to the family and other character-building institutions. Juvenile offenses in traffic and drug misconduct have received increased official attention. The tolerance of such "marginal deviance" is less but still exists. One consequence is that the probation offices are receiving the more extreme examples of problematic personalities among the juveniles caught up in the "dragnet" of the criminal justice system. Two case histories illustrate the consequence for probation offices.

Male probationer, aged sixteen years, traffic offense. The family court placed A. A. on probation when referred for theft of a motorcycle and driving without a license. He had graduated from junior high school but, rather than enrolling in high school, became a construction worker. While on probation, contrary to the conditions for conditional release into the community, he continued to associate with questionable persons, wandered around until late at night, and ignored his parents' instructions to be at home by a reasonable hour.

He ignored the requirements to report periodically to the VPO, who was unable to contact him. His parents were unable to control him. The PPO found supervision impossible, although referral to the family court for action was pending at the time of the report.

Male probationer, aged seventeen years, organic solvent abuse. The parents of T. Y. were divorced when he was aged two years. The father died without contacting him; the mother vanished. He was raised by his maternal grandparents. The PPO described his personality as "mentally underdeveloped, faint hearted, and dependent. He had lost self-confidence and volition to wrestle with problems of his own accord."

On probation T. Y. began work as a construction laborer for an uncle. Although a dedicated worker, he began inhaling paint thinner after two weeks in spite of being cautioned by the VPO. He told the PPO that he used paint thinner out of boredom and that he doubted he was a burden to his grand-parents. The PPO persuaded the grandmother to attend group counseling sessions explaining the harmful effects of solvents and how to influence abusers.

T. Y. increased the use of paint thinner, quit work, and acted violent in the home while under the influence of the drug. The grandparents summoned the police. It was decided that medical treatment was necessary.

At the hospital, T. Y. told the PPO: "It is no use having a grudge against my mother. I must stand on my own two feet and make a living. If I return home, it is feared that I will repeat the same failure." The grandparents said to the PPO: "We have lost confidence to live with him. We have done our level best."

T. Y. and the grandparents agreed that he should go to a rehabilitation aid hostel, but, after leading a regular life as a construction laborer for a time, he was discovered in his hostel room under the influence of paint thinner. The VPO at the hostel and the PPO failed to change his conduct. The PPO was negotiating with a nonprofit organization specializing in the treatment of drug abusers, but T. Y. broke into a paint shop to steal a bottle of paint thinner. Arrested, he was returned to a juvenile training school.

Juvenile Classification Homes and Age of Delinquency Onset

The Ministry of Justice publishes data relating age of juve-niles to other variables for juveniles admitted to juvenile clas-sification homes (JCHs). Although such data are not supplied for juvenile probationers and parolees, the JCH statistics have at least suppositional value as a substitute. First, the policies of the family courts make for previous contacts with "guid-ance counseling" of juveniles by the police, referral to child wel-fare agencies, and perhaps probation before this referral to

Table 6.2
Age at Onset of Delinquency by Age
When First Admitted to Juvenile Classification Home, 1989

Age at Onset of Delinquency	Age at First Admission to Juvenile Classification Homes							
	14	15	16	17	18	19	All Ages	Mean Age at JCH Admission
	Percentage Distribution							
Males								
Under 10	5.9	3.1	2.1	2.2	2.1	1.3	2.4	16.40
10	8.1	5.7	4.0	2.8	2.2	2.3	3.5	16.32
11	5.6	3.3	1.9	2.2	1.7	1.5	2.3	16.41
12	17.2	9.9	7.9	5.4	3.9	3.9	6.6	16.24
13	35.3	23.1	12.9	11.9	10.1	8.2	13.9	16.30
14	27.5	39.0	30.7	25.4	22.7	20.4	26.4	16.73
15	—	15.6	26.8	24.7	22.4	20.7	20.9	17.24
16	—	—	13.2	16.2	15.8	14.8	12.3	17.57
17	—	—	—	8.4	7.5	7.2	5.0	17.91
18	—	—	—	—	10.5	7.9	3.8	18.42
19	—	—	—	—	—	10.5	2.1	19.00
Unknown	0.4	0.3	0.5	0.8	1.1	1.3	0.8	—
Mean age at onset	12.51	13.24	13.92	14.31	14.77	15.21	14.27	—
Total number	728	1,054	1,719	2,177	2,058	1,970	9,706	—
Females								
Under 10	1.6	1.1	1.0	0.8	0.5	1.2	1.1	15.70
10	3.4	3.6	2.2	1.1	1.1	0.6	2.3	15.31
11	4.1	1.6	1.5	1.6	0.5	—	1.8	15.13
12	9.6	6.1	6.6	4.4	2.6	3.0	6.0	15.49
13	40.7	17.9	10.5	9.3	9.5	2.4	17.1	15.07
14	40.6	44.3	27.9	18.7	16.3	19.6	30.6	15.53
15	—	24.9	29.1	20.6	17.4	10.1	18.1	15.93
16	—	—	20.0	22.3	13.7	17.3	11.1	17.01
17	—	—	—	19.5	10.5	10.1	5.5	17.50
18	—	—	—	—	24.2	8.9	3.1	18.24
19	—	—	—	—	—	25.0	2.1	19.00
Unknown	—	0.5	1.2	1.7	3.7	1.8	1.2	—
Mean age at onset	13.06	13.70	14.27	14.94	15.56	16.23	14.31	—
Total number	386	442	409	364	190	168	1,959	—

Source: Research and Training Institute (1990, 38).

JCHs. Second, family court referrals imply the judges seek more reliable assessment of the particular individuals before final dispositions. Odds favor the ultimate choice of either probation or training schools for juveniles who do not receive case dismissals. Those sent to training schools are highly likely to become parolees.

In one study reported by the Research and Training Institute (1990, 38), 9,706 males and 1,959 females had entered JCHs for the first time in 1989 and were discharged that year (see table 6.2). The age of their first delinquent incident was related to their age at first admittance to JCHs. Most of these persons, the Research and Training Institute (1990, 37) notes, had had some contact with community-oriented programs, but this was the first contact with JCHs or institutional corrections. Both sexes are arrayed by age (14–19 years) for the first admission to JCHs. Ages of first delinquent incident range from under 10 years (as reported in the source data) through 19 years. The ages of first delinquent incident were obtained from public records prepared by the juvenile guidance program of the police, statements of the juveniles themselves, and statements of the juveniles' family members.

For the 9,706 male juveniles, 2.4 percent had been involved in their first delinquent act before age 10 years; they had entered JCHs subsequently as they grew older, from 14 to 19 years. Half of the males in table 6.2 had been admitted to JCHs after their first delinquent incident, when their ages were less than 14 years.

For the 1,959 juvenile females, the onset of delinquency was more gradual; only 1.1 percent of the JCH admissions of girls were first involved in delinquency at ages less than 10 years. Only 28.3 percent of those entering JCHs by age 19 years had been first involved in delinquency before age 14 years. However, as for the boys, the onset of delinquency has come for a significant number of Japanese youngsters at an earlier age than so-called "common sense" would lead us to expect. For the full age span of Japanese juveniles (less than

20 years), ages 14 and 15 years for males, being the time of delinquency onset, had delivered 47.3 percent of the JCH admissions by age 19 years. For girls, the equivalent figure was similar (48.7 percent). These peak ages correspond with American and European experiences (McKissack 1967; Blumstein and Graddy 1982, 82; Farrington 1986, 219–21).

The early onset of delinquency continues to affect the flow of juveniles into classification homes. To measure the continuing impact, the mean age of the onset of delinquency is listed for each age of JCH admissions. For boys, the mean age at onset rose from 12.51 years for admissions at age 14 to mean age of 15.21 years at onset for admissions at age 19 years. As the age of JCH admission increased, the youngest ages at onset lost some of their earlier impact but continued to be influential. The girls also exhibited the continuing effect of early onset of delinquency, but, as shown by the mean age at onset, they had shorter spans of years between onset and JCH admission. For age 19 years at admission to JCH, girls had first become delinquents on average at age 16.23 years.

Age and Admissions to
Juvenile Classification Homes

The published statistics on JCH admissions also provide a plausible documentation on the relationship between age of juveniles and various offenses (Research and Statistics Section 1996c, 40–41). The offenses are compared by mean ages and the percentage share held by the oldest juveniles (18–20 years) referred to JCHs in 1995. Table 6.3 reports on the total admissions but drops two kinds of offenses from the offense categories: those with numbers less than 39 (the figure for homicide), and those not specifically described ("other" offenses). The limited number of certain offenses does not permit meaningful percentage distributions and mean ages. For total offenses, the mean age is 17.16, with the vast majority accumulating in ages

16 and 17 years. A few individuals were at the extreme ages, 13 and 20 years.

Homicide is tilted toward the older end of the continuum of average ages (17.60), with the majority in ages 18 and 19 years. Of the two "heinous" offenses, robbery has a wider percentage distribution and lower mean age (17.08). Of the three varieties of robbery, "simple" robbery had both a wide distribution and the same mean age (Research and Statistics Section 1996c, 40–41). Robbery-rape had the fewest incidents (only 35) but were concentrated in the ages 18 and 19 years (77.2 percent) with the highest mean age (17.89 years). The oldest teenagers were prone to this brand of violence. Robberies resulting in death average 16.99 in age and about half in the ages 16 and 17 years. Ineptness of young robbers appears to be one of the reasons for the fatalities; also juveniles involved in fatal robberies were more apt to be referred to public prosecutors if they were older than 17 years.

Violent offenses (see table 6.3) cover a wide range of incidents to average out similar to robbery, but with a higher mean age (17.14). Bodily injury, the most numerous of violent offenses, pushed the general mean upward with its own mean of 17.18. Assault had similar effect. Also numerous, extortion exerted a counterinfluence (mean of 17.08). The Law for Punishment of Acts of Violence (the violence law) involved 85 percent of the juvenile violators in ages 16–19 years (mean of 17.06) largely through public demonstrations by young motorists of their driving "proficiency" on crowded streets (Research and Statistics Section 1996c, 40–41). Limitations on the possession of swords dates back to the Tokugawa era. From 1946, various ordinances and laws culminated in the Firearms and Swords Control Law. Public prosecutors received 10,129 juvenile violators of the Law in 1963, but the referrals dropped sharply to number only 525 in 1988 (Shikita and Tsuchiya 1990, 12, 243). The few admissions to JCHs in 1995 were distinctly of older juveniles (average age of 17.41 years).

Elements of property offenses also ranged variously

Table 6.3
Age by Crimes at Admission to Juvenile Classification Homes, 1995

Offense Categories	Total Juveniles	Age at Admission to JCH					Mean Age
		13	14–15	16–17	18–19	20	
		Percentage Distribution					
Heinous	522	—	64	233	225	—	17.12
Percent	100	—	12.3	44.6	43.1	—	—
Robbery	484	—	12.4	45.7	41.9	—	17.08
Homicide	38	—	10.5	31.6	57.9	—	17.60
Violent	3,438	2	467	1,474	1,494	1	17.14
Percent	100	0.0	13.6	42.9	43.5	0.0	—
Bodily injury	1,846	0.1	14.5	39.4	46	—	17.18
Extortion	1,207	—	12.8	47.2	40	0.0	17.08
Violence law	217	—	12.0	50.2	37.8	—	17.06
Assault	113	—	15.0	40.7	44.3	—	17.16
Firearms	41	—	4.9	46.3	48.8	—	17.41
Property	4,571	1	625	1,922	2,017	6	17.15
Percent	100	0.0	13.7	42.1	44.1	0.1	—
Larceny	4,305	0.0	13.9	42.4	43.6	0.1	17.13
Intrusion	109	—	10.1	42.2	47.7	—	17.33
Fraud	65	—	—	23.1	76.9	—	18.26
Arson	47	—	14.9	29.8	55.3	—	16.62
Sex	370	—	28	127	213	2	17.55
Percent	100	—	7.6	34.3	57.6	0.5	—
Rape	232	—	7.3	34.5	57.3	0.9	17.53
Indecent assault	116	—	9.5	37.1	53.4	—	17.47
Drugs	1,659	—	109	547	992	11	17.69
Percent	100	—	6.6	33.0	59.8	0.6	—
Stimulants	873	—	3.2	23.5	72.4	0.9	18.06
Organic solvents	770	—	10.4	43.9	45.3	0.4	17.26
Traffic	1,798	—	54	835	908	1	17.50
Percent	100	—	3.0	46.4	50.5	0.1	—
Predelinquency	983	29	543	303	106	2	15.48
Percent	100	3.0	55.2	30.8	10.8	0.2	—
Total	13,844	36	1,925	5,597	6,260	26	17.16
Total percent	100	0.3	13.9	40.4	45.2	0.2	—

Source: Research and Statistics Section (1996c, 40–41).

around the mean age of 17.15 years. The few cases of fraud drew the older juveniles (mean age of 18.26 and 76.9 percent in the ages 18 and 19 years). Chapter 37 of the Penal Code links fraud and extortion. Article 247 speaks of a breach of trust, but Article 248 on "constructive fraud" offers a better basis for juvenile offenses. Older juveniles are more likely to take "advantage of the lack of knowledge or experience of a minor or the weak-mindedness of another [to obtain] a surrender of such person's property or illegally obtains or causes a third person to obtain illegally any economic benefit."

Larceny-theft, the most numerous offense against property, is a traditional crime, along with arson and intrusion. Juvenile theft comes in many versions: theft from houses, vehicles, and vending machines; shoplifting; and stealing bicycles and motorbikes (Research and Training Institute 1995, 43). Larceny-theft was the major contributor to the wide percentage distribution and middle mean age of property crimes. Arson is more oriented to the older juveniles. Chapter 9 of the Penal Code refers to burning of inhabited and uninhabited structures, "buildings, railroad trains, electric cars, vessels, or mines." Intrusion upon a habitation resembles housebreaking but takes in a greater variety of structures. Chapter 12 of the Penal Code defines it as a "person who, without good reason, intrudes upon a human habitation or upon the premises, structure or vessel guarded by another, or who refuses to leave such a place upon demand."

The sex offenses of rape and indecent assault have similar mean ages, but rape draws more of the older teenagers. Article 177 of the Penal Code defines rape as sexual intercourse with a female person of not less than 13 years of age "through violence or intimidation" or sexual intercourse with a person under 13 years of age. Article 176 treats indecency through compulsion as an indecent act, "through violence or intimidation . . . upon a male or female person of not less than 13 years of age" or an indecent act "upon a male or female person under 13 years of age."

Abuse of organic solvents and stimulants has put a substantial number of drug offenders in JCHs; only narcotic abusers (16) were few. All three types had high average ages: stimulants 18.1, narcotics 17.9, and organic solvents 17.3 years. Ages
18–20 years held high percentage shares of the respective admissions in the same order: 73.3, 68.7, and 45.8 percent (Research and Statistics Section 1996c, 40–41).

Half of the traffic offenders referred to JCHs (50.6 percent) were in the ages greater than 17 years. Two elements of
the law are applied to traffic offenders: the Penal Code and
the Road Traffic Law, among the "special laws." The distinction is explained in chapter 5. Several differences mirror the
distinction of the laws. The juveniles convicted for "professional negligence" are older on average (18 years) than those
convicted under the Road Traffic Law. The same relationship
holds for average number of previous admissions to JCHs
(1.47 versus 1.24 times); percent of JCH juveniles previously
in JTSs (11.9 versus 7.2 percent); and percentage of JCH juveniles who were members of various juvenile gangs (71.5 versus 16.1 percent) (Research and Statistics Section 1996c, 40–
43; 46–47; 62).

The predelinquency policy assumes that some juveniles
are vulnerable to their "character or environment" in terms
of future law violations. The policy targets the younger juveniles for *protective* measures. Of all the juveniles entering
JCHs, predelinquents had the lowest mean age (15.5 years)
and the smallest percentage share devoted to ages 18 and 19
years (10.8 percent). In admissions to probation, the 912 predelinquents in 1985 (3.4 percent of all admissions) dropped to
264 (1.4 percent) in 1995. In admissions to parole, the 452 predelinquents in 1985 (8.1 percent) dropped to 165 (4.4 percent)
in 1995 (Research and Statistics Section 1990, 70–77; 1991a, 70–
77; 1996a, 70–77).

For the five years 1990–1995, the Research and Training
Institute (1996, 25) reports, the admissions to probation and
parole have differed for the "heinous offenses," homicide and

robbery. *Heinous* denotes these crimes as especially wicked or nefarious. Article 199 of the Penal Code states: "A person who kills another shall be punished with death or imprisonment for life or not less than three years." Article 236 defines the penalty for simple robbery: "A person who deprives another of the property through violence or intimidation thereby commits the crime of robbery and shall be punished with imprisonment at forced labor for a limited term of not less than five years." Although simple robbery is included among heinous crimes, the other two versions draw the most severe sanctions. Article 240 deals with injury of the victim during a robbery and imposes imprisonment at forced labor or "for not less than seven years." If the victim is killed, "death or imprisonment at forced labor for life shall be imposed."

Comparing Admissions: Probation, Parole, or Juvenile Training Schools

When facing the choice between probation or training schools, family courts have turned to probation increasingly over the decades. In the 1950s two juveniles were placed on probation for every one sent to training schools (see table 6.4). That ratio grew rather consistently over the decades to top 17 in 1990, then sagging slightly in 1995 when the absolute number of admissions dropped for both probation and training school admissions. The gain in ratios had been due, first, to an irregular increase in the absolute number of probationers and, second, to a decline in the number of JTS admission from 1960 to 1980.

The age-specific rates connect admissions to the number of juveniles in Japan from which the delinquents were drawn each year. Criminologists have established that fluctuations in proportional share of juveniles and young adults in the nation's population have great influence on the general crime rate. Here age-specific rates measure whether or not admissions to probation and training school keep pace with changes

Table 6.4
Admissions to Juvenile Probation, Parole,
and Training Schools, 1950–1995

Years	Juvenile Probation	Training Schools	Ratios[a]	Juvenile Parole	Ratios[b]
1950	13,291	6,867	1.93	3,121	0.45
1955	17,094	8,604	1.99	7,375	0.86
1960	24,408	8,992	2.71	7,797	0.87
1965	28,173	7,874	3.58	6,301	0.80
1970	27,383	3,965	6.91	3,167	0.80
1975	21,384	2,549	8.39	1,593	0.62
1980	56,322	4,720	11.93	4,063	0.86
1985	71,411	6,029	11.84	5,585	0.93
1990	73,779	4,234	17.42	4,333	1.02
1995	51,075	3,828	13.34	3,782	0.99
Rates per 100,000 Japanese Aged 14–19 Years					
1950	128.0	66.1	—	30.0	—
1955	161.4	82.8	—	69.6	—
1960	225.6	83.1	—	72.1	—
1965	218.3	61.0	—	48.8	—
1970	256.7	37.2	—	29.9	—
1975	224.7	26.8	—	16.7	—
1980	579.6	48.6	—	41.8	—
1985	651.4	55.0	—	50.9	—
1990	616.8	35.6	—	36.6	—
1995	513.3	38.5	—	38.0	—

Sources: Shikita and Tsuchiya (1990, 374); Research and Statistics Section (1981c, 102; 1991c, 102; 1996a, 102; 1996c, 102).

[a]Number of probationers per training school inmate.
[b]Number of parolees per training school inmate.

in the representation of individuals, ages 14–19 years, in the Japanese population. The general trend for juvenile probation admissions has been upward. Meanwhile, after a rise in certain age-specific rates from 1950 to 1960, the trend for JTS admissions has declined from 83.1 in 1960 to 38.5 in 1995.

The JTS admissions come earlier than releases from training schools. The number of parole admissions per JTS admission does not precisely capture the availability of parole candidates, but in lieu of a better alternative, table 6.4 records a slight increase after 1950 in the use of parole. The age-specific rates for juvenile paroles peaked in 1960 and, in an erratic trend, have moved downward since then. The statistics mirror a close relationship between parole and JTS admissions.

Correction Bureau reports on training schools compare two kinds of discharge of inmates back into the community: expiration of sentence or parole (Research and Statistics Section 1996c, 86–87). The heavy reliance on juvenile parole is made clear. In 1950 the Correction Bureau reported 2,986 releases from training schools and only 71 discharges upon expiration of sentence. Paroles held 97.6 percent of all JTS releases. From 1950 to 1975, the percentage of paroles declined to 77.1 percent, then climbed into the 90 percentages, and reached 95.5 in 1995.

The numerical superiority of probation among admissions held for all offense categories in 1995. Admissions to training schools and parole were about equal; almost all discharges from training schools were via parole. However, the three correctional settings differed in the relative importance of the various offenses. Again family courts were responsible for the differences between probation admissions and training school admissions because the offense was among the criteria for decisions in dispositions. Admissions to training schools and parolees had greater similarity, but availability for parole does not exactly match the number of JTS admissions at the particular time.

The comparisons in table 6.5 are based, first, on the percentage distributions of probation admissions, JTS admissions, or parole admissions and, second, on the two ratios. One ratio divides the absolute number of probation admissions by the number of JTS admissions. For all offense, the ratio is 5.01 (18,917 divided by 3,776). The heavy representation of juvenile probationers on the traffic program (ratio of 18.91) makes for other offense categories having a ratio less than 5.01. The comparison must be in terms of narrowing the difference between that general ratio and the ratio for other particular offense categories. The second ratio compares probation and

Table 6.5
Admissions by Selected Crimes to Juvenile Probation, Training Schools, and Parole, 1995

Selected Offenses[a]	Juvenile Probation (A)	Training Schools (B)	Juvenile Parole (C)	Ratio A/B	Ratio A/C
Heinous	351	196	207	1.79	1.70
Percent	1.85	5.19	5.54	—	—
Robbery	1.80	4.63	5.11	1.95	1.79
Homicide	0.05	0.56	0.43	0.43	0.56
Violent	3,361	804	766	4.18	4.39
Percent	17.77	21.29	20.51	—	—
Bodily injury	10.41	11.07	11.9	4.71	4.42
Extortion	5.07	8.32	6.19	3.05	4.15
Violence law	1.24	1.09	1.29	5.70	4.87
Assault	0.84	0.50	0.75	8.32	5.64
Property	5,515	1,486	1,481	3.71	3.72
Percent	29.15	39.35	39.65	—	—
Larceny	27.34	37.42	38.23	3.66	3.95
Embezzlement	0.73	0.48	0.24	7.72	15.44
Intrusion	0.49	0.37	0.40	6.64	6.20
Fraud	0.25	0.37	0.27	3.43	4.80
Sex	196	189	191	1.04	1.03
Percent	1.04	5.01	5.11	—	—
Indecent assault	0.55	0.95	0.88	2.89	3.15
Rape	0.38	4.00	4.15	0.48	0.46
Drugs	1,459	532	482	2.74	3.03
Percent	7.71	14.09	12.91	—	—
Organic solvents	5.50	4.32	4.98	6.39	5.60
Stimulants	2.18	9.69	7.90	1.13	1.40
Traffic	7,771	411	443	18.91	17.54
Percent	41.08	10.89	11.86	—	—
Predelinquency	264	158	165	1.67	1.60
Percent	1.40	4.18	4.42	—	—
Total number	18,917	3,776	3,735	—	—
Total percent	100	100	100	5.01	5.06

Sources: Research and Statistics Section (1996a, 70–77; 1996c, 104–5).

[a]Excludes firearms and swords, intimidation, forgery, arson, stolen property, prostitution, pornography, narcotics, and public order crimes because they are too few for meaningful comparisons. Other penal and special law offenses are excluded because they are not specified.

parole admissions against a general ratio of 5.06 (18,917 divided by 3,735). The general ratio is dominated by the probation program for juvenile traffic offenders.

In percentage distributions, property offenses are the most "popular" among juveniles; they rank second to traffic among probation admissions and first among training school admissions. The absolute number of property offenders among JTS admissions reduces the ratio to 3.71. Larceny is very influential. Probation is granted juvenile embezzlers especially, not for "embezzlement in the conduct of business," but for "conversion" of property lost by another person or "drifting" or "any other property which belongs to another person and is in no one's custody" (Penal Code, Article 254).

In percentage distribution, violent offenses rank next for both probation and training schools because of bodily injury and extortion. The violence law (Law for Punishment of Acts of Violence) and assault are linked partially with public demonstrations; for juveniles, the bosozoku are prominent among those offenders. They have special access to probation when they show evidence of not being "real delinquents," but the ratios suggest that the family courts sent a greater absolute number to JTSs.

Drug offenses generate a larger percentage of JTS admissions than of probationers because of stimulant drugs. Organic solvents, especially abused by juveniles, are more likely to gain probation (ratio of 6.39). Heinous offenses—primarily robbery—tend to go to training schools (ratio of 1.79). Sex offenses—primarily rape—also are highly likely to be referred to JTSs; indecent assault has the greater ratio. This is true for predelinquents as well; the family courts usually resort to JTSs for juveniles needing "protective measures."

Changes in Admissions from 1965 to 1995

Juvenile probationers are more numerous than juvenile parolees, but that superiority has varied over recent years. Table

Table 6.6

*Admissions to Juvenile Probation and Parole
by Crime Categories and Ratios, 1965–1995*

Crime Categories	1965	1970	1975	1980	1985	1990	1995
Total admissions[a]							
Probation	26,719	27,092	20, 665	24, 869	26,646	23,131	18,934
Parole	6,216	3,174	1,556	3,998	5,522	4,278	3,737
Ratios[b]	4.30	8.61	13.28	6.22	4.82	5.41	5.07
Property							
Probation	10,339	7,449	5,103	6,434	8,143	6,127	5,515
Parole	3,439	1,833	822	1,864	2,610	1,951	1,481
Ratios	3.01	4.06	5.79	3.45	3.12	3.14	3.72
Traffic							
Probation	6,521	14,250	12,242	11,252	11,657	11,284	7,771
Parole	4	54	76	293	460	421	443
Ratios	1,630.25	263.89	161.08	38.40	25.34	26.80	17.54
Violence							
Probation	6,009	3,141	1,990	3,052	2,929	2,429	3,378
Parole	1,150	433	175	563	793	709	768
Ratios	5.22	7.25	11.37	5.42	3.69	3.43	4.30
Sex							
Probation	2,019	1,081	588	484	338	228	196
Parole	630	347	168	246	247	209	191
Ratios	3.20	3.11	3.50	1.97	1.37	1.09	1.03
Predelinquency							
Probation	1,163	773	447	769	912	588	264
Parole	617	286	134	419	452	316	165
Ratios	1.88	2.70	3.34	1.83	2.02	1.86	1.60
Heinous							
Probation	661	385	226	249	162	185	351
Parole	367	194	113	143	170	143	207
Ratios	1.80	1.98	2.00	1.74	0.95	1.29	1.70
Drugs							
Probation	7	13	69	2,629	2,505	2,290	1,459
Parole	9	—	8	470	790	530	482
Ratios	0.78	—	8.62	5.59	3.17	4.32	3.03

Sources: Research and Statistics Section (1966, 72–75; 1971a, 80–83; 1976a, 78–81; 1981a, 68–71; 1986a, 70–73; 1991a, 70–73).

[a]Excludes gambling and lotteries, public order, and "other" crimes in source tables.
[b]The number of probation admissions divided by the number of parole admissions.

6.6 lists the ratios (number of probationers per parolee) for the years 1965 to 1995. The ratio was 4.30 in 1965, rose to 13.28 in 1975, dropped to 6.22 in 1980, and has stabilized around 5.00. The number of juvenile probationers has declined, but the fluctuation of the ratios has responded mostly to the up-and-down movement of parole admissions. The movements of parole, in turn, reflect changes in the distribution of offenses.

Two statistics measure those changes. The ratios for crime categories in table 6.6 show how parole admission made gains or losses in approaching the number of probation admissions. The comparisons are for each of the years. The crime categories are arrayed in order of the number of probation admissions in 1965, from 10,339 for property offenses to only 7 for drug offenses. From 1965, the ratios measure the up-and-down movement of the probation-parole relationship in response to the major trends for community-oriented corrections in Japan.

The second statistic (presented in table 6.7) measures the percentage distribution of each crime category along the continuum of years. The purpose is to portray the changes over the years in the relative importance of each crime category among all crime categories. For juveniles, traffic offenses and drug offenses (to a more limited extent) mirrored changes in public policy that brought previously marginal deviants into community-oriented corrections.

Ratios in table 6.6 show that property offenses were most numerous in 1965 for both probation and parole. (Table 6.7 shows that in 1965, property offenses held 38.7 percent of all probation admissions and 55.3 percent of all parole admissions.) Both programmatic admissions lost numbers in later years. Parole failed to keep pace with probation admissions until 1980, when the relationship settled around a three-to-one relationship. Property offenses would have held a reasonably steady dominance of admissions in percentage share if the traffic and drug admissions had not interfered.

Probation admissions of juvenile traffic offenders were in

Table 6.7
Admissions to Juvenile Probation and Parole
by Crime Categories, 1965–1995

Crime Categories	1965	1970	1975	1980	1985	1990	1995
Probation	26,719	27,092	20,665	24,869	26,646	23,131	18,934
Parole	6,216	3,147	1,556	3,998	5,522	4,278	3,737
			Percentage Distribution				
Property							
Probation	38.7	27.5	24.7	25.9	30.6	26.5	29.1
Parole	55.3	58.2	56.7	46.6	47.3	45.6	39.6
Traffic							
Probation	24.4	52.6	59.3	45.2	43.7	48.8	41.1
Parole	0.1	1.7	4.9	7.3	8.3	9.8	11.9
Violence							
Probation	22.5	11.6	9.6	12.3	11.0	10.5	17.8
Parole	18.5	13.8	11.2	14.1	14.3	16.6	20.6
Sex							
Probation	7.6	4.0	2.8	1.9	1.3	1.0	1.0
Parole	10.1	11.0	10.8	6.1	4.5	4.9	5.1
Predelinquency							
Probation	4.3	2.9	2.2	3.1	3.4	2.5	1.4
Parole	9.9	9.1	8.6	10.5	8.2	7.4	11.4
Heinous							
Probation	2.5	1.4	1.1	1.0	0.6	0.8	1.9
Parole	5.9	6.2	7.3	3.6	3.1	3.3	5.5
Drugs							
Probation	—	—	0.3	10.6	9.4	9.9	7.7
Parole	0.2	—	0.5	11.8	14.3	12.4	12.9

Sources: Research and Statistics Section (1966, 72–75; 1971a, 80–83; 1976a, 78–81; 1981a, 68–71; 1986a, 70–73; 1991a, 70–73).

high numbers in the 1970 to 1990 years, while parole admissions had a much more modest gain after 1980. A serious crisis of traffic accidents and fatalities appeared in the years between 1955 and 1970, and a national counter-effort was instigated that brought more traffic offenders to corrections. In 1977 a short-term program increased probation admission from family courts. The family courts also became increasingly involved after 1975 in cases of juvenile drug offenses, especially abuse of organic solvents. Paroles drew few drug abusers, until 1975.

Juvenile violators of laws against traffic misconduct and drug abuse illustrate the principle of marginal deviants becoming unprecedented targets of the juvenile criminal justice system as a consequence of heightened concern about a public crisis. Previously, juvenile and adult drivers who engage in traffic "acrobatics" were tolerated, perhaps sometimes admired. Juvenile and adult drug abusers were tolerated as rather strange persons but not as "real" criminals or delinquents. The escalation of the number of these marginal deviants, plus a sharp decline in the level of public tolerance, has brought legislative changes and revision of public policy that have led to a greater flow of young traffic and drug-law offenders into the juvenile justice system.[6]

When I eliminated the traffic and drug offenses from probation admissions listed in table 6.7, the property offenders gained larger percentage shares of all probation admissions, from 51.2 percent in 1965 to a peak of 61.1 percent in 1985. The adjusted ratios also signal increased numerical superiority for property offenses of probation admissions over parole admissions: 5.87 in 1965, 7.00 in 1970, 9.47 in 1975, 5.89 in 1980, 4.78 in 1985, 4.90 in 1990, and 6.55 in 1995.

Violence held third position, after traffic property and traffic offenses, in the number of probation admissions in 1965. As measured by ratios, probation gained further ascendancy over parole through 1975 and then tapered off. Bodily injury incidents, an offense with a variety of situations and motives for juveniles, accounted for the family courts' willingness to grant the intermediate level of tolerance to violent offenders. The comparison of percentage distributions in table 6.7 shows violent offenses were most strongly represented after 1975 among parole admissions, and, in that respect, the representation among paroles was greater in those years than the representation of violent offenses among probation admissions. Overall, for those years, family courts were especially reluctant to grant probation to violent offenders in general; those juveniles sent to training schools became later candidates for parole.

Juvenile sex offenders recorded even lower ratios that declined over the years. Table 6.7 shows a lower proportion of all probationers who had been involved in sex offenses than the share of all parolees who had been sent to juvenile training schools for sex offenders. The same pattern held for heinous offenses and predelinquency. The family courts preferred case dismissals and probation over referrals to JTSs for predelinquents (see table 5.3), but, as stated previously, the training schools were treated in this matter as refuges for young victims of intolerable conditions in the family or community settings.

Attributes and Experiences of Individuals

Their youth cultivates singular characteristics and experiences that differentiate juvenile probationers from juvenile parolees and both groups from adults. Juvenile parolees (mean age 18.05 years in 1995 admissions) are older on average than juvenile probationers (mean age 17.29 years). Ten percent of the parolees and 5.7 percent of the probationers are less than 16 years old. None of the probationers are older than 19 years, but 15.7 percent of the parolees are in the age group 20 to 22 years because Article 42 of the Offenders Rehabilitation Law authorizes the family court to "fix the term of probationary supervision . . . within the period before the person reaches 23 years of age" (Research and Statistics Section 1996a, 90).

Upon admission in 1995, juvenile parolees were more likely to be unemployed (62.1 percent) than juvenile probationers (21.1 percent), but the term *unemployment* is more dependable for adults than juveniles. Many juveniles, especially the youngest, are not supposed to be full-fledged wage earners, but the data attest to the lower economic position of juvenile parolees. Of them, only 32.9 percent were employed in-come earners, 4 percent were students, and 1 percent engaged in "household work" (presumably family enterprises). Com-paratively, 57.9 percent of the juvenile probationers were employed, 20.2 were students, 0.9 were in household work, and the rest neither employed nor students. The very general description of income status indicates small representation of the well-to-do for both juvenile probationers (2.8 percent) and juvenile parolees (1.8 percent), but the parolees had more in the subaverage category (Research and Statistics Section 1996a, 88).

Juvenile probationers had more schooling, a mean of 10.1 years over 9.5 years for juvenile parolees. Both have few with-out education or completion of only sixth grade. Parolees (62.6 percent) tended to terminate their schooling with graduation from junior high school; only 36.1 percent of the probation-ers did so. Of the probationers, 4.8 percent had dropped out of school before completing junior high school. The proba-tioners had the advantage in attendance of senior high school (62.2 versus 37.3 percent), graduation from senior high school (12.5 versus 2.6 percent), and college attendance (only 1.7 versus .1 percent) (Research and Statistics Section 1996a, 87).

Japanese juveniles on probation or parole tend to be mem-bers of intact families in spite of the popular image of family disorganization spawning delinquency. Of those entering probation in 1995, 62 percent had been living with both par-ents and another 26 percent with either their mother or father in a broken home. Juvenile parolees also had lived with both their parents (54 percent) but were more likely to have been with either the father or mother (34 percent). Only 4 percent of the parolees had been in halfway houses (.2 percent of the probationers) as evidence of a prior contact with the juvenile justice system (Research and Statistics Section 1996a, 86).

Compared to juvenile probationers, a greater proportion of juvenile parolees had had previous experience with the juvenile justice system (see table 6.8). All of those measures

Table 6.8

Previous Exposure to Protective Measures of Juveniles Admitted to Probation or Parole, 1995

Age Categories	Total Numbers[a]	JTS	Probation	Percentage Distribution of Protective Measures		Dismissal of Case Hearing	Dismissal of Case No Hearing	No Record
				Social Agencies				
Juvenile probationers								
Under 16	1,955	0.1	3.9	2.2		14.3	10.3	69.2
16–17	7,700	0.6	14.6	1.5		25.6	15.8	41.9
18–19	9,630	2.6	26.6	0.4		21.4	11.3	37.7
Total	19,285	1.5	19.5	1.0		22.4	13.0	42.6
Juvenile parolees								
Under 16	217	4.6	12.9	22.6		3.7	2.8	53.4
16–17	1,151	11.1	38.9	7.2		9.1	5.9	27.8
18–19	1,816	23.6	46.3	1.9		9.2	4.0	15.0
20–22	592	39.4	38.5	0.5		5.4	4.0	12.2
Total	3,776	21.1	40.9	4.5		8.3	4.5	20.7

Source: Research and Statistics Section (1996a, 91).

[a]Unknown cases are excluded.

are described as "protective measures." The table presents a continuum of decreasing severity of the previous exposure, from JTS at one extreme to dismissal without a hearing by the family court at the other extreme. Probationers had benefited more than parolees in having no previous exposure to the workings of the juvenile justice system; when so exposed, the family courts tended toward dismissal of cases or sending few of them to juvenile training schools. Parolees had had significant experience in training schools, but, as a sign of a rather favorable assessment of earlier family courts, they had even more previous exposure to probation.

For both probationers and parolees, the share without protective measures declines with greater age. The youngest individuals have had the least opportunity for earlier contacts and the greatest possibility of having been referred to social agencies. Both probationer and parolees (especially parolees) have had more exposure to training schools as they move up the age continuum. Parolees have the greater contacts with social agencies, and that was chiefly for the youngest parolees. Probationers show the greater evidence of earlier favorable treatment by the family courts in the form of case dismissals, but the relationships with age was mixed.

Delinquent Groups as Marginal Deviants

The Ministry of Justice publishes statistics on several variables related to four kinds of "delinquent groups" or "juvenile gangs": at schools, in neighborhoods, the bosozoku, and affiliates of the yakuza (professional criminal gangs). The membership of these youth groups hover variously between marginal deviants and outright juvenile criminals. The distinctions between the marginal deviants and outright juvenile criminals are particularly cloudy in Japan. Our immediate interest here is how the distinctions apply to admissions to probation and parole of Japanese juveniles.

Marginal deviants are members of a particular group—the Ministry of Justice identifies four such groups—receiving unusual attention in the given community or society. The members of the marginal group are less the target of attention as members than as individuals per se. The members are "strangers at home" because persons in positions of social power (norm-enunciators) doubt their eligibility for full participation in the benefits of community life. The deviance from accepted behavioral standards is not simply tolerated by the norm-enunciators; rather their conduct is not condemned as being outside the pale of social acceptability. The marginal deviants are not excluded from the social affairs of the community.

Japan presents particular prospects for continued tolerance of marginal deviance—tolerance that springs from the impact of modernization and affluence on the social institutions of Japan, especially on families, schools, and employing organizations. Continued tolerance is part of the analytic equation because of the possibility of redefining a larger proportion of the juvenile marginal deviants into ranks of juveniles treated as young criminals.

Marginal deviants, especially among juveniles, have benefited from the trends of Japanese history and from the philosophy underlying the dispositions of family courts. The imagery of "protective measures" colors the judicial and correctional branches of the juvenile justice system even for referrals to juvenile training schools. More significantly, the Japanese people generally place a degree of trust in their adolescents. As discussed earlier in this chapter, intergenerational conflict is muffled by toleration of contradictions between the general and youth cultures, by the rather superficiality of the expressionistic emphasis of youthful consumerism, and the "soft individualism" of adolescents and young adults.

Table 6.9 relates the four "delinquent groups" to the offenses reported when their members were admitted to juvenile classification homes (JCHs) in 1995. The family courts referred some of the juveniles to JCHs because of the need for diagnostic evaluation. The selection among all juveniles received by the family courts produced a crude sample of the "most problematic personalities" likely to raise special public concern.

Note that, in this crude sample, half of the juveniles were not identified with any delinquent group. Perhaps for at least some of them, the conduct that had brought them to the family courts were symptoms of the status passage from childhood through adolescence to incipient adulthood. Referrals to JCHs suggest the awareness of family court judges of such a possibility. Nevertheless, among these nonmembers of groups, an important share had been sent to the family courts because of involvement in serious crimes. Table 6.9 shows that juveniles without linkage to any delinquent group made up 69 percent of the sex crimes, 62.3 percent of the drug cases, 58.7 percent of the property cases, and 56 percent of the "heinous" cases. Companionate factors were more instrumental in traffic, violent, and predelinquent offenses.

School delinquency, the National Police Agency (1993, 84–86) declares, includes violent acts against teachers and "bullying" defined as giving "pain to one or more particular persons by repeated and continuous attacks on the body of the victim or victims, or by psychological pressure on such victim or victims, such as intimidation by words or acts, harassment and snubbing."

Members of student groups entering JCHs were represented among predelinquents who are primarily considered to be victims of an adverse environment. Their representation among violent crimes was high, mostly bodily injury; only one juvenile was accused of intimidation; larceny was the most numerous offense (Research and Statistics Section 1996c, 64).

Neighborhood groups are creatures of local communities where people live, and their local institutions affect their lives in intimate ways. For the juveniles, intense social relationships may exist outside the social-psychological arena of their families, arenas that in Japan, as well as elsewhere, are expected

Table 6.9

Admissions to Juvenile Classification Homes by Group Affiliations, 1995

Offenses[a]	Number	Group Affiliation				
		Student	Neighborhood	Bosozoku	Criminal	No Group
		Percentage Distribution				
Heinous	518	12	162	30	23	291
Percent	3.9	1.9	5.5	1.1	6.5	4.4
Robbery	480	1.7	5.4	1.0	5.4	3.9
Homicide	38	0.2	0.1	0.1	1.1	0.5
Violent	3,419	212	854	655	154	1,544
Percent	25.8	32.8	28.8	24.9	43.6	23.3
Bodily injury	1,837	19.4	15.5	16.0	20.1	11.4
Extortion	1,201	9.6	10.8	4.1	11.9	10.1
Violence law	217	1.7	1.5	3.1	8.5	0.8
Assault	110	1.7	0.6	1.5	1.4	0.5
Firearms	40	0.2	0.2	0.1	0.8	0.4
Property	4,524	189	1,133	504	41	2,657
Percent	34.2	29.2	38.1	19.2	11.6	40.1
Larceny	4,259	28.0	36.3	18.3	9.4	37.5
Fraud	64	0.2	1.4	0.1	1.1	0.7
Intrusion	109	0.3	1.0	0.4	0.8	1.0

Table 6.9 cont. on next page

Table 6.9 continued

Offenses[a]	Number	Group Affiliation				
		Student	Neighborhood	Bosozoku	Criminal	No Group
Property						
Embezzlement	33	0.5	0.3	0.3	0.3	0.2
Arson	47	0.2	0.1	—	—	0.7
Sex	364	5	86	18	4	251
Percent	2.8	0.7	2.9	0.7	1.2	3.8
Rape	232	0.5	2.6	0.6	0.9	2.0
Indecent assault	114	0.2	0.3	0.1	—	1.5
Drugs	1,643	35	399	103	82	1,024
Percent	12.4	5.4	13.4	3.9	23.2	15.4
Stimulants	860	1.8	5.6	1.5	19.5	8.6
Oganic solvents	767	3.6	7.7	2.4	3.7	6.6
Traffic	1,787	12	125	1,266	13	371
Percent	13.5	1.9	4.2	48.1	3.7	5.6
Predelinquency	977	182	212	54	36	493
Percent	7.4	28.1	7.1	2.1	10.2	7.4
Total offenses	13,232	647	2,971	2,630	353	6,631

Source: Research and Statistics Section (1996c, 64).

[a]Excludes public order and "other" offenses, and unreported gang affiliation with groups.

along with the schools to be the control instruments of social control during adolescence. The large absolute number of JCH referrals from neighborhood groups suggests much of the problems of the juvenile status passage exist in the neighborhood.

JCH staffs emphasize the victimization of the youngsters who are sent to them for psychological diagnoses, but the offenses that bring them to the JCHs are titled slightly toward the property crimes of larceny and fraud, and the violent offenses of bodily injury, extortion, robbery, and rape. Predelinquency is a minor factor, indicating that members of neighborhood groups have higher average ages than student groups. Drug offenses were more prevalent among neighborhood groups and also suggest older average ages. The National Police Agency (1993, 84) reported for 1992 that job-holding juveniles given guidance by the police were 40 percent of the paint thinner sniffers and 47 percent of the stimulant drug abusers.

The bosozoku, as pointed out earlier, dominate juvenile traffic offenses. Sato (1991) describes their modification of motor vehicles to create noise and give them special features. Sato sees the bosozoku (a term meaning "wild tribe") as engaged in "extreme expressiveness and playfulness." Kersten (1993) assesses the bosozoku, along with street youth and the yakuza, as subcultural entities who are particularly noteworthy exceptions to the emphasis on conformity in Japan. From another perspective, the police (National Police Agency 1991, 114) talk of "groups of hot-rodders annoying residents with violent exhaust noise after midnight," intergroup fighting, and "attacks against patrol cars and general citizens' vehicles." "Since 1985," the National Police Agency (1993, 84) concludes, "the ratio of those who have been charged with larceny or bodily injury has been high." The agency also declares "that many juvenile hot-rodders are under the strong influence of *boryokudan*.[7]

In the official view, "delinquent groups" are affiliated with the yakuza (or boryokudan) and are especially problematic because the members are particularly alienated from conventional society in Japan. When precisely applied, the term *gang* implies some sort of recognizable leadership and various roles adapted by followers. For juvenile gangs, the members drop in and drop out as they move through the sequence of juvenile ages. Attitudes favorable to deviance are acquired primarily through companions and by participation in small, intimate groups such as gangs in much the same manner as in law-abiding groups.

JCH admissions of delinquents believed to be affiliated with the yakuza were especially involved in violent and drug offenses. They composed the smallest of the four groups, but these juveniles were well represented in all varieties of violence, including robbery and the very few homicide cases. Drug offenses are especially attributed to the yakuza. The "delinquent group" tended to be older on average; that pattern is implied by the heavy involvement in stimulant drugs as characteristic of adults.

Companionship and Probation or Parole

The Ministry of Justice publishes statistical data on previous membership of juvenile probationers and parolees in various groups. The kinds of memberships are reported according to the three programs for probationers: general probation, a short-term program for juvenile traffic offenders on probation, and a short-term program for other young probationers. Juvenile parolees are distinguished according to the three programs to which they were assigned while in JTSs (see table 6.10).

Two-thirds of the probationers had no previous group affiliation. The bosozoku were most numerous among group members as an effect of the probationers assigned to the short-term probation program for traffic offenders. Neighborhood groups were in second place, and a few young probationers had affiliations with fellow pupils in schools; their numbers are few in spite of the recent concern about bullying at schools. Associations with yakuza were very exceptional among probationers.

The general probation program drew the largest number

Table 6.10

Juvenile Probationers and Parolees by Pre-Admission Affiliation with Delinquent Groups, 1995

Programs	Number	Group Affiliation Before Admission					
		Student	Neighborhood	Bosozoku	Criminal Affiliates	Other Groups	No Group
		Percentage Distribution					
Juvenile probation admissions							
Total	19,293	3.6	12.4	17.6	0.9	1.5	64.0
General probation	8,893	5.2	20.1	13.2	1.5	2.4	57.6
Short traffic	7,699	0.3	2.5	26.5	0.3	0.3	70.1
Short special	2,701	8.1	14.9	7.0	0.3	2.1	67.6
Juvenile parole admissions							
Total	3,771	2.0	19.0	30.5	6.9	1.9	39.7
JTS long	2,148	1.9	19.6	23.5	9.8	1.8	43.4
JTS short	1,307	2.2	19.5	36.4	3.8	2.0	36.1
JTS special	316	1.6	12.7	53.5	0.6	2.2	29.4

Source: Research and Statistics Section (1996a, 92).

of probationers, although challenged by the short-term program for traffic offenders. Nonmembers were numerous but short of the share of juveniles in the other two probation programs. Neighborhood and delinquent groups were at a maximum, but delinquent groups drew very limited membership.

The short-term traffic program had 70 percent of its probationers without a group membership, and most of the affiliations devoted to the bosozoku, an obvious connection between probation and traffic offenses of adolescents. The selection of probationers for the special program also produced a high percentage of nonaffiliations. Neighborhood and student groups held most of the group members.

Juvenile parole admissions were associated with a lower level of nonaffiliations (40 versus the 64 percent for probationers). Perhaps affiliations were linked with more serious transgressions that sent juveniles to JTS. Delinquent groups were represented more than among probationers but at a modest level because the long-term stay at training school received a noteworthy share of those juveniles having some connection with the yakuza. The bosozoku were especially numerous among parolees generally, especially in the JTS special program. Except for that program, parole matched the general probation program for neighborhood affiliations.

Number of Participants and Locale

The companionate factor in juvenile delinquency can also be measured by the number of persons involved in the delinquent incident, whether or not a group affiliation marked the incident. Table 6.11 shows that a third of the juveniles entering JCHs in 1995 had been apprehended alone and another 22 percent had one companion, but some 30 percent had three or more companions.

The mean number of codefendants singles out several offenses for being exceptions to the companionate factor: indecent assault, predelinquency, and homicide. Homicides

Table 6.11

Codefendants by Offense in Admissions to Juvenile Classification Homes, 1995

Offense Categories	Total Admissions	Mean Number	Number of Codefendants				
			None	One	Two	Three or More	"Many"
Heinous	521	2.8	84	94	120	222	1
Percent	100	—	16.1	18.1	23.0	42.6	0.2
Robbery	483	2.94	11.4	19.0	24.9	44.5	0.2
Homicide	38	0.97	76.3	5.3	—	18.4	—
Violent	3,436	2.78	772	759	620	1,171	114
Percent	100	—	22.5	22.1	18.0	34.1	3.3
Bodily injury	1,845	3.08	22.8	17.4	15.7	40.3	3.8
Extortion	1,206	1.95	21.3	32.2	23.5	22.9	0.1
Violence law	217	4.48	6.4	15.7	14.7	54.4	8.8
Assault	113	4.68	31.9	12.4	8.8	26.5	20.4
Property	4,558	1.76	1,399	1,376	855	896	32
Percent	100	—	30.7	30.2	18.7	19.7	0.7
Larceny	4,292	1.80	29.7	30.5	18.8	20.3	0.7
Intrusion	109	1.24	37.6	29.4	17.4	14.7	0.9
Fraud	65	1.23	36.9	30.8	23.1	9.2	—
Embezzlement	33	1.54	60.6	21.2	6.1	9.1	3.0

Table 6.11 cont. on next page

Table 6.11 continued

Offense Categories	Total Admissions	Mean Number	None	One	Two	Three or More	"Many"
					Number of Codefendants		
Sex	370	2.39	153	27	41	146	3
Percent	100	—	41.3	7.3	11.1	39.5	0.8
Rape	232	3.42	18.9	5.6	16.4	58.2	0.9
Indecent assault	116	0.55	81.1	8.6	1.7	8.6	—
Drugs	1,649	1.08	722	580	196	146	5
Percent	100	—	43.8	35.2	11.9	8.8	0.3
Stimulants	864	1.04	40.5	40.7	11.2	7.2	0.4
Organic solvents	769	1.12	47.2	29.3	12.6	10.7	0.2
Traffic	1,792	6.47	509	63	19	652	549
Percent	100	—	28.4	3.5	1.1	36.4	30.6
Predelinquency	979	0.66	846	59	17	30	27
Percent	100	—	86.4	6.0	1.7	3.1	2.8
Total	13,789	2.54	4,705	3,053	1,910	3,364	757
Percent	100	—	34.1	22.1	13.9	24.4	5.5

Source: Research and Statistics Section (1996c, 62).

[a]"Unknown" cases were excluded.

were few in number, but some incidents involved three or more juveniles. Predelinquency and indecent assaults were more numerous but were even more non-companionate. Of 979 predelinquents, only 74 (7.6 percent) had two or more codefendants. Of the 116 incidents of indecent assault, only 10.3 percent had two or more codefendants.

The numerous property and drug offenses were intermediate in exhibiting companionship. Stimulants exceeded organic solvents in having one companion, but multiple companions gave organic solvents the higher mean number of companions. Among property offenses, larceny drew the largest number of codefendants.

Traffic offenders had the highest mean number (6.47) of fellow participants because of the groupism of the bosozoku. Unlike indecent assault, rape tended to be a group activity; 58.2 percent of the incidents involved three or more juveniles. The number of codefendants in violent offense were raised by Unlawful Assembly with Dangerous Weapons (mean of 4.68), the Law for Punishment of Acts of Violence (mean of 4.48), and bodily injury (mean of 3).

In addition to several groupings displayed in table 6.11, the Ministry of Justice publishes data (table 6.12) on the locations where juvenile offenders participated with fellows in delinquent incidents. Table 6.12 deals only with incidents involving more than one juvenile. The locales reported by the Ministry of Justice are schools, places of amusement (recreation), places of employment, relatives (family setting), a delinquent group, an institution to which juveniles had been referred (inmates), and a chance contact (no previous acquaintance with fellow participants).

The most important settings (85.2 percent) were recreation and delinquent groups. School mates were a distant third, and the remaining four settings rather trivial. The so-called leisure activities are supposed to be pregnant with juvenile opportunities for questionable conduct. Japan is not an exception. For several offense categories, recreation mates have held more than their percentage share (58.4) of all JCH admissions: drugs 74.8 percent, sex 72.7 percent, property 72.2, predelinquents 60.6 percent, and violent offenses 58.3 percent. Although recreation mates take over a large proportion (67.6 percent) of stimulant drugs, they tend even more toward organic solvents (82.7 percent) in the fashion of young drug abusers in Japan. The dominance of indecent assault (85 percent) is even greater. Juvenile involvement in robbery is greater than homicide for heinous crimes; recreation mates also are the leaders among the several group settings. Their dominance persists for property offenses because of intrusion (similar to housebreaking), fraud, and larceny. Larceny, a collection of petty thefts, is common among juveniles; here, we find it also is especially active in the course of relationships of friends in the quest of pleasure. In JCH admissions, predelinquents were largely (86.6 percent) in the recreation and school settings. This pattern is consistent with the low average age of predelinquents among JCH referrals: 15.5 years compared with 17.3 years for non-predelinquents (Research and Statistics Section 1996c, 40–41).

Delinquent groups, were heavily concentrated in traffic offenses (90.6 percent). Homicides were few in absolute numbers of JCH admissions, but they were proportionately important for members of the delinquent groups. The delinquent groups also had a heavy proportion of violations of the Law for Punishment of Acts of Violence and Unlawful Assembly with Dangerous Weapons (assault), as already noted for table 6.9.

The schools are in third place, but far behind, after recreational and delinquent groups, as settings for the appearance of delinquency. The high number of predelinquents among the school-based delinquents suggests a larger proportion of the youngest pupils. Probably what the police call "initial-type delinquency" operates within this context: shoplifting, bicycle theft, motorcycle theft, stealing, and lost property (National Police Agency 1993, 82–83). Initial-type delinquency has gained in ratio of all delinquency, the police warn,

Table 6.12

Group Setting of Offenses by Codefendants Admitted to Juvenile Classification Homes, 1995

Offense Categories	School Mates	Recreation Mates	Work Mates	Relatives	Delinquent Group	Inmates	Chance Contact
Heinous	39	314	13	4	57	4	2
Percent	9.0	72.5	3.0	0.9	13.2	0.9	0.5
Robbery	9.2	73.6	2.8	1.0	12.0	1.0	0.4
Homicide	—	22.2	11.1	—	66.7	—	—
Violent	281	1,536	78	33	667	18	20
Percent	10.7	58.3	3.0	1.2	25.3	0.7	0.8
Bodily injury	10.7	53.7	3.8	1.3	29.4	0.4	0.7
Extortion	11.2	72.3	2.2	1.4	10.5	1.4	1.0
Violence law	7.5	35.5	1.0	0.5	55.0	—	0.5
Assault	12.0	33.3	1.3	—	53.4	—	—
Property	266	2,226	92	73	323	71	31
Percent	8.6	72.2	3.0	2.4	10.5	2.3	1.0
Larceny	8.8	72.1	3.0	2.3	10.6	2.4	0.8
Intrusion	1.5	81.8	—	3.0	9.1	1.5	3.0
Fraud	5.3	73.7	2.6	2.6	5.3	—	—

Table 6.12 cont. on next page

Table 6.12 continued

Offense Categories	School Mates	Recreation Mates	Work Mates	Relatives	Delinquent Group	Inmates	Chance Contact
Sex	15	154	10	—	27	3	3
Percent	7.1	72.7	4.7	—	12.7	1.4	1.4
Rape	6.9	73.3	4.3	—	13.9	1.6	—
Indecent assault	10	85.0	—	—	5.0	—	10.5
Embezzlement	7.7	46.1	15.4	7.7	23.1	—	—
Drugs	38	608	38	13	60	7	49
Percent	4.7	74.8	4.7	1.6	7.4	0.8	6.0
Stimulants	3.8	67.6	6.2	1.7	9.3	0.5	10.9
Organic solvents	5.2	82.7	3.1	1.5	5.4	1.3	0.8
Traffic	10	107	—	1	1,158	1	2
Percent	0.8	8.4	—	0.0	90.6	0.0	0.2
Predelinquency	33	77	—	1	8	6	2
Percent	26	60.6	—	0.8	6.3	4.7	1.6
Total number	702	5,160	249	129	2,363	113	113
Percent	7.9	58.4	2.8	1.5	26.8	1.3	1.3

Source: Research and Statistics Section (1996c, 63).

Note: Excludes lone defendants, "other" codefendants, and no codefendants.

because of more illegal parking of bicycles and motorcycles, heightened vigilance of the clerks against shoplifting, and the erosion of juvenile morality. The relatively high proportion of property offenses is relevant for school-based offenses. The specifics of robbery, extortion, and bodily injury are so broad that the school-based incidents could be attributed to a premature quest for material goods.

Work mates apparently were too old for predelinquency and avoided traffic violations. Otherwise, their variety is suggested by a high incidence of embezzlement (an occupation-related offense in this instance) and the violence of homicide and rape. Stimulant abuse was more characteristic than organic solvents.

Chance acquaintanceships and inmate codefendants were least in numerical importance. Stimulant drug abuse stood out as the basis of the chance contacts. Taking illegal means of gaining an economic advantage (fraud) lends itself to casual relationships. Inmates in various institutions engaged primarily in offenses against property, but, a few of them were treated as predelinquents. Their small numerical representation among the codefendants stands in contrast to the usual image of "inmates" being especially disreputable.

7
Supervision in the Japanese Fashion

REGARDLESS OF THE OPERATIVE PHILOSOPHY and method-
ology of community-oriented corrections, the merits are tested
in the actualities of case supervision. The supervisor and probationer or parolee meet with one another as flesh-and-blood
human beings in the complexities of social interaction. Each
party has his or her self-interests, biographical background,
and personal characteristics. One represents official authority;
the other is subject to that authority but plays a vital role in determining whether the period of supervision will have a satisfactory outcome for the agency, the supervisor, and the client.

Supervisors usually are thrust into unfamiliar situations
when they enter the social world of their clients. Radest (1993,
117) contrasts being at "home" versus becoming a "tourist"
in another person's social world: "Generally, we have dependable ground on which to stand as long as we remain at
home. . . . Leaving home, however, we experience the anxiety of relativism. We step aside as observers and enter as visitors from another place."

The merits of community-oriented corrections are tested
in case supervision. The decision making of the courts for probationers and parole boards for parolees is being inspected
pragmatically. The rehabilitative claims of correctional institution must pass muster when parolees confront the realities
of being restored to community life. Can and will the probationers and parolees accept their responsibilities? Is the supervisor capable of striking a balance between control and the
client's legitimate needs? Should supervision be based on
cynicism about the client's capability for character reform or

261

on humanitarian concern for the disadvantaged client? Is there the possible match between the supervisor and supervisee in personal characteristics and perspectives? Can parolees and probationers be treated as equivalents?

The Involuntary Client and Probationary Supervision

Supervision in the community can be conceived as interaction between flesh-and-blood actors. In studying this process, Thibault and Kelley (1969, 21–24) postulate how members of a dyad (a two-person relationship) evaluate the outcomes of a transaction and whether or not they persist in the relationship. One evaluative criterion measures outcome satisfaction. The second evaluative criterion emphasizes the existence of alternative relationships available to the dyad member for deciding whether to remain in the present relationship. If the outcome falls below the lowest level of acceptability by the second criterion, the actor should be expected to leave the relationship. But such departure hinges on the availability for the actor of the alternative opportunities that are superior to those of the present relationship.

The relevance to probationary supervision appears when Thibault and Kelley turn to *nonvoluntary* relationships in which the outcome of the interaction is less than satisfactory for the actors, but they are forced to stay regardless of their preference. "The person remains in relationships of this sort," Thibault and Kelley (1969, 169) say, "only because heavy costs are in some manner associated with being in better ones." Rooney (1992, 6–7) distinguishes between the *involuntary client* and the *mandated client*. The involuntary client is forced to seek, or feels the pressure to accept, contact with a helping professional. The pressure comes from agencies, other referral sources, family members, and events outside those sources. The mandated client must work with a practitioner because of a legal mandate or court order.

American helping professionals prefer to believe that all their clients come to them ready to participate actively in the healing process; they tend to ignore involuntary clients or consider them to be in a state that is preliminary to becoming voluntary clients. Rooney explains that tendency in three ways. First, the greatest source of prestige of the helping profession is the practice of psychotherapy with voluntary clients. Second, psychotherapy theorists ignore the power the healer holds over the healed. Third, some theorists have argued that a counseling relationship cannot be maintained when the healer has authority over the client.

Probationary supervision (including parole) is an exercise of a flesh-and-blood relationship between the supervisor and the "mandated clients." The backgrounds, personalities, and perspectives of both parties influence the outcome, but, unlike some social transactions in the community, the client has been forced into the relationship. The probationers—and probably even more so for parolees—have exceptionally grave doubts that the relationship with the supervisor will be a happy one for them but, if they have any expectation about their future fate, are forced to stay within the relationship until supervision ends. The costs of doing else would exceed any advantage of deserting the relationship. The mandated clients differ from one another along a range of efforts to meet the conditions intended to qualify them as "proper citizens." The efforts range from sincere dedication through lip-service adjustment to mere manipulation for the moment.

The supervisors also differ from one another in background, personality, and perspective. American research has isolated at least two extreme types of parole officers: the "punitive officer," who vacillates between protecting the parolee from adverse conditions and protecting the community from the parolee, and the "welfare officer," who tries to move the parolee toward individual adjustment within the limits of the client's capacity (see Irwin 1970, 163–64).

Supervision of "Mandated Clients" in Japan

The interrelationships between the Japanese "mandated clients" and their probationary supervisors are attuned to the particulars of their culture and social patterns. Jedlicka (1990, 131–32) puts it rather simplistically: The Japanese "still know [believe] that they are God's children and that there is a unique purpose to their being on this planet." He argues that Japanese children grow up "firmly subscribing to a national cultural view that they have internalized." The oyabun-kobun relationship and its supporting principles of giri press the supervisor and client to adopt "brotherly" or "father-son" roles. Social ties are along the vertical rather than the horizontal dimension through attachments of oyabun (persons of superior rank: parent, patron, boss, and so on) with the kobun (persons of subordinate rank: child, client, employee, and so on) (Nakane 1984, 24–26, 44–45).

In a very general way, both the supervisors and "mandated clients" in Japan differ significantly in background, personality, and perspectives as they interact with one another. Probationers are more likely than parolees to approach sincerely the obligations of supervision. The unsophisticated juvenile may raise problems but, unlike the experienced criminal, usually will avoid mere pretended conformity and artful manipulation. The vocationally inept and disorganized personality will aggravate difficulties of finding them a place in the community.

Five categories of supervisees are authorized by the Offender Rehabilitation Law (1949), the Law for Probationary Supervision of Persons under Suspension of Execution of Sentences (1954), and the Antiprostitution Law (1958): juvenile probationers, adult probationers, training school parolees,

Table 7.1

Admissions to Community-Oriented Corrections, 1950–1995

Years	Total Admissions	Juvenile Probation	Juvenile Parole	Adult Probation	Adult Parole
			Percentage Distribution of Cases		
1950	59,739	22.2	5.2	0.4	72.2
1955	61,265	27.9	12.0	7.1	57.0
1960	71,554	34.1	10.9	11.9	43.1
1965	62,254	45.3	10.1	13.4	31.2
1970	55,319	49.5	5.7	12.5	32.3
1975	44,958	47.6	3.5	15.7	33.2
1980	83,649	67.3	4.9	9.6	18.2
1985	101,971	70.0	5.5	7.0	17.5
1990	97,801	75.5	4.4	4.9	15.2
1995	71,851	71.1	5.2	6.8	16.9
			Age-Specific Rates per 100,000 Population		
1950	107.5	128.0	30.0	0.5	95.4
1955	99.7	161.4	69.6	8.6	63.8
1960	107.0	225.6	72.1	15.2	55.0
1965	82.8	218.3	48.8	13.4	31.2
1970	68.7	257.7	29.7	9.9	25.6
1975	52.1	224.6	16.7	9.2	19.5
1980	92.0	574.6	41.8	9.9	18.7
1985	105.2	651.4	50.9	8.3	20.7
1990	95.3	622.8	36.6	5.3	16.4
1995	67.0	481.9	35.7	5.0	12.5

Sources: Shikita and Tsuchiya (1990, 374); Research and Statistics Section (1996c, 54–55).

prison parolees, and women's guidance home parolees. "Probationary supervision" in Japan includes management of parolees as well as probationers by the "probation offices."

Admissions to women's guidance homes have vanished, ending such paroles. The Antiprostitution Law was framed to suppress street prostitution by prohibiting solicitation; loitering and following a prospective partner in public places; calling attention to the service; and recruiting a girl by force, intimidation, or other influences (Koshi 1970). However, the nature of commercial sex has moved away from street prostitution, and, from a peak in 1960, admissions to women's guidance homes dropped to zero in 1991.[1]

The supervisory caseload has increased rather erratically in the forty-five years since community-oriented corrections in the modern form came to Japan (see table 7.1). Juvenile probationers have accomplished the most noteworthy and consistent increase. Adult parolees held the dominant share of cases in the decade after World War II, but thereafter juvenile probationers took over. Short-term probation for juvenile traffic offenders has been very influential. Adult parolees have been in second place, behind juvenile probationers, since about 1960 but, along with juvenile parolees and adult probationers, have lost percentage share rather consistently.

The age-specific rates per 100,000 Japanese in the given age-category measures whether or not the caseload has kept pace with the changes in the pool of all Japanese who possibly could have become probationers or parolees. Juvenile probationers have more than kept pace over the decades. The pattern for juvenile parolees tilted upward until 1965; thereafter, it has been erratic. Adult probationers followed suit but at a considerably lower level. Adult parolees started very high, but their rate of decline was sharpest.

Procedures for Supervision in Japan

Juveniles may be placed on probation by the family courts for at least two years or until they reach the age of twenty years. The directors of probation offices have the authority to discharge them from supervision prior to those limits. If the probationers violate the conditions for probation, the directors ask the family court to make a new disposition. Paroles are decided by seven regional parole boards; supervision is usually until the juvenile parolees become twenty years of age. When the director of the probation office recommends, the board may authorize an earlier discharge from supervision.

When parole conditions are violated, the director of the probation office asks the family court to recommit the juvenile to the training school or to issue a revocation.

Criminal courts place adults on probation through suspension of the execution of sentences already pronounced. The court sets the period of supervision from one to five years. The regional parole board may provisionally suspend adult probation, but there is no special provision, as for juvenile probationers, for early termination of supervision. When probation conditions are violated, the director of the probation office may apply to the criminal court, through the public prosecutor, for a revocation and the court's determination of a new disposition.

The parole boards authorize paroles from adult prisons with parole supervision lasting until the end of the prison sentence that had been set by the sentencing court. Pardon is the only means for ending parole supervision before that time.[2] The parole board may revoke a parole upon application to the director of the probation office. Revocation sends the adult parolee back to prison for the entire length of the original parole period.

The Offenders Rehabilitation Law, Article 18, specifies "the business" of probation offices to be (1) probationary supervision and (2) "prevention of offenses" through their responsibility "to indoctrinate and guide the public to arouse their opinion, to make efforts to improve social environments and to promote the activities of the local residents which aim at the prevention of offenses."

When probation is granted, the individual is expected to report immediately to the probation office. Parolees are told to report within forty-eight hours after leaving prison. The professional probation officer (PPO) for the area of supervision interviews the probationer or parolee. The PPO prepares a summary of the case record and a treatment plan. The case summary is developed from the information provided by any police report available, by the court for probationers, by a juvenile classification home (when available), or by the prison or juvenile training school for parolees. Copies of the case summary and treatment plan are mailed to the volunteer probation officer (VPO) whom the PPO selects for the case. Usually, the PPO has only an hour's interview with the client to determine the best match of VPO and client in terms of personality characteristics of each.

VPOs meet with their clients in the VPO's home, the client's residence, workplace, or elsewhere. To avoid unnecessary public demonstration of supervision, the privacy of the residences are preferred. The client is expected to meet the VPO two or three times a month. The frequency and mode of contacts vary among cases. The VPO submit a standardized monthly report to the PPO. To assist the RPB's study of a parole application, the VPOs investigate the circumstances for the prisoner's return to the community. The Volunteer Probation Officer Law calls upon the VPOs to promote crime prevention by working with public and private organizations.

Previous Exposure to Criminal Justice Agencies

Presumedly, repeated apprehension for law violations raises chances for imprisonment, but criminal justice policy in Japan reduces those chances, especially when the offender expresses repentance and tries to reduce the impact of the offense upon the victim. That policy operates within the offices of public prosecutors to reduce significantly the flow of adult defendants to the courts. The courts also practice leniency through suspension of sentences. The family courts follow that policy through a range of dispositions other than to juvenile training schools.

That policy brings relatively unpromising candidates[3] for fundamental behavioral change to the probation offices as probationers or parolees. The difficulties of supervising experienced offenders are raised when the caseloads of

Table 7.2

Juveniles Admitted to Probation or Parole by Their Previous Exposure to Protective Measures, 1995

Programs or Ages of Juveniles	Number of Juveniles	Previous Exposure to Protective Measures					
		Training Schools	Probation	Social Agencies	Case Dismissals		No Record
					Hearings	No Hearings	
		Percentage Distribution					
Juvenile Probation							
General Long Program	8,891	2.64	18.30	1.89	22.75	14.43	39.99
Traffic Short Program	7,694	0.75	25.55	0.27	21.34	9.74	42.35
General Short Program	2,700	0.08	6.18	0.48	24.07	17.37	51.82
Under 16	1,955	0.10	3.89	2.15	14.32	10.33	69.21
16–17	7,700	0.57	14.62	1.51	25.57	15.78	41.95
18–19	9,630	2.59	26.56	0.46	21.45	11.26	37.68
Total	19,285	1.53	19.50	1.05	22.37	12.97	42.58
Juvenile Parole							
JTS Long Program	2,155	32.53	34.48	6.26	6.26	3.39	17.08
JTS Short General	1,305	6.90	50.88	2.60	10.04	4.75	24.83
JTS Short Special	316	2.22	43.35	0.32	14.56	11.39	28.16
Under 16	217	4.61	12.90	22.58	3.69	2.76	53.46
16–17	1,151	11.04	38.92	7.21	9.12	5.91	27.80
18–19	1,816	23.57	46.25	1.93	9.20	4.02	15.03
20–22	592	39.36	38.51	0.51	5.41	4.05	12.16
Total	3,776	21.14	40.89	4.50	8.26	4.53	20.68

Source: Research and Statistics Section (1996a, 91).

Note: Unreported cases are excluded.

probationers and parolees carry a history of repeated acts of leniency by the several agencies of criminal justice. The Ministry of Justice publishes statistics on the previous contacts of probationers and parolees, admitted to the programs in 1995, to the juvenile and adult criminal justice agencies (see table 7.2).

Juvenile probationers and parolees, because of their youth, have had more limited chances to become familiar with adult corrections. There has been no imprisonment, and adult probation is very rare. Fines—almost all for traffic offenses—are numerous but have been applied to chiefly to ages eighteen and nineteen years (Research and Statistics Section 1996a, 90). Their lack of exposure approaches 100 percent, with fines absorbing almost all of the remainder. The juvenile justice system speaks of "protective measures" to connote a policy preference for meeting clients needs rather than serving only community security. The much larger probation caseload than the parole caseload suggests a commitment to that preference. Forty-three percent of the juvenile probationers, compared to 21 percent of the juvenile parolees, had no record of earlier protective measures, but the difference lies in the kinds of prior protective measures. Probationers were more likely to have benefited by dismissals with or without a hearing. Parolees had greater exposure to juvenile training school and the implication of earlier doubts of family courts. Yet, they also had a record of greater referrals to probation and, slightly, to social agencies caring for the young.

Adults had a record of less exposure to protective measures and that exposure was limited to juvenile training schools and juvenile probation. The record of prior exposure to the adult system was very strong; only 35.2 percent of the adult probationers and 14 percent of the adult parolees had avoided prior contacts with adult courts and corrections (see "total number" column in table 7.3). Parolees were inclined heavily toward imprisonment and marginally toward probation. Probationers had a more modest background of suspended sentences without probation and fines, and a slight advantage for suspended prosecution.

The Ministry of Justice publishes statistics on the previous exposure to the adult criminal justice system by adult probationers and parolees (see table 7.3). Previous exposure could be imprisonment, probation, release unconditionally into the community (suspended prison sentence without probationary supervision), or fines. Of all the individual's previous contact with the criminal justice system, the table lists the most rigorous in his or her history.

The kinds of previous exposure are arrayed in table 7.3 along a continuum from greatest rigor (imprisonment) to fines. "No record" refers to those probationers or parolees who had no previous exposure, at least as far as the classification workers of the Correction Bureau could determine. The "no record" supervisees are outside the continuum, but they measure the affect of "first offenders."

Table 7.3 includes the ratios: the number of parolees per probationer. The ratios capture the relative importance of parole and probation in previous exposure to an array of sanctions imposed by the criminal justice system for adults. For all sanctions, the ratio of 2.55 means that for every one of the 4,679 probationers (admitted to probation in 1995), there were 2.55 parolees (11,927 admitted to parole in 1995). The ratio is a summary statistic that permits us to examine that relationship between adult parole and adult probation in regard to a variety of sanctions imposed by the criminal justice system. As will be considered below, the age-specific ratios in table 7.3 will enable us to explore the variations by age of individuals in previous exposure to the various sanctions.

The "total number" column in table 7.3 traces the previous history of exposures to the sanctions for adult probationers and parolees, respectively. The two distributions of previous sanctions are instructive. Parolees are more likely than probationers (51.1 versus 11.5 percent) to have been imprisoned previous to the last sentence. A record for previous imprisonment increases chances for another term in prison and, perhaps, subsequent parole. Parolees also are slightly more likely to have been on probation (9.1 versus 6.3 percent). On

Table 7.3

*Adults Admitted to Probation and Parole by Age and
Previous Exposure to the Criminal Justice System, 1995*

Criminal Justice Measures[a]	Total Number	Ages at Admission to Probation or Parole						
		Under 22	23–29	30–39	40–49	50–59	60+	Mean Age
Adult Probation								
Prisons	536	2	7	118	187	159	63	47.9
Probation	295	9	54	80	90	47	15	40.6
No probation	1,299	93	358	358	295	159	36	37.0
Fines	830	187	288	160	120	58	17	32.0
No record	1,719	793	538	213	103	58	14	27.1
Total number[b]	4,679	1,084	1,245	929	795	481	145	34.0
Percent	100	23.2	26.6	19.8	17.0	10.3	3.1	—
Adult Parole								
Prisons	6,097	17	711	1,610	1,969	1,318	472	43.8
Probation	1,088	33	460	290	192	96	17	34.5
No probation	2,254	40	742	654	519	246	53	36.9
Fines	801	29	203	182	212	136	39	39.8
No record	1,687	180	483	386	335	212	91	37
Total number[b]	11,927	299	2,599	3,122	3,227	2,008	672	40.4
Percent	100	2.5	21.8	26.2	27.1	16.8	5.6	—
Ratios of Parolees to Probationers								
Prisons	11.37	8.5	10.16	13.64	10.53	8.29	7.49	—
Probation	3.69	3.67	8.52	3.62	2.13	2.04	1.13	—
No probation	1.73	0.43	2.07	1.83	1.76	1.55	1.47	—
Fines	0.96	0.15	0.70	1.14	1.77	2.34	2.29	—
No record	0.98	0.23	0.90	1.81	3.25	3.65	6.50	—
Totals	2.55	0.27	2.09	3.36	4.06	4.17	4.63	—

Source: Research and Statistics Section (1996a, 90).

[a]Suspended prosecution is excluded because it is not a criminal justice sanction.
[b]Unreported cases are excluded.

average, parolees are older and more apt to have benefited from probation on an earlier confrontation with the courts. "No probation" means that when the court suspended a prison sentence for an earlier offense, the defendant was returned to the free community without probationary supervision. Current probationers had previously experienced this level of leniency to a greater degree than current parolees (18.9 versus 27.8 percent), but both groups had benefited. When their criminal justice records were limited to monetary fines, again the probationers exceeded the parolees (6.7 versus 17.7 percent). The probationers did best (14.2 versus 36.7 percent) when absence of any previous contact with criminal justice was considered. All in all, as the expectations for probation systems would require, Japanese probationers presented a more satisfactory previous record than parolees, even though most of these individuals had failed to meet the principles of a justice system that enunciated a policy of leniency when feasible.

Table 7.3 lists the relationship between age on probation and parole, respectively, and goes on to distinguish the relationship for each of five criminal justice sanctions. The relationship is especially relevant for adults because juvenile probationers and parolees have a much more restricted range of ages. Half of all probationers are less than thirty years of age, but fines (those ages hold 57.0 percent of all fines) and "no record" (those ages hold 77.4 percent of all probationers without previous exposure) are most responsible. For the young adults, previous imprisonment was grossly underrepresented. They were better represented among probationers exposed either to probation or were unconditionally returned to the community when judges suspended a prison sentence. The young adults had a smaller share (24.3 percent) of all parolees but outdid the young adult probationers in their proportionate share of previous exposure to imprisonment and probation.

The age-specific ratios for all supervisees present a consistent increase from a ratio of .27 (probation is in control) for ages less than twenty-two years to a ratio of 4.63 for ages sixty years and over. As age rises, the number of parolees narrows its numerical disadvantage when compared with the number of probationers. The older the individual, the odds increase that parolees will exceed probationers in the numbers being supervised by the probation offices. That pattern varies among the various criminal justice measures.

The pattern is very strong for individuals who had no contact previous to the current probation or the prison sentence from which they have just been paroled. The fundamental criminal justice policy of Japan makes for a low and declining imprisonment rate. Among the criteria is the tendency to imprison the serial offenders—those who appear repetitively in the rolls of criminal justice agencies. Recidivism takes time to repeat offenses. Young adults are more likely to appear for the first time. The possibility of being a first offender declines with age, but, of those older adults who do offend, the odds of a prison sentence increase.

Fines are the least stringent measure and present a consistent increase in ratios, but less strong than the "no record" group. Fines draw the least loss of reputation for the offender and are less likely to be the sole previous exposure, but they would be more characteristic of probationers. Parole offenders experiencing only previous fines usually are considered officially to be first offenders, but, to have been on parole, they usually were involved in a comparatively serious crime. The ratios reflect increased importance of parole with advancing age. That trend reflects the tendency of older adults, proportional among all offenders, to be more involved in offenses meriting imprisonment culminating in parole.

Previous imprisonment was less likely to merit probation over repeated imprisonment and later parole. The ratios for all sanctions reflect growing reliance on parole with increased age, but the trend slacked off for ages fifty years and more. Both probation and parole lost similarly in absolute numbers, but the decline was greater for probationers. That scenario also holds for the two versions of suspended prison sentence— probation and return of the offender unconditionally to the community. Of the two measures, unconditional release was most likely to gain probation in a recent appearance before a judge. That advantage peaked for those in their twenties but faded progressively in higher ages.

The situation for elderly persons (those over 50 years of

age, according to Japanese policy) merits special consideration. For all kinds of criminal justice sanctions, the number of parolees per probationer rises consistently from .27 for ages less than 23 years to reach 4.63 for ages 60 years and more. However, the ratios for previous imprisonment drop after ages 30 to 39 years. After age 22 years, "probation" and "no probation" follow suit. That leaves "fines" and "no record" to generate the high ratio (a particular emphasis on parole) for the elderly persons now on probation or parole.

The importance of "fines" and "no record" alerts us to the so-called "latecomers to crime." These are the older persons who first become clients for criminal justice processing without a record of previous lawbreaking. However, these latecomers often were involved in crimes that, in spite of their favorable previous conduct, motivated the courts to order imprisonment ending in parole.

Repeated Admissions to the Programs

The number of times on probation or parole is a clue, first, to the level of previous experience with community-oriented corrections and, second, to the leniency granted repeated offenders who were so benefited when appearing before courts or regional parole boards. Parolees had had greater previous experience than probationers, probably because, when compared with outright return of prisoners to the streets, parole provides supervision of even the dedicated criminal at least during the initial period of release.

Adults admitted to parole in 1995 had been on parole a mean of 2.76 times,[4] and 35.3 percent were on parole for the first time (Research and Statistics Section 1996a, 89). Ages 18 to 30 years averaged 2.47 admissions to parole; the average dropped to 2.39 for ages 30–39 years and then gradually increased to 3.76 for parolees aged more than 59 years. In a reverse pattern, the percentage share of first experience with parole confirmed the relationship between age and prior experience with parole. Ages 18–29 years had 35.7 percent on parole for the first time. The percentage rose to 37.4 for ages 30–39 years and then slipped progressively to reach 29.6 for parolees aged 60 years and over.

Adult probationers would have more previous experience with probation than with parole if we may properly assume that sentencing courts prefer probation over imprisonment. Since Japanese courts would return convicted defendants to the free community without supervision when feasible, are judges likely to continue to place offenders on probation even when they have been on probation previously?

It appears that they are, but to a more limited extent than regional parole boards put ex-parolees on parole again. In 1995 the admitted adult probationers had a rate of 1.78 admissions (including the current admission). The 18–29 years group had a rate of 1.91, dropping to 1.55 for the 30–39 years group, and followed by an increase to 2.10 for parolees aged over 59 years. The adult probationers also were less likely than adult parolees in percentage share (56.3) of persons on the program for the first time. The youngest adults were least likely to be on probation for the first time (48.2 percent); other age groups hovered around 65 percent, except the 56 percent for those over 59 years of age.

As expected, juveniles were less likely than adults to be repeaters because of their limited age span and restricted opportunity for previous exposure to criminal justice sanctions. However, the juveniles follow the pattern of adult first offenders who have greater chances of being placed on probation than serial offenders, but juvenile parolees are more likely to be repeaters than juvenile probationers. Juvenile parolees had greater prior exposure to parole (means of 1.81 versus 1.24) than juvenile probationers had to probation. The means increased with advancing ages of juveniles. First admissions were more characteristic of juvenile probationers (79 versus 38.1 percent) than of juvenile parolees. The percentage shares of first admissions were 96 for probationers and 82.5 percent for parolees less than fifteen years of age. The percentages declined consistently with greater ages in the span of juvenile ages (Research and Statistics section 1996a, 89).

Crimes Committed During Probationary Supervision

Decision makers for probation and parole inevitably risk failures because they deal usually with "problematic personalities," because encrusted habits of trouble-prone living tend to persist, because of the practical contingencies of return to the dynamics of life in the community, and because restored offenders often encounter communal doubts about their "rehabilitation." In short, even the component selection of presumably "trustworthy" candidates for probation and parole will have some disappointing outcomes. The risk goes with commitment to community-oriented corrections when alternatives to imprisonment are feasible. Japanese corrections provide the opportunity for that commitment to determine outcomes.

Of the probationers and parolees completing supervision in 1995, crimes during supervision had been committed by 3,320 juvenile probationers, 864 by juvenile parolees, 143 by adult parolees, and 1,620 by adult probationers (see tables 7.4 and 7.5). The new crimes illustrate the possibility of continued lawbreaking, even by those offenders who have benefited by return to life in the community, although under supervision, or who have been granted earlier release from prison or juvenile training school.

"Offenses resulting in suspension" actually refers to canceling of the court's decision to hold up (to "suspend") its previous order to send the offender to a correctional institution. The stub columns of tables 7.4 and 7.5 are headed "offenses resulting in suspension" to refer to various offenses that were suspended to put juveniles or adults on probation. However,

Table 7.4

Offenses Resulting in Suspension by Offenses During Suspension for Juvenile Probationers and Parolees, 1995

Offenses Resulting in Suspension	Total First Offenses[a]	New Offenses While on Probationary Supervision[b]						
		Violence Against Persons	Threats to Community	Offenses Against Property	Drug Offenses	Sex Offenses	Traffic Offenses	Predelinquency
		Percentage Distribution						
Juvenile probation								
Property	1,420	11.3	6.3	42.3	8.5	2.2	27.9	1.5
Traffic	870	11.6	5.2	15.4	8.6	0.9	57.5	0.8
Violence against persons	389	17.3	9.6	17.6	12.8	3.2	37.1	2.4
Drugs	325	7.6	4.4	16.0	36.5	2.8	30.8	1.9
Threats to community	173	17.9	16.8	19.1	13.3	0.6	30	2.3
Predelinquency	72	8.3	1.4	33.3	18.1	—	22.2	16.7
Others	50	23.9	—	19.6	6.5	—	50.0	—
Sex	21	—	9.5	28.6	—	19.0	42.9	—
Total	3,320	12.1	6.6	28.0	12.2	2.0	37.3	1.8
Juvenile parole								
Property	456	14.5	4.2	55.8	8.5	0.9	14.3	1.8
Violence against persons	116	22.0	7.3	27.5	11.9	2.8	25.7	2.8
Drugs	86	2.4	13.1	9.5	52.4	—	17.8	4.8

Table 7.4 cont. on next page

Table 7.4 continued

Offenses Resulting in Suspension	Total First Offenses[a]	New Offenses While on Probationary Supervision[b]						
		Violence Against Persons	Threats to Community	Offenses Against Property	Drug Offenses	Sex Offenses	Traffic Offenses	Predelinquency
Juvenile parole								
Traffic	69	12.3	7.7	16.9	15.4	3.1	43.1	1.5
Predelinquency	59	7.0	1.7	31.6	31.6	—	8.8	19.3
Threats to community	42	17.5	20.0	30.0	17.5	5.0	7.5	2.5
Sex	21	9.5	4.8	23.8	14.3	23.8	23.8	—
Other	15	14.3	—	28.6	21.4	7.1	28.6	—
Total	864	13.6	6.3	40.4	16.2	2.0	18.1	3.4

Source: Research and Statistics Section (1996a, 140–45).

[a]These offenses resulted in supervision.
[b]Excludes "other" offenses, as so described in source data.

to simplify the tables, the meaning of "offenses resulting in suspension" was stretched to cover also RPB decisions to parole inmates of juvenile training schools or adult prisons. The term is taken beyond its technical boundaries to include RPBs shortening the period of confinement. Then, the stub columns in the two tables refer to those offenses that put these persons "on the streets."

"Offenses while on probationary supervision" occurred while the persons were on the streets after being granted probation by courts or parole by RPBs. These were offenses that ended the condition of conditional freedom of these probationers and parolees. Most of the offenses recorded by the Ministry of Justice were too few to survive the analyses reported in tables 7.4 and 7.5. I grouped the offenses to capture their essential meanings. "Violence against persons" refers to offenses such as bodily injury (mostly), assault, robbery, and a few homicides. "Threats to community" concentrate on violent offenses that are directed against corporate society—the unified body of the Japanese people. Those offenses are extortion (chiefly); conduct against the Law for Punishment of Acts of Violence; a scattering of violations of the Firearms and Swords Control Law; and (rarely) intimidation and escape. "Offenses against property" are largely larceny-theft; a few cases of housebreaking (somewhat like burglary) and embezzlement; and rarely possession of stolen property, fraud, or arson. "Drug offenses" are stimulants, organic solvents (primarily among juveniles), and, very seldom, narcotics. "Sex offenses" are rape and indecent assault; in an unorthodox way, I have added the very few instances of prostitution and pornography. "Others" refer to a collection of offenses so listed in the source tables without exact specification. Traffic offenses are obvious, and predelinquency was defined earlier.

The two tables are intended to answer two general questions. First, how did the four classes of cases differ in the distributions of offenses of persons who had been granted conditional release to the free community? Second, how did the classes of offenses "while on probationary supervision," re-spectively, compare with the crimes linked with the earlier granting of conditional release to the community?

In each of the tables, the earlier offenses are ranged in order of their members. Offenses against property are always more numerous; their diversity and the emphasis of legal codes on protection of private property explain the universal priority given these offenses. From that point, the order of offenses differs among probationers versus parolees and adults versus juveniles.

For juvenile probationers, the juvenile courts' special program for traffic offenders puts them in second place. Table 5.3 in chapter 5 demonstrates the great number of traffic cases handled by family courts and their numerical dominance among referrals for probation. Violence against persons held third place; these offenses hold the same position among pro-bation decisions by family courts. Drug offenses hold fourth position in the same way. Predelinquency draws few proba-tion cases and offenses while on probation, but sex cases are most exceptional.

Caseloads for juvenile parole are considerably less than for juvenile probation; that trend helps explain the fewer ju-venile parolees represented in table 7.4. The family courts' selection of juvenile cases for training schools—from which parolees were drawn—emphasized cases of heinous and vio-lent offenses (see table 5.3). Drug and traffic offenders were few among canceled paroles; sex offenders were even fewer.

For adults, the heavy caseloads went to parole; table 3.1 lists 4,856 admissions to adult probation and 12,138 admis-sions to adult parole in 1995. Nevertheless, adult probationers had a greater number of case failures than adult parolees (see table 7.5). The differential outcomes among offenses cannot be evaluated here without detailed information on specific case histories, but I suggest several relevant factors (see chapter 8 for further discussion). The length of supervision is funda-mental; judges set the period of supervision for probation

Table 7.5

Offenses Resulting in Suspension by Offenses During Supervision for Adult Probationers and Parolees, 1995

Offenses Resulting in Suspension	Total First Offenses[a]	New Offenses While on Probationary Supervision[b]					
		Violence Against Persons	Threats to Community	Offenses Against Property	Drug Offenses	Sex Offenses	Traffic Offenses
		Percentage Distribution					
Adult probation							
Property	751	4.9	2.7	74.1	9.0	0.3	9.0
Drugs	462	5.2	3.1	7.7	73.0	0.2	10.8
Traffic	134	7.7	3.1	7.7	6.2	0.8	74.4
Threats to community	107	20.4	18.4	19.4	16.5	1.0	24.3
Violence against persons	103	30.0	10.3	10.3	22.7	5.1	21.6
Others	32	16.7	8.3	16.7	16.7	8.3	33.3
Sex	31	3.3	3.3	30.0	10.0	10.0	43.4
Total	1,620	7.9	4.5	40.5	28.4	1.0	17.7
Adult parole							
Property	54	4.0	—	66.0	8.0	2.0	20.0
Drugs	39	2.8	—	2.8	72.2	—	22.2
Violence against persons	33	6.7	3.3	6.7	10.0	—	73.3
Threats to community	7	14.3	14.3	14.3	28.6	—	28.6

Table 7.5 cont. on next page

Table 7.5 continued

Offenses Resulting in Suspension	Total First Offenses[a]	Violence Against Persons	New Offenses While on Probationary Supervision[b]				
			Threats to Community	Offenses Against Property	Drug Offenses	Sex Offenses	Traffic Offenses
Adult parole							
Sex	6	—	20.0	20.0	—	—	60.0
Traffic	2	—	—	—	—	—	100.0
Others	2	—	—	—	100.0	—	—
Total	143	4.6	2.3	29.0	27.4	0.8	35.9

Source: Research and Statistics Section (1996a, 146–49).

[a]These offenses resulted in supervision.
[b]Excludes "other" offenses, as so described in source data.

from one to five years, whereas parole is for the unexpired portion of the original prison term as set by the sentencing judge. Because approvals of parole usually come late in the sentence as served in prison, the length of parole supervision can be too brief for reliable evaluation of the parolee's performance and increases chances that the parolee can stay out of trouble. Also, among former prisoners, especially those with repeated prison sentences, many are more experienced in coping with the realities of being supervised by agents of the government.

Within the context of the underrepresentation of parolees, the numbers of drug offenders for both probationers and parolees are second numerically only to offenses against property. The policy makers have given strong attention to drug abuse and trafficking in recent decades, especially violation of the Stimulant Drugs Control Law. Although far short of the management of juvenile offenders, adult probation has given more attention to traffic offenders than adult parole. There were only two traffic parolees because the relative tolerance of traffic offenders as being noncriminals had reduced the length of many other prison terms. Similarly, some of the crimes that threatened the community order were more likely to draw probation than imprisonment. Violence against persons was more characteristic of adult parolees than adult probationers—a byproduct of the courts' doubts about extending leniency to such criminals. Sex offenders were in short supply in table 7.5

How did the new offenses compare with the crimes that resulted in these juveniles being placed on probation? Tables 7.4 and 7.5 array them according to the same typology as for the earlier offenses. Did the juvenile probationers duplicate their earlier offenses? If not, how serious were the new offenses compared to the earlier ones? Did the repeaters raise the degree of their victimization of other Japanese? The answers are in terms of the general offense categories, not the specific component offenses within each category. For example, in offenses against persons, the original bodily injury may be followed by assault, another kind of violence against persons.

The juvenile probationers tended to commit the same general type of offense; usually traffic and property offenses played an important part. The latter pattern was strongly demonstrated by total offenses. Property offenders often repeated themselves (42.3 percent of new offenses) and invested secondarily in traffic violations. Traffic showed the same pattern; 57.5 percent traffic and 15.4 percent property offenses. Violence against persons reduced its coercive impact; only 17.3 percent were repetitive, and traffic and property offenses consumed larger shares of new offenses. Drugs continued their appeal (36.5 percent of new crimes), but traffic and property were well represented. The expectation that drug abuse is especially habitual was only partially borne out. Threats to the community (only 19.1 percent of repeated offenses) and predelinquency avoided reoccurrence even more.

Juvenile parolees who committed crimes while being supervised had especially been property offenders. In overall earlier offenses, they exceeded juvenile probationers in emphasis on property and drug offenses; for both groups, the repetition of earlier general categories of offenses was especially common for property and drug offenses. Because of the heavy use of probation for juvenile traffic violations, parolees trailed in the representation of traffic offenses in both earlier and new incidents. Violence against persons and drugs increased their relative position among earlier offenses of juvenile parolees. Property offenses were heavily repetitive; violence against persons competed with traffic for a distant second place among new offenses of juvenile parolees. In new crimes for violence against persons, repetition was rather infrequent; new offenses against property and traffic crimes took precedence. The threat to other Japanese was eased. Repetition was high for drug and traffic violations. The few predelinquents usually had been apprehended for property or drug incidents. Threats to the community also were few among earlier offenses and were scattered among property, community threats, and organic solvents. Sex and "other" earlier offenses were too few for a meaningful conclusion.

Adults ape the pattern for juvenile probationers and parolees by giving priority to property offenses among the earlier offenses, but drugs (primarily stimulants for adults) gain ascendancy, and traffic violations drop away. Predelinquency is absent for adults, of course. The study of the new crimes is problematic for adult paroles because their small numbers are insufficient for detailed categorization.

For total adult probationers, new property and drug offenses hold the majority share. The crimes resulting in supervision are usually duplicated by the new crime. At least two-thirds duplication is recorded by property, drug, and traffic crimes. Sex and "other" offenses are too few for reliable analysis of new crimes. Duplication of earlier crimes is low for threats to the community and violence against persons.

Only three original crimes of juvenile parolees are in sufficient numbers to justify treatment of the distribution of new crimes. Property and drug offenses record a high degree of repetition; traffic offenses hold a reasonable share of new incidents. Violence against persons deteriorates as a threat to other Japanese because 73.3 percent of new crimes are traffic violations.

The Process of Volunteerism in General

Volunteerism is a process in that, as a form of human behavior, is a series of actions intended to serve an end. "To volunteer is to choose to act in recognition of a need," Ellis and Noyes (1990, 4) propose as a definition, "with an attitude of responsibility and without concern for monetary profit, going beyond one's basic obligations."

Elaborating on the definition, Ilsley (1990) identifies eight "elements of volunteerism." *Altruism* connotes selfless commitment to others and/or to the good of society. For some persons *commitment* is primarily to individuals; some are committed to an ideal such as social justice; others are loyal to an organization or other volunteers. *Free will* is the power to make a choice uncoerced by fate, other individuals, or an organization. Opportunity for *learning* is a powerful motivation. Volunteers differ from employees by the *absence of financial remuneration*. *Organization* lends efficiency to volunteerism through planning, funding, staffing, and controlling activities. Motivations for volunteers include the *psychological benefits* of good feelings from doing something worthwhile, opportunities for personal growth, or trying new skills in a risk-free environment. All volunteers *sacrifice* their time; others sacrifice more.

Volunteerism is popularly conceived as "amateurism" in the sense of being the opposite of professionalism. From that perspective, the regular members of the agency staff are likely to see unpaid volunteers as competitors or invaders of their professional turf. The staff may resent the burden of training and supervising volunteers who do not appear for scheduled duties and quit when most needed (Fischer and Schaffer 1993, 151–52). This emphasis on the possibility of competition, however, overlooks the distinction between *formal volunteerism* and *informal volunteerism*. Formal volunteerism, Ilsley (1990, 5) explains, is "service that is addressed to a social need, or needs, defined by an organization, performed in a coordinated way in an organizational context, and rewarded by psychological or other benefits." He sees informal volunteerism as a spontaneous expression of service toward meeting a personally perceived social need, performed without organizational constraints and often without any thought of reward.

Formal volunteerism fits the characteristics of the VPO system as defined and performed according to the expectations of the Rehabilitation Bureau. Moreover, the VPO system tends to follow the Japanese conception of volunteerism as described by Plath (1964, 141): "Americans tend to underline the voluntary aspects of association membership. Japanese are more aware of compulsory facets—of the moral pressure of the *waku* (the system of social control)." He sees the distinction to be porous, because some Japanese see participation to be exciting and personally satisfying, and some Americans feel they are being pressured to participate. But, Plath is convinced that Japanese tend to be more accepting of control by organizations than Americans.[5]

The Rise and Nature of Japanese VPO System

During the Meiji Restoration, delegations went to Europe and the United States for quick studies of Western social institutions, including legal codes and criminal justice systems. Among the possibilities for study were the "patronage societies" funded by the French government for supervision of paroled adults and of juveniles not adequately managed by parents. Patronage societies were privately directed but authorized by the state and funded by private donations and state subsidy. After 1885, misdemeanants with good conduct could be released to the patronage societies after serving half their sentences (O'Brien, 1982).

The earliest example of volunteers in Japanese community-oriented corrections appears in 1913, but only in part of the country. They became a part of the official scheme in 1923 in the "old" law on juveniles providing volunteer probation officers as official agent for supervising juveniles. Another statute in 1939 extended the responsibility to discharged offenders (Shiono 1969).

Immediately after World War II, when the present version of community-oriented corrections was set in place, a question for debate was whether or not a professional service should be established for supervision of probationers and parolees. The choice was to combine a professional staff with volunteer workers. "The shortage of funds at that time precluded the realization of overall-professionalization," the Rehabilitation Bureau (1990, 13) recalls. "But the even greater reason making a determination to maintain volunteers obviously lays in the fact that the trust of the authorities in the potential of volunteer workers was so overwhelming."

Volunteer visitors also have come to Japanese prisons and juvenile training schools since 1953. At a UNAFEI seminar chaired by Masako Saeki (1996), the program in 1993 was described. From 12,290 volunteers, the services were education 225, literature 222, religion 183, community-oriented treatment 156, and legal matters 95. Voluntary chaplains had 14,857 consultations and 1,513 services. Of 840 volunteer visitors to juvenile training schools, 335 were women; juvenile inmates benefited from 16,082 consultations.

The Volunteer Probation Officer Law, Article 1, defines the mission of VPOs serving the Rehabilitation Bureau: "To contribute to the welfare of the individual and the public by helping persons who have committed criminal offenses to improve and be rehabilitated and at the same time by leading public opinion for the prevention of offenses and by cleaning up the community, in the spirit of social service." The law authorized the Minister of Justice (who may delegate the duty to the chair of the regional parole board) to appoint the VPO with these qualifications: holds the confidence and popularity of the community; exhibits enthusiasm for his work and has time for such work; possesses financial stability; and is healthy and active.

The law sets the term of service as two years, subject to renewal, as a precaution against retention of unqualified persons. A selection committee,[6] not exceeding fifteen members, is set for screening a list of candidates prepared by the director of the probation office. The VPOs are assigned to one of the 883 rehabilitation areas of Japan, according to their place of residence.

The VPOs receive no monetary compensation, but the government reimburses some expenses: a maximum of 4,270 yen per month for supervising a probation or parolee; 1,000 yen for an employment-residence investigation; 800 yen for a day's attendance at a training session; and mileage, with the limits of budgeted funds, for the investigation and training if the travel exceeds a specified distance (Rehabilitation Bureau, 1990).

In interpreting the implications of the official mission statement, Satoh (1988, 10–11) specifies VPO duties other than supervision:

> They inquire into and make adjustments of, on a voluntary basis, the environment where the inmate of a correctional institution is expected to return; they locate a probationer or parolee who had moved from another area and take over his supervisory casework; they conduct preliminary investigations in the case of candidates for pardons; and they assists offenders' families. . . . In the promotion of crime prevention . . . they collaborate with public and private organizations in exploring and coordinating social resources in the community; they spread the rehabilitative philosophy and efforts to individual neighbors or to the public as a whole; and they attempt to eradicate crime-precipitating conditions in cooperation with community residents.

Article 20 of the Offenders Rehabilitation Law calls upon VPOs to "assist the professional probation officer and make up for inadequacies of the latter's work." However, Article 39 gives both PPOs and VPOs the responsibilities of guidance, supervision, and rehabilitation aid. The Law for Aftercare of Discharged Offenders defines "rehabilitation aid" as helping eligible persons to return home "and furnishing or lending money or articles to them . . . if such persons can not receive aid from the relatives, friends, etc."

The probation office of the particular area provides three kinds of training. Initial orientation for one day introduces the VPO recruit to such rudimentary subjects as basic laws and regulations, agency procedures, report writing, and interviewing. Periodic refresher training deals with various topics such as criminal policies, history of the rehabilitation system, and the organization of the system. Special sessions bring together experienced VPOs for study of a selected topic, such as case conferences, role playing, casework, conditions of supervision, management of traffic offenders, procedures for granting parole, methods of interviewing, client relationships at work, and supervision of abusers of paint thinner or glue sniffing.

"When I was appointed VPO the probation office had a one-day training program," a male VPO reported. "Very basic things, like don't go to the client at night-time. If possible, go day-time, or you must make an appointment. Many things like that. Also our VPO association has a special video program about difficult cases. We train each other; you should do this or that or you should not do that. Sometimes there is a traffic law change or jail house law. A person from the probation office gives a speech. A special program every two or three months is about a new law or a special case."

VPOs Explain Their Willingness to Participate

Since they draw no salary, the participation of VPOs cannot be derived from material benefits. "What motivates a VPO is a sense of mission," Hough (1995, 184) says, "and the gratification he/she derives from seeing a good response to the help he/she provides. Public recognition and social prestige also are possibilities." In an interview in 1990, I asked a number of VPOs to explain their participation. At a day office in Shinjuku (a section of Tokyo), a woman told me how she become a VPO and what the work has meant to her.

> About a quarter century ago, I and my family were in Pittsburgh, Pennsylvania, for two years. Some members of the Pittsburgh Council of International Visitors took care of us and told me about volunteers in the United States. I noticed that there are many differences in history, culture and customs between Japan and U.S.A. There are various ways of life and social systems in the world; so I think it is very important to know and understand each other. After I came back to Japan, I volunteered to help patients and students from Southeast Asia at a hospital. A friend, who is an expert VPO, asked me to serve as a VPO. Knowing noth-

ing about the law and probation, I had no confidence to achieve this work. I consulted my husband and finally decided to serve.

Up to now I have taken care of more than 30 cases— thieves, persons who did violence, prostitutes, and paint-thinner sniffers who were young offenders. Adult offenders were swindlers, narcotic or stimulant users or sellers, prostitutes, and a murderer. Some were parolees. Sometime women but many men. When I started VPO activity, I was afraid to meet them, but soon my fear and tension have disappeared. They are like general citizens in nature. It is very important to build up a good relationship, to keep an equal standpoint with them, and to accept them with kindness and strictness.

If some troubles happened to them, I consulted a probation officer how to help them. A stimulant-drug abuser had had a hallucination, I took him to a hospital. A gangsters threatened a girl; a probation officer, a policeman, and I met the gangster with her. Now I have two offenders who are in prison. I am sending a letter once a month to them.

I love this job very much and want to continue as possible as I can. Support of my family is very important. When an offender visits me in the evening or holiday, my husband and my daughter usually join our conversation.

In another interview in Yokohama, another woman reported that she turned to VPO work when her two sons became adults.

I never had paid work, but I had been a volunteer at my children's school and, while a college student, at a hospital. After seeing my sons growing up, I want to work for young people. At that time a friend was a judge and persuaded me to be a VPO. My mother had volunteered for a family court. I have been satisfied with probationers but quite often disappointed. I have noticed that problems can be overcome by mutual trust. I try to mediate, to be a go-between . . . patiently, slowly and tenderly between the probationer and the family . . . between son or daughter and parents.

A juvenile, fifteen years old, lived with his father because his parents divorced when the boy was three years old. When he was in junior high school, the father worked from early morning to late at night. Lonesome, the son brought friends to the home, and they inhaled paint-thinner there and in public parks. Otherwise he had no delinquencies and attended school. The father decided to move, hoping the son would change if living elsewhere, but paint-thinner abuse continued. The son was sent to training school. The father would drive some 10 hours to see the son at the training school. I had had the boy while he was on probation; the father asked me what gifts to bring to the training school. After coming home, the son was assigned to me as a parolee. The father-son spirit returned. The son works hard in the same office as the father. This has been one of my successful cases.

In another interview in Yokohama, a man described his twenty-two years of VPO service.

My father entered the restaurant business almost fifty years ago. Now the family has a Japanese restaurant, a Western restaurant, a Chinese restaurant, and an Italian restaurant. Because I was active in town affairs, prefectural officials asked me some twenty years ago to go to Europe with other people interested in youth for study of youth houses. When I got back, the prefectural officials said: "Now that you have spent taxpayers' money to go abroad, you should do volunteer work." My family also expected me to do something without pay. So, I said, "O.K., I will be a VPO." I feel I must do something for my town, and I saw some boys going to nightclubs where there are criminals. Maybe I can help them. Perhaps my VPO work will steer some people to my business. If I know people well, it is good for me too.

Sometimes I am very glad to be a VPO because of many successful cases. One case fifteen years ago was a young guy and a girl who lived with him. When seventeen or eighteen, she became pregnant. Her parents told her she didn't need a baby and she should see a doctor. They asked me and I said: "If you go to a doctor, it is like murder. If you marry now, you can have a baby." They have a baby and were married later. He works hard, and his wife helps him. At my house we celebrated a happy marriage with their three-year-old daughter.

Arguments Favorable to the Emphasis on VPOs

"Community treatment is a process through which the community participates in the rehabilitation of offenders," Angata (1990, 2) declares. "The offenders come from the community; in a sense, the community produces offenders." In that context, he emphasizes that both the VPOs and the probationers and parolees live in the same community; that, figuratively speaking, the VPOs have been nominated by local citizens; that the VPOs have lived in the community for many years; and that the VPOs know the community. PPOs are likely to be transferred among the prefectures, but the VPOs usually live continually in the neighborhood. They may be accessible to clients even when the period of formal supervision has ended.

Satoh (1988, 6) adds another advantage to the frequent contacts between supervisor and client: "This contributes to the effective control and supervision of probationers and parolees." In that vein, Ono (1970, 12) comments: "Not only does it [the VPO system] have the advantage of being local in nature and voluntary, but also the moral influence of these volunteer workers affects greatly the rehabilitation of offenders, and therefore there are many reasons why we must continue to depend on their work in the future." The "moral influence" is among the possible effects of the low caseload—as low as one client per VPO—that Thornton and Endo (1992) consider "one of the great virtues of the VPO system."

The advantage of the VPO's constant presence in the neighborhood, Angata (1990, 8) advises, also raises the possibility of conflicts with probationers and parolees. The conflict may stem from political interests, religious beliefs, or social issues dividing members of the local community. Membership in the community also may persuade the VPO to keep the probation office ignorant of the client's "realistic situation."

Extensive use of VPOs is inevitable in Japan, Satoh (1988) postulates, because there are only 750 PPOs to handle the great number being admitted to probation offices (see table 7.1). (The Rehabilitation Board listed 1,025 PPOs in 1995.) Without the VPOs, the burden of PPO responsibilities would be impossible. Shiono (1969, 28) points out that PPOs, even though freed from most direct supervision, are "engaged primarily in such special tasks as arrest, discharge, revocation of probation or parole and the like, as well as case assignment and consultation with volunteers."

In comparing the roles and functions of VPOs and PPOs, Satoh (1988, 17) believes the VPOs are more informal and less threatening from the client's perspective; are more optimistic, accepting, and sympathetic with clients; have more contact with clients and access to community resources; comprehend clients' lifestyles better; and are quicker in assisting their coping with daily problems. The PPOs have more authority and responsibility; understand the legal system, the assessment of client needs, and the process of supervision; and know relevant agencies. In an interview, a VPO told me: "I am a common citizen. If I give very common advice to my probationers they will understand. If I speak like a policeman or professional probation officer, they will not understand or feel attraction."

In a similar vein, Angata (1990, 6–7) sees the volunteers as antidotes for the excessive inflexibility and bureaucratism of "officialism." He sees VPOs having more discretion because PPOs "as government officials must work with clients within the framework of procedures required by the government agency." He believes the VPOs can reduce the hostility of clients and their parents against governmental authority. "Governmental agencies have fixed office hours, and officials are not available during early morning or late hours."

Questioning the Emphasis on VPOs

"Along with changes in our society at large," Hashimoto (1983, 186) summarizes, "the VPO system itself has faced several problems: Inequality of treatment, the age gap between VPOs and offenders, and difficulty in recruiting qualified VPOs from urban areas." As an example of inequality of treatment, Hashimoto cites situations in which two probationers show the same progress, but one may be discharged after a favorable report by a lenient VPO while the other remains under supervision because of a negative report of a strict VPO. "Japanese probation and parole services do not suffer from over-professionalization," Tomita (1971) comments, but a state of "over-laicisation" may be a problem.

VPOs approach their clients with views derived from personal experience, Angata (1990, 7–8) cautions. They usually lack the specialized knowledge and technical skills of an expert in dealing with human problems. "Many VPOs need intensive training and have poor susceptibility to training." He says that PPOs cannot provide professional treatment in all cases.

Persons older than 50 years have taken larger and larger shares of the VPO group. The mean age was 53.2 years in 1953 and reached 61 years by 1987. (The Rehabilitation Bureau reported the mean age to be 62.3 years in 1994.) Persons over 59 years of age made up 8.21 percent of the population of Japan in 1920, 8.80 percent in 1960, and 16.96 percent in 1989 (Statistics Bureau 1992, 36–37). The trend mirrors the increasing difficulty of recruiting younger persons, the willingness of experienced VPOs to continue the service, and changes in the conditions in Japanese society that had been favorable to tapping a wide range of groups in the community. Noting that small entrepreneurs over 50 years of age are especially willing to volunteer for community service, Wagatsuma and DeVos (1984, 29) describe it as a means of gaining prestige but also as a continuation of "Japanese paternalistic responsibilities."

They explain: "Whereas in the past the individually successful Japanese felt himself responsible to his employees for their
well-being, he is now universalizing some of this energy into
a feeling of responsibility for community service."

The age gap between VPOs and their clients has been
aggravated by the increased representation over the years of
juveniles in the caseload of probation offices (see table 7.1).
Even most of the adult clients are considerably younger than
VPOs. The mean age of adults admitted to parole in 1995 was
40.3 years, and 51.1 percent were less than 40 years of age. For
adults admitted to probation, the mean age was only 34.1 years,
and half were less than 30 years of age (Research and Statistics Section 1996a, 89). The age gap for adult probationers, for
example, signifies differences in life experiences because of
developments in Japanese society over the decades. VPOs,
aged 65 in 1995, would have been born in 1930 and experienced
Japan's postwar chaos at age 15 years. Adult probationers,
aged 30 in 1995, would have been born in 1965 and experienced
Japan's greater affluence when reaching age 15 years in 1980.

Acknowledging the problematics of the age gap, Shiono
(1969) argues that the "oriental culture" presses the young to
respect the elderly. However, he agrees that the PPOs and
VPOS are disturbed about those problematics and the consequences in weakening the effectiveness of supervision.

Closely associated with the age gap is the growing representation of housewives and retired men among VPOs in
the last four decades. Other occupational categories have lost
share. Farming and fishing, the best index of VPO participation by ruralites, held the largest share in 1958 but has lost
representation since then. Members of religious orders have
been especially active, climbing to third place in spite of a percentage loss. Managers and sales personnel were the only
other occupational categories with significant numerical representation. Teachers and social workers have low representation but surpass the very few physicians, dentists, and practicing attorneys.

"Some observers from abroad," Shiono (1969, 27) concedes, have pointed to class distinctions as a barrier to communication between clients and VPOS drawn from the middle or upper strata of Japanese society. In Japan, however, he contends: "Class distinctions are not as great as in many other countries nor is the gap between different group subcultures so wide that close relationships cannot be established." A few countries have made wider use of "indigenous workers" from the lower class or minority groups, he says, "but such a need appears to be relatively small in Japan."

Social Changes and the VPO System

Massive socioeconomic changes have had a great effect on the Japanese and weaken the efficacy of official justification for the heavy use of VPOs. Sometimes the effect is attributed to sources outside Japan. One VPO explained to me the intergenerational problem: "I think it comes from the United States. Japanese boys and girls copy very quickly what is on television. They watch what singing is going on, what playing is going on."

More generally, the term *urbanization* is supposed to encapsulate the diverse sources of the age gap in value beliefs and behavior patterns. Hirata (1985, 8) adopts that explanation: "Since they come from different social and cultural backgrounds, people in urban areas are characterized by their individualism. They pay little attention to other persons in the community. Social control of crime and delinquencies is very weak. . . . It is difficult to recruit the VPOs in urban areas, since there are few residents who are well qualified to be VPOs and who have interest in such activities. Moreover, it is difficult for the VPOs in urban areas to perform fully their duties, since human relations among residents . . . are so weak."

Under urbanization as a blanketing concept, more specific developments should be recognized, such as increased employment in large-scale enterprises that limit occupational self-direction and, thereby, reduce the pool of VPO candidates. Jobs have consequences for workers' lives outside the workplace. In reviewing the American literature on that linkage, Wilson and Musick (1997) note that volunteering is a form of work but is most prevalent among persons with jobs at the top of the occupational ladder—people of higher status even when the volunteers try to help persons of lower status. They point to research findings that volunteering is more characteristic of occupations that demand or encourage the use of initiative, thought, and independent judgment at work. "People whose ego is boosted and not deflated by their work," Wilson and Musick (1997, 269) say, "are more willing to give themselves outside work." Among their conclusions, they warn that the limits on occupational self-direction at work dilutes the pool of volunteer candidates.

Expanding PPOs' Direct Role in Supervision

In light of the perceived crisis of growing offenses of juveniles, the Ministry of Justice issued in 1960 a directive calling for tighter probationary supervision. "Probation offices about the nation, on receiving the note," Shikita and Tsuchiya (1990, 219) recall, "began strengthening the supervision of those who were prone to commit another dreadful crime." After experimentation on the roles of PPOs and VPOs, "onset supervision" was introduced at probation offices in Tokyo and Osaka in 1974. While directly supervising, for one to three months, selected cases considered especially difficult, PPOs would diagnose the probationer or parolee and assess personal problems. When turning supervision over, the PPO would advise the VPO on the nature and ways to manage the individual.

The involvement of PPOs was further increased by the direct supervision model introduced in Tokyo and Osaka in 1974. Judges may recommend direct supervision, but the director of the probation office has that authority. Especially

Evaluation Item	Alternative Choices	Score
1. Age at admission	15 years or less	3
	16-17 years	2
	18 years or more	0
2. Offense	Sniff paint thinner	4
	Other offenses	3
	Property, predelinquent	2
	Heinous, violent, sex,	
	stimulant drugs	0
3. Family conflicts	Applicable	3
	Not applicable	1
4. Parents fail to		
control juvenile	Applicable	3
	Not applicable	0
5. History of		
problematic conduct	Applicable	2
	Not applicable	1
6. Ran from home and		
wandered about	Applicable	2
	Not applicable	1
7. Record of drug use		
or addiction	Applicable	2
	Not applicable	1
8. Record of juvenile		
training schools	Applicable	5
	Not applicable	0
Total score	Points	A if 18 or more
		B if 17 or less

Source: Rehabilitation Bureau's scaling instruction sheet.

Note: Preliminary Evaluation: After totaling the score items, classify the juvenile as either A or B.

Fig. 7.1. Criteria for classification of juvenile probationers and parolees

Evaluation Item	Alternative Choices	Score
1. Age at admission	29 years or less	2
	30–39 years	1
	40–49 years	2
	50–59 years	1
	60 years or more	0
2. Offense	Larceny-theft	4
	Murder, property (except larceny-theft)	2
	Robbery, violent and drug offenses	2
	Other offenses	0
3. Length of parole	6–12 months	5
	12 months or more	3
	3–6 months	1
	Less than 3 months	0
4. Living situation	Others	3
	Single with parents	2
	Halfway house	1
	With spouse	0
5. Unstable lifestyle	Applicable	5
	Not applicable	0
6. Member or link with yakuza	Applicable	4
	Not applicable	0
7. Experience of drug addict or alcoholic	Applicable	2
	Not applicable	1
8. Recidivist	Applicable	2
	Not applicable	1
9. Unsatisfactory rating of conduct on probation	Applicable	3
	Not applicable	1
10. Inadequate nature of occupation	Applicable	3
	Not applicable	0
Total score	Points	A if 18 or more B if 17 or less

Source: Rehabilitation Bureau's scaling instruction sheet.

Note: Preliminary Evaluation: After totaling the score items, classify the individual as either A or B.

Fig. 7.2 Criteria for classification of adult parolees

troublesome cases became the responsibility of several PPOs without referral to VPOs. The particular probationers or parolees may be skillful in only pretending compliance with official rules. Perhaps neighborhood stigmatization of a client would stimulate special concern.

Broadly speaking, the individuals considered to require direct treatment would have certain characteristics. They might have mental problems interfering with their social adjustment but short of requiring hospitalization. They may have social difficulties not attributable to mental disorder. There may be disadvantages in their social environment, especially the family, such as in intergenerational conflicts or mental disorder of parents. Foreigners may have unusual difficulties in adjustment to Japanese society.

A more sophisticated classification system differentiates between persons expected to have acute behavioral difficulties requiring direct supervision (Group A) and those not so requiring (Group B). The rating scale is presented in figure 7.1 for juvenile probationers and parolees and in figure 7.2 for adult parolees. The scales are not applied to traffic offenders. The rating scales are advisory only and to be ignored in favor of personal assessment. PPOs may decide on special intervention in spite of a Group A rating if the individual shows a strong commitment to character reform, has a stable lifestyle, or has support persons with a positive influence. The low score may be canceled if there is marked drug or alcohol addiction, yakuza affiliation, strong antisocial attitudes, or mental illness.

Day offices are a device for bringing certain PPOs into direct supervision. They are satellites of the probation office to which PPOs go to meet directly with probationers or parolees who require more attention than usually provided by VPOs. The location is a municipal office, public hall, or youth center in a neighborhood convenient to the interviewees. In that sense, the PPOs and their interviewees are guests of another agency.

I accompanied a staff member of the Tokyo Probation Office to Shinjuku, a section of the metropolis, to meet with five parolees. Three had been serving a life sentence for homicide; one had been a thief. The fifth was a juvenile probationer who had used paint thinner. The interviews were for regular reports on the clients' current situation. Two VPOs also were interviewed.

At the day offices, PPOs interview their own clients, confer with VPOs, counsel family members who have grievances or special concerns, meet with school teachers and employers, or take advantage of liaison of community agencies. In 1988 the PPOs had 28,645 interviews with probationers and parolees; 8,085 with employers, family members, and other persons; and 18,843 with VPOs (Correction Bureau 1990).

8
Return to the Community:
Outcomes and the Reentry Crisis

IN CHOOSING PROBATION RATHER than imprisonment, Japanese judges place a bet that social ties of family and community have the advantage over the deterrent effect of imprisonment in pressing convicted offenders from further crimes. Parolees and prisoners discharged upon completion of sentence join probationers in facing the difficulties of finding a responsible and self-satisfying place in the community. For them, aftercare services become instruments and expressions of the dualism of community attitudes toward former offenders. Consideration of their legitimate needs is motivated by humaneness and the hope that restoration to the benefits of community membership will forestall continued criminality. The double nature of community attitudes also draws on the public unease that victimization will persist at the hands of Japanese criminals who are incapable of "self-correction." Probation and parole require a balance between, first, treating the "former offender" as an individual with unique needs and personal qualities and, second, supervisory controls dedicated to protecting the community against possible recidivism.

This final chapter of the book centers attention on important questions. What are the results of the supervision of probationers and parolees? Among releases from prisons and juvenile training schools, what is the comparative share of parole versus discharge upon completion of the term ordered by the courts? How does the comparison differ along the course of increasing length of sentence? Are parolees less likely to

304

commit new crimes than persons serving their full prison term? How do rehabilitation aid hostels alleviate the reentry crisis? In what ways does the Rehabilitation Bureau ease the difficulties of reentry through "rehabilitation aid"?

The return of inmates to the free community becomes a testing ground for the purposes and operations of the criminal justice agencies that processed them from the first experience of apprehension to the current experience of departure from probation or parole. As a concept, the word *career* points attention to the regularized occupational experiences of agency employees. The policemen, the public prosecutors, judges, prison officers, and probation officers have duties and functions that are supposed to achieve agency purposes. The ultimate success of agency purposes is tested now that these probationers and parolees are being released from the probation office's control. That same can be said for the personnel of the various agencies. In carrying out the details of agency purposes, will the various kinds of personnel be pleased by what the probationers and parolees do upon return to the community?

The Reentry Crisis for Criminal Justice and Offenders

Reentry into the free community is a crucial turning point in the "careers" of persons who had been locked up in prisons or juvenile training schools. The term *career* connotes a somewhat orderly passage through a series of related jobs, with incentives motivating the aspirant to learn prerequisite skills and to persist in dedicated service to an occupation. The concept is appropriate for the employees of correction agencies who are recruited and evaluated at the entry level by the National Personnel Authority. The accepted candidates are trained by the Bureaus' in-service programs and motivated by reward systems of pay increases, promotions, and retirement allowances.

In Japan, the field of corrections follows the lifetime employment system of the large-scale organizations whereby key employees are recruited directly from schools as "corporate citizens," are taught specific skills and management philosophy through training provided by the employing organization, are given career paths for further development of competences useful to the organization, and are encouraged by a set of benefits to be loyal to the organization.[1] The seniority-based reward system rotates the promising employees through a series of jobs; a "career path" maps the progressive experiences of ultimate executives.

Career should be applied with care to the probationers and parolees. Among them are "career" criminals who develop skills of a kind of crime and assume the basic attitudes and moral values of a criminal livelihood. In a much looser sense of "career," others have had a sequence of regularized experiences in being exposed to the workings of the criminal justice system. The probationer and parolee have been apprehended, tried, convicted, and sentenced. The parolee has also experienced imprisonment.

There are rhythms and similarities of being treated as a suspect, defendant, convict, and probationer or parolee. Those experiences merge with the offenders' personal inclinations and the influences of their community setting in shaping what they do when freed of official supervision. They too are tested for the qualities of "rehabilitated" offenders in attitudes, capacities, resourcefulness, and emotional flexibility. Do they receive the benefits of acceptance by family, friends, associates, and the community in general? Did the sentencing court make the proper decision in putting them on probation or ordering them to a prison or training school and thereby shaping their correctional experiences? Did the probationer or parolee take advantage of whatever services the correctional agencies offered?

Considering the High Success Rate

To what extent is supervision of probationers and parolees successful from an official point of view? The answer takes on a particular Japanese flavor in keeping with the general policy of returning offenders to the community whenever feasible.

In reviewing the official data on case outcomes, this chapter reports a very high rate of successes. Perhaps that remarkable outcome is due to the persistence of traditional emphasis on maintaining harmonious relationships with other persons by subordinating self-interests to the interests of the group. A substantial proportion of Japanese probationers and parolees may differ from similar persons in Western societies because they as Japanese accept, in the social status of probationers or parolees, the duty of subordinating their own interests to the norms enunciated by agents of the Rehabilitation Bureau.

Perhaps the sentencing judges had been effective in distinguishing among convicted offenders those most capable of self-correction if returned to the community. The most capable convicted defendants receive a suspended prison sentence and are released without probationary supervision.[2] Those requiring a measure of control and transitional assistance go on probation. The least promising prospects are sentenced to prison. Some prisoners are benefited by either the deterrent effect of imprisonment or by the rehabilitative services of the prison. They are released early on parole.

As another possible explanation, the administration of community-oriented corrections in Japan may be a major factor. Noting that adult probationers have higher revocation rates than adult parolees, Nishikawa (1994, 239) offers an example of the effects of administrative differences. "Since there are no basic differences in method or intensiveness between the supervision of probationers and the supervision of parolees, except for small differences in the restrictiveness of the conditions imposed," he says, "the reason for this may be found in the fact that parole is more selectively applied to adult cases, thus excluding poor risks."

He also notes that parole supervision generally is too brief for clear distinctions between good and poor adjustment in evaluating the quality of the supervisee's conduct. In brief supervision, even the dedicated criminal can feign compliance, exploit the sympathy of a naive supervisor, and await the opportunity to assume the life course that had put him or her in prison. Adult probationers would risk greater chances for negative evaluation because of a longer period of supervision. The relatively brief period of supervision gives the questionable parolee the opportunity to survive without being penalized.[3] Courts use probation selectively, in contrast to unconditional return to the community, for offenders who reveal greater "criminal tendencies."

Nishikawa does not mention another selective factor: By being exposed to imprisonment, parolees are more likely to be experienced with managing the status of an inferior person in relationships with persons in positions of authority. Less experienced in that regard, at least some probationers are less knowledgeable and skillful than most parolees in avoiding "trouble" and possibly artfully manipulating relationships with the supervisors.

The quality of supervision also affects the outcomes of Japanese probation and parole. The merits and disadvantages of volunteer probation officers have already been considered. The dedication and enthusiasm of VPOs are supplemented by the prevalence of oyabun-kobun relationships. Those traditional roles, familiar to the Japanese, add viability to the VPO-supervisee relationship.

Among the parolees and probationers are "marginal deviants" who have not committed themselves to criminal conduct and values; rather, their law violations reflect flagrant (although somewhat concealed) rejection of the general norms. The simplistic supervision of VPOs may free the marginal lawbreakers to move into the ranks of conformists, whereas "professional" enforcement of official behavioral standards may exert demands excessive in the immediate situation and escalate the failure rate.[4] This possibility, however, must be balanced against the chances that inadequate supervision will breed further crimes.

Outcomes: Juvenile Probation and Parole

The juvenile justice policy of Japan is dedicated to the "wholesome rearing" of youngsters. Although probation is favored over referral to juvenile training schools, the family courts treat both as "protective measures." Parole becomes a device for assisting the socially deprived youngsters in their efforts to find a personally satisfying and responsible place in the community. As table 8.1 attests, the family courts have favored probation over referral to the training schools that supply candidates for juvenile parole. Ignoring probation in particular cases where the juvenile's situation in the community is untenable and unpromising, the family courts are likely to turn to correctional institution as a positive setting in comparison.

Juvenile probationers appear to surpass juvenile parolees in share of successful outcomes, largely because of the high proportion of "early terminations" (see table 8.1). Article 33 of the Offenders Rehabilitation Law authorizes that probationary supervision be "suspended or rescinded even during the term of probationary supervision, if it is deemed unnecessary." The heavy use of early terminations implies conscientious selection by family courts when they choose between probation and referral to training schools. Juveniles sent to training school also do well on parole but trail probationers in gaining early terminations.

Completion of the full term of supervision is especially marked for the case outcomes of juvenile parolees.[5] Differences

Table 8.1
Outcomes of Juvenile Probation and Parole by Previous Exposure to Protective Measures, 1995

Previous Exposure	Total Outcomes Number	Total Outcomes Percent	Early Termination	Outcome of Juvenile Probation or Parole[a] Completion	Abscond	Arrest	Revoked
				Percentage Distribution			
Juvenile probation							
Social agencies	209	1.0	49.76	15.31	6.22	9.60	27.75
Training schools	311	1.6	40.19	34.08	7.72	1.61	16.40
Probation	4,159	20.5	72.03	15.15	1.61	0.58	10.63
Dismissal, hearing	5,153	25.4	72.43	13.35	1.59	0.27	12.36
Dismissal, no hearing	1,876	9.3	75.37	11.67	2.03	0.48	10.45
No exposure	8,555	42.2	80.78	8.22	1.24	0.26	9.50
Total persons	—	100.0	75.42	11.74	1.63	0.37	10.84
Number	20,263	—	15,283	2,377	330	76	2,197
Juvenile parole							
Social agencies	146	3.7	13.70	36.99	8.90	2.74	37.67
Training schools	839	21.2	8.94	60.55	5.84	5.48	19.19
Probation	1,659	42.0	21.28	60.70	2.95	2.05	13.02
Dismissal, hearing	364	9.2	31.59	52.20	1.92	2.20	12.09
Dismissal, no hearing	145	3.7	29.65	56.55	3.45	2.07	8.28
No exposure	797	20.2	35.26	43.91	3.01	1.38	16.44
Total persons	—	100.0	22.46	55.47	3.72	2.68	15.67
Number	3,950	—	887	2,191	147	106	619

Source: Research and Statistics Section (1996a, 115).

[a]"Other" outcomes are excluded.

in the average length of supervision is among the reasons for this pattern. Compared with early terminations, completion is more frequent for juvenile parole than probation. Early terminations do exist, but the age of the juvenile parolee determines the length of supervision, and it ends usually at age twenty. For juvenile probationers, family courts set the length of supervision from one to five years, leaving room for early terminations.

Revocations (return of the case to training schools) are more frequent among juvenile parolees, but, along with juvenile probationers, the revocation rate is low. Absconding (unauthorized evasion of supervision) and arrest (apprehension for a new offense) add modestly to the failures. Again parole is more prominent. These outcomes are separate from revocations because the "extinction" is added to the nonsuccessful outcomes, but it is an administrative device for eliminating cases from the active files without positive conduct of the supervisee. Article 27 of the Penal Code states: "When a period of suspension elapses without the revocation of the pronouncement of suspension of execution of sentence, the sentence loses its effect."[6]

In two general respects, table 8.1 measures the emphasis on "protective measures" in the juvenile justice system. First, the family courts' degree of tolerance in earlier dispositions is suggested by arraying decisions from the relative sternness of referrals to training schools to the greatest tolerance in case dismissals without a formal hearing. Second, the outcomes of probation and parole supervision are arrayed similarly from the high degree of case success in early termination to the other extreme of revocation of supervision as the clearest pronouncement of case failure.

Among probationers, those with training school experience had a high number in revocations, absconding, and arrests, but even this background did not undermine the record of completions and early terminations. Previous probation experience was second only to dismissals without a hearing in favorable outcomes of the most recent probation experience; absconding, arrest, and revocations were about average. Performance on probation was particularly unsatisfactory for those who had been referred to social agencies. Of course, not all juveniles were sent earlier to social agencies when very young and ended up on probation later, but for some the initial behavioral problems signaled persistent delinquency. Dismissals with hearings were more common than dismissals without a hearing; the family courts' preference for formal consideration of these earlier cases suggests a degree of caution. However, probation outcomes differed little for those exposed to either of the two versions of dismissal.

Compared to juvenile probationers, the previous exposure of juvenile parolees has moved away from dismissals and toward training schools and earlier probation. A second general pattern has been the emphasis on completion and weakening of early terminations. However, parole continues to be associated with highly favorable outcomes in spite of the ponderable gain over probation in revocations and other kinds of case failures.

The case failures stand out for juvenile parolees who had been referred to social agencies. Family courts had found those "social agency alumni" especially inadequate in sending them to training schools from which they had been paroled. Juvenile parolees "graduating" from training schools balanced favorable outcomes against a relatively high level of case failures. Probation experience led to a more positive outcome on parole. Perhaps the previous experience of being supervised had improved the performance on parole. Dismissals by family courts of earlier cases were associated with comparatively better performance on parole, with a slight advantage going to dismissals without a hearing. Perhaps the family courts had detected factors that signaled in these individuals qualities and capacities later brought forth during parole.

Table 8.1 provides evidence that the juvenile probationers terminated in 1995 had benefited more through the earlier decisions of the family courts than the juvenile parolees terminated in 1995. The probationers had continued to hold that advantage because they were completing probation again, whereas the parolees, whether or not they had been on probation previously, were ending parole supervision after being in training school. Note, however, juvenile paroles had exceeded juvenile probationers in previous exposure to protective measures.

In that total range of exposures, a greater proportion for parolees than for probationers had been in training schools and on probation. Recall that from the perspective of the family court judges in making dispositions, probation would be a more stern disposition than dismissals, with all dispositions believed to be "protective measures" for juveniles. The greater proportion of parolees had the previous referrals to social agencies. Some present parolees were younger than subsequent probationers at first court appearance.

Much of the advantage for probationers was in "no exposure," indicating that they were considerably more likely to be first offenders and to have been assessed as proper candidates for the recent probation than for referral to training schools and subsequent parole. Nevertheless, probationers had a clear advantage in earlier dismissals with or without a formal hearing.

The probationers' more positive background of exposure is further demonstrated by ratios of the absolute number of probationers divided by the absolute number of parolees for each type of previous exposure. For the relatively stern dispositions, the ratios were training schools .37 (311 divided by 839) and probation 2.50. Probationers had an advantage for previous probation, but the advantage was much greater for case dismissals: with hearings 14.16 and without hearings 12.93. The greater advantage for dismissals with a formal hearing is tentative evidence of greater care by the family courts in earlier dispositions. Probationers also had an advantage in "no exposure": a ratio of 10.73.

Overall, the case outcomes reported in table 8.1 are more favorable to juvenile probationers than juvenile parolees. Regardless of kind of previous exposure to protective measures, the probationers were granted more early terminations and fewer revocations than the parolees. The positive case outcomes for parolees rested on completion of the supervisory period, not its early termination, even when the parolee had no previous experience with the family courts. At the negative end of case outcomes, the probationers had smaller shares of revocations and arrests. Probationers surpassed parolees in absconding when both had previous referrals to training schools; this was the only exception. Generally, probationers with previous training school experience trailed other probationers in case outcomes.

Outcomes: Adult Probation and Parole

Adults have many more parolees than probationers, and parolees are more successful in completing supervision than probationers (see table 8.2). Only probationers can be rewarded for good conduct by "provisional suspension" of supervision. Article 25-2-2 of the Penal Code authorizes "provisionally" discharge from supervision "by a disposition of the administrative authorities." Only 18 percent of the probationers' outcomes were provisional suspensions. Completions (45 percent) produced a total success rate of 62 percent, short of the 91 percent rate for adult parolees.

The Law for Probationary Supervision of Persons under Suspension of Execution of Sentence, Article 8, amplifies on the administration: "[T]he provisional discharge . . . shall be decided on by means of a ruling of the regional parole board (RPB) having jurisdiction over the area wherein the probation office handling the probationary supervision of the subject person locates, on the application of the chief of such probation office." Article 8 also authorizes the RPB to cancel the provisional discharge "when it deems it proper to recommence the probationary supervision in view of his [the probationer] behavior."

In short, as a peculiar twist of *probation* administration, the *parole* board has the authority to free an adult *probationer* from supervision. The word *provisional* is apt because only the court can terminate probation supervision completely. Probation is linked directly to the court's suspension of a prison sentence. Also, the probation period continues unless otherwise terminated.

The ratios (absolute number of probationers divided by the absolute number of parolees) are affected by the much greater number of adult parolees than adult probationers (see table 8.2). Overall, there were only 39 probationers (ratio of .39) for every 100 parolees. Nevertheless, as for juveniles, adult probationers held the advantage of higher ratios for the more tolerant previous dispositions of the courts than held by the adult parolees: suspended prosecution 5.00, general fines 1.25, and traffic fines 1.14. "No exposure" had a neutral ratio of 1.01. Adult probation was underrepresented: imprisonment only .06, probation .26, and suspended sentence without probation .62.

As discussed earlier in this chapter, adult parolees score more favorable outcomes than adult probationers. All adult parolees "complete" supervision at the rate of 91.3 percent, without any provisional suspensions of supervision. Adult probationers benefit from provisional suspension but trail the success rate of adult parolees even when completions and provisional suspensions are combined for adult probationers. The revocation rate of probationers (30.3 percent of outcome) clearly exceeds the parolees' rate (7.4 percent). Absconding duplicates the comparison, but arrests are similar. Extinction, a minor factor, is exclusive to adult parole.

For adult probationers, previous imprisonment or suspension of prosecution was associated with the least satisfactory outcomes of recent probation. Suspended prosecution

Table 8.2

Table 8.2

Outcomes of Adult Probation and Parole by Previous Exposure to Criminal Justice, 1995

Previous Exposure	Total Outcomes		Outcome of Adult Probation and Parole[a]					
	Number	Percent	Provisional Suspension	Completion	Extinction	Absconding	Arrest	Revoked
				Percentage Distribution				
Adult probation								
Imprisonment	409	8.7	10.76	43.52	—	9.29	0.49	35.94
Probation	270	5.8	15.19	41.48	—	8.89	1.85	32.59
Suspended sentence w/o probation	1,354	28.9	23.26	43.06	—	5.17	0.52	27.99
General fine	366	7.8	12.57	43.72	—	6.28	—	37.43
Traffic fine	560	12.0	22.86	47.86	—	4.46	0.54	24.28
Suspended prosecution	100	2.1	8.00	35.00	—	11.00	2.00	44.00
No exposure	1,622	34.7	16.59	46.24	—	6.84	0.37	29.96
Total persons	—	100.0	18.18	44.56	—	6.45	0.54	30.27
Number	4,681	—	851	2,086	—	302	25	1,417
Adult parole								
Imprisonment[b]	6,385	53.1	—	89.49	0.92	0.38	0.30	8.91
Probation	1,030	8.6	—	88.45	0.97	0.19	0.58	9.81
Suspended sentence w/o probation	2,189	18.2	—	91.18	0.69	0.09	0.27	7.77
General fine[c]	293	2.4	—	96.63	0.34	—	—	2.73

Table 8.2 cont. on next page

Table 8.2 continued

Previous Exposure	Total Outcomes		Outcome of Adult Probation and Parole[a]					
	Number	Percent	Provisional Suspension	Completion	Extinction	Absconding	Arrest	Revoked
Adult parole								
Traffic fine	490	4.1	—	97.14	0.61	—	—	2.25
Suspended prosecution	20	0.2	—	95.00	—	—	5.00	—
No exposure[d]	1,606	13.4	—	97.45	0.44	0.06	0.12	1.93
Total persons	—	100.0	—	91.28	0.79	0.24	0.28	7.41
Number	12,013	—	—	10,965	95	29	34	890

Source: Research and Statistics Section (1996a, 114).

[a]"Other" outcomes are excluded.
[b]Includes one stay at a Women's Guidance Home.
[c]Includes four cases of penal detention and minor fine.
[d]Includes one indeterminate sentence.

had been rare, but the high revocation rate (44 percent) suggests that the earlier decision of public prosecutors had not turned these individuals toward "self-correction." Imprisonment as a previous experience drew a higher completion rate and lower revocation rate.

Earlier suspended prison sentence without probation and traffic fines had the best outcomes, but revocations were frequent. Traffic fines had a better record than general fines. Traffic offenders are believed to be less criminalistic than "real" criminals, and their self-images tend to be consistent with that popular belief. Probationers previously on probation stood in the mid-quality of outcomes. Again courts tend to select probationers as being too worthy for imprisonment but short of unconditional release. Even without previous exposure to the adult criminal justice system, probationers could not keep pace with adult probationers who earlier had received only a general fine.

Adult parolees without previous exposure to the adult criminal justice system had the highest completion rate and the lowest revocation rate among parolees. Previous exposure to imprisonment or probation generated remarkably high performance on most recent parole, but the completion rates were lowest of all kinds of previous contact with criminal justice. Suspended prison sentences without probation had a higher success rate than suspensions with probation (identified simply as "probation" in table 8.2), but short of the performance of fined individuals. The very few instances of suspended prosecution scored remarkably well, but the instances were too few to tell much about the ultimate consequences of suspended prosecution.

Gang Membership and Marginal Deviance

As discussed in chapter 6, the Ministry of Justice publishes statistics on four juvenile groups that have been referred to juvenile classification homes as delinquents requiring diagnostic examination. The four groups—school, neighborhood, bosozoku, and criminal affiliates—are examples of marginal deviants who at least temporarily do not receive the public stigmatization applied to "genuine" criminals. The withholding of stigma is consistent with the juvenile justice preference for protection of youngsters from the effects of an adverse familial relationship and other environmental circumstances. Membership in one of the delinquent groups offers clues to the relationship between the juvenile's background and case outcome.

In quality of case outcomes, juvenile probationers performed at a more satisfactory rate than juvenile parolees. That comparison is consistent with the other findings of the two programmatic outcomes. Here, attention turns to the comparison of the members of the four delinquent groups. Juveniles without gang membership outnumbered the gang members— an indicator of the secondary importance of the companionate factor in Japanese delinquency—especially for probationers. Table 8.3 shows that juveniles not members of gangs hold 67 percent share of the probationers and 45.3 percent of parolees. Family courts would have found gang membership a reason to question the appropriateness of probation when case dismissal was not feasible. Probationers outperform parolees for all kinds of gangs and no gang membership. For both versions of community-oriented corrections, the bosozoku performed best in outcomes among the four kinds of gang. For bosozoku probationers, 77.4 percent of the outcomes were early terminations, and the revocations held a relatively low 12.3 percent. The parolees gained only 33.7 percent in early terminations but added 50.7 percent completions. Again revocations held the 12.1 percent share. As expected, the bosozoku offenses were concentrated in traffic violations (48.1 percent) in JCH admissions in 1995 (Research and Statistics 1996c, 64).

Traffic offenders, whether juvenile or adult, see themselves

Table 8.3

Gang Membership and Drug Abuse in Outcomes of Juvenile Probation and Parole, 1995

	Total Cases		Early Termination	Completion	Absconding	Arrest	Revoke
	Number	Percent	Percentage Distribution				
Juvenile gangs							
Juvenile probation							
Bosozoku	3,676	18.2	77.4	9.4	0.7	0.2	12.3
Student	582	2.9	72.5	6.5	1.0	0.2	19.8
Neighborhood	2,085	10.3	64.9	15.0	2.1	0.6	17.4
Criminal affiliates	331	1.6	48.9	26.8	4.8	1.7	17.6
None	13,516	67.0	77.3	11.7	1.7	0.4	8.9
Total number	20,190	100	15,247	2,367	324	78	2,191
Percentages	—	—	75.5	11.7	1.6	0.4	10.8
Juvenile parole							
Bosozoku	1,158	29.8	33.7	50.7	2.0	1.5	12.1
Student	60	1.5	28.3	41.7	1.7	3.3	25.0
Neighborhood	608	15.7	19.7	50.2	4.3	3.6	22.2
Criminal affiliates	301	7.7	9.3	73.4	4.7	4.7	7.9
None	1,758	45.3	18.4	57.9	4.4	2.7	16.6
Total number	3,885	100	879	2,155	141	104	606
Percentages	—	—	22.6	55.5	3.6	2.7	15.6

Table 8.3 cont. on next page

Table 8.3 continued

	Total Cases		Early Termination	Completion	Absconding	Arrest	Revoke
	Number	Percent					
Drug abuse							
Juvenile probation							
Opium, hemp	134	0.7	79.9	9.7	2.2	—	8.2
Stimulants	405	2.0	68.2	18.8	4.4	0.7	7.9
Organic solvents	4,184	20.7	59.7	19.5	2.2	0.7	17.9
None	15,484	76.6	79.5	9.4	1.4	0.3	9.0
Total number	20,207	100	15,247	2,367	324	78	2,191
Percentages	—	—	75.5	11.7	1.6	0.4	10.8
Juvenile parole							
Opium, hemp	29	0.7	24.1	69.0	—	—	6.9
Organic solvents	1,588	40.4	19.0	55.2	4.3	2.7	18.8
Stimulants	393	10.0	12.2	70.0	4.8	3.3	9.7
None	1,920	48.9	27.3	52.5	3.0	2.5	14.7
Total number	3,930	100	881	2,180	146	104	619
Percentages	—	—	22.4	55.5	3.7	2.6	15.8

Source: Research and Statistics Section (1996a, 118–19).

as law-abiding persons, and the general public also questions the treatment of them as "common criminals." The background of the bosozoku lends some support to that point of view when we consider some of the characteristics reported for bosozoku entering JCH. Of the four gangs, they have the greatest percentage of members living with their family (84.1 percent) and having both parents as guardians (58.2 percent). In their previous exposure to the juvenile justice system, experiences of juvenile traffic offenders include a significant contact with social agencies for juveniles and case dismissals by the family court, while non-traffic offenders have had more exposure to juvenile training schools and probation (Research and Statistics Section 1996c, 124–25, 128–29, 158–59).

In second place among the gangs in the percentage distribution, neighborhood gangs depended on completions, along with early terminations, to top the student gangs in quality of outcomes for probationers. Criminal affiliates took over second place for juvenile parolees. In JCH admissions, members of neighborhood gangs were especially involved in robbery and rape—in relative terms rather than in magnitude—and in abuse of organic solvents, but larceny situation was second only to the members of the bosozoku; 72.1 percent were in an intact family, and 50.8 percent had both parents. Broken families were a source of the problems of another 13 percent (Research and Statistics Section 1996c, 56–57, 64–65).

Student gangs represented a modest share of case outcomes, especially for parole, but held one of the best performances for probation in spite of a high revocation rate. Those on parole had the least satisfactory outcomes in regard to revocations. In JCH admissions, the student gangs were noteworthy in the unusual number of predelinquents (28.1 percent) who had a mean age of 15.8 years. However, larceny and bodily injury were also highly represented but had higher average ages (about 17 years). Student gangs tended to suffer from broken homes; 54 percent had only one biological parent as guardian, although 66.2 percent lived in a familial situation.

Juveniles having some connection with the yakuza also had favorable outcomes in supervision, especially those on parole (Research and Statistics Section 1996a, 118). The official identification of them with criminal organizations was related to those members involved with violence and stimulant drugs who were at least 17 years in age. Those juveniles identified with criminal gangs tended to live outside the bonds of their families and were more likely among the members of various kinds of gangs to be living with a girlfriend or a delinquent friend. Their guardians were either one biological parent (41 percent) or a stepparent (10.5 percent).

Drug Offenses and Marginal Deviance

The public has been given the image of a growing crisis of drug offenses. Abuse of opium, marijuana, and narcotics has been limited, but abuse of stimulant drugs (amphetamines) grew after World War II, when the drugs produced for the military became available to the public. Strengthened penalties helped ease the crisis of drug abuse, but it reappeared after 1970, when juveniles became involved. Around 1962, some juveniles experimented with sniffing organic solvents (toluene and acetone) used for paint thinning. Admissions to juvenile probation for stimulant drugs were only five in 1969, increased gradually to reach 197 in 1976, to 876 in 1982, and declined to 363 by 1993. Sniffing of organic solvents appeared abruptly in 1979, when 1,781 juveniles were admitted to probation when charged with the offense. The number of admissions grew irregularly to 2,093 in 1991 and has eased off since then.[7]

Table 8.3 reports on the involvement with drugs of juveniles departing from probation and parole supervision in 1995. Some of the drug users had been convicted of offenses other than drugs. Probationers had less involvement than parolees. As for juvenile drug abusers generally, organic solvents

Table 8.4
Outcomes of Probation and Parole by Selected Crimes, 1995

Community Programs	Number	Outcomes of Supervision			Chi–Square	Level of Significance
		Success	Intermediate	Revoked		
Percentage Distribution						
Total crimes						
Juveniles					331.9	0.001
Probation	20,296	87.13	2.01	10.86	—	—
Parole	3,958	77.92	6.39	15.69	—	—
Ratios	5.13	5.73	1.61	3.54	—	—
Adults					1,985.8	0.001
Probation	4,700	62.68	7.04	30.28	—	—
Parole	12,030	91.27	1.32	7.41	—	—
Ratios	0.39	0.27	2.08	4.89	—	—
Traffic						
Juveniles					27.2	n.s.
Probation	8,306	93.05	0.87	6.08	—	—
Parole	497	88.33	3.02	8.65	—	—
Ratios	16.71	17.61	4.80	11.74	—	—
Adults					170.2	0.001
Probation	829	83.23	2.66	14.11	—	—
Parole	1,163	98.97	0.17	0.86	—	—
Ratios	0.71	0.60	11.00	11.70	—	—
Extortion						
Juveniles					8.5	0.02
Probation	818	86.31	2.57	11.12	—	—
Parole	203	80.79	7.39	11.82	—	—
Ratios	4.03	4.30	1.40	3.79	—	—
Adults					136.0	0.001
Probation	170	44.12	23.53	32.35	—	—
Parole	325	91.69	0.31	8	—	—
Ratios	0.52	0.25	40.00	2.11	—	—
Bodily Injury						
Juveniles					28.7	0.001
Probation	1,840	87.12	1.52	11.36	—	—
Parole	471	83.23	5.73	11.04	—	—
Ratios	3.91	4.11	1.04	4.02	—	—
Adults					83.0	0.001
Probation	280	70.36	7.14	22.5	—	—
Parole	474	94.52	0.63	4.85	—	—
Ratios	0.59	0.44	6.67	2.74	—	—

Table 8.4 cont. on next page

Table 8.4 continued

| Community Programs | Number | Outcomes of Supervision | | | Chi–Square | Level of Significance |
		Success	Intermediate	Revoked		
Larceny						
Juveniles					92.2	0.001
Probation	5,654	79.48	3.18	17.33	—	—
Parole	1,525	69.64	7.67	22.69	—	—
Ratios	3.71	4.23	1.54	2.83	—	—
Adults					719.4	0.001
Probation	1,556	49.10	10.86	40.04	—	—
Parole	3,722	84.44	2.58	12.98	—	—
Ratios	0.42	0.24	1.76	1.29	—	—
Indecent assault						
Juveniles					3.15	0.1
Probation	109	93.58	0.92	5.50	—	—
Parole	328	1.25	6.25	12.50	—	—
Ratios	3.41	3.92	0.50	1.50	—	—
Adults					10.4	0.01
Probation	859	2.94	—	7.06	—	—
Parole	47	72.34	8.51	19.15	—	—
Ratios	1.81	2.32	—	0.67	—	—
Stimulant drugs						
Juveniles					0.019	n.s.
Probation	335	87.46	5.37	7.17	—	—
Parole	287	87.46	5.57	6.97	—	—
Ratios	1.17	1.17	1.12	1.20	—	—
Adults					740.8	0.001
Probation	1,024	59.57	4.20	36.23	—	—
Parole	3,493	93.39	0.83	5.78	—	—
Ratios	0.29	0.19	1.48	1.84	—	—

Source: Research and Statistics Section (1996a, 110–13).

exceeds stimulant drugs on the rolls for juvenile probationers and parolees. Abuse of opium and marijuana are exceptional, and the few juvenile admissions score very well in
supervisory performance.

Again, probationers performed better than parolees, because of the high proportion (75.5 versus 22.4 percent) of early
terminations for probationers. Parolees depended on completion of the full supervisory term. Probationers had the lower
rates for revocations, absconding, and arrest.

Probationers also were in the advantageous position over parolees for those juveniles not involved in drug abuse. Performance exceeded the benchmark of the quality of outcome set by total probationers and parolees, respectively. Stimulant drug abuse is mostly characteristic of adults, and organic solvent abuse is limited largely to juveniles. Therefore, admissions for organic solvents exceed in number the admissions for stimulant drugs for both probationers and parolees. Stimulant drug offenders have a supervisory record superior to that of organic solvent offenders. The more advanced age of the stimulant drug abusers is a factor in that greater compliance. The supervisees would be more likely to be returned to training schools as a protective measure if the younger probationer or parolee suffered adverse situations in the community.

Crimes: Comparing Probation and Parole Outcomes

The crimes for which probationers and parolees were convicted offer clues to their qualities and the standards of the judges as decision makers. The particular crime reflects the administration of criminal justice more than of the specific behaviors entailed in the crime's situation. The legal definition of crime, which underlies the decisions of criminal justice agents, pivots on what the code of law singles out in setting the kind and degree of punishment.

A social definition of crime goes beyond legal norms and examines the meanings of the misconduct from the offender's perspective and in terms of the impact on the community. That approach is relevant to the Japanese consideration of a crime and its place along a continuum of seriousness. The Japanese tend to accept wide discretion in the interpretation of legal codes during the processing of specific cases. There seems to be a "disposition to lay a greater emphasis upon intuitive sensible concrete events, rather than upon universals" (Nakamura 1964, 35). In that sense, the crime categories in Japan come closer to the behavioral meanings.

In regard to the offenses for which they had been convicted, how did probationers and parolees differ in their performance while being supervised? Table 8.4 presents two modes of comparison. The percentage distribution of the outcomes compares how they are concentrated in the successes or failures. For example, 87.13 percent of the total juvenile probationers had finished the period of supervision, 2.01 percent were intermediate cases that hovered between full-fledged success and failure, and 10.86 percent were revocations and clear-cut failures. Those figures serve as standards for comparing outcomes for various crimes.

Administrative differences in outcomes and between juvenile versus adult cases can create laborious discussion of outcomes. To avoid those obstacles to clear explanation of outcome, the more general category "success" includes more specific categories of favorable outcomes: early termination, provisional suspensions, and case completions. "Intermediate outcomes" include absconding, arrest, and extinction. "Revocation" is retained here as a general category. Secondarily, the broader categories have the additional advantage of reducing the effect on statistical comparisons of the excessively few instances of the components now merged into the three general categories of outcomes.

Many offenses are insufficient in absolute numbers to survive for meaningful analysis the array of the various programmatic outcomes. The insufficiency is further aggravated by the dispersal of outcomes between probation and parole plus between juveniles and adults. Table 8.4 presents six offenses that survive these difficulties reasonably well. The six offenses constitute a crude sample of the various types of offenses.

Ratios, the second kind of comparison, are the absolute number of probationers per parolee for each crime and also for each of the three general categories of outcomes. For juveniles, there are more probationers than parolees; that difference varies among crimes and outcomes. How do the differences change along the continuum of outcomes? For all juvenile offenses, probation had a 5.73 advantage over parolees in successes but lost some of the advantage (ratio of 3.54) for revocations and had even more loss (ratio 1.61) for intermediate outcomes. In spite of strongly edging out parolees in successes, juvenile probationers drew a considerable number of revocations and approached equality in the "twilight zone" of intermediate outcomes.

The six selected offenses are arrayed in table 8.4 according to the ratio for juveniles from 16.71 for traffic offenses to 1.17 for stimulant drugs. The short-term probation program for juvenile traffic offenders has inflated the advantage of juvenile probation over parole. The ratios for adults are much less in value—indicating the numerical superiority of adult parole over adult probation—and do not follow the pattern for juvenile ratios.

Another statistical device—the chi-square test—measures whether or not the outcomes are distributed about the same along the continuums of probation and parole, respectively. We should expect that the distributions will differ, but is the difference great enough to be beyond mere chance? The chi-square values in table 8.4 for all offenses indicate that the difference between probation and parole was considerably greater for adults than juveniles. Chi-square values were beyond chance for both juveniles and adults. Adults had the more impressive difference in performance of parolees over probationers.

Juvenile traffic offenders were particularly numerous in probation because of the special program for juvenile probationers; that also explains the high success rate. Perhaps the selection of the least promising juvenile traffic offenders for training schools explains the lower success rate and higher revocation rate of the parolees. The consequences are high ratios for both successes and revocations.

Adult parolees were more numerous than adult probationers for traffic offenders, not an unusual relationship for adults, but even more impressive is the general performance of paroled traffic offenders. Their traffic offenses probably justified imprisonment, but their conduct as parolees suggests that most of them saw themselves as non-criminals. The chi-square value (170.2) points to a noteworthy difference between probation and parole, but the unusual feature is a ratio for success (.6) approaching equality. The revocations exhibited the greatest difference (ratio of 11.7) and then because probationers had such a high share of cases (14.11).

In the Penal Code, extortion is listed along with fraud and thereby creates different legal platforms for juveniles and adults. Article 249 deals with "extortion" thusly: "A person who, by intimidation, causes another to surrender property shall be punished with imprisonment at forced labor for not more than 10 years." The statement is relevant to the offenses of both juveniles and adults. Article 247 (Breach of Trust) swings to the adult side: "When a person who administers the affairs of another performs, for the purpose of promoting his own interest or that of a third person or inflicting damage on such other person, commits an act in violation of his duties and causes damage to property of such person, imprisonment at forced labor for not more than five years or a fine of not more than 1,000 yen shall be imposed."[8] Fluctuating between possible juvenile and adult offenses is "constructive fraud" (Article 248): "A person who, by taking advantage of the lack of knowledge or experience of a minor or the weak-mindedness of another, obtains a surrender of such a person's property or causes a third person to obtain illegally any economic benefit shall be punished with imprisonment at forced labor for not more than 10 years."

The combination of force and illicit economic gain in extortion lacked the rather ambivalent consent the public grants most traffic offenders. Extortion drew fewer juvenile probationers, relative to parolees, than traffic offenses but had a higher ratio (4.03) than the other selected offenders. The quality of performance slipped from the traffic offenders for the juvenile probationers associated with extortion; the percentage shares dropped to 86.31 for successes and rose to 11.12 for revocations. Juvenile parole followed suit, narrowing the difference from juvenile probation; the chi-square value (8.5) declined from that of juvenile traffic offenders.

As common for adults, extortion was more characteristic of adult parolees than adult probationers, although the ratio (.52) was very low. Adults involved in "breach of trust" primarily—perhaps even in forcible intimidation—have sufficient linkage with white-collar offenses to be overwhelmed psychologically by imprisonment sufficiently to respond positively to parole supervision. Adult probationers were especially prone to revocations, intermediate outcomes, and a very low success rate. The high chi-square value confirms the sizable differences between probation and parole in outcomes.

Bodily injury represents violence against persons in our crude sample, but such offenders and offense situations come in wide variety. Injury of a victim may be deliberate thuggery or stem incidentally from a dispute. For juveniles and adults, outcomes of both probation and parole deviate sufficiently for sizable and statistically significant values of chi-square. Probationers have the greater percentage shares for both successes and revocations. The heterogeneity of the criminal incidents is especially reflected in adult probation with relatively low percentage share devoted to successes and a high percentage to revocations. That pattern stands in sharp contrast to that of adult parole; the ratios mirror that contrast.

Larceny is an even more heterogeneous affair and the most popular of offenses against property. That conformation holds for both juveniles and adults, with parole trailing probation in quality of juvenile outcome and parole even more intensively outscoring probation in adult outcomes. Adults associated with larceny are more likely to be recidivists than juveniles and, familiar with the operations of criminal justice, are more likely than juveniles to be compliant parolees. Then too, juveniles' outcomes reflect the use of parole as a "protective measure" that lends weight to the return of the parolee to the training school because of victimization by others in the community.

Indecent assault represents sex offenses that are low in recidivism and are among the infrequent admissions to juvenile and adult probation and parole. Small numbers weaken the comparisons in table 8.4, but indecent assault is included in our "sample" because rape is even less frequent. The chisquare values indicate that the difference between probation and parole is marginal for both juveniles and adults. Probationers are more numerous than parolees for both juveniles and adults, with probationers having the greater advantage for juveniles. The percentage share for success is high at about the same degree for both age groups, but adult parolees fall behind adult probationers to the greater extent.

Abuse of stimulant drugs is more an adult offense than characteristic of juveniles, but its incidence is more common among all drug offenses than organic solvents. Juvenile probation and parole are essentially similar in quality of outcome, resulting in low ratios and a nonsignificant value of chi-square. Adult probation falls far behind adult parole in quality of outcome. Drug abuse tends to be habitual and especially tests the capacity of probation supervision to deal with the personal and social conditions that favor repetition.

Ambivalence Toward Parole

Parole is dedicated simultaneously to ease the reentry crisis of inmates from correctional institutions and to supervise them against the possibility of new law violations. The inherently contradictory purposes of the agency are matched by the ambivalence among the parolees. Welcoming help mingles with resentment against official authority.

As a "protective measure" parole emphasizes safeguard-

Table 8.5

Table 8.5

Trends of Parole among Releases from Prison, 1950–1995

| Years | Total Releases | Referrals to RPBs | Percentage of Total Releases | | | |
			Termination	Paroles	Referrals to RBPs	Rate of RPB Approvals[a]
1950	57,586	53,887	26.82	73.18	93.58	77.89
1955	50,520	55,060	36.27	63.73	69.40	93.80
1960	44,930	34,395	31.56	68.44	76.55	90.00
1965	33,978	24,314	42.81	57.19	71.52	81.28
1970	28,870	20,941	38.15	61.85	72.53	86.25
1975	26,669	17,801	44.01	55.99	66.75	84.29
1980	29,342	18,191	48.19	51.81	62.00	84.43
1985	31,938	19,928	44.28	55.72	62.40	91.30
1990	26,453	16,226	43.69	56.31	61.34	92.55
1995	21,371	13,222	43.20	56.80	61.87	94.17

Sources: Research and Statistics Section (1971a, 5; 196a, 3; 1991b, 162; 1996b, 170); Shikita and Tsuchiya (1990, 372–73).

[a]Number of approvals per 100 referrals to RPBs.

ing youngsters from the adverse social circumstances in the community. The long-term trend has been toward parole's near monopoly of releases from juvenile training schools. From approaching zero in the 1940s, parole reached the 80 percent shares of releases from training schools in the 1950s, dipped to 67 percent in 1970, and thereafter has climbed into the 90 percentages (Shikita and Tsuchiya 1990, 317).

Parole also is popular in adult corrections in Japan, but the percentage share of all prison releases is considerably less and has declined over the years (see table 8.5). Parole held 79.7 percent of all releases in 1949, when prisons were over-populated (Shikita and Tsuchiya 1990, 373). Parole lost share over the following decades to reach 56.8 percent in 1995 (Research and Statistics Section 1996b, 170). The number of all persons leaving the prisons also has dropped. The general decline has been a side effect of Japan's long-lasting retreat from imprisonment.

The significance of that downward trend of the parole

rate, however, also lies in the complexities of parole decision making for adults. Juveniles have a shorter age span than adults, and juvenile parole ends at age twenty. The average length of training school sentences is considerably shorter than those for prisons; length of stay is less a factor for juveniles in parole decision making than for adults. In 1995 all juvenile releasees averaged 9.2 months in training schools. From the short-term program of the training schools, 321 were released on parole (average stay 2.6 months) and 1,313 departed at expiration of sentence (4.9 months stay). Parole was considerably more characteristic of the long-term program and its average stay of about 12.5 months. The numbers of releases from the long-term program were 2,150 on parole and 180 at expiration (Research and Statistics Section 1996c, 166–73).

Adult supervision also is limited by its length being set by the unserved portion of the prison sentences. Short sentences discourage the officials from accepting an excessively brief length of parole supervision and persuade prisoners that they will gain little advantage. The twin reasons for limited use of parole are among the sources for the decreasing proportion of paroles of all releases from prison, but, as table 8.5 documents, a third factor must be considered: the influence of the wardens' authority as gatekeepers to the inmates' access to parole. Table 8.5 lends support to the following list of fundamental facts:

- The total releases from prison have dropped from 57,586 in 1950 to 21,371 in 1995. This 62.9 percent drop is due to the noteworthy retreat from the use of imprisonment as the major means of dealing with criminality.

- Paroles have held a declining share of total releases—from 73.18 percent in 1950 to 56.8 percent in 1995—while increasing percentages have been devoted to unconditional discharges upon completion of the prison sentence. In that respect, community-oriented corrections has experienced a twofold loss of this part of its caseload. The pool of inmate-candidates for parole has been significantly drained by the major reduction of Japan's imprisonment rate. Second, a smaller proportion of prisoners are being referred to regional parole boards.

- The wardens' referrals of parole applications have declined over the decades from 1950 (when prisons were crowded during the postwar crisis) to 1995. Paroles held the largest share of all prison releases in 1950, when referrals were 93.6 percent of the total number of ultimate discharges from prison in 1950. In contrast, referrals to the RPBs were 61.9 percent (a respective but lower figure) of the 1995 releases.

- The declining parole rate cannot be attributed to any policy change by the RPBs. Table 8.5 lists the rates of RPB approvals of parole applications, from 93.8 percent in 1955, down to 81.3 percent in 1965, and upward to 94.2 percent by 1995. That rate is the number of RPB approvals of 100 parole applications forwarded by prison wardens. That rate after 1950 is consistently greater than the rate of wardens' referrals per 100 total releases from prison. The deviation shows that proportionately fewer referrals are among the major explanations for the reduced parole rate.

- RPBs have approved for parole a very high proportion of the wardens' applications. Conversely, the RPBs' rate of denials had dropped considerably. Applications may be withdrawn from RPB deliberations because of violations of prison regulations or because of inadequacies discovered in the residence-employment plan for the prisoner. Of the cases withdrawn in 1995, 65 percent were derived from a prison report and 35 percent from a probation office report. Forty-six percent of the cases received a favorable RPB decision later (Research and Statistics Section 1996a, 45).

The parole rate also can be affected by changes in the distribution of length of prison sentences. As table 8.6 reports, 80 percent of prisoners had prison sentences ranging from 6 to 36 months in duration, but 87 percent (10,554 of 12,138) re-

Table 8.6
Releases from Adult Prisons by Length of Imprisonment, Expiration of Sentence Versus Parole, 1995

Length of Imprisonment in Months	All Releases Number	All Releases Percent	Expiration of Sentence Total Expiration	Parole Denied	No Parole Requested	Release on Parole
Number of Inmates						
Under 3	674	3.1	664	3	661	10
3–6	1,437	6.7	999	13	986	438
6–12	4,876	22.8	2,000	72	1,928	2,876
12–24	8,542	40.0	3,120	257	2,863	5,422
24–36	3,749	17.6	1,493	167	1,326	2,256
36–60	1,487	7.0	716	80	636	771
60–84	278	1.3	120	10	110	158
+ 84	328	1.5	121	12	109	207
Total	21,371	100	9,233	614	8,619	12,138
Mean months	21.16	—	19.80	26.41	19.32	22.20
Percentage Distribution						
Under 3	—	—	98.5	0.4	98.1	1.5
3–6	—	—	69.5	0.9	68.6	30.5
6–12	—	—	41.0	1.5	39.5	59.0
12–24	—	—	36.5	3.0	33.5	63.5
24–36	—	—	39.8	4.4	35.4	60.2
36–60	—	—	48.2	5.4	42.8	51.8
60–84	—	—	43.2	3.6	39.6	56.8
+ 84	—	—	36.9	3.7	33.2	63.1
Total	—	—	43.2	2.9	40.3	56.8

Source: Research and Statistics Section (1996b, 170).

ceived paroles. Sentences less than 6 months were likely to result in terminations other that parole. Sentences greater than 36 months composed only 9.8 percent of all releases, but those inmates also were likely to be paroled.

On average, the releasees had served only 21 months before discharge. Total releasees at expiration had the shorter stay (mean of 19.8 months) than total parolees (22.2 months) because inmates with shorter sentences are more likely to be released on completion of the full term than to be paroled. Those denied a parole upon application had a longer stay

(26.4 months) than those subject to a parole request (19.3 months). The latter difference is attributable to the number of RPB appearances of some long-term prisoners before approval. In 1995, only 6,469 out of 12,451 RPB case approvals (52.6 percent) came on first appearance; an average of 2.4 appearances had occurred before the approval.

The number leaving parole, as compared with completion of probation, is reported in table 8.7. Adult parolees outnumber adult probationers among returns to the community in 1995. Successful completion of the full supervision period (expiration) was the dominant (91 percent of all endings) among parolees. The administrative device of "extinction" took up less than 1 percent (.79 percent). Among programmatic failures, revocations were prominent but only 7.4 percent of all endings. Arrests (.29 percent) and absconding (.24) were few.

As already explained, adult probationers had inferior performance in case outcomes than adult parolees. Revocations (30.3 percent of case endings), absconding (6.5 percent), and arrests (.53 percent) topped the probationers' failures. Probationers (44.6) also trailed for expiration (44.6 percent) but added provisional suspensions (18 percent), a reward for exceptional conduct that is not available to adult parolees.

Juvenile probation has three programs: general probation, a short-term program for traffic offenses, and a special short-term program. Juvenile parole is linked with three programs of the training schools: long-term, general short-term, and special short-term. The supervisory outcomes for the five programs are given in table 8.8.

Juvenile probation has the reward of early termination that was the most prominent among supervisory outcomes. The special probation program was very selective, with the result that its early terminations represented 93 percent of all of its case completions; revocations (7 percent) were the only other possibility. The traffic probation program also had exceptional outcomes. It was almost as selective but drew considerably more juvenile offenders—almost eight times more. Nevertheless, early terminations (87 percent of all case endings) and expiration (7 percent) were most characteristic. Revocations (6 percent), absconding, and arrests even more minuscule.

The general program for juvenile probationers was in the orthodox model, drew the largest caseload, and also had a high success rate, although short of the other more selective juvenile programs. Early terminations (65.4 percent of outcomes) and expiration (16.6 percent) mirrored high favorable ratings by supervisors. Revocations (14.9 percent) were highest of the three programs. Absconding (2.5 percent) and arrests (.6) were unusual.

Juvenile parole caseloads were lower than for juvenile probation. The long-term program of the juvenile training schools delivered the most juvenile parolees, but the general short-term program of the schools paroled a significant number of inmates. The JTS special program had fewest inmates and parolees. Except for three juveniles leaving the JTS general short-term, juvenile parolees did not receive the early terminations available to juvenile probationers. Most outcomes were either at termination of the JTS sentence from which they were paroled or completion of the parole period.

Counting the combination of terminated JTS sentences and expirations as successes, the selective special program of the training schools were at the top (89.7 percent), over the general short-term (81.8 percent) and the general long-term (73.5 percent). Revocations, absconding, and arrest were in opposite order in representation among the programs.

Length of Supervision and Outcomes for Adults

The supervision of probationers and parolees, of course, is a series of events colored by the personal characteristics and attitudes of participants—both the supervisors and supervisees. We are interested in the outcomes of the relationships between the two sets of participants: the favorable reward of early termination; penalization of forbidden conduct by revocation of probation and parole; the supervisee's premature with-

Table 8.7
Length of Supervision of Adult Probationers
and Parolees for Cases Ending in 1995

Dispositions	Total Cases[a]	Mean Length	Length of Supervision in Months				
			Under 12	12–24	24–36	36–48	48–60
			Percentage Distribution				
Adult probation							
Total number	4,700	31.61	503	569	2,016	1,215	397
Total percent	100	—	10.70	12.11	42.89	25.85	8.45
Provisional suspension	851	38.74	—	1.17	47.00	37.02	14.81
Expiration	2,095	36.99	0.05	2.29	53.13	33.79	10.74
Absconding	306	35.45	—	5.23	56.86	29.41	8.50
Revocation	1,423	18.49	35.28	34.78	22.21	6.61	1.12
Arrest	25	38.64	—	—	52.00	32.00	16.00
Adult parole							
Total number	12,030	5.67	11,196	524	126	40	144
Total percent	100	—	93.07	4.35	1.05	0.32	1.20
Expiration	10,980	4.91	94.74	3.95	0.86	0.20	0.25
Extinction	95	64.88	—	—	—	—	100
Absconding	29	3.69	96.55	—	3.45	—	—
Revocation	891	8.67	82.35	9.88	3.48	2.02	2.24
Arrest	35	6.44	91.43	5.71	—	—	2.86

Source: Research and Statistics Section (1996a, 108–9).

[a]"Other" outcomes are excluded. "Total cases" column disagrees with table 8.2 because of differences in exclusions.

drawal (absconding); and arrest. The outcomes were defined earlier in this chapter. Table 8.7 relates the outcomes for adult probationers and parolees to the lengths of case supervision.

The mean has the advantage of directly comparing the times, but the mean is affected by extreme values. Two programs may have similar means, but one lumps most supervisees in the middle range of months under supervision, while the second program has many supervisees leaving early and many leaving after a high number of months. The balance between the extremes is similar to that of a seesaw in a playground for children. Small children at the far end of the plank can balance the heavier weight of an adult near the fulcrum.

Tables 8.7 and 8.8 present the means but supplement them with percentage distributions of the times of supervision that reveal the muffling effect of means. For comparisons, the time continuum is divided into five units of the total spread of supervision. Table 8.7 illustrates the advantage of percentage distributions by highlighting the bunching of case endings for adult parolees in the first twelve months of supervision and the wide dispersion for adult probationers.

Adult probation exceeds adult parole in length of supervision because the courts, when suspending a prison sentence and substituting probation, set the length of supervision from one to five years. The length of supervision for adult parole is for the unserved portion of the prison sentence yet to be served in prison at the time of release on parole.

Among the outcomes, the provisional suspensions of supervision—authorization of early ending supervision of adult probationers—reduce the length of supervision, but those probationers average the greatest time of supervision. The paradox is due to their longer periods of supervision by the sentencing courts, presumably largely because of the crimes for which they were convicted. Expiration is interrelated with the length of supervision set by the courts; then, the case endings bunch up at two- to three-year periods of probation.

Of probationers beginning supervision in 1995, 48.5 percent had probationary periods set at two to three years, whereas of equivalent parolees, 94.9 percent had probationary periods at less than a year and only .9 percent at two to three years (Research and Statistics Section 1996a, 86). Probationers had very early expirations, a case outcome much more frequent for them than parolees. As endemic to that outcome exclusive to parole, extinction came very late. Otherwise, revocations, absconding, and arrests came earlier in the scenario for parolees than probationers.

Table 8.8
Length of Supervision of Juvenile Probationers and Parolees for Cases Ending in 1995

Dispositions	Total Cases[a]	Mean Length	Length of Supervision in Months				
			Under 6	6–9	9–12	12–24	24+
			Percentage Distribution				
Juvenile general probation							
Total number	11,029	19.83	237	579	524	7,446	2,243
Total percent	100	—	2.15	5.25	4.75	67.51	20.34
Early termination	7,213	17.63	0.22	4.81	4.30	77.15	13.52
Expiration	1,832	29.79	—	—	—	55.13	44.87
Absconding	269	30.76	—	—	—	52.79	47.21
Revocation	1,646	16.12	13.43	14.09	13.00	41.98	17.50
Arrest	69	31.42	—	—	—	55.07	44.93
Juvenile traffic offenders							
Total number	8,214	11.10	281	4,524	1,176	1,846	387
Total percent	100	—	3.42	55.08	14.32	22.47	4.71
Early termination	7,110	9.70	2.66	62.33	15.33	17.65	2.03
Expiration	550	26.04	—	—	—	67.64	32.36
Absconding	61	24.96	—	—	—	80.33	19.67
Revocation	484	12.78	19.01	19.01	17.77	33.88	10.33
Arrest	9	26.33	—	—	—	66.67	33.33
Juvenile special probation							
Total number	1,053	6.69	77	938	38	—	—
Total percent	100	—	7.31	89.08	3.61	—	—
Early termination	980	6.77	3.98	92.86	3.16	—	—
Revocation	73	5.70	52.05	38.36	9.59	—	—
Juvenile parole from JTS long-term							
Total number	2,181	13.03	8.22	233	208	557	361
Total percent	100	—	37.69	10.68	9.54	25.54	16.55
Termination of JTS sentence	228	19.73	0.88	6.58	14.47	52.19	25.88
Expiration	1,375	11.19	52.14	8.73	6.91	16.73	15.49
Absconding	107	18.61	27.10	3.74	10.28	29.91	28.97
Revocation	393	13.92	13.23	22.39	15.78	36.64	11.96
Arrest	78	13.69	28.21	7.69	8.97	41.03	14.10
Juvenile parole from JTS general short-term							
Total number	1,466	16.27	104	399	211	458	294
Total percent	100	—	7.09	27.22	14.39	31.24	20.06
Early termination	3	6.83	33.33	66.67	—	—	—
Termination of JTS sentence	479	14.44	4.39	21.71	21.92	42.38	9.60
Expiration	720	16.83	8.47	33.89	8.89	24.17	24.58

Table 8.8 cont. on next page

Table 8.8 continued

Dispositions	Total Cases[a]	Mean Length	Length of Supervision in Months				
			Under 6	6–9	9–12	12–24	24+
Juvenile parole from JTS general short-term							
Absconding	39	23.53	—	33.33	—	15.39	51.28
Revocation[b]	199	16.78	10.05	14.57	20.10	33.17	22.11
Arrest	26	20.52	3.85	26.92	7.69	34.62	26.92
Juvenile parole from JTS special program							
Total number[a]	311	13.18	25	86	64	107	29
Total percent	100	—	8.04	27.65	20.58	34.40	9.33
Termination of JTS sentence	183	12.00	7.65	34.97	16.94	35.52	4.92
Expiration	99	15.27	5.05	19.19	27.27	31.32	17.17
Absconding	1	30.00	—	—	—	—	100.00
Revocation	26	13.00	23.08	11.54	19.23	38.46	7.69
Arrest	2	11.50	—	—	50.00	50.00	—

Source: Research and Statistics Section (1996a, 108–9).

[a]"Other" outcomes are excluded.
[b]Includes a few "returns to juvenile training schools."

Length of Supervision and Outcomes for Juveniles

Juvenile probationers are under supervision for a shorter time than adult probationers. The juvenile probation period is until age twenty years or a maximum of two years of supervision has been reached, whichever is greater. Supervision of adults is for at least one year and cannot exceed five years after the sentence to prison would have taken effect.

Juvenile parolees are under supervision for a longer time than adult parolees. Unlike juveniles, adults are in parole only for the remaining portion of the prison sentence not served. The adults' supervisory period usually is shortened by the few months remaining on the sentence when going on parole.

The three probation programs for juveniles draw greater caseloads than the three parole programs. Both approaches diversify the average lengths of supervision, with probationers holding the higher averages for all constituent programs.

The juvenile parole and probation are the same in relative importance of long-term programs. The 11,029 on the general program represented 54 percent of all juvenile probationers. The 2,181 from the JTS long-term program were 55 percent of all juvenile parolees. However, the general probationers averaged 19.8 months (the highest for juvenile probation), whereas the juveniles from the JTS long-term program averaged 13 months, and that average was short of the 16.3 months for the JTS general short-term program. (See table 8.8.)

The general probation program has the greatest tilt toward the longest supervision along the time continuum, with early termination more influential. Expiration came late for both the general and traffic programs. Termination of the JTS sentence had that function for parole but short of the trend for the general probation program.

The effect was parole's greater programmatic failure in revocations (chiefly), absconding, and arrests. Successes, however, were more prominent for parole as well as probation. Expiration, absconding, and arrests came late along the time continuum for the general and traffic probationers. Parolees were distributed throughout the continuum, but many instances of expiration came in the early months for parole from the JTS long-term program.

The relative success of special probation is at least partly explained by the heavy concentration of cases in six to nine months of supervision, due primarily to early terminations as a reward for exemplary conduct. This program was designed to single out the most promising juveniles. The brevity of the remaining time for supervision minimized the possibility of violations of probation conditions, but half of the revocations came in less than six months.

Back to Prison: Parole Versus Expiration

Probably, the most popular conception of a test for parole is whether or not the individual ever returns to prison for a new crime or other serious violations of parole conditions. Less obvious is another benefit of parole: Does the parolee who is reimprisoned avoid revocation for a longer time than the person who had been discharged after serving the full sentence to prison? That longer period of freedom without victimizing other persons is a secondary benefit for parole.

In publishing statistics on that issue, the Ministry of Justice distinguishes between males and females. The differences between expiration and parole were traced for seven years, through 1995, when prisoners released in 1988 could have been in the community for various times up to seven years. In 1988 the male releases from prison were 13,006 upon expiration of the sentence and 15,563 on parole. The women were fewer, as in all data about the operations of correctional agencies. In 1988, 291 women were released at expiration and another 977 were parolees. As reported in table 8.9, parolees composed 43.7 percent of the men leaving prison in 1988, and 66.5 percent of the women were parolees.

Releases on parole in 1988 were more numerous than discharges from prison upon completion of the sentence set by the court: 54.5 percent of the men and 76.9 percent of the women. How did the parolees compare with the "terminees" in length of time in the community before being returned to prison for some failure, primarily a new crime? Table 8.9 presents three statistical devices for answering the question: first, the percentage share of parolees of all 1988 dischargees returned to prison in each of the following seven years; second, the accumulated percentage share of all expirations or paroles, respectively, for each of the years; third, ratios of the absolute number of expirations divided by the number of paroles for each year.

The male parolees who ultimately were returned to prison stayed out on average more months than the male prisoners released after completion of their prison sentences. This relative delay in sending the parolees back to prison had two benefits for the community. The parolees were in the free community for a longer time without posing threats to other members

Table 8.9

Readmissions of Prisoners Released in 1988 by Year
of Readmission, Expiration of Sentence Versus Parole, 1995

| Year | Number by Type of Release | | Parole as % of Total Releases | Accumulated Percent of Readmissions | | Ratios A/B |
	Expiration (A)	Parole (B)		Expiration	Parole	
Males						
Total releases	13,006	15,563	54.5	—	—	0.84
1988	1,529	512	25.1	11.8	3.3	2.99
1989	2,827	1,959	40.9	33.5	15.9	1.47
1990	1,452	1,355	48.3	44.7	24.6	1.07
1991	794	808	50.4	50.8	29.8	0.98
1992	498	561	53.0	54.6	33.4	0.89
1993	353	414	54.0	57.3	36.0	0.85
1994	212	267	55.7	58.9	37.8	0.79
1995	152	198	56.6	60.1	39.0	0.77
Total returned	7,817	6,074	43.7	60.1	39.0	1.29
Females						
Total releases	291	977	76.9	—	—	0.30
1988	37	23	38.3	12.7	2.4	1.61
1989	55	97	63.8	31.6	12.3	0.57
1990	30	82	73.2	41.9	20.7	0.37
1991	16	46	74.2	47.4	25.4	0.35
1992	11	29	72.5	51.2	28.3	0.38
1993	4	19	82.6	52.6	30.3	0.21
1994	5	12	70.6	52.9	31.5	0.42
1995	3	11	78.6	55.3	32.6	0.27
Total returned	161	319	66.5	55.3	32.6	0.50

Source: Research and Statistics Section (1996b, 165).

of the community. (Cynics might say that, at least, any threats were not detected officially.) Also the taxpayers did not bear the financial cost of keeping those parolees locked up.

Of the 6,074 male parolees who were back behind bars by 1995, table 8.9 lists their percentage share of all releases from 25.1 percent in 1988 and through successive years to reach 56.6 by 1995. Note that parolees were underrepresented in the earlier years, but, after 1990, their share progressively moved more and more above 50 percent. Parolees discharged in 1988 were more numerous (54.5 percent share) than "terminees" after terminees lost their advantage in the earlier years. Parolees tended to stay in the community for more months than the prisoners who had been discharged after completing the full prison sentence.

The second statistical method confirms the conclusion but emphasizes the accumulative nature of the reimprisonment of those parolees. Initially, parolees were in the minority, but gradually they moved toward equality with terminees. Note the more gradual increase of accumulated percentage shares parolees held of all 1988 releases from prison.

The third device shows even more clearly the increased prevalence of parolees among returns to prison as the years unfold. The longer presence in the community of even failed parolees is confirmed again. The total male returnees had a ratio of .84 parolees per terminee, but the greater ration in 1988 (2.99) dropped consistently over subsequent years to approach equality in 1991. Thereafter, the parolees assumed numerical superiority—the ratios dropped from .89 to .77.

All three statistical devices confirm that conclusion for women parolees who are reimprisoned. They surpass men in percentage share of parolees for each of the years. Female parolees, in comparison with female terminees, are even more gradual than male parolees in delaying their return to prisons. Women parolees occupy a 38.3 percentage share of 1988 returns to prison (versus 25.1 percent of men); that share grows somewhat consistently to 78.6 percent (versus the male share of 56.6 percent) in 1995. (The female parolees are so few in total that they do not always flesh out their percentage distribution over the span of eight years.) Female parolees follow the male pattern of tardiness of parolees in maintaining the terminees' pace in growth of accumulated percentage of prison admissions. The ratios demonstrate a pattern of greater irregularity, but their general trend is toward decreasing representation of terminees as the years proceed.

"Rehabilitation Aid" as a
Response to the Reentry Crisis

The Law for Probationary Supervision of Persons under Suspension of Execution of Sentence (Article 6) defines the purposes of "rehabilitation aid" as assistance in addition to the services of hostels. The law puts supervision under the authority of the chief of the probation office. Article 6 states: "In giving guidance and aid, aid shall be given so that the subject person may secure employment or necessary vocational guidance, medical treatment, living quarters, etc., by obtaining the assistance of public institutions of health, welfare, etc., and his environments shall be adjusted, and such measures shall be taken as giving counsel and making arrangements necessary for the subject person's rehabilitation, etc."[9]

The probation offices are expected to emphasize referrals to other agencies in meeting the physical and social needs of probationers that are unfulfilled otherwise. What if referrals are insufficient? Article 6 continues: "In case there is apprehension that the subject person will be prevented from being rehabilitated due to the fact that he can not obtain necessary aid only from the methods mentioned in the preceding paragraph, expenses for traveling to his release destination, clothing, food, etc. may be supplied, medical treatment, or living quarters may be made available for him and other aid necessary for his rehabilitation may be given."

The Law for Aftercare of Discharged Offenders lists a remarkable variety of persons eligible for rehabilitation aid, including hostel services:

1. A person who has completely served his sentence of imprisonment with or without forced labor[10] or penal detention.[11] These prisoners are discharged at "expiration" of the sentence set by the court.

2. A person whose execution of sentence of imprisonment with or without forced labor or penal detention has been excused. They had had their prison sentence suspended and were placed on probation.

3. A person who has been granted the suspension of execution of sentence to imprisonment with or without forced labor and whose sentence has not yet become final. An unusual situation has interrupted the administrative processing of persons to be granted the suspension of a sentence.

4. A person who has been granted the suspension of execution of sentence to imprisonment with or without forced labor but has not been placed under probationary supervision. The court has returned the convicted offender to the community without conditions.

5. A person who has not been prosecuted because it has been found unnecessary (suspended prosecution). The public prosecutor has ended the case by deciding not to send the defendant to court for formal trial.

As table 8.10 summarizes, the rehabilitation aid hostels are more a vehicle for Aid I than the probation offices in the sense of being the final party. Probation offices make the decisions on applications. Adults, especially parolees, consume the bulk of the assistance provided by both hostels and probation offices. Adults encounter greater reentry crises than juveniles.

The percentage distribution of emergency aid by probation offices suggests the differential impact of the reentry crisis on four classes of community-oriented programs. Acquiring food is essential to physical survival as well as a social priority. Adult parole created the greatest demand for emergency aid and that demand was unusual in calling for clothing. Adult probation's demand was especially for food and travel in relative terms because of more brief withdrawal from the community on average. Juvenile probation placed a heavy emphasis on food in emergency Aid I. Juvenile parole had even less representation in emergency aid, and half of that aid

Table 8.10

Rehabilitation Aid by Type of Recipient, 1995

Recipients	Aid at Hostels	Aid at Probation Offices	Emergency Aid Given at Probation Offices				
			Total	Food	Clothes	Travel	Medical
		Percentage Distribution					
Aid I							
Adult parole	85.5	74.7	827	26.2	56.2	16.0	1.6
Adult probation	7.9	12.8	333	54.1	8.1	37.5	0.3
Juvenile parole	4.1	4.7	120	50.0	23.3	25.9	0.8
Juvenile probation	2.5	7.8	206	69.4	2.0	28.6	—
Total percent	100	100	100	40.4	35.3	23.3	1.0
Total number	4,904	2,686	1,486	600	524	347	15
Aid II							
Terminated	70.3	60.6	1,644	41.4	15.7	42.6	0.3
Suspended sentence	15.4	16.5	541	42.7	15.7	41.4	0.2
Suspended prosecution	14.3	22.9	729	44.0	15.1	40.5	0.4
Total percent	100	100	100	42.3	15.5	41.9	0.3
Total number	2,852	4,097	2,914	1,232	453	1,220	9

Source: Research and Statistics Section (1996a, 156–57).

was devoted to food. However, the relatively longer stay in juvenile training schools created a demand for clothing.

The Law for Aftercare of Discharged Offenders announces the purpose of Aid II: "[t]o ensure immediate and appropriate rehabilitation aid . . . with a view of their release from physical restraint inflicted upon them by criminal procedure, and smoothly to render emergency help to persons under probationary supervision." Article 3 limits temporary aid to six months after release from physical restraint. Article 40 of the Offenders Rehabilitation Law supplements that statement by referring to "emergency help" when a supervisee "may be prevented from rehabilitation by reason of injury or sickness or by lack of proper temporary lodging, residence or job."

Table 8.10 presents three categories of persons eligible for Aid II drawn from the five groups the Law for Aftercare of Discharged Offenders lists as acceptable for aftercare. "Terminations" cover prisoners completing their full sentence (group 1); "suspended sentences" refers to three groups who had been granted suspension of the execution of sentence; "suspended prosecution" represents defendants diverted from formal trial by public prosecutors (group 5).

The percentage distribution of emergency aid is about the same for the three general kinds of recipients. Food and travel compose most of Aid II; clothes drop away to third position; and medical care is rare. Hostels dominate assistance to discharged adult prisoners and training school inmates, but probation offices also are involved, especially for persons benefited by suspended prosecution. The difference between the two organizations is slight for suspended sentences of courts.

Rehabilitation Aid Hostels: Cushioning the Reentry Shock

The family is expected to be the primary buffering agency for those defendants and convicted offenders who return to the community, but, for many of them, the family cannot provide—or prefers to withhold—the social-psychological and material resources especially vital in the early weeks of the return. Rehabilitation aid hostels (halfway houses) are the primary substitute for the family in cushioning the search for jobs, residence, and social acceptance. History and public policy has given chief responsibility for hostels to private organizations.

The Law for Aftercare of Discharged Offenders authorizes the chief of the probation office to commission hostels to engage in aftercare. The private organizations are required to send the minister of justice a written account of activities and any plan to seek financial donations. Article 12 specifies a government grant "within the limits of the budget," to the hostels for clerical expenses, improvement of physical plants, and the "commissioning of rehabilitation aid."

Rehabilitation aid is defined in Article 2 as helping specified persons "to become law-abiding good members of the society and assist them quickly to be rehabilitated." The chief of the probation office can grant "temporary aids" for helping "them return home and furnishing or lending money or articles to them." The hostels provide "continuous aids" intended "to help them obtain necessary culture, training, medical treatment, recreation or employment and effecting the betterment and adjustment of their environments, if such persons can not receive aid from their relatives, friends, etc., or when they cannot obtain medical treatment, lodging accommodations, employment or other protection from public health, welfare or other institutions or in case it is feared that they may not be rehabilitated merely with such aid or protection."

The primary reliance on the family and social agencies is consistent with the government's preference to rely on private organizations. The involvement of private parties in aftercare came about a century ago when the first post-release facility for juveniles opened in 1888 in Shizuoka Prefecture. Meizen Kimbata, a philanthropist who pioneered the movement, was greatly disturbed by the suicide of a released prisoner rejected by his family. Charity-minded and religious groups established two hostels in 1891, twenty-six by 1900, sixty-one by 1910, more than one hundred by 1920, and eight hundred by 1927 (Hyotani 1985; Udo 1990; Shikita and Tsuchiya 1990).

The early involvement of private parties, Shigemi Satoh (1988, 8) explains, stemmed from traditional community solidarity and strong family ties that opposed the "deviant behavior of individual members." The royal family and government encouraged the rapid growth of hostels, he notes, and "religious organizations began simultaneously to make extensive contributions to corrections." The expansion of privately operated hostels accompanied the rapid modernization undertaken by the Meiji regime. Lacking resources to finance all modern infrastructure, Kunpei Satoh (1989, 1) declares, "the government requested religious groups, mainly Buddhist organizations, as well as voluntary organizations to provide financial assistance and moral support for ex-offenders."

Operations of the Rehabilitation Aid Hostels

In 1995 Japan had 99 rehabilitation aid hostels—7 serving youths (one for girls), 89 for males (64 housing both youths and adults), and 3 receiving both sexes (one for adults) (Research and Training Institute 1996). The rehabilitation regions range in the capacity of their hostels from 73 in Shikoku (the island south of Hiroshima) to 2,267 in Kanto (includes Tokyo).

The government pays a subsidy that meets part of the costs of meals, housing, maintenance, and staffing. The rehabilitation aid organization sponsoring the hostel must meet the rest of the expenses through donations or special projects. To obtain a governmental subsidy for a reasonable portion of the expenses, a hostel would have to maintain an average of about 80 percent utilization of bed space, but the population fluctuations and the low average number of residents are problematic. Theoretically, the residents can stay for their entire probation and parole period; some juvenile probationers could stay more than two years. However, the limitations on the governmental budget shortens the stay considerably.

The hostels function as temporary refuges for discharged prisoners, parolees, and suspects benefiting from suspended prosecution. The function is directed toward those individuals who are not assisted by families and nonfamilial groups in the community. Aftercare policy emphasizes the obligation of the extended family to meet the needs. Members of families are parents, spouses, siblings, and other relatives. Nonfamilial groups in the community are friends, acquaintances, employers, social welfare agencies, and others.

Families helped most released prisoners, 55.9 percent; nonfamily groups, 21.5 percent; and the hostels, 22.6 percent. Families were more likely to help parolees (60.5 percent) than other released inmates. Of those completing the sentence, only 7.3 percent had been denied a parole. Hostels followed suit; 80.6 percent of their admissions were parolees; of those discharged without parole, 6.8 percent had been denied a parole. The nonfamily groups took up the slack; 77.9 percent of those they helped had completed the prison sentence, but only 5.7 percent of the expirations had followed denial of a parole application (Research and Statistics Section 1996b, 200).

Most persons leaving prison do not obtain rehabilitation aid (90.7 percent), but those sent to hostels are more likely to seek aid—in 1995, 88.1 percent did not receive aid. No aid was received by 91.5 percent helped by families and 91.3 percent helped by nonfamily groups. Aid was primarily for travel expenses. Hostel residents were more likely (12.5 percent of the aid) to need clothing. The equivalent figures were 3.2 percent of the families and 10 percent of the nonfamily group (Research and Statistics Section 1996b, 200).

While parole candidates are still in prison, aftercare arrangements are being made. The probation offices will contact appropriate hostels when there are no families willing or able to lend support and no other residence is available. Representatives of the rehabilitation aid associations meet periodically to establish criteria for admission to hostels in the area. The criteria usually require the candidate to be mentally and physically healthy, without linkage to the yakuza, and, mainly, unlikely to bring objections to his presence from the hostel's neighbors. Repeated imprisonment would be less important than the probability of controversy.

The probation office receives the dossiers prepared by the RPB staff. The dossiers describe inmates without an adequate employment-residence plan because they lack of a family connection or other arrangements in the community. A representative of the office brings the dossier to appropriate hostels. Any unsatisfied questions are referred to the prisoner for more information. The hostel makes the final decision on admissions.

The inmate is not able to choose a particular hostel. In unusual cases, an individual is welcomed because of a favorable previous stay at the hostel. Since the candidates usually lack any family connections, the particular neighborhood of the hostel is less important than finding a place to stay and access to employment in the initial phase of release. Few residents become permanent members of a particular neighborhood. After leaving the hostel, they usually settle down elsewhere. The hostel staff defines their responsibilities largely to helping residents develop positive habits, such as saving money or not wasting money. The staff checks in an indirect way on how residents use what they earn. The hostel does not collect the wages.

The chief of the probation office technically sets the time limit on hostel residence. For parolees, the maximum is the unserved portion of the prison sentence. A prisoner discharged at expiration of the sentence is eligible for up to six months after discharge. Technically, the judge sets the maximum stay at the hostel of probationers by ruling on the length of probation from one to five years. The resident is supposed to stay for the full period of probation. In practice, however, the government's subsidy is determined by the allocation within the Rehabilitation Bureau's budget; it usually covers an average stay of two months. The hostel decides whether or not the resident can stay beyond the average of two months. If the staff and resident reach an agreement for an extended stay, the resident is responsible for the payments.

Background and Idiosyncrasies of the Hostels

Within the general contours of their histories and operations, the ninety-nine rehabilitation aid hostels present a variety of specific functions and approaches. Several hostels were visited to learn how their staffs try to cope with the practicalities of management. I report on what I was told and observed about the human dimensions of hostel operations.

In Sendai, Miyagi Prefecture (north of Tokyo, on the coast of the Pacific Ocean), Miyagi Tokakai originated on its present site when a voluntary association purchased 14,000 square meters of farmland. Earlier religious persons had tried to ease the reentry crisis, before the association in Sendai was created in 1908 by judges, public prosecutors, members of the bar association, and the warden of Miyagi Prison.

Miyagi Prison is a historic treasure for Japan because it originated as the castle of a feudal lord. Today there are remnants of the original moat and century-old trees. During the Meiji Restoration, it confined samurai who had fought against the Meiji regime and were defeated in battle. For lack of a release facility in the latter decades of the nineteenth century, the discharged prisoners without access to help in adjusting to freedom were temporarily housed in the prison. In 1911 the voluntary association purchased farmland, and a building was erected in 1917. That building was replaced in 1969 by a two-story structure with a capacity for twenty-one male adults and four male juveniles. Additional construction in 1990 expanded the capacity to thirty.

As for Japanese hostels in general, the government's perdiem subsidy is insufficient to meet operating expenses. Since the visit to Miyagi Tokakai of Prince Chichibu, brother of the late Emperor Hirohito, some three decades ago, the hostel has received contributions from the royal family. The major source of income stems from lease of land for construction of a private apartment building. The hostel staff believes that the lease arrangement deters residents from joining some other neighborhood in protesting against the local presence of hostels.

The hostel's staff consists of the director, the chief guidance officer, two guidance officers, and a female cook. Most residents are from Sendai, but one or two are accepted from other prefectures. A juvenile released from a training school elsewhere was believed to be an associate of the yakuza. Unable to place him in a nearby hostel because of that belief, the training school contacted Miyagi Tokakai, where he was accepted. Because becoming a painter was his ambition, he was placed with a construction firm as a probationer. He left the hostel with a job as an expert painter.

Keiwa-Yen ("Respect Harmony") was established in 1958 in the Nakano district of Tokyo by the Tokyo Rehabilitation Aid Association. The building was enlarged in 1961 and accommodated both sexes (it was originally for males only). When I visited it in 1990, it served male juveniles, but young adults could be admitted. The capacity was eighteen; only ten were present: seven juvenile parolees and three on "temporary probation" from the juvenile courts.[12] Their average age was eighteen years, one being fifteen. Most residents averaged a stay of one month. Occupancy had to be 80 percent for financial solvency, but ten out of eighteen was only 55 percent. Annual income of 4,000,000 yen from a parking lot erased part of the deficit.

The chief guidance officer had been chief of a probation office and member of a regional parole board. His experience had alerted him to the greater difficulty of managing juvenile residents compared to adults. Those who come here, he explained, have not had a stable family situation. He could not recall a relative visiting a young resident. Fortunately, he said, all the residents present at that time were employed and thus too involved to raise difficulties. "The kids know everything," I was told. "The family court can send them back to a juvenile training school for serious misconduct. Short of that, we cannot react. We can do nothing about absconding if we can not find them before they become 20 years of age." Keiwa-Yen posts its own house rules: no smoking or drinking of alcohol; no fighting; keep yourself and your own room clean; no eating in your own room; be back to the hostel by 10 P.M. and don't leave thereafter.

The hostel staff endeavors to find jobs. New residents are asked, "What do you want to do?" "Be a driver or a restaurant waiter?" Employers in the neighborhood are asked to employ a new resident. The part-time employment is in gasoline stations, garages, assistant drivers for trucking companies, gardening, janitorial labor, and construction labor. The wages are marginal. In 1988 instruction in plumbing was introduced for those unable to be employed immediately.

The staff members are VPOs; they report any behavioral problem to the probation office. Eight PPOs in that office constitute the aftercare section; each is responsible for one or two hostels. Once or twice a month, they stay overnight at a hostel to interview the residents. Every Monday, they telephone to determine whether or not their presence is necessary.

The Wachukai Hostel in Osaka merits special attention because of the size of the facility and its success in establishing a sound financial base. The Federation of Buddhist Temples established it in 1912, when amnesty was given to many prisoners at the death of Emperor Meiji. In 1945 an air raid destroyed the facility. Makeshift quarters had to make due until two 3-story buildings were constructed in 1960 and 1971. A multistory brick building costing about 400,000,000 yen was opened in 1987 to replace the wooden structure. Now the previous buildings provide twenty-eight rooms for residents, living quarters for staff, and a garage. The largest building houses sixty-eight residents in single rooms and fourteen in double rooms. Each of the dormitory floors has a lounge and storage rooms. Offices, counseling rooms, and conference rooms are on the first floor. A large dining hall, a kitchen, and a meeting room are on the second floor.

In addition to the donations that financed construction of the brick building, thirty private companies contribute 8,000,000 yen annually to support the operations. Private companies in the neighborhood hire residents. Volunteers provide 30,000 yen annually to the budget and supplement the hostel staff.

Shinkou Kai ("New Beginning House") was opened in the Toshima district of Tokyo in 1952, rather soon after legislation in 1949 authorized hostels. A newspaper reporter donated the land and financed construction of the building during the postwar crisis. His concern for the reentry crisis of prisoners stemmed from his work in prisons as a volunteer chaplain. In 1988, reconstruction reduced the bed capacity to thirty from forty.

The reporter's widow became a member of the staff, which, unlike most hostels, had no former officials of prisons and juvenile training schools. The members included a retired official of Tokyo's government and a retired probation official. Personnel were receiving pensions that supplemented the modest salaries of hostels. Budgetary constraints prevented salaries attracting younger persons.

This hostel receives adult parolees, primarily, and adult probationers. The crimes are of great variety; only sex offenders are not accepted, because a kindergarten is nearby. The staff reported that in the previous year, 62 percent of the departures were after successful stays; 16 percent had absconded. Usually the absconders feared return to prison because of disputes among residents, at workplaces, or with other persons. Residents worked mostly in construction and truck driving. Most were single, separated, or divorced. The neighbors had raised objections to Shinkou Kai. The staff explained that some residents return late and pound on the door for admission. Second, some residents go to nearby bars without money; the bar owners call the hostel demanding payments.

One former parolee had been rejected by his wife because she felt shame that he had committed a crime. The parolee was forty-seven years old, a first offender, and a father of two boys aged twelve and sixteen years. He had been an efficient worker with high wages but had lost money in gambling. On a train, he stole two bags to sell for money, and was sentenced to two years and six months. A guidance worker at Shinkou Kai talked to his wife during her three visits to the hostel. To persuade her to drop her plan for a divorce, the staff member pointed out his good record and his essential worthiness. When his wife accepted him, the parolee rejoined the family, although at the hostel for only half of his four-month parole period.

Kofu Ryo ("Light and Wind Dormitory") in Nakanosho in Shiga Prefecture traces its history back to 1897, when the warden and chaplain of Zeze Prison (now Shiga Prison) rented a house for discharged inmates. In 1901 the minister of justice approved a nongovernmental foundation to operate the Shiga Prefecture Aid Hostel. In 1950 the hostel joined the reorganization of the system of rehabilitative services. In 1980 a two-story concrete building was named "Kofu Ryo." The advisory board members are the governor of Shiga Prefecture, the president of the Shiga's Association of Town Headmen, the chief of the Otsu district office of public prosecutors, the warden of Shiga Prison, and the head priest of the Ishiyama Temple.

Korakukai Rehabilitation Aid Hostel in Itabashi-Ku, Tokyo, was established when the warden of Fuchu Prison provided a house he owned. He took the initiative because of his concern about the plight of inmates without resources being released during the extensive social disorder immediately after World War II. On the site, a woodworking shop offered jobs for the residents.

When I visited the facility in 1988, Japan was at the height of an economic boom, and the labor market was tight. Job hunting was simple, and local employers were receptive. The government's subsidy met a third of the operating expenses. For the remainder of the budget, the workshop had been abandoned and converted into a storage warehouse, and a parking lot was created. Private companies paid rent for the two services.

How Hostels Met the Reentry Crisis

The various rehabilitation aid hostels function in particular ways because they are arms of voluntary organizations, rather than only instruments of a centralized governmental agency. Second, the criminal justice policy in Japan prefers to depend largely on the family and the community to meet the problems of released offenders. In reaching out to voluntary organizations and their hostels, the Rehabilitation Bureau specifically and Japan's government generally are seeking a partnership with a segment of the communal organization. Third, only a small proportion of their potential clientele come to the hostels; adults are more likely to come than juveniles, and parolees more likely than probationers. Table 8.11 distinguishes those four groups of clients and their respective outcomes in 1995 referrals to hostels.

Of the numerous juveniles ending supervision as probationers, only 50 were admitted to hostels: a rate of 2.46 per 100 juvenile probationers. Of the adult probationers, 180 were referred to hotels: a rate of 38.30 per 100 adult probationers. Juveniles exceeded adults in access to probation, largely because adolescent offenders are more likely to be seen officially as victims of their adverse living situation. Probation was imbued with the imagery of "protective measures" taken to remedy those deficiencies. Nevertheless, since the rate of hostel referrals is so low, some substitute for the family was mobilized for the majority of juvenile probationers. The rate of hostel referrals for adult probationers was almost 15.6 times that of the rate for juvenile probationers. The number of adult probationers is considerably less, but even in absolute numbers, the adult probationers made the greater demands for the hostel's services.

Table 8.11
Supervisory Outcomes by Reasons for Referral to Hostels, 1995

Source of Hostel Referrals by Supervisory Outcomes	Number of Supervisory Outcomes	Referrals to Hostels Number	Referrals to Hostels Rate	Resident's Reason for Hostel Referral[a] (Percentage Distribution) No Relative Available	Kin Rejected Resident	Resident Rejected Kin	Resident Wanted Services
Juvenile probation							
Successes	17,685	23	130.00	15.0	15.0	30.0	40.0
Intermediate outcomes	408	4	9.80	25.0	50.0	—	25.0
Revocations	2,203	23	10.44	9.5	33.3	14.3	42.9
Total	20,296	50	2.46	13.3	26.7	20.0	40.0
Juvenile parole							
Successes	3,084	73	23.67	25.0	46.9	12.5	15.6
Intermediate outcomes	253	29	114.62	30.8	53.8	15.4	—
Revocations	621	37	59.58	28.1	46.9	9.4	15.6
Total	3,958	139	35.12	27.0	48.4	12.3	12.3
Adult probation							
Successes	2,946	50	16.97	67.3	13.4	14.0	5.3
Intermediate outcomes	331	43	129.91	73.2	9.7	12.2	4.9
Revocations	1,423	87	61.14	70.4	16.0	9.9	3.7
Total	4,700	180	38.30	67.3	13.7	13.7	5.3

Table 8.11 cont. on next page

Table 8.11 continued

Source of Hostel Referrals by Supervisory Outcomes	Number of Supervisory Outcomes	Referrals to Hostels		Resident's Reason for Hostel Referral[a]			
		Number	Rate	No Relative Available	Kin Rejected Resident	Resident Rejected Kin	Resident Wanted Services
Adult parole							
Successes	10,980	2,972	270.67	57.4	18.4	20.9	3.3
Intermediate outcomes	159	104	654.09	73.8	10.7	13.6	1.9
Revocations	891	483	542.09	61.4	19.3	17.4	1.9
Total	12,029	3,559	295.87	58.4	18.3	20.2	3.1

Source: Research and Statistics Section (1996a, 128–29).

Note: "Other" outcomes and "other" reasons are excluded.
[a]Number of referrals per 1,000 supervisory outcomes.

The Ministry of Justice publishes four specific reasons given by hostel residents for needing a hostel. Three reasons emphasize the importance of the family: no family members exist for potential resources; the relatives exist but refuse to be of help; and the resident rejects the relatives. Fourth, the resident expressed a desire for the hostel's services, although the nature of the desire is not specified.

For juvenile probation, the fourth reason was dominant (40 percent), but rejection by the family ran second. The juveniles were slightly more likely to reject their relatives than relatives rejected them. VPOs and PPOs gave the impression that the juveniles referred to family courts suffered greatly from family inadequacy and neglect. Table 8.11 does not picture juvenile probationers in that light. Their rate of referrals to hostels is low, and those sent to hostels do not report a high incidence of family problems. Perhaps young victims are reluctant to make such statements. Family courts select juvenile probationers, versus referrals to training schools, for having comparatively better family situations.

Adult probationers are more inclined to seek hostel admissions for lack of family support (67.3 percent) than the juveniles. Hostel admissions include a high proportion of single persons and histories of separation from family ties. Rejection by relatives is balanced with the resident's rejection of relatives. Adult probationers have a greater range of ages, and, over those years, they are more likely to have a history of divorce, separation, or death of spouse.

Older ages and, sometimes, a history of slender ties with the family are mirrored in reasons for the admissions to hostels of adult probationers. Successful ending of probation was associated with the lowest rate of referrals to hostels. Revocations drew a high rate, but the intermediate outcomes had the highest rate. Regardless of the supervisory outcome, the reasons for referrals were heavily weighted by the unavailability of relatives.

For successful ending of probation supervision, juveniles

had a low rate of hostel referrals, and they were inclined either to want the services or to reject their kin. Intermediate outcomes had too few referrals for reliable analysis. Those being revoked had a higher referral rate and tended to either seek hostel services or be rejected by relatives.

Whether juveniles or adults, parolees exceeded probationers in the rate of hostel referrals for lack of assistance from relatives. Both groups had greater difficulty than probationers without the help of rehabilitation aid hostels. The demand was much stronger for adult parolees than adult probationers—referral rates of 296 versus 38, respectively. Juvenile parolees were especially vulnerable to rejection by kin. Adult parolees experienced greater unavailability of kin but tended to rebuff the possibility of their help.

As reported in table 8.12, the departures from the hostels were classified in six ways: auspicious (favorable) outcomes to self-reliance, auspicious outcomes to social agencies for continued assistance, change in rehabilitation aid without hostel involvement, left by accident (not the resident's fault), asked to leave (disapproved by hostel staff for continued residence after government's subsidy ended), and left hostel without notice (resident disappeared, but abrupt departure is not punishable). The outcomes are arrayed in table 8.12, most favorable to least favorable. The table distinguishes three categories referred to hostels: inmates discharged from prison on parole or at expiration of sentence; probationers; or suspended prosecution (the public prosecutor's decision to drop the case).

Releasees from prison were most numerous among the three categories of offenders and had a high share (75.7 percent) of "auspicious outcomes." Departure for self-support indicates that former prisoners were able to take care of themselves with or without family assistance. Although especially reliant on hostels, former prisoners utilized them effectively. A few depended on further help, social agencies in this instance. Change in the form of rehabilitation aid (also dependent on Rehabilitation Bureau's funds) was of minor impor-

Table 8.12

Outcomes of Hostel Stay by Residents' Reasons for Assignment to the Hostel, 1995

Outcomes of Stay in Hostels	Total Residents		Resident's Reason for Hostel Referral[a]			
	Number	Percent	No Relative Available	Kin Rejected Resident	Resident Rejected Kin	Resident Wanted Services
		Percentage Distribution				
Released from prison						
Auspicious outcomes	1,449	75.7	70.5	12.5	15.7	1.3
Self-support	(1,410)	(73.7)	(70.1)	(12.4)	(16.2)	(1.3)
Social agency	(39)	(2.0)	(84.6)	(15.4)	(—)	(—)
Change of aid	136	7.1	69.8	11.8	17.6	0.8
Left by accident	59	3.1	62.7	13.6	20.3	3.4
Asked to leave	70	3.7	75.7	17.2	7.1	—
Left w/o notice	200	10.4	71.0	17.0	12.0	—
Total	1,914	100	70.4	13.1	15.3	1.2
Probation						
Auspicious outcomes	146	37.8	84.2	9.6	4.1	2.1
Self-support	(131)	(33.9)	(84.0)	(9.1)	(4.6)	(2.3)
Social agencies	(15)	(3.9)	(86.7)	(13.3)	(—)	(—)
Change of aid	182	47.2	72.0	13.7	12.6	1.7

Table 8.12 cont. on next page

Table 8.12 continued

Outcomes of Stay in Hostels	Total Residents Number	Percent	No Relative Available	Kin Rejected Resident	Resident Rejected Kin	Resident Wanted Services
Probation						
Left by accident	2	0.55	0.0	—	50.0	—
Asked to leave	12	3.15	8.4	33.3	8.3	—
Left w/o notice	44	11.4	79.5	9.1	11.4	—
Total	386	100	76.9	12.2	9.3	1.6
Suspended prosecution						
Auspicious outcomes	251	67.1	83.7	4.8	10.7	0.8
Self-support	(244)	(65.2)	(83.6)	(4.9)	(10.7)	(0.8)
Social agencies	(7)	(1.9)	(85.7)	(—)	(14.3)	(—)
Change of aid	17	4.5	76.5	17.6	5.9	—
Left by accident	4	1.1	50.0	—	50.0	—
Asked to leave	18	4.8	77.7	11.1	5.6	5.6
Left w/o notice	84	22.5	82.1	8.3	7.2	2.4
Total	374	100	82.4	6.4	9.9	1.3

Resident's Reason for Hostel Referral[a]

Source: Research and Statistics Section (1996a, 164–65).

Note: "Other" outcomes and unreported reasons for referral to hostels are excluded.

tance, but the reasons "left by accident" and "asked to leave" were frequent. Departures without notice held a percentage share short only of departure to social support.

All former prisoners suffered an absence of family assistance. Some left the hostels but turned to social agencies. Those leaving hostels with self-support included a few who snubbed any possible connection with kin. Change of aid and departures by accident also included rejection of kin by residents. Seventy residents had wanted to continue occupancy after their subsidy ran out but were denied; they too were heavily represented among those either without relatives or relatives who refused to help. The same can be said about the 10 percent who left the hostels without notice.

The total probationers trailed the former prisoners in the quality of their outcomes of being at the hostels. Only 37.8 percent had auspicious outcomes, compared with 75.7 percent of the former prisoners, but these probationers also had the greater proportion without the availability of relatives. That reason for referral to hostels was more characteristic of probationers, than of parolees, who left the hostel in a commendable fashion. However, probationers were particularly likely to leave the hostels due to a change of rehabilitation aid. Few probationers left by accident or were asked to leave. For those leaving without notice, probationers resembled former prisoners in absence of family assistance.

Suspended prosecution would seem to be the mark of especially worthy offenders. Their auspicious outcomes were second only to former prisoners, but, as an explanation for their appearance at the hostels, these successes were obtained by persons with a high proportion lacking relatives. Another noteworthy feature was the high proportion of persons leaving without notice and also with a special concentration of unavailable relatives.

Former prisoners averaged 52.6 days at the hostels regardless of their departure; those benefiting from suspended prosecution were there for an average of 49 days; and probationers only 26.2 days (see table 8.13). Those differences in average stay measure the relative need for hostel services and are related to the outcomes of the hostel stay. The percentage distributions of stays in days compare how early or late various outcomes happened.

For former prisoners, change of aid drew longer average stays (91.1 days), with 62.3 percent coming at 90 days or more after the government's subsidy had been exhausted. Self-support followed with the second average stay (53.3 days) and the buildup coming after 20 days. Former prisoners going to social agencies left the hostels early (mean of 39.1 days); possibly lack of family assistance was among the justifications for the social agencies agreeing to help. Departures without notice, stimulated often by fear of impending reimprisonment, came early (mean of 37.9 days). Accidental and requested departures were distributed throughout the continuum of time.

Probationers spent fewer days at the hostels than former prisoners. Avoiding imprisonment, they were able to reassume their previous status before arrest, but, among them, some suffered a shortage of resources. The two residents who left by accident had the least time in the hostel in spite of great absence of family involvement. Change of aid and departures without notice came almost as soon (average stays less than 25 days). Auspicious outcomes took about a month in spite of these probationers being highly penalized by unavailability of relatives. As for former prisoners, probationers asked to leave the hostel had a high average stay.

Among the persons with a longer stay at hostels were most of those who had been excused by public prosecutors. The average of 49 days may be attributed to lack of family support. Change of aid came with the longest stay, an average of 105 days and 70.6 percent in 3 months or more. Persons asked to leave averaged 53.9 days; most were out before 2 months in spite of a grave reluctance of the family to intervene. Departures by accident were few, and departures without notice more common; both spent only a month in the hostels.

Table 8.13

Length of Stay in Hostels by Outcomes of Referrals to Hostels and Source of Referrals, 1995

Referral Outcomes by Referral Source	Number of Hostel Residents	Mean Days of Stay	Length of Stay in Days				
			Under 5	5–20	20–60	60–90	90+
			Percentage Distribution				
Releases from prison							
Auspicious outcomes	1,467	52.9	14.9	18.9	27.9	14	24.3
Self-support	(1,426)	(53.3)	(14.4)	(18.7)	(28.2)	(14.4)	(24.3)
Social agency	(41)	(39.1)	(29.3)	(26.8)	(19.5)	(2.4)	(22.0)
Change of aid	138	91.1	3.6	4.4	16.7	13.0	62.3
Left by accident	60	42.2	13.3	30.0	30.0	10.0	16.7
Asked to leave	70	41.9	15.7	27.2	31.4	11.4	14.3
Left w/o notice	201	37.9	25.4	22.9	26.4	13.4	11.9
Total	2,005(b)	52.6	16.3	18.7	26.9	13.3	24.8
Probation							
Auspicious outcomes	153	33.1	32	32.7	13.1	7.2	15
Self-support	(137)	(33.5)	(29.9)	(34.3)	(13.2)	(8.0)	(14.6)
Social agency	(16)	(30.0)	(50.0)	(18.7)	(12.5)	(—)	(18.7)
Change of aid	182	22.5	7.7	81.3	2.2	1.7	7.1
Left by accident	2	8.7	50.0	50.0			—
Asked to leave	13	50.6	7.7	30.8	30.8	7.7	23.0
Left w/o notice	44	24.9	36.3	38.6	11.4	2.3	11.4
Total	439(b)	26.2	26.2	51.7	7.8	3.6	10.7

Table 8.13 cont. on next

Table 8.13 continued

Referral Outcomes by Referral Source	Number of Hostel Residents	Mean Days of Stay	Length of Stay in Days				
			Under 5	5–20	20–60	60–90	90+
Suspended prosecution							
Auspicious outcomes	252	54.5	14.7	22.6	26.6	5.2	30.9
Self-support	(245)	(55.3)	(14.3)	(22.1)	(26.9)	(5.3)	(31.4)
Social agencies	(7)	(26.8)	(28.6)	(42.8)	(14.3)	(—)	(14.3)
Change of aid	17	105.0	—	—	5.9	23.5	70.6
Left by accident	4	32.5	—	25.0	25.0	—	—
Asked to leave	18	53.9	—	16.7	44.4	22.2	16.7
Left w/o notice	85	30.9	36.5	27.0	14.1	10.6	11.8
Total	408(b)	49.0	22.3	20.8	23.3	7.4	26.2

Source: Research and Statistics Section (1996a, 168).

Note: "other" hostel outcomes are excluded.

Suspended prosecution was associated with longer time in the hostel (55 days). Those who gained self-support or later assistance by social agencies had the high percentage without available relatives. Those benefited by social agencies spent only 26.8 days on average at the hostel.

Age and Admissions to Rehabilitation Aid Hostels

Admissions to halfway houses escalate as the age of the new residents increases (see table 8.14). The age distribution of admissions to parole or probation is compared with the age distribution of residents leaving the hostels. The distributions do not exactly meet the requirements of the comparison, but, since the ideal statistics are not available, this crude relationship will be used. To calculate rates, the absolute number of hostel departures in 1995 is divided by the number of persons admitted to probation or parole in 1995, and that figure is multiplied by 100. Table 8.14 presents rates for each age for prison releasees and probationers respectively.

The age-specific rates are greater for prison releasees than for probationers. Regardless of age, former prisoners on average have a greater need for halfway houses than probationers. Prisoners have been withdrawn from community life for a longer time than probationers. Probationers are selected from all convicted offenders for a firmer linkage with the community's social system and avoiding a record of repeated imprisonment. The rates of hostel departures for released prisoners range consistently from 5.81 per 100 parolees at ages less than 30 years to 43.9 per 100 parolees at ages 60 years and over. Hostel departure rates for probationers also rise consistently but from 3.43 per 100 probationers at ages less than 30 years to 22.15 per 100 probationers at ages 60 years and over.

The comparative need for hostels as an interim refuge also differs for former prisoners and probationers. The difference is measured by the percentage distribution of the days

Table 8.14
Ages of Hostel Residents by Length of Stay, 1995

Ages by Referral Sources	Admissions to Parole or Probation (A)	Departures from Hostels (B)	Rates: B/A[a]	Length of Hostel Stay in Days			
				Under 10	10–30	30–60	60+
				Percentage Distribution			
Releases from prison							
Under 30	2,977	173	5.81	23.1	23.1	17.9	35.9
30–39	3,223	363	11.26	26.7	19.6	17.9	35.8
40–49	3,249	622	19.14	25.9	21.1	15.4	37.6
50–54	1,212	291	24.01	21.0	16.5	24.0	38.5
55–59	805	261	32.42	24.5	17.6	18.0	39.9
60+	672	295	43.90	23.4	19.0	16.6	41.0
Total percent	—	—	—	24.5	19.5	17.9	38.1
Total number	12,138	2,005	16.52	492	392	358	763
Probation							
Under 30	2,420	83	3.43	41.0	42.2	3.6	13.2
30–39	970	78	8.04	38.5	46.2	3.8	11.5
40–49	816	128	15.69	28.9	50.0	4.7	16.4
50–54	298	58	19.46	34.5	48.3	6.9	10.3
55–59	203	59	29.06	35.6	44.1	3.4	16.9
60+	149	33	22.15	45.4	27.3	9.1	18.2
Total percent	—	—	—	35.8	45.1	4.8	14.3
Total number	4,856	439		157	198	21	63

Source: Research and Statistics Section (1996a, 91, 169).

[a]Rates are the number of hostel departures per 100 admissions to either parole or probation.

spent at the halfway houses for each age. The releasees spend more days there than the probationers: 38.1 percent of the releasees and only 14.3 percent of the probationers were at the hostels for 60 days or more.

For each age, the distribution of the stays at halfway houses can be compared with the distribution for all releasees or probationers, respectively. As the comparison moves through the ages in sequence, the general tendency is to move away from the shorter stays towards the stays of 30 days or more. The concentration in the longer stays is considerably less for the probationers.

The disparate demand for hostels by age has been aggravated over the years. The Research and Training Institute (1991, 44–45) reports changes in the ages of hostel residents: "The percentage of those in their fifties increased from 15.1 percent of 1,479 residents as of September 1, 1990, and those who were 60 years of age increased by 5.6 percent to 8.7 percent respectively." The Institute described an age-specific difference in duration of stay: "The more advanced the age group is, the higher the percentage of those who will stay long."

Also, the older the residents, the weaker their physical health. The Research and Training Institute (1991, 45) summarized: "Those who were evaluated as having feeble constitution accounted for 1.7 percent in those who were under 20 years of age, 3.6 percent in their twenties and thirties respectively, 4.4 percent in their forties, 12.3 percent in their fifties, and 23.3 percent of those who were over 60 years of age."

Reprise: Community-Oriented Corrections in Japan

Reaching the end of the exploration of the intersection of community and corrections in Japan we—you the reader and I—may well repeat the theme expressed in chapter 1.

The Japanese reluctance to employ imprisonment rests in part on a faith that most offenders have the capacity for self-correction without intervention of the criminal justice system. The officials have that faith, but, even more important for the community-oriented corrections, the general public believes that if the criminals are repentant and capable of self-correction, they should be returned to the fellowship of the family and community.

Public policy radiates beyond the usual conception of formally designed and implemented programs and enlists the motivational forces of community life. The implementation is characterized by prosecutorial discretion, the suspension of prison sentences by courts, the unconditional return to the community of a substantial share of convicted offenders, the use of probation as a sanction for many of the offenders believed to be lacking a capacity for self-correction, commitment to correctional institutions of the remainder of the undercommitted offenders, and parole as an inducement for reaching the undercommitted upon the return of some inmates to the free world. All of these elements of community-oriented corrections have risen, and operate, within the context of the particular history, social structure, and cultural perspectives of the Japanese.

The term *community* has a variety of meanings and implications for its possible partnership with corrections within that Japanese context. A very diffused literature on the community was compressed in chapter 2 into four interpretations: consensual community, territorial community, community as an element of social organization, and community of interests. As characteristic of other societies and criminal justice systems, the inclination of the Japanese and the Japanese correctional system is to prefer the consensual community for idealizing the past and making it the model for solving the problems of the contemporary society. That revival of the past community, as idealized, usually is associated with restoring the influence of the family as the basic element of the society's organization and with limiting the functions of government in delivering social services. Probation and parole represents part of an effort to bring the family and other intimate groups into the management of criminality and, thereby, mobilizing the community as a substitute resource for the government's functions in that regard.

Only the future will determine whether or not the imagery of consensual community will collapse under the impact of massive sociopolitical changes reshaping the world in general and Japan specifically. Territorial community has lost much of its earlier significance. Of increasing relevance are community as an element of social organization and community of interests. At several points, previous chapters have outlined the effects of demographic and other major trends in contemporary Japan and concerns about delinquency and crime. For example, developments within the nuclear family have sapped the vitality of the traditional ie as a social unit—through rising divorce rate, delay in marriage by young adults who prefer the pleasures of being single, greater employment of women outside the family, and other reasons for the decreasing birthrate. More directly, for community-oriented corrections in Japan, the faster pace of urbanization and strengthened influence of social forces external to Japan bring into unprecedented question the efficacy of the heavy reliance on volunteer probation officers as ultimate agents of consensual community.

The Rehabilitation Bureau (1990, ii) notes that corrections is not immune to change: "Industrialization, cultural sophistication and accelerated mobility of population, with many other aspects of recent changes, have been posing problems which have never been encountered before by corrections." A Japanese research team speaks of the diminishing of the household head's authority over family members, the greater concern about the family's role in personality formation, increased juvenile delinquency, greater adult recidivism, and more female offenders. "Recently Japanese people have become aware of the fact," they (Buendia 1989, 351–52) say, "that affluence in terms of material wealth does not necessarily bring about the extermination of crime and criminality."

A basic and valid principle of comparative criminology insists that each society provides its own cultural and social frameworks for the reactions to criminals and criminality. Japan is no exception. In my research, I encountered an unanticipated result of the Japanese experimentation with criminalization as a policy reaction to major social crises. Admissions to prison increased for traffic offenders, female drug abusers, foreigners, elderly Japanese, gangsters, and juvenile traffic and drug offenders. But, after a period of deviation from the more general decline in institutional admissions, the trend turned downward as the factors opposing imprisonment resumed their grip (see Johnson 1997). I learned to be more confident in my conviction that although Japan's modernization in the last century was strongly influenced by the principles and practices of the West, this society and its system of corrections will go on in its own way.

Notes

References

Index

Notes

1. Introduction: The Setting and Tasks of the Rehabilitation Bureau

1. For probationers, the restrictions on rights is automatically eliminated when the full term of supervision is completed. Prison releasees have their criminal record wiped out when ten years have elapsed without further conviction (Rehabilitation Bureau 1990, 51).

2. The history summarized in this section draws heavily on Soejima (1974).

3. *Meiji Restoration* is a translation of the Japanese term *Meiji renovation*. Sims (1991, 318) prefers *Meiji renovation* because of the "epoch-making transformation." *Restoration* commemorates the formal restoration of the emperor to power; *Meiji* means enlightened government.

4. "The roots of the system lie in a Ministry of Justice directive of 1885 allowing public procurators (predecessors of the present public prosecutor) to request investigations into crime even though they could not conduct such investigations themselves. In time, public procurators came to have their own power to carry out investigations and decide whether or not to institute prosecution; it is out of that tradition that the contemporary power to suspend institution of or to institute prosecution has come" (Research and Training Institute 1979, 27).

5. For more on family courts, see chapter 5.

2. Community and Corrections: Historic and Contemporary Japan

1. "Gift relationship" refers to the variety of reasons persons volunteer services, from altruism to awareness of its value. The rea-

sons were supposed to be an index of the cultural values and qualities of human relationships in a given society.

2. "In some cases this traditional 'community' is given the attributes of warmth and affectivity," Imamura (1987, 6) comments. "In contrast, the urban dweller's 'community' is not so clear-cut. . . . this image is characterized by instrumental relationships and less warmth but greater individual freedom."

3. Kawamura calls this "a *gemeinschaft* type of social organization." Ferdinand Toennies, a German sociologist, developed two models: *gemeinschaft* (community) and *gesellschaft* (society). He conceived of them as two ways in which human beings establish relationships with one another. To him, the two models merged to different degrees in reality rather than being polar opposites. "Community" was a place of intimacy and trust. "Society" was anonymous and public.

4. Scalapino (1953, 17–18) notes that the bakufu contributed to Japan's isolation from the outside world. The Portuguese first landed in Kyushu soon after 1540 to open contacts. "With the arrival of Spanish traders and Franciscans, the implications of foreign religious and commercial strife took on a serious aspect." The Tokugawa policy turned to rigid isolation to cope with "the inevitable intrusion of Western religious and commercial ideologies into a precariously balanced internal structure."

5. The system had existed in China before the birth of Christ (Hozumi 1943). It existed in Japan until 1888, but the principle of group responsibility survived in local associations established to perform wartime functions in the 1930s (Tonomura 1992).

6. In high-rise housing subsidized by companies for higher status employees, Smith (1955, 151) says, "any sense of community comes from sharing a common workplace." But the families aspire to move to their own places. "Expectations of short-term stays produce low commitments in the housing complex."

7. Kraus, Rohlen, and Steinhoff (1984, 392–93) describe new issues and new patterns of conflict in the 1970s: pollution and quality of life, Japan's low level of welfare services, and the expansion of rights for low-status groups such as women and *burakumin* ("people of the hamlet," a term applied to hereditary outcasts). "Clearly these new sources of conflict bubbling up from below and involving heterogeneous collections of citizens," they say, "are reminiscent of the type of conflict most prevalent in the West."

8. Aoki (1997) contends that the warrior class—only 6 percent

of the population—was the only defender of the patriarchal nature of parent-child relationships.

9. The legal dominance of the ie over the individual, Fukutake (1981) says, was eroded by the "diminishing consciousness" of the extended family, new laws favoring marriage by mutual consent, and other stimulants of the increased number of nuclear families.

10. Beasley cites Minear (1970, 80) as the source of this quotation.

11. Yoshizumi (1995) notes that loss of love between a married couple is not usually viewed as a sufficient reason for divorce, keeping the divorce rate low. However, more middle-aged and older wives, once the children are grown, are initiating divorce.

3. Adult Probation and Parole: Administrative Features

1. "In general supervision periods for paroled prisoners are quite brief. . . . Parole supervision under Japanese law cannot exceed the maximum length of the original sentence to imprisonment" (Research and Training Institute 1979, 36).

2. Some prison systems use a scale of reductions of time served as a substitute for monetary payment for prison labor and for exemplary conduct. Japanese prisoners receive a modest "remuneration" (the value set along a scale of ten grades) for labor in workshops. In a progressive-stage system, promotions in rank provide increasing number of privileges earned by diligence in prison labor, exemplary conduct, and showing a sense of responsibility. Hagiwara (1982) refers to another function of parole; for those inmates not deemed worthy of parole for merit, parole late in the prison career provides supervision in the community as another means of assuring their proper conduct after release from prison.

3. For further discussion of Japan's criminalization of traffic offenders, see Johnson (1997, 123–39).

4. The yakuza are considered especially poor prospects for parole because of their commitment to criminal values. Their share of prison admissions rose from 16.4 percent in 1970 to 26.3 percent in 1985, trailed off to 25.8 percent in 1990, and to 17.5 percent in 1995 (Research and Training Institute 1985, 54; 1989, 80; Research and Statistics Section 1991b, 60, 132; 1996b, 60, 132).

5. The term *parole officer* is confusing here because management of both parolees and probationers is carried out by "probation officers," as they are called in Japan. Nevertheless, certain "probation officers" are assigned to regional parole boards for services other than case supervision.

6. "Volunteers carry out many forms of activities subsumed under the concept of community organization," Hashimoto (1983, 184) says. "They collaborate with public and private organizations in exploring and coordinating social resources in the community. They interpret rehabilitative philosophy and efforts to individual neighbors, or to the public as a whole, and they attempt to eradicate environmental conditions generating crime, in cooperation with the community residents."

4. Adult Probationers and Parolees

1. The 1996 data do not report on the income of admitted prisoners. Statistics for 1993 were substituted.

2. The Law for Punishment of Acts of Violence, promulgated in 1930, provided heavy punishment for aggravated crimes of assault, intimidation, and destruction committed by a group of offenders. In 1964 the law was amended to introduce an aggravated crime of bodily injury committed with firearms and swords. Heavier penalties were set for habitual offenders involved in crimes of violence (Shikita and Tsuchiya 1990, 45, 83).

3. Social agencies are child guidance centers, centers of the prefectural government, child education and training homes, and homes for dependent children.

4. The term *deviance* implies that crime is only one version of aberrations, caprices, vagaries, or anomalies that differ from conventional "normality."

5. The Research and Training Institute (1969, 1) outlines another dichotomy: "The Penal Code comprises such offences as larceny or homicide, that is acts which have been condemned by all societies as 'natural crimes.' In contrast, the Special Law offenses, Road Traffic Law for example, are referred to as 'statutory crimes,' in that they are violations of laws specifically promulgated for the purpose of maintaining the administrative control of a given society at a given time."

6. In more detail, Johnson (1997) analyzes the effects on Japanese prisons of the criminalization of traffic offenses (chapter 4), drug offenses of women (chapter 3), and traffic and drug offenses of juveniles (chapter 5).

5. Juvenile Corrections in the Community: Family Court and Juvenile Classification Homes

1. The Juvenile Law, Article 51, specifies, for persons less than eighteen years of age, that the death penalty will be reduced to life imprisonment and that a sentence of imprisonment for life will be converted to a minimum of ten years and a maximum of fifteen years.

2. The Juvenile Law, Article 56, requires that juvenile sentences to prison "shall be executed in prisons specially established for the purpose, or in special compartments provided in prisons." Further, even after a juvenile "has become twenty years of age, the execution (of juvenile sentences) may be continued . . . until he becomes twenty six years of age."

3. In 1992 the police reported that of 85,621 juvenile larcenies, 18.6 percent were shoplifting, 18.5 percent motorbike theft, 12.6 percent bicycle theft, and 14.3 percent "other" (National Police Agency 1993, 83).

4. Serious questions have been raised about predelinquency as a target for criminal justice agencies, since formal action is taken for juveniles who have not been apprehended for law violations. The merger of "predelinquents" with young law violators extends social opprobrium *in advance* of apprehended delinquency; the stigmatization may press the predelinquent toward criminal acts. The concept ignores the causal complexity of delinquency in assuming the youngsters will become delinquents unless "protective measures" are taken. If certain symptoms and conditions exist in childhood, the youngsters are assumed to move inexorably toward delinquency and, perhaps later, toward the crimes of an adult. That underlying premise is very uncertain.

5. Admissions to the short-term probation program for juvenile traffic offenders were 33,083 in 1981, 35,642 in 1982, 41,772 in 1983, 42,924 in 1984, 44,361 in 1985, 45,499 in 1986, 45,565 in 1987, 44,099

in 1988, 46,586 in 1989, 50,298 in 1990, and 48,021 in 1991 (Research and Training Institute 1984, 161; 1987, 159; 1990, 182; 1992, 166).

6. The information was obtained from personal correspondence.

7. Of the fifty-three JCHs, Miyako (11 referrals) and Yaeyama (23 referrals) had received only family court referrals. The two JCHs were dropped from the analysis. Because their few referrals were only from family courts, they would skew the conclusion.

6. Juvenile Probationers and Parolees

1. In contemporary Japanese families, Befu (1986) reports, the mother and children frequently form a coalition against the father, who is supposed to be the disciplinarian of children but is mostly absent from the family circle in performing work obligations. The coalition is less likely in Japan when both parents work in a family business and in the United States, where parents usually share responsibility for the children.

2. When he prepared the paper in 1974, Kazuho Soejima was superintendent of the Tama Juvenile Training School. In 1990 he provided the author a copy of the paper and a translation in English.

3. The chief of outcastes was a shogunate official, who among his responsibilities for managing criminals would assign juvenile delinquents to tasks such as rag picking.

4. School violence and bullying, Kawasaki (1994, 193–94) says, became a serious problem in the 1980s. "For example, in 1982 there were 1,400 cases of violence in lower secondary schools, while bullying cases numbered 100,000 in elementary schools in 1985. . . . the most serious educational problem has been 'students refusing to attend school'; 40,000 lower secondary school students refused to go to school in 1990."

5. The National Police Agency (1993, 82–83) defines "initial-type delinquency" as offenses that "could lead to more serious delinquent acts, such as violence and drug abuse." The term refers to four categories of offense, that is, shoplifting, bicycle theft, motorcycle theft, and stealing lost property. Yokoyama (1997, 14–16) summarizes the police involvement in prevention of juvenile delinquency.

6. Johnson (1997, 8–14, 157–71) discusses more fully the process

of criminalization and its application to juveniles as a consequence of a perceived crisis of traffic and drug offenses.

7. *Boryokudan* is the term the Japanese police apply to the yakuza.

7. Supervision in the Japanese Fashion

1. For further discussion of the Antiprostitution Law and women's guidance homes, see Johnson (1997, 29–31).

2. "Other" reasons for ending the parole case are hospitalization for illness or mental disorder or other unusual circumstances.

3. I say "relative" to emphasize that "unpromising candidates" should be defined in the Japanese context within which conformity to the dominant sociocultural norms among officially defined "criminals" is more likely than in Western societies.

4. The rate of 2.76 includes the current admission; the parolees on average had been on parole 1.76 times *before* the current admissions.

5. Dore (1958, 254, 258) makes the point that giri acts "spring from a sense of obligation rather than from spontaneous inclination." Roughly speaking, giri stands for indebtedness, duties, and obligations linked to honest desire and spontaneous feelings for others in social relationships.

6. The Rehabilitation Bureau (1990, 15) explains: "This committee includes representatives of [the] apparatus of justice, the prosecution, the Bar, institutional corrections, probation and parole and other public commissions as well as 'learned citizens.'"

8. Return to the Community: Outcomes and the Reentry Crisis

1. Johnson (1996, 59–77) elaborates on the recruiting, training, and motivating of the correctional personnel in Japan.

2. In suspending a prison sentence, courts choose between unconditional return to the free community (suspension *without* supervision) versus probation (suspension *with* supervision). In that context, those convicted offenders placed on probation are evaluated as

inferior prospects. Imprisonment, of course, implies an even less favorable evaluation than probation.

3. The length of adult parole supervision is the unserved portion of the sentence to prison. The supervision is sharply limited when the prison sentence is comparatively short. When the RPB does not approve parole the first time, even longer prison sentences may lead to rather brief parole supervision.

4. The reluctance to "criminalize" the marginal deviant is a basic argument in favor of the diversion of suspects and defendants away from imprisonment. That argument has special relevance to Japan's low imprisonment rate.

5. Satisfaction of conditions to the end of the supervisory period can be called "expiration," but I prefer *completion* as the term to avoid confusion with expiration of the sentence to prison.

6. In Japan, probation of adults is derived from the courts' authority to suspend the sentence to prison. The principle inherent in Article 27 also applies to juvenile parole.

7. For further discussion, see Johnson (1996, 236–42); and Johnson (1997, 162–63, 174–79, 182–83).

8. The amounts of fines specified in the Penal Code are raised as the exchange rate of the yen changes.

9. The Offenders Rehabilitation Law, Articles 37 and 39, adds supervision of parolees to the responsibilities of *probation* offices.

10. The Penal Code, Article 9, lists "the order of gravity" of the categories of punishment: death, imprisonment at forced labor, imprisonment without forced labor, fine, penal detention, and minor fines. Imprisonment with forced labor is defined as more grave, but imprisonment without forced labor is described as less punitive because the inmate does not have to work. In practice, however, inmates almost always volunteer for work.

11. The Penal Code, Article 18, applies the term *penal detention* to the placing in a workhouse (a detention facility) "a person unable to pay his fine . . . for a term not less than one day nor more than two years." If the detainee pays only part of the fine, the length of detention "shall be reduced by a period of days which bears the same ratio as the total period of detention for non-payment . . . originally imposed as the amount of fine . . . actually paid bears to the total fine . . . originally imposed."

12. Temporary probation is defined in chapter 5.

References

Abe, Hakaru. 1963. "Education of the Legal Profession in Japan." *Law in Japan: The Legal Order in a Changing Society*. Ed. Arthur Taylor Von Mehren. Cambridge, MA: Harvard University Press. 153–87.

Allinson, Gary D. 1979. *Suburban Tokyo: A Comparative Study in Politics and Social Change*. Berkeley: University of California Press.

Ancel, Marc. 1971. *Suspended Sentence*. London: Heinemann Educational Books.

Angata, Shizuo. 1990. "Some Aspects of Volunteer Probation Officer (*Hogoshi*) System in Japan." Unpublished paper. Tokyo: United Nations Asia and Far East Institute for Prevention of Crime and Treatment of Offenders.

Aoki, Yayoi. 1997. "Independent Scholar and Critic." *Broken Silence: Voices of Japanese Feminism*. Ed. Sandra Buckley. Berkeley: University of California Press. 1–31.

Aoyagi, Kiyotaka. 1983. "Visible traditions in Urban Japan: *Matsuri* and *Chonaikai*." *Town–Talk: The Dynamics of Urban Anthropology*. Ed. Haus Ansari and Peter J. M. Nas. Leiden: E. J. Brill.

Araki, Nobuyoshi. 1985. "The Flow of Criminal Cases in the Japanese Criminal Justice System." *Crime and Delinquency* 31: 601–27.

Aries, Philippe. 1962. *Centuries of Childhood*. Trans. Robert Baldick. New York: Alfred A. Knopf.

Asano, Yoshimasa. 1991. "Changes of the Application of Diversion by Public Prosecutors in Japan." Unpublished paper. Tokyo: United Nations Asia and Far East Institute for Prevention of Crime and Treatment of Offenders.

Asia Crime Prevention Foundation. 1983. "Family and Crime." *ACPF Today*, 107–17.

Beardsley, Richard K., John W. Hall, and Robert E. Ward. 1959. *Village Japan*. Chicago: University of Chicago Press.

Beasley, William G. 1972. *The Meiji Restoration*. Stanford, CA: Stanford University Press.

————. 1990. *The Rise of Modern Japan*. Tokyo: Charles E. Tuttle.

Becker, Carl B. "Report from Japan: Causes and Controls of Crime in Japan." *Journal of Criminal Justice* 16: 425–35.

Befu, Harumi. 1986. "The Social and Cultural Background of Child Development in Japan and the United States." *Child Development and Education in Japan*. Ed. Harold Stevenson, Hiroshi Azuma, and Kenji Hakuta. New York: W. H. Freeman. 13–26.

Ben-Ari, Eyal. 1991. *Changing Japanese Suburbia: A Study of Two Present Day Localities*. London: Kegan Paul International.

Bestor, Theodore C. 1985. "Tradition and Japanese Social Organization: Institutional Development in a Tokyo Neighborhood." *Ethnology* 24.2: 121–35.

Blumstein, Alfred, and Elizabeth Graddy. 1981–82. "Prevalence and Recidivism in Index Arrests: A Feedback Model." *Law and Society Review* 16.2: 265–90.

Braibanti, Ralph J. D. 1948. "Neighborhood Associations in Japan and Their Democratic Potentials." *Far Eastern Quarterly* 7.2: 136–64.

Buendia, Hernando Gomez, ed. 1989. *Urban Crime: Global Trends and Policies*. Tokyo: United Nations University.

Christopher, Robert C. 1987. *The Japanese Mind: The Goliath Explained*. Tokyo: Charles E. Tuttle.

Clinard, Marshall B., and Daniel J. Abbott. 1973. *Crime in Developing Countries: A Comparative Perspective*. New York: John Wiley and Sons.

Clinard, Marshall B., Daniel J. Abbott, and Robert F. Meier. 1985. *Sociology of Deviant Behavior*. 6th ed. New York: Holt, Rinehart and Winston.

Correction Bureau. 1967. *Correctional Administration in Japan*. Tokyo: Ministry of Justice.

————. 1990. *Correctional Institutions in Japan*. Tokyo: Ministry of Justice.

————. 1995. *Correctional Institutions in Japan*. Tokyo: Ministry of Justice.

Craig, Albert M. 1961. *Chosu in the Meiji Restoration*. Cambridge, MA: Harvard University Press.

DeVos, George A. 1973. *Socialization for Advancement: Essays on the Cultural Psychology of the Japanese*. Berkeley: University of California Press.

DeVos, George A., and Keniichi Mizushima. 1973. "Delinquency and Social Change in Modern Japan." *Socialization for Achievement:*

Essays on the Cultural Psychology of the Japanese. Ed. George A. DeVos. Berkeley: University of California Press. 325–68.

Doi, Takeo. 1981. *The Anatomy of Dependence.* Trans. John Bester. Tokyo: Kudansha International.

Dore, Ronald P. 1958. *City Life in Japan: A Study of A Tokyo Ward.* Berkeley: University of California Press.

Durkheim, Emile. 1938. *The Rules of Sociological Method.* New York: Free Press.

————. 1947. *The Division of Labor in Society.* Trans. George Simpson. Glencoe: Free Press.

Ellis, Susan J., and Katherine H. Noyes. 1990. *By the People: A History of Americans as Volunteers.* San Francisco: Jossey-Bass.

Erikson, Kai T. 1966. *Wayward Puritans: A Study in the Sociology of Deviance.* New York: John Wiley and Sons.

Farrington, David P. 1986. "Age and Crime." *Crime and Justice: An Annual Review of Research.* Ed. Michael Tonry and Norval Morris. Vol. 7. Chicago: University of Chicago Press. 189–250.

Fischer, Lucy Rose, and Kay Banister Schaffer. 1993. *Older Volunteers: A Guide to Research and Practice.* Newbury Park, CA: Sage.

Foucault, Michel. 1980. "Prison Talk." Power/Knowledge: Selected Interviews and Other Writings by Michel Foucault, 1972–1977. Ed. Colin Gordon. Brighton, Eng.: Harvester Press.

Fukutake, Tadashi. 1981. *Japanese Society Today.* 2d ed. Tokyo: University of Tokyo Press.

————. 1989. *The Japanese Social Structure: Its Evolution in the Modern Structure.* 2d ed. Tokyo: University of Tokyo Press.

George, B. J., Jr. 1988. "Discretionary Authority of Public Prosecutors in Japan." *Law and Society in Contemporary Japan: American Perspectives.* Ed. John O. Haley, 263–88. Dubuque, IA: Kendal-Hunt.

Gillis, John R. 1974. *Youth and History: Tradition and Change in European Age Relations 1770–Present.* New York: Academic Press.

Hagiwara, Yasuo. 1982. "Parole in Japan." Unpublished paper. Tokyo: United Nations Asia and Far East Institute for Prevention of Crime and Treatment of Offenders.

Haley, John Owen. 1991. *Authority Without Power: Law and the Japanese Paradox.* New York: Oxford University Press.

Hall, John Whitney. 1966. *Government and Local Power in Japan 500 to 1700.* Princeton, NJ: Princeton University Press.

Hara, Hiroko, and Mieko Minagawa. 1996. "From Productive Dependents to Precious Guests: Historical Changes in Japanese Children." *Japanese Childrearing: Two Generations of Scholarship*. Ed. David W. Shwalb and Barbara J. Shwalb. New York: Guilford Press. 9–30.

Hashimoto, Nobura. 1983. "Japan's Use of Volunteers in Community-Based Treatment." *Proceedings of 112th Annual Congress of Corrections of American Correctional Association*. Toronto, Canada. 183–89.

Hayashi, Shuji. 1972. *Culture and Management in Japan*. Trans. Frank Baldwin. Tokyo: University of Tokyo Press, 1988.

Hiramatsu, Yoshiro. 1972. "History of Penal Institutions in Japan." *Law in Japan* 6: 1–48.

———. 1973. *History of Penalty Theory and Practice of Penalties* (in Japanese). Tokyo: Sobunsha.

Hirano, Ryuichi. 1963. "The Accused and Society: Some Aspects of the Japanese Criminal Law." *Law in Japan: The Legal Order in a Changing Society*. Ed. Arthur Taylor Von Mehren. Cambridge, MA: Harvard University Press. 274–96.

Hirata, Keiko. 1985. "Collaboration Between the Probation Officer and the Volunteer Probation Officer in Japan." Unpublished paper. Tokyo: United Nations Asia and Far East Institute for Prevention of Crime and Treatment of Offenders.

Hirst, Paul. 1994. *Associative Democracy: New Forms of Economic and Social Governance*. Amherst: University of Massachusetts Press.

Hodge, Robert W., and Naohiro Ogawa. 1991. *Fertility Change in Contemporary Japan*. Chicago: University of Chicago Press.

Hough, Mike. 1995. "Variations in Probation Function." *Probation Round the World: A Comparative Study*. Ed. Koichi Hamai, Renaud Ville, Robert Harris, Mike Hough, and Ugljesa Zvekic. London: Routledge.

Hozumi, Shihgetoh. 1943. "The *Tonari-Gumi* of Japan." *Contemporary Japan* 12.8: 984–90.

Hyotani, Toshiyuki. 1985. "Rehabilitation Services and Criminal Policy." Unpublished paper. Tokyo: United Nations Asia and Far East Institute for Prevention of Crime and Treatment of Offenders.

Ifukube, Shunji, and Sachiko Sugihara. 1979. "Study on Parole Examinations." *Bulletin of the Criminological Research Department*. Tokyo: Research and Training Institute, Ministry of Justice. 13–15.

Ignatieff, Michael. 1981. "State, Civil Society, and Total Institutions: A Critique of Recent Social Histories of Punishment." *Crime and*

Justice: An Annual Review of Research. Ed. Michael Tonry and Norual Morris. Vol. 3. Chicago: University of Chicago Press. 153–92.

Ilsley, Paul J. 1990. *Enhancing the Volunteer Experience*. San Francisco: Jossey-Bass.

Imafuku, Shoji. 1997. "The Criminal Justice System in Japan: Rehabilitation in the Community." Unpublished paper. Tokyo: United Nations Asia and Far East Institute for Prevention of Crime and Treatment of Offenders.

Imamura, Anne E. 1987. *Urban Japanese Housewives: At Home and in the Community*. Honolulu: University of Hawaii Press.

Irwin, John. 1970. *The Felon*. Englewood Cliffs, NJ: Prentice-Hall.

Ishida, Takeshi. 1971. *Japanese Society*. New York: Random House.

———. 1983. *Japanese Political Culture: Changes and Continuity*. New Brunswick: Transaction Books.

Ishii, Ryosuke. 1980. *A History of Political Institutions in Japan*. Tokyo: University of Tokyo Press.

Ishikawa, Hiroshi. 1986. "Characteristic Aspects of Japanese Criminal Justice System." Unpublished paper. Tokyo: United Nations Asia and Far East Institute for Prevention of Crime and Treatment of Offenders.

Ito, Shigeki. 1986. "Characteristics and Roles of Japanese Public Prosecutors." Resource Material Series No. 30. Tokyo: United Nations Asia and Far East Institute for Prevention and Treatment of Offenders. 67–75.

Ives, George. 1944. *A History of Penal Methods*. London: Stanley Paul.

Iwao, Sumiko. 1993. *The Japanese Woman: Traditional Image and Changing Reality*. New York: Free Press.

Janowitz, Morris. 1967. *The Community Press in an Urban Setting*. Chicago: University of Chicago Press.

Jedlicka, Allen. 1990. *Volunteerism and World Development: Pathway to a New World*. Westport, CT: Praeger.

Johnson, Elmer H. 1996. *Japanese Corrections: Managing Convicted Offenders in an Orderly Society*. Carbondale: Southern Illinois University Press.

———. 1997. *Criminalization and Prisoners in Japan: Six Contrary Cohorts*. Carbondale: Southern Illinois University Press.

Jones, Randall S. 1988. "The Economic Implications of Japan's Aging Population." *Asian Survey* 28: 958–69.

Kasai, Akio. 1973. "Some Causes of the Decrease of Crime in Japan." Resource Material Series No. 6. Tokyo: United Nations Asia and

Far East Institute for Prevention of Crime and Treatment of Offenders. 134–37.

Kasarda, John D., and Morris Janowitz. 1974. "Community Attachment in Mass Society." *American Sociological Review* 39: 328–39.

Kashiwagi, Keiko. 1986. "Personality Development in Adolescents." *Child Development and Education in Japan*. Ed. Harold Stevenson, Hiroshi Azuma, and Kenji Hakuta. New York: W. H. Freeman. 167–85.

Kawamura, Nozumu. 1994. *Sociology and Society of Japan*. London: Kegan Paul International.

Kawasaki, Kenichi. 1994. "Youth Culture in Japan." *Social Justice* 21. 185–203.

Kersten, Joachim. July 1993. "Street Youths, *Bosozoku*, and *Yakuza*: Subculture Formation and Societal Reactions in Japan." *Crime and Delinquency* 39: 277–95.

King, Joan F. S. 1958. *The Probation Services*. London: Butterworth.

Kinoshita, Yasuhito, and Christie W. Kiefer. 1992. *Refuge of the Honored: Social Organization in a Japanese Retirement Community*. Berkeley: University of California Press.

Kishimoto, Koichi. 1988. *Politics in Modern Japan: Development and Organization*. 3d ed. Tokyo: Japan Echo.

Koshi, George M. 1970. *The Japanese Legal Advisor: Crimes and Punishment*. Tokyo: Charles E. Tuttle.

Kouhashi, Hiroshi. 1985. "Courts' Selection of Offenders to Be Placed Under Probationary Supervision." Unpublished paper. Tokyo: United Nations Asia and Far East Institute for Prevention of Crime and Treatment of Offenders.

Krauss, Ellis S., Thomas P. Rohlen, and Patricia G. Steinhoff. 1984. "Conflict and Its Resolution in Postwar Japan." *Conflict in Japan*. Ed. Ellis S. Krauss, Thomas P. Rohlen, and Patricia G. Steinhoff. Honolulu: University of Hawaii Press. 377–97.

Lanham, Betty B. and Regina J. Garrick. 1996. "Adult to Child in Japan: Interaction and Relations." *Japanese Childrearing: Two Generations of Scholarship*. Ed. David W. Shwalb and Barbara J. Shwalb. New York: Guilford Press. 97–124.

Lincoln, James R., and Arne L. Kalleberg. 1990. *Culture, Control, and Commitment: A Study of Work Organization and Work Attitudes in the United States and Japan*. Cambridge, Eng.: Cambridge University Press.

Maeda, Hiroshi. 1982. "Ad Hoc Lecture." Unpublished paper. To-kyo: United Nations Asia and Far East Institute for Prevention of Crime and Treatment of Offenders.

Maguire, Kathleen, and Anne L. Pastore. 1995. *Sourcebook of Criminal Justice Statistics—1994*. Washington: U.S. Department of Justice.

Masland, John W. 1946. "Neighborhood Associations in Japan." *Far Eastern Survey* 15.23: 355–58.

McKissack, I. J. 1967. "The Peak Age for Property Crime." *British Journal of Criminology* 7: 184–94.

Minami, Yoshimi. 1991. "Japan Adjusts to Demographic Changes at the Local Level." *Public Management* 73: 8–9.

Minear, Richard H. 1970. *Japanese Tradition and Western Law*. Cambridge, MA: Harvard University Press.

Moran, Frederick A. 1945. "The Origins of Parole." National Probation Association Yearbook. 71–75.

Moreland, Donald W. 1941. "John Augustus and His Successors." *National Probation Association Yearbook*. 3–9.

Morioka, Kiyomi. 1986. "Privation of Family Life in Japan." *Child Development and Education in Japan*. Ed. Harold Stevenson, Hiroshi Azuma, and Kenji Hakota. New York: W. H. Freeman. 63–74.

Moriyama, Tadashi. 1995. "The Structure of Social Control in Japan: Why Do We Enjoy a Low Crime Rate?" *Psyche-Law-Society: In Honor of Manfred Rehbinder. Publications in Psychology of Law* 1: 47–66.

Najita, Tetsuo. 1974. *Japan*. Chicago: University of Chicago Press.

Nakajima, Hiroshi. 1991. "Current Trends of Criminal Activities and the Practices of Criminal Justice in Japan." Unpublished paper. Tokyo: United Nations Asia and Far East Institute for Prevention of Crime and Treatment of Offenders.

Nakamura, Hajime. 1964. *Ways of Thinking of Eastern People: Asia, China, Tibet, Japan*. Ed. Philip P. Wiener. Honolulu: East-West Center Press.

Nakane, Chie. 1984. *Japanese Society*. Tokyo: Charles E. Tuttle.

Namiki, Hiroyuki. 1980a. "Relations Between the Correctional Institution and the Aftercare Agency." Unpublished paper. Tokyo: United Nations Asia and Far East Institute for Prevention of Crime and Treatment of Offenders.

———. 1980b. "Functions of the Probation Officer Attached to the Secretariat of the Regional Parole Board." Unpublished paper.

394

REFERENCES

Tokyo: United Nations Asia and Far East Institute for Prevention of Crime and Treatment of Offenders.

National Police Agency. 1991. *White Paper on Police 1991 (Excerpt)*. Tokyo: Japan Times.

———. 1993. *White Paper on Police 1993 (Excerpt)*. Tokyo: Japan Times.

Nishikawa, Masakazu. 1990. "Adult Probation in Japan: A Case Study of Alternatives to Imprisonment." Tokyo: United Nations Asia and Far East Institute for Prevention of Crime and Treatment of Offenders. Photocopy.

———. 1994. "Adult Probation in Japan." *Alternatives to Imprisonment in Comparative Perspective*. Ed. Uglejesa Zveric. Chicago: Nelson-Hall. 203–49.

Norbeck, Edward. 1954. *Takashima: A Japanese Fishing Community*. Salt Lake City: University of Utah Press.

O'Brien, Patricia. 1982. *The Promise of Punishment: Prisons in Nineteenth-Century France*. Princeton, NJ: Princeton University Press.

Ogawa, Shigejiro, and Kosuke Tomeoka. 1910. "Prisons and Prisoners." *Fifty Years of New Japan*. 2d ed. Comp. Shibenobu Okuma. English version 1970. Ed. Marcus Huish. New York: Kraus Reprint. 296–319.

Ogawa, Taro. 1976. "Japan." *Criminology: A Cross-Cultural Perspective*. Ed. Dae Chang. Vol. 2. Durham, NC: Carolina Academic Press.

Ohbayashi, Hiroshi. 1990. "The Discretionary Power of Prosecution and the Prevention of Its Abuse." *Asian Journal of Crime Prevention and Criminal Justice* 8: 148–51.

Ono, Seiichiro. 1970. "Criminal Justice, Correctional Treatment and Rehabilitation in Japan." Address to Fourth United Nations Congress on Prevention of Crime and Treatment of Offenders, Kyoto. 1–18.

Ooms, Hermon. 1985. *Tokugawa Ideology: Early Constructs, 1570–1680*. Princeton, NJ: Princeton University Press.

Osgood, D. Wayne, Lloyd D. Johnston, Patrick M. O'Malley, and Jerald G. Bachman. 1988. "The Generality of Deviance in Late Adolescence and Early Adulthood." *American Sociological Review* 53: 81–93.

Passim, Herbert. 1968. "Japanese Society." *International Encyclopedia of the Social Sciences*. Ed. David L. Sills. Vol. 8. New York: MacMillan.

Pempel, T. J. 1982. *Policy and Politics in Japan: Creative Conservatism.* Philadelphia: Temple University Press.

Pharr, Susan. 1981. *Political Women in Japan: The Search for a Place in Political Life.* Berkeley: University of California Press.

Plath, David W. 1964. *The After Hours: Modern Japan and the Search for Enjoyment.* Berkeley: University of California Press.

Radest, Howard B. 1993. *Community Service: Encounter with Strangers.* Westport, CT: Praeger.

Radzinowicz, Leon. 1956. *A History of English Criminal Law and Its Administration from 1750.* Vol. 2. London: Stevens and Sons.

Rehabilitation Bureau. 1990. *Community-Based Treatment of Offenders in Japan.* Tokyo: Ministry of Justice.

Reischauer, Edwin O. 1988. *The Japanese Today: Change and Continuity.* Cambridge, MA: Harvard University Press.

Research and Statistics Section. 1956. *Annual Report of Statistics on Correction for 1955.* Vol. 2. Tokyo: Secretariat, Ministry of Justice.

———. 1961. *Annual Report of Statistics on Correction for 1960.* Vol. 2. Tokyo: Secretariat, Ministry of Justice.

———. 1966a. *Annual Report of Statistics on Correction for 1965.* Vol. 2. Tokyo: Secretariat, Ministry of Justice.

———. 1966b. *Annual Report of Statistics on Rehabilitation for 1965.* Tokyo: Secretariat, Ministry of Justice.

———. 1971a. *Annual Report of Statistics on Rehabilitation for 1970.* Tokyo: Secretariat, Ministry of Justice.

———. 1971b. *Annual Report of Statistics on Correction for 1970.* Vol. 1. Tokyo: Secretariat, Ministry of Justice.

———. 1976a. *Annual Report of Statistics on Rehabilitation for 1975.* Tokyo: Secretariat, Ministry of Justice.

———. 1976b. *Annual Report of Statistics on Correction for 1975.* Vol. 1. Tokyo: Secretariat, Ministry of Justice.

———. 1981a. *Annual Report of Statistics on Rehabilitation for 1980.* Tokyo: Secretariat, Ministry of Justice.

———. 1981b. *Annual Report of Statistics on Correction for 1980.* Vol. 1. Tokyo: Secretariat, Ministry of Justice.

———. 1981c. *Annual Report of Statistics on Correction for 1980.* Vol. 2. Tokyo: Secretariat, Ministry of Justice.

———. 1986a. *Annual Report of Statistics on Rehabilitation for 1985.* Tokyo: Secretariat, Ministry of Justice.

———. 1986b. *Annual Report of Statistics on Correction for 1985*. Vol. 1. Tokyo: Secretariat, Ministry of Justice.

———. 1988a. *Annual Report of Statistics on Correction for 1987*. Vol. 1. Secretariat, Ministry of Justice.

———. 1988b. *Annual Report of Statistics on Correction for 1987*. Vol. 2. Secretariat, Ministry of Justice.

———. 1990. *Annual Report of Statistics on Rehabilitation for 1989*. Tokyo: Secretariat, Ministry of Justice.

———. 1991a. *Annual Report of Statistics on Rehabilitation for 1990*. Tokyo: Secretariat, Ministry of Justice.

———. 1991b. *Annual Report of Statistics on Correction for 1990*. Vol. 1. Tokyo: Secretariat, Ministry of Justice.

———. 1991c. *Annual Report of Statistics on Correction for 1990*. Vol. 2. Tokyo: Secretariat, Ministry of Justice.

———. 1993a. *Annual Report of Statistics on Rehabilitation for 1992*. Tokyo: Secretariat, Ministry of Justice.

———. 1993b. *Annual Report of Statistics on Correction for 1992*. Vol. 1. Tokyo: Secretariat, Ministry of Justice.

———. 1996a. *Annual Report of Statistics on Rehabilitation for 1995*. Tokyo: Secretariat, Ministry of Justice.

———. 1996b. *Annual Report of Statistics on Correction for 1995*. Vol. 1. Tokyo: Secretariat, Ministry of Justice.

———. 1996c. *Annual Report of Statistics on Correction for 1995*. Vol. 2. Tokyo: Secretariat, Ministry of Justice.

Research and Training Institute. 1969. *Summary of the White Paper on Crime*. Tokyo: Ministry of Justice.

———. 1979. *Summary of the White Paper on Crime*. Tokyo: Ministry of Justice.

———. 1984. *Summary of the White Paper on Crime*. Tokyo: Ministry of Justice.

———. 1985. *Summary of the White Paper on Crime*. Tokyo. Ministry of Justice.

———. 1987. *Summary of the White Paper on Crime*. Tokyo: Ministry of Justice.

———. 1988. *Summary of the White Paper on Crime*. Tokyo: Ministry of Justice.

———. 1989. *Summary of the White Paper on Crime*. Tokyo: Ministry of Justice.

———. 1990. *Summary of the White Paper on Crime*. Tokyo: Ministry of Justice.

———. 1991. *Summary of the White Paper on Crime.* Tokyo: Ministry of Justice.

———. 1992. *Summary of the White Paper on Crime.* Tokyo: Ministry of Justice.

———. 1993. *Summary of the White Paper on Crime.* Tokyo: Ministry of Justice.

———. 1994. *Summary of the White Paper on Crime.* Tokyo: Ministry of Justice.

———. 1995. *Summary of the White Paper on Crime.* Tokyo: Ministry of Justice.

———. 1996. *Summary of the White Paper on Crime.* Tokyo: Ministry of Justice.

Riley, Matilda White. 1987. "On the Significance of Age in Sociology." *American Sociological Review* 52: 1–14.

Rooney, Ronald H. 1992. *Strategies for Work with Involuntary Clients.* New York: Columbia University Press.

Rosenberger, Nancy R. 1996. "Fragile Resistance, Signs of Status: Women Between State and Media in Japan." *Re-Imaging Japanese Women.* Ed. Anne E. Imamura. Berkeley: University of California Press.

Saeki, Masako. 1996. "Public Participation in the Treatment of Offenders." Resource Material Series No. 48. Tokyo: United Nations Asia and Far East Institute for Prevention of Crime and Treatment of Offenders.

Sakai, Fumio. 1985. "Suspension of Prosecution System in Japan." Unpublished paper. Tokyo: United Nations Asia and Far East Institute for Prevention of Crime and Treatment of Offenders.

Sansom, George. 1963a. *A History of Japan to 1334.* Tokyo: Charles E. Tuttle.

———. 1963b. *A History of Japan, 1334–1615.* Tokyo: Charles E. Tuttle.

———. 1963c. *A History of Japan 1615–1867.* Tokyo: Charles E. Tuttle.

Sasaki, Kazuo. 1995. "On Suspension of Prosecution." Unpublished paper. Tokyo. United Nations Asia and Far East Institute for Prevention of Crime and Treatment of Offenders.

Sato, Ikuya. 1991. *Kamikaze Biker: Parody and Anomy in Affluent Japan.* Chicago: University of Chicago Press.

Sato, Tsuneo. 1990. "Tokugawa Villages and Agriculture." *Tokugawa Japan.* Trans. Conrad Totman. Ed. Chie Nakane and Shizaburo Oishi. Tokyo: University of Tokyo Press. 37–80.

Satoh, Kunpei. 1989. "Rehabilitation Services in Japan: Present Situation and Problems." Unpublished paper. Tokyo: United Nations Asia and Far East Institute for Prevention of Crime and Treatment of Offenders.

Satoh, Shigemi. 1988. "The Criminal Justice System in Japan." Unpublished paper. Tokyo: United Nations Asia and Far East Institute for Prevention of Crime and Treatment of Offenders.

Satsumae, Takeshi. 1977. "The Practice of Suspension of Prosecution." Unpublished paper. Tokyo: United Nations Asia and Far East Institute for Prevention of Crime and Treatment of Offenders.

Scalapino, Robert A. 1953. *Democracy and the Party Movement in Prewar Japan*. Berkeley: University of California Press.

Schlossman, Steven L. 1977. *Love and the American Delinquent*. Chicago: University of Chicago Press.

Schore, Leo F. 1967. "The Community." *Sociology: An Introduction*. Ed. Neil J. Smelser. New York: John Wiley and Sons. 79–150.

Shibusa, Shingo. 1985. "Exercise of Prosecutorial Discretion as to Suspension of Prosecution in Japan." Unpublished paper. Tokyo: United Nations Asia and Far East Institute for Prevention of Crime and Treatment of Offenders.

Shikita, Minoru. 1985. "Violence and Urbanization: The Experience in Large Japanese Cities." *Crime and Criminal Policy*. Ed. Pedro N. David. Rome: United Nations Social Defense Research Institute.

Shikita, Minoru, and Shinichi Tsuchiya. 1990. *Crime and Criminal Policy in Japan from 1926 to 1988*. Tokyo: Japan Criminal Policy Society.

Shiono, Yasuyoshi. 1969. "Use of Volunteers in the Non-Institutional Treatment of Offenders in Japan." *International Journal of Criminal Policy* 27: 25–31.

Sims, R. L. 1991. *A Political History of Modern Japan, 1868–1952*. New Delhi: Vikas Publishing House.

Smith, Herman W. 1995. *The Myth of Japanese Homogeneity: Social-Ecological Diversity in Education and Socialization*. Commack, NY: Nova Science Publishers.

Smith, Robert J. 1983. *Japanese Society: Tradition, Self, and the Social Order*. Cambridge, Eng.: Cambridge University Press.

Smith, Thomas C. 1955. *Political Change and Industrial Development in Japan: Government Enterprise, 1868–1880*. Stanford: Stanford University Press.

Soejima, Kazuho. 1974. "History of Regulations for Juvenile Delinquents in Japan." Unpublished paper. Tokyo: United Nations

Asia and Far East Institute for Prevention of Crime and Treatment of Offenders.

Sonoda, Hidehiro. 1985. "The Provinces." *Seventy-seven Keys to the Civilization of Japan*. Ed. Tadao Umesao. Osaka: Sogensha. 201–4.

Statistics Bureau. 1992. *Japan Statistical Yearbook 1991*. Tokyo: Management and Coordination Agency.

Steiner, Kurt. 1965. *Local Government in Japan*. Stanford: Stanford University Press.

Supreme Court of Japan. n.d. *Justice in Japan*. Tokyo: Supreme Court.

———. 1989. *Guide to the Family Court of Japan*. Tokyo: Supreme Court.

Suzuki, Yoshio. 1979. "Corrections in Japan." *International Corrections*. Ed. Robert J. Wicks and H. A. A. Cooper. Lexington, MA: Lexington Books. 141–61.

Takigawa, Seijiro. 1972. *A History of Prison Administration in Japan* (in Japanese). Tokyo: Seikeibou.

Tanaka, Toshihiko. 1986. "Criminal Justice System in Japan (I)." Unpublished paper. Tokyo: United Nations Asia and Far East Institute for Prevention of Crime and Treatment of Offenders.

Tanigawa, Akira. 1982. "Public Participation and the Integrated Approach in Japanese Rehabilitative Services." *Criminal Justice in Asia: the Quest for an Integrated Approach*. Ed. B. J. George, Jr. Tokyo: United Nations Asia and Far East Institute for Prevention of Crime and Treatment of Offenders.

Thibault, John W., and Harold H. Kelley. 1969. *The Social Psychology of Groups*. New York: John Wiley and Sons.

Thornton, Robert Y., with Katsuya Endo. 1992. *Preventing Crime in America and Japan: A Comparative Analysis*. Armonk, NY: M. E. Sharpe.

Toennies, Ferdinand. 1940. *Fundamental Concepts of Sociology*. Trans. Charles P. Loomis. New York: American Book.

Tokuoka, Hideo, and Albert K. Cohen. 1987. "Japanese Society and Delinquency." *International Journal of Comparative and Applied Criminal Justice* 11: 13–22.

Tomita, Shozo. 1971. "How to Utilise Volunteers in the Field of Probation." Resource Material Series No. 1. Tokyo: United Nations Asia and Far East Institute for Prevention of Crime and Treatment of Offenders.

Tonomura, Hitomi. 1992. *Community and Commerce in Late Medieval Japan: The Corporate Villages of Tokuchin-ho*. Stanford: Stanford University Press.

Traffic Safety Policy Office. 1985. *White Paper on Transportation Safety in Japan '85.* Tokyo: International Association of Traffic and Safety Sciences.

———. 1994. *White Paper on Transportation Safety '94.* Abridged edition. Tokyo: International Association of Traffic and Safety Sciences.

Tsubochi, Kosuke, Tsuneko Sato, Takaaki Hama, Shigeo Hashisako, Kiyofumi Koita, and Yoshikazu Yuma. 1990. "Research on Consciousness of Norms and Correctional Programs Regarding Boys Housed in Juvenile Training Schools" (summary in English). Tokyo: Research and Training Institute, Ministry of Justice. 10–11.

Udo, Guro. 1990. "Rehabilitation Aid Hostels in Japan." Unpublished paper. Tokyo: United Nations Asia and Far East Institute for Prevention of Crime and Treatment of Offenders.

Ueno, Chizuko. 1994. "Women and the Family in Transition in Postwar Japan. *Women of Japan and Korea: Continuity and Changes.* Ed. Joyce Gelb and Marian Lief Palley. Philadelphia: Temple University Press. 23–42.

Vaughn, Michael S., and Frank F. Y. Huang. 1992. "Delinquency in the Land of the Rising Sun: An Analysis of Juvenile Property Crimes During the Showa Era." *International Journal of Comparative and Applied Criminal Justice* 16: 272–300.

Verba, Sidney, Steven Kelman, Gary R. Orren, Ichiro Miyake, Joji Watanuki, Ikuo Kabashima, and G. Donald Ferree, Jr. 1987. *Elites and the Idea of Equality: Comparison of Japan, Sweden, and the United States.* Cambridge, MA: Harvard University Press.

Wagatsuma, Hiroshi, and George A. DeVos. 1984. *Heritage and Endurance: Family Patterns and Delinquency Formation in Urban Japan.* Berkeley: University of California Press.

Wagatsuma, Hiroshi, George A. DeVos, and Arthur Rosett. 1986. "The Implications of Apology: Law and Culture in Japan and the United States. *Law and Society Review* 20: 461–98.

Watanabe, Kazuhiro. 1979. "On Suspension of Prosecution." Unpublished paper. Tokyo: United Nations Asia and Far East Institute for Prevention of Crime and Treatment of Offenders.

Watanuki, Joji. 1986. "Is There a `Japanese-type Welfare Society'?" *International Sociology* 1: 259–69.

White, Merry. 1993. *The Material Child: Coming of Age in Japan and America.* New York: Free Press.

Wilson, John, and Marc A. Musick. 1997. "Work and Volunteering: The Long Arm of the Job." *Social Forces* 76: 251–72.

Wuthnow, Robert. 1991. "The Voluntary Sector: Legacy of Past, Hope for the Future." *Between States and Markets: The Voluntary Sector in Comparative Perspective*. Ed. Robert Wuthnow. Princeton: Princeton University Press. 3–29.

Yamamura, Yoshaki. 1986. "The Child in Japanese Society." *Child Development and Education in Japan*. Ed. Harold Stevenson, Hiroshi Azuma, and Kenji Hakuta. New York: W. H. Freeman.

Yokoyama, Minoru. 1982. "How Have Our Prisons Been Used in Japan?" Paper delivered at World Congress, International Sociological Association, Mexico City.

———. 1989. "Net-Widening of the Juvenile Justice System in Japan." *Criminal Justice Review* 14: 43–53.

———. 1990. "Criminalization Against Traffic Offenders in Japanese Criminal Justice System." *Kokugakuin Journal of Law and Politics* 27: 1–27.

———. 1997. "Juvenile Justice: An Overview of Japan. *Juvenile Justice Systems: International Perspectives*. Toronto: Canadian Scholars' Press. 1–28.

Yoshino, Michael Y. 1968. *Japan's Managerial System: Tradition and Innovation*. Cambridge, MA: MIT Press.

Yoshitake, Mitsuyo. 1989. "Juvenile Classification Homes in Japan." *American Jails* 3: 88, 93–97.

Yoshizumi, Kyoko. 1995. "Marriage and Family: Past and Present." *Japanese Women: New Feminist Perspectives on the Past, Present, and Future*. Ed. Kumiko Fujimura-Fanselon and Atsuko Kamedo. New York: Feminist Press of City University of New York. 186–97.

Index

White, Merry, 212, 213–14

Wicks, Robert J., 4

Wilson, John, 298

Women, employment of, 60, 126,
    214, 374

Women's guidance home, 75, 266

Women's prisons, 74, 108, 110

Wuthnow, Robert, 44

Yakuza (criminal syndicate), 75, 81,
    87, 90, 131–32, 142, 155, 180,
    245, 250, 253, 381n. 4, 385n. 7

Yamada, Akiyoshi, 24

Yamamura, Yoshaki, 211

Yatsuka, Hozumi, 58

Yokoyama, Minoru, 55, 175, 223,
    384n. 5

Yoshino, Michael Y., 136

Yoshitake, Mitsuyo, 162

Yoshizumi, Kyoko, 381n. 11

Youth culture, 207, 214, 246

Yuma, Yoshikazu, 210

ELMER H. JOHNSON was born in Racine, Wisconsin, and received his Ph.D. in sociology from the University of Wisconsin at Madison in 1950. He taught at North Carolina State University at Raleigh from 1949 to 1966, worked as a parole supervisor for the North Carolina Board of Paroles in 1956, and served as the assistant director of the North Carolina Prison Department, 1958–60. From 1966 until his retirement in 1987, he taught at Southern Illinois University at Carbondale in the Center for the Study of Crime, Delinquency, and Corrections and in the Department of Sociology, where he attained the rank of distinguished professor. His books include *Crime, Correction, and Society*, 4th ed. (1978), *Japanese Corrections: Managing Convicted Offenders in an Orderly Society* (1996), and *Criminalization and Prisoners in Japan: Six Contrary Cohorts* (1997), and he edited the two-volume *International Handbook of Contemporary Developments in Criminology* (1983) and the *Handbook on Crime and Delinquency Prevention* (1987).

CAROL H. JOHNSON is a graduate of North Carolina State University at Raleigh and has specialized in gerontology. While in Japan she studied services for the elderly and traditional Japanese crafts.